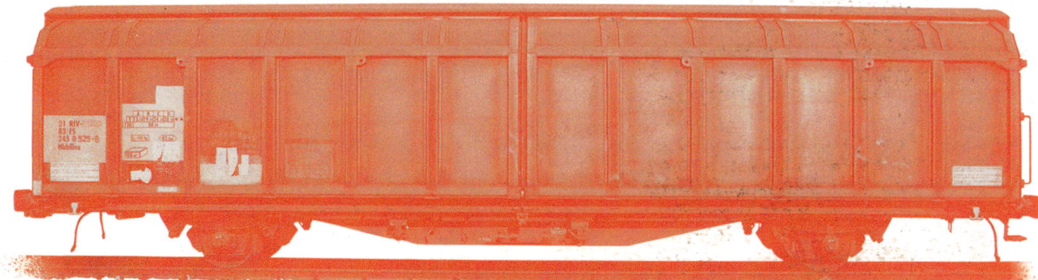

无妥协方式
NO APOLOGIES

N° 3   2021 年

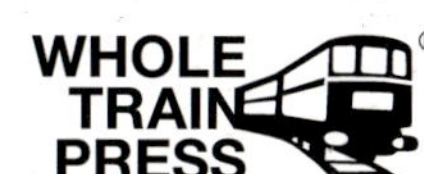

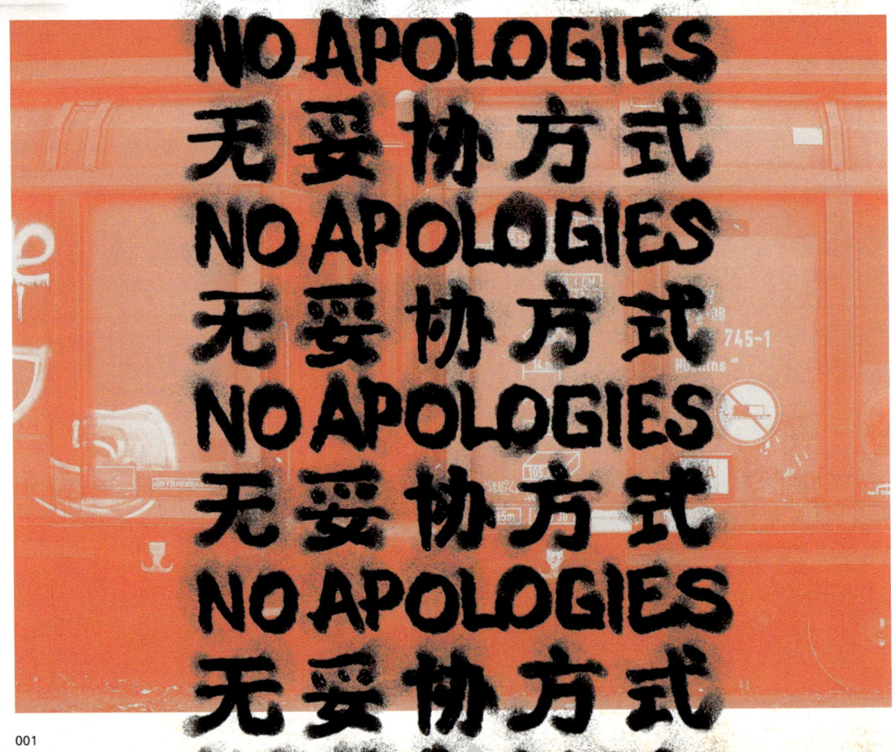

"我们所经历的涂鸦背后都一定充满故事和冒险。[...]当我们发掘城市的切入点与一般民众不同的时候,或者说那些被遗忘的角落,我们与这座城市之间产生了某种特殊的连接" HENCE (C&F)

几个月前,《无妥协方式》开始筹划新一期的内容,并商讨哪些写手将可以出现在杂志中。经过一番激烈的讨论与筛选,我们最终确定了这一期出现的写手,与我们共同分享他们对涂鸦的热情,以及来自世界各地宝贵的涂鸦智慧。

女士们先生们,在新一期的杂志中,您将会感受到我们带来的一场精彩纷呈的狂欢,虽然地球还在与疫情作斗争,生活方式也与以往更加不同了。但是我们所挑选的是来自东西方真正的涂鸦英雄:正是他们对待涂鸦的纯粹精神及独特个性,才得以体现其城市特有涂鸦文化。从快节奏的纽约到慢生活的阿姆斯特丹,从年轻疯狂的马德里到世界古都罗马,从极度寒冷的赫尔辛基到中国的俩座城市中心:北京与广州。尽管每个写手的风格及态度都是独一无二的,但是我们仍然可以在他们之间找到相似之处,这也更好的让读者理解他们在这一期杂志集中呈现的理由。

我们选择了来自欧洲及美国的涂鸦老手,这是一帮从80年代末期到90年代中就开始涂鸦的写手,当周遭的世界不断变化,涂鸦文化也不断的发展,他们从懵懂少年成长成需要面对工作、责任的成人,但是他们仍然通过三、四十年不断的努力来让这些名字发光,换句话说,他们的经历铸就了他们的现在。当然也包含涂鸦,他们的作品从客运列车画到货运火车,从地铁画到繁忙的街道、隧道、铁轨、高速公路等等地点都可以见到这些名字,同时也通过他们的一次次旅行将名字散播到了世界各地。你可以肯定的是,他们了解涂鸦的历史和传统,并且从他们的行为中看到影子:不论是充满灵魂的签名,还是富有节奏的Throwup,以及深思熟虑的Burner。虽然他们的涂鸦是粗糙的,但是却透露出一种自然的优雅,每一笔都经过深思熟虑。

在世界的另外一端,我们选择了来自年轻时代的中国力量。尽管他们年纪尚小,但是在中国的环境下成长为一名写手是困难的,在这里涂鸦是一种全新的、未被充分理解的现象,但这些年轻的写手们有着与生俱来的天赋和献身精神。也许有一天他们的成就将会达到杂志中其他西方写手的地位,成为激励世界各地写手的标杆。

我们挑选的写手都是来自世界各地真正的地下王者,这也就是为什么他们会出现在这一期的原因。这些都是我们所期待看到的涂鸦。

无妥协方式

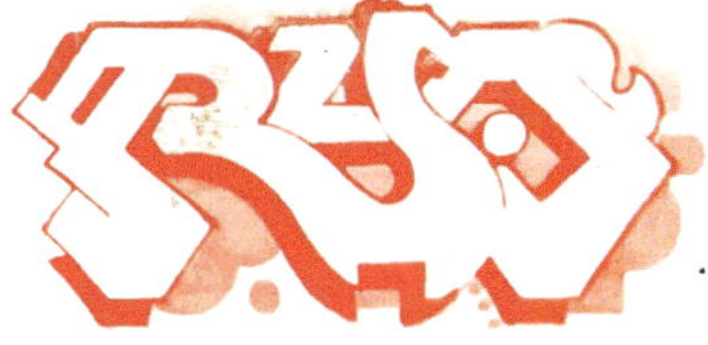

Some months ago, during a reunion of the NO APOLOGIES team, we began questioning ourselves about who deserved to be featured in the upcoming issue and why: names were discussed and possible line ups were scheduled, then finally most of the selected writers accepted enthusiastically to share their gems and their wisdom with us and the world.

Ladies and gentlemen, here we go again with another juicy concentrate of dopeness, while the planet earth is still fighting the pandemic and life seems weirder than ever. For this issue, we picked up some true heroes of the western and eastern world: few unique personalities who really embody the pure spirit of the peculiar graffiti culture of their cities, from the hectic New York to the chilled out Amsterdam, from the crazy Madrid to the ancient Rome, from the extra-cold Helsinki to the heart of China with Beijing and Guangzhou. Even though their style and attitude are pretty unique, we still can identify some affinities that make us understand better why we are here to read about them.

Of the writers from Europe and the US, none of them is a new jack: we are talking about grown-up men who started scribbling their moniker possibly between the late '80s and the mid-'90s and kept bombing through the span of 3-4 decades, while the world around them was changing, the graffiti culture itself was changing, and they were changing as well, evolving from allegedly restless kids to adults who have to pay bills, facing jobs and other responsibilities; in other words, they have been through a lot. Their graffiti also went through a lot, shifting from passenger trains to freights, from subways to busy streets, tunnels, track-sides, highways, and so on, but also spreading around the world through their trips. You can be sure those guys are aware of the graffiti history and traditions, and traces of that can be seen in what they do: their stuff is crude but still elegant, spontaneous, and thought-out at the same time, from soulful tags to funky throwies to well-built burners.

To represent the other side of the world and the younger generations we also selected two wild warriors from China. Despite their young age and the difficulties of growing as a writer in a country like China—where graffiti is a quite new and underrepresented phenomenon—these young guns have raw talent and dedication. Maybe one day they will reach the status of their western counterparts in this magazine, and they will be the veterans that inspire people from all around the world.

The writers we selected are true kings and that's why they are on these pages. These are the graffiti we all want to see.

NO APOLOGIES

在杂志的结尾，我们对 RYO 致上最高的敬意，一位近期离世的特殊朋友，我们会深深地怀念他。他也是 WHOLE TRAIN PRESS 的创始人，为保护这种文化做了许多奋斗。他将永远活在我们心里。
—
At the end of the magazine, you will find a tribute to RYO, a special person who passed away recently and that will be deeply missed. He was the founder of WHOLE TRAIN PRESS and did a lot for the preservation of this culture.. he will always have a place in our hearts.

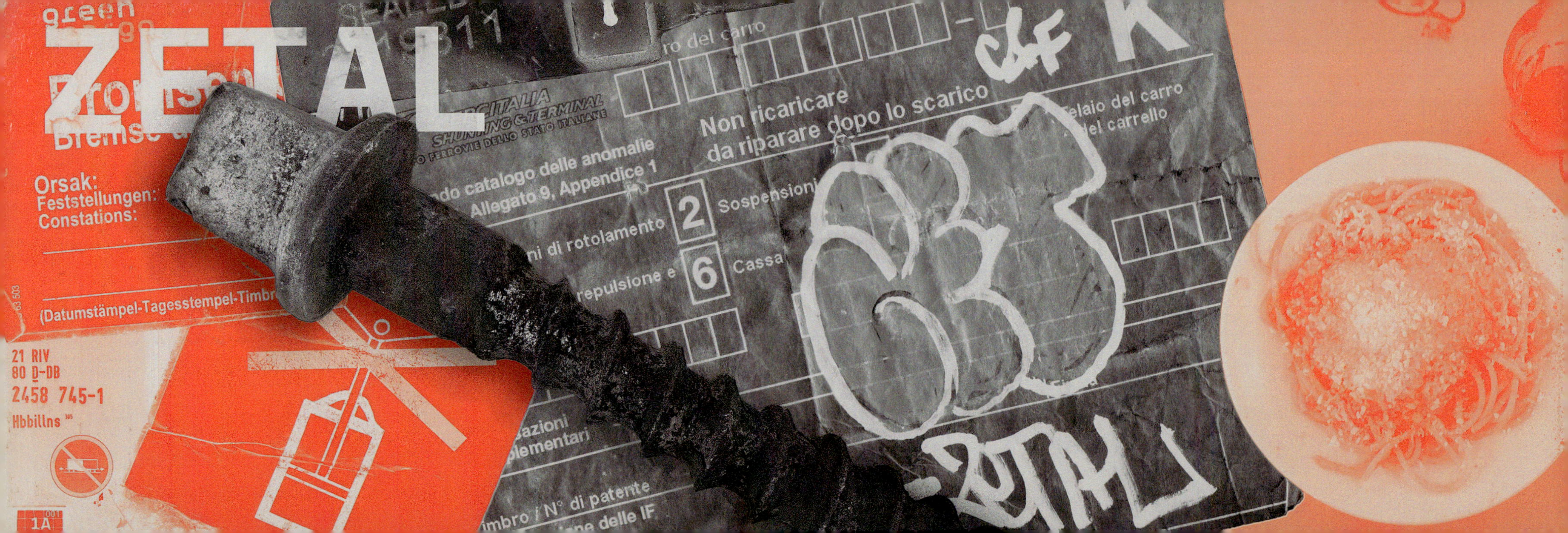

green
zago
ZETAL
Bremse
Orsak:
Feststellungen:
Constations:
(Datumstämpel-Tagesstempel-Timbr
21 RIV
80 D-DB
2458 745-1
Hbbillns
1A
SEALED
1911
ro del carro
RCITALIA
SHUNTING & TERMINAL
O FERROVIE DELLO STATO ITALIANE
Non ricaricare
da riparare dopo lo scarico
do catalogo delle anomalie
Allegato 9, Appendice 1
ni di rotolamento
2 Sospensioni
6 Cassa
repulsione e
elaio del carro
del carrello
azioni
plementari
imbro / N° di patente
ne delle IF
63 503

ZETAL
永恒的叛逆者

当你看到 ZETAL 的涂鸦，总会让人联想到罗马，在那里的写手充满原生的疯狂，而这也让罗马变成一个独立于欧洲内部的多彩宇宙。能聊聊你与这座城市之间的关系吗？

能把涂鸦写手的名字与一座城市联系起来，或许这是对他们的最高赞美——这也是我的荣幸。我所创作的作品都是为了在街头争取更大的视觉印象而产生的。每一个涂鸦写手都必须时刻关注和接纳周遭的事物，并将自己的感受转化到作品中，只有这样，他的作品才会具有个性和表现力。

因此，罗马成为了我作品的一部分，他存在于我用五金店的工业喷漆滋出来的线条上，他也存在于我涂鸦线条的天性与速度上。甚至我的故乡伊特鲁里亚城市的历史都存在于作品之中，这些灵感来自于伊特鲁里亚人的布克凯洛[1]陶器。并不是我创造了"罗马风格"，在我之前，有类似 TRV、ZTK 和 CB 这样的团队，尤其是他们的早期风格带给了我很大灵感。而对我影响最大的罗马写手是来自 CB 团队的DOME[2]，是他第一次将原装喷头递到我的手上，那种感觉就像是 The Tenacious D[3] 在电影中强而有力的吉他弹拨。我仍然记得这个人生分水岭的一天，那是在罗马古堡小镇的马里诺饮食店——"Il Bujaccaro"，桌面上摆放的是一盘 Amatriciana[4] 传统意大利面和一杯红酒，以及一整鞋盒的"Commando Beasts"的照片。我的团队"黑手"（Black Hand）无疑延续了他们与生俱来的风格。至于罗马的涂鸦氛围，从2000 年代中期开始我就再也没有关注过，他让我觉得无聊、空洞，而且失去了"对未来的遐想"。

罗马的涂鸦历史充斥了疯狂的故事。你能和我们分享你在"永恒之城"一些涂鸦经历吗？

好的，我知道涂鸦写手最热衷的是那些关于罗马地铁的故事。但是我事先申明，出于家庭原因，我从 2004 年 5 月 1日起就没有在地铁涂鸦了，那天我在 Magliana 地铁站被抓了，不过那也是另一回事了。

最近有一位墨西哥人访问了罗马，他是经由一位我信任的朋友介绍的，每个人说他是一个认真，可靠的角色，所以我在家招待了他（和一些我不认识的人在一起）那时他正在意大利旅行，但是在预定到达的那个晚上他放了我鸽子，我为了准备他的房间还取消了约会，他的延迟让我很恼火。

一小时后，他打电话给我，为给我带来的不便道歉，我决定再给他一次机会。从他到达那一刻，神奇的友谊就诞生了，我们就像老朋友一样聊了很久。我带他去吃了一顿不错的意大利面[5]，然后尝试去喷了一辆双层火车，但那天晚上铁路上几乎全是工人。我们只能将任务延迟，并一直等到深夜，在我们的一次聊天中，他向我坦承，他真的很欣赏我们的木偶艺术，而我也很欣赏的社会政治主题涂鸦。于是，创造一个首尾相连的火车涂鸦的想法诞生了。 很长一段时间以来BICER是他的涂鸦代号。他一直致力于用影像记录南美那些拼命想进入美国的"勇敢移民"。

他让我相信这些"勇敢的移民"是值得我们在罗马地铁上为他们创作一幅涂鸦的。虽然我已经退出这个地铁游戏很多年了，而我也不能冒险在没有侦查过的地方创作。不过我知道有一段时间，Rome 到 Lido 的铁路线上会有一些旧车厢停在离 Magliana 车站几百米远的地方，那是一些比较外围、不太受监控的区域，于是他接受了这个建议。我们非常兴奋的勾勒出一个首尾相连的整车涂鸦手稿，BICER[6] 负责"移民的英勇"（MIGRANTES VALIENTES）几个字母，而我则负责人物的

部分: 我选择了圣经中摩西分开水面的故事，在他乘坐的马车尾部是俩重波浪，而水面则是由俩只带着断裂手铐的黑人双手分开。我们想到了可以把字母平躺在海床上，周围的墓碑刻着边境地区的首字母，每天都有许多移民在那里冒着生命危险为了寻找更美好的未来。简而言之，这是我们俩都感兴趣的话题。第二天，在快速检查现场环境后，我们偷偷地在晚餐时间潜入停车区域，在 20 分钟内我们已经完成了手，一重波浪以及所有字母的填色，但我们意识到有一辆保全的车停到离我们不远的地方。于是我卧倒注视着他们的举动，确保我们能在最短时间逃脱成功。大约等了 20 分钟后，又来了一辆保全车，他们开始在车外聊天，然后其中一个人操着急促带有威胁性的步伐像我们逼近。

我们认准了时机准备逃走，在离开围墙范围的时候就试图与保全进行对话，说服他这里停放的不过是一些僵尸列车，但是我们并没有说服他，接着他威胁道我们即将被全面包围。我们带着没有画完的遗憾消失在黑暗之中。第二天，BICER 并不想放弃，因为这将是他在罗马的最后一晚，而涂鸦也几乎快要完工。于是我们决定等到稍微晚一些再回来完成作品。今晚这一区域看起来没什么工人，几分钟之后，我就开始攀爬梯子为第二只手填色，而 BICER 则开始填充他字体的背景。我们在里面没有待到五分钟，就听到有一辆车全速向我们的方向驶来。这一次我无法救出我的梯子，只救回了喷漆。我们不相信他们这么快就赶到现场，也不相信他们会如此努力地保卫那些被僵尸列车。这次的任务又失败了，而 BICER 第二天就要离开了，但是我们还剩下一些喷漆，所以我们决定不管怎样都要把这个主题做完。临近上午，我把他带到一个废弃的仓库里，我们将所有的愤怒都宣泄在这面墙上。虽然我们已经尽了最大的努力，但有时计划总是事与愿违。然而，我们之间的强烈友谊诞生了，于是彼此承诺终有一日我们将一同喷完一辆首尾相连的列车。

在这个时代，加入团队往往是一条通往涂鸦圣殿的捷径。BLACK HAND，你的团队里，拥有着一群怀揣共同目标的真兄弟。你能告诉我们一些背后的故事吗？

我相信存在着两种类型的团队，一种是铁哥们团队，另一种是涂鸦写手团队。BLACK HAND 诞生于 2000年左右，他是为了我与 DRES 的友情所起的名字。几年后，我们的朋友圈扩大了，但我们都拥有一个共同的目标，那就是成为更铁的铁哥们。这么多年后，我们中的一些人离开了团队，生活把他们带到别的地方，不幸的是，这些铁哥们中也有些人离世了。而那些留下的人仍然充满激情与奉献着自己的涂鸦精神，他们比以往任何时候都更希望团队更加强大。你想知道为什么我们团队能如此长寿吗？因为我们互相激励彼此，设定目标，并强迫自己做得更好，将简单的字母与重复使用的颜色变化出惊奇的涂鸦。虽然我不想傲慢地说，我们不再把罗马作为一个参照点，但现在存在的竞争只有在我们团队之间发生，这是属于我们最珍惜的彼此。当夜晚降临，我与我的铁哥们一起出动，像一直以来在街上涂鸦那样创作，分享我们所感受的触动，这会给你一种生活在继续，但有些事情永远都不会改变的感觉。

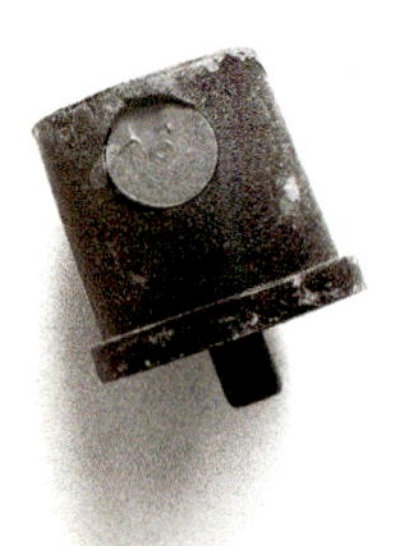

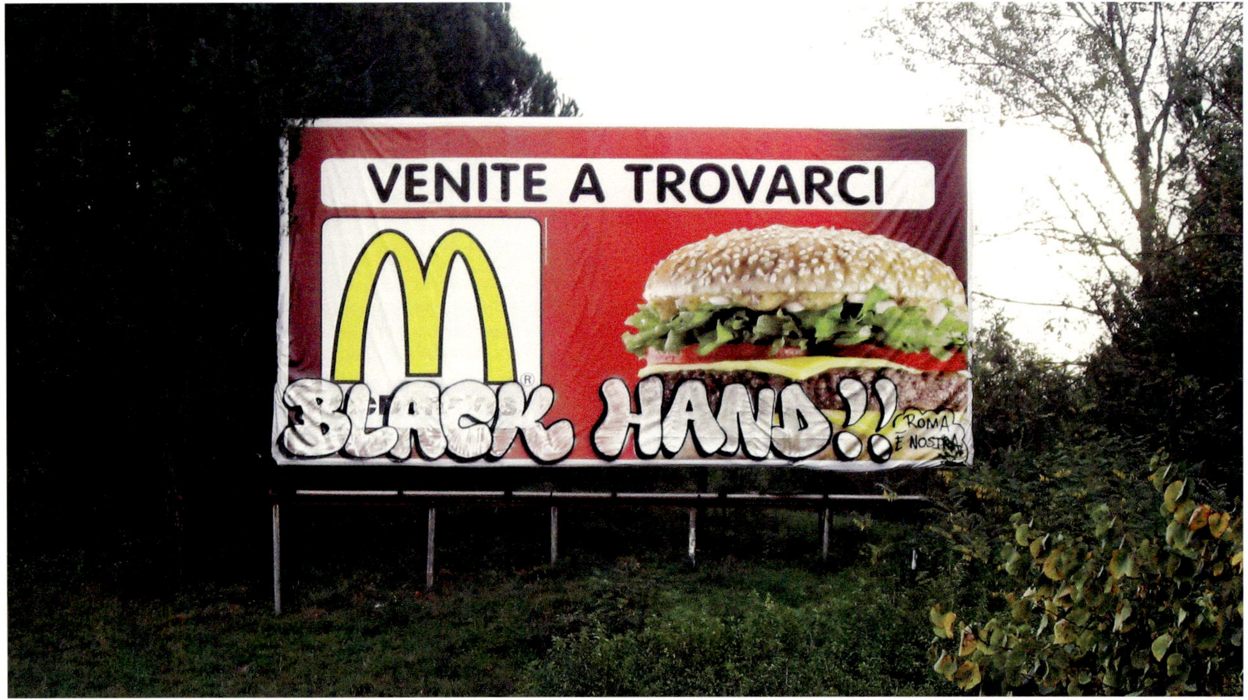

这个巨大的广告牌矗立在通往罗马的一座小山坡上。我们认为所有沿着奥雷里亚线前往梵蒂冈的游客都能看到它。而这也是我们这支"永恒的团队"欢迎您来到永恒之城的特殊仪式。

广告牌上写着："Venite a trovarci"（来拜访我们），黑手，"Roma è nostra"（罗马是我们的）。
—
This large advertising sign stands on a hill at the entrance of Rome. We like to think that all tourists heading to the Vatican along the Aurelia line can see it. Our "Eternal Crew" welcomes you to the Eternal City.

On the billboard: *'Venite a trovarci'* (come to visit us'), BLACK HAND, *'Roma è nostra'* (Rome is ours).

这么多年以来，你喷了很多货运火车，我们时常能看到你的涂鸦挂在意大利半岛上行驶的生锈货运火车（merci）上。为什么你决定在这上面喷大量的涂鸦？

我敢说，喷货运火车的热爱是 OZER 和 GIOEL 灌输给我的，但真正促使我行动的是 BUNY 和 HENCE，他们是真正的涂鸦哲学家。我一直追寻新的创作目标，而 BUNY 的世界集装箱项目在我心中久久回荡不曾离去。你必须知道自己为什么涂鸦，并且找到一种方法来与那些试图阻断你梦想的行为说不。所以我承袭了 BUNY 的"征服世界"的想法，我们的梦想不仅仅局限于罗马，而是将我的名字传播到尽可能远的地方。对货运火车的喜爱还有另一个重要的原因:我已经厌倦了看涂鸦被重复清理，这蛮浪费时间跟金钱，并且我还需要冒着风险去喷，这已经不是我这个年纪所能承受之轻。但是继续四处探险的欲望仍然很强烈，于是我决定遵循"经典必须经过长时间的考验，方能到达更远的彼岸"。为了做到这一点，我也开始在通勤火车顶部喷涂鸦，而且我发现这让涂鸦持续长达好几个月不被清理，反而比画在火车车窗以下的涂鸦来得有效。能够看到我的涂鸦一直待在又高又亮的火车顶端，这让我感到欣慰。然而，没有人意识到这个转变。最近，我看到BRUS 的一幅涂鸦也出现在火车上，只是相比起来它是如此的精致与完美，但是在他的正上方，却有一块我一年多前画的"一小时"计划的一部分;几天后，我又看到了那列火车， BRUS 的涂鸦已经被清理掉了，但我的完好无损。他们花了很多时间来清理那副完美的涂鸦，却忘记了顶端还有我的作品。比起创作一幅完美的涂鸦，我的目标是为了让我的名字能够在火车上留的更长的时间。但是没关系，每个写手的目标都不同。

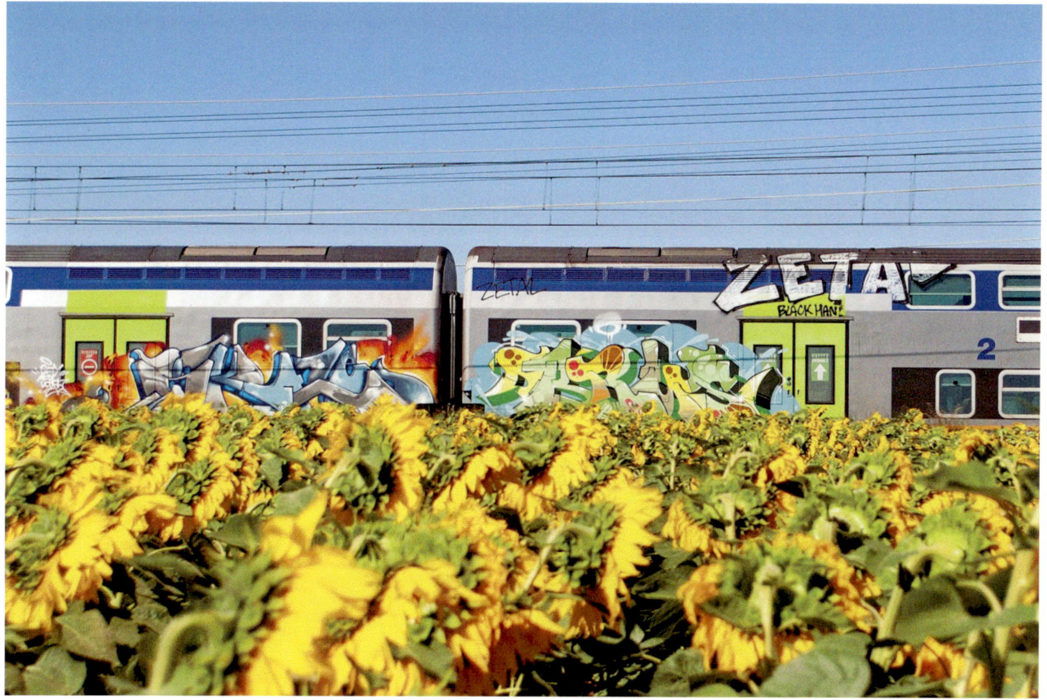

每位写手都对涂鸦有着不同的看法;有些人认为它是一项运动，有些人则更注重风格，还有一些人则认为这是一种很酷的方式来摧毁体制。你对这个经典的命题有什么看法?你认为涂鸦只是一种个人的修行，还是涂鸦会对我们的社会存在某种影响？

几年前，有人问了我一个类似的问题，想知道我是如何定义自己的，究竟是一位艺术家，还是一位破坏者？我一直觉得自己是个不守规矩的叛逆者。我所向往的是那些出现在 70 年代里，试图将整个城市系统画满涂鸦的写手。我比那个时代晚了些出生，这也许是不幸，也可能是注定。这一代总是在纽约的涂鸦先驱之后出生。这一代也都晚于1970 年代有人将"政府之心"喷在了罗马街头。然而一遍又一遍将我的名字重复书写也许是一种伟大的行为。但是我也不放弃任何一个书写句子的机会，将我对某个话题或某个不公正的想法留在街头，希望有人能理解它。而我不仅仅是一位破坏者，更是一个永恒的叛逆者。

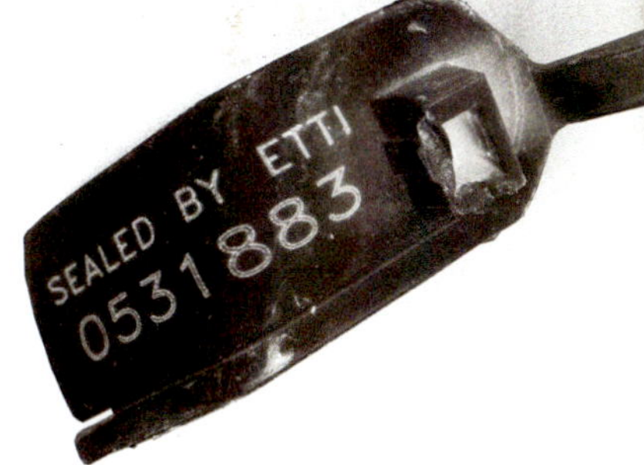

ZETAL
The eternal rebel

The greatest compliment you can give to a writer is to associate his name with the style of a city- I am honored. Every piece I made has been designed to get that visual impression in the observer. A graffiti artist must always be attentive and receptive to what surrounds him and translate his feelings into his pieces, only in this way his work will be personal and expressive.

Rome, therefore, lives in my pieces, in the dirty line of the original cap from the hardware's spray, in the outline of the piece carried with instinct and speed. Even the history of my small Etruscan city lives in my pieces' textures, which are inspired by the Etruscan Bucchero[1]. It wasn't me who forged the "Roman-style" but those who came before me, crews like TRV, ZTK, and CB were a source of inspiration, especially in their early years. The Roman writer who inspired me the most is certainly Dome (CB)[2], he put the original cap in my hands for the first time, giving it to me as if it was the powerful guitar pick of the Tenacious D's movie[3]. I still remember that day, a clear dividing line event for me, in a trattoria in Marino - a small town of the Castelli Romani - called "Il Bujaccaro", between

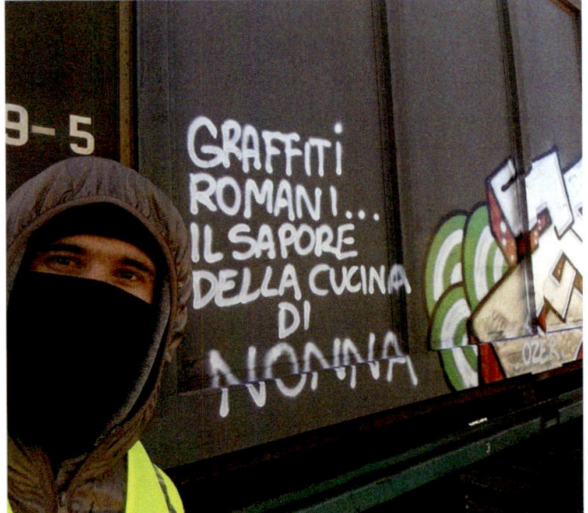

罗马的涂鸦就像是奶奶煮的饭菜 "Roman graffiti… like grandma's cooking flavor"

an Amatriciana[4] and a glass of wine with a shoebox full of epic photos of the "Commando Beasts" on the table. My crew, Black Hand, has certainly continued a stylistic path that was born with them. As for the Roman scene, I have not followed it since the mid-2000s, I find it boring, empty, and without any "vision of the future".

Rome graffiti history is also full of crazy stories. Can you share with us some of your experiences while painting in the Eternal City?

Ok, I know that the stories graffiti artists are most passionate about are those concerning the Rome metro. I start by saying that for family reasons, that I am not going to explain, I have not painted the metro since May 1st, 2004, the day I was caught inside the Magliana depot, but that is another story.

A Mexican guy recently visited Rome, he was recommended to me by trusted friends, everyone talked about him as a serious, reliable guy, so I convinced myself to host him at home —a rare event with people I don't know— he was doing a tour around Italy and the evening he was due to arrive he stood me up, I had canceled appointments and prepared his room, I was very annoyed by his delay.

He called me hours later apologizing for the inconvenience, and I decided to give him another chance. When he arrived, a friendship was immediately born, and from the beginning, we had long chats as if we were old friends. I took him for a nice Carbonara[5] and then we tried to paint a double-deck train, but that evening the workers were surrounding the train. The

mission was only postponed and in the late evening, during one of our conversations, he confessed to me that he really appreciated our puppets, and I, vice versa, appreciate his graffiti with socio-political themes. From there the idea of creating an end2end together was born. BICER is his tag and for a long time, he has been committed to documenting the exodus of the South American "brave migrants" who are desperately trying to enter America[6].

He convinced me that those people deserved a piece on the Rome metro. I've been out of the game for too many years and I couldn't take the risk of painting in places that would need a preliminary study. However, I knew that for some time some old carriages of the Rome-Lido line had been parked a few hundred meters from the Magliana depot, a peripheral and not very controlled area and he accepted the compromise. We get carried away and we sketched an end2end, BICER was in charge of painting the letters 'MIGRANTES VALIENTES' and I would have taken care of the figurative part: the biblical scene of Moses opening the waters, with two top2bottom waves at the ends of the wagon, and two black hands open, with broken chains at the wrists. We thought of the letters lying on the seabed, surrounded by tombstones engraved with the initials of the border areas where many migrants risking their lives every day to find a better future. In short, a heart-felt subject for both of us. The next day, after a quick check, we sneaked in around dinner time, the situation was calm and in 20 minutes we had already done our hands, a wave and filled out all the letters of the piece, but we realized that a machine of the security had come to park not far from us. We laid down to observe them, sure that with a short run we would be out. After waiting for around 20 minutes a second car arrived, they started chatting outside the cars, then one of the two started walking towards us with a rapid and threatening pace.

At that moment we decided it was time to take our bags and go, once we got out of the fence we tried to establish a dialogue with the energetic security, to convince him that the car was nothing more than an iron carcass, but we did not persuade him and he threatened that soon we would be surrounded. We disappeared into the dark with the regret of having left our work unfinished. The following day BICER did not want to give up, it would be his last night in Rome and we were very close to finish the work. We decided to return, this time a little later. The area seemed clear and in a few minutes I was on the ladder coloring the second hand and my partner doing the background for the letters, we had been inside for no more than a few minutes when suddenly we heard a car coming towards us at full speed. This time I couldn't save the ladder, only the colors. We were incredulous at how fast they arrived, and at their diligence to defend those abandoned cars. The mission failed once again and the next day BICER would have left, but we still had the colors so we decided we would make the theme anyway. In the morning I took him into an abandoned warehouse and we painted with all the dedication and anger possible. We had done our best, but sometimes things don't go as planned. However, a strong friendship was born and the promise to return one day to close that e2e together.

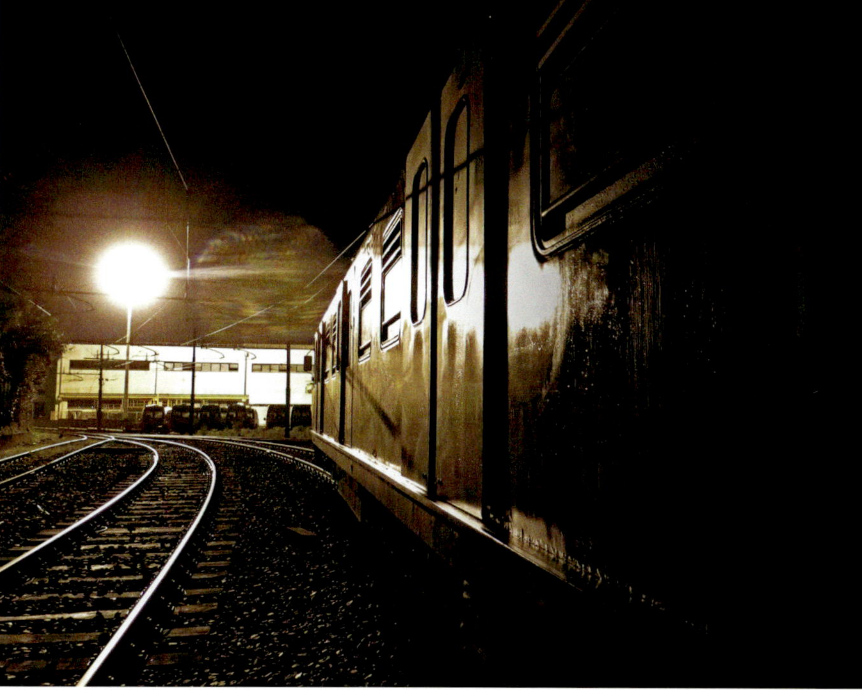

罗马，丽都线，马格利亚纳车站。
—
Rome, Lido Line, Magliana Depot.

In an era where crews are often a shortcut to reach some kind of graffiti status, BLACK HAND, your crew, seems made of a bunch of real brothers with a shared mission. Can you tell us the story behind it?

I am convinced that there are two types of Crew, those made by real brothers and those made by graffiti writers, the Black Hand is born around the 2000s, from my and Dres' need to give a name to our friendship. A few years later the circle of friends expanded, but we all had the same purpose, to bring our partnership up. After so many years some of us have moved away, life has taken them elsewhere and unfortunately, others have passed away. Those who are left are still full of passion and dedication to the cause and they push our crew with more intensity than ever. Do you want to know the secret of our longevity? We push each other, we set goals, we impose ourselves to do better, to amaze, to go beyond the routine of simple graffiti made of letters, loops, and colors. I don't want to be arrogant in saying that today we no longer look at Rome as a reference point, but nowadays the competition is between us and the crews beyond the border, the ones we value the most. Hanging out at night with my lifelong friends, painting together as we painted many years ago, sharing the sensations that those places instill, it gives you the feeling that life goes on but some things do not change.

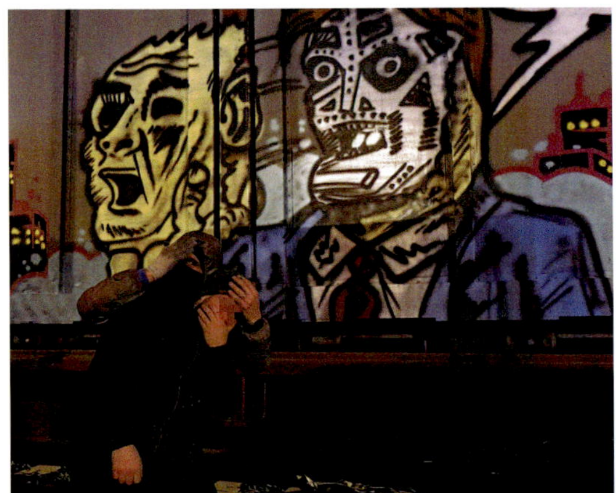

Keepsake 拍摄的 ZETAL 与 DEM 一同创作的首尾相连的火车涂鸦，这是一个具有人类特征的木偶机器人。有时我们也把自己想象成机器人，因为我们不停的在喷涂鸦。与这些金属列车接触的时间让我们变成了钢铁侠。

Keepsake shot of the ZETAL-DEM end2end with a robot puppet with human features. Sometimes we consider ourselves machines too because of the number of pieces we paint. The time spent in contact with all this metal makes us a bit like iron-men.

You have painted a lot of freights for many years now and it is common to spot your tag running on the rusty side of a 'merci'7 in the Italian peninsula. Why did you decide to invest a lot of work on this kind of surface?

The love for freight trains was passed to me - I would dare to say instilled - by OZER and GIOEL, but the real boost was given to me by BUNY and HENCE, true philosophers of writing. I'm always looking for new goals and BUNY's Container World project "rang a bell" in me. You have to think ahead, you need to understand why you paint graffiti and find a way to avoid those who want to suffocate and repress your dreams without distorting what you do. So I embraced BUNY's idea of "conquering the world", of not being limited to the metropolitan area of Rome to send my name to the furthest place possible. There is another important aspect for why I prefer freight trains: I am tired of seeing my graffiti buffed, it is a waste of time, money, and a risk that, at my age, I can no longer afford. The desire to stay and go around is still great so I decided to follow the philosophy of "it must run for a long time and to the furthest place". To do so I also started painting the roofs of commuter trains and I discovered that they run for much longer before being buffed, sometimes even for many months, nothing to compare with the few days of life of the classic windows-down pieces. It is wonderful to see my pieces standing alone, high and shiny on the roof of a car, they are a beautiful sight. Yet no one has perceived the turning point. Recently I saw a piece of Brus running, it was so refined and polished, at least a '1-hour' piece and exactly above him, on the roof, there was a piece of mine from a year before; a few days later I saw the same wagon again, the Brus piece had been buffed, mine was still there, intact. they had spent time removing his burner, oblivious of my work. My aim is to have my name running for longer more than creating the most precise and accurate piece. Each one has its own goals.

Every writer has a different perspective on what graffiti is; some think is just a sport, some focus more on the style, and others think is a cool way to bomb the system. What is your view on this classic dilemma? Do you think graffiti is just a personal journey or it has some kind of impact on our society?

They asked me a similar question a few years ago, wondering how I defined myself, an artist, or a vandal? I've always felt like a non-conformist rebel. I would have liked to be one of those timeless rebels who tried to overthrow the system in the 70s, unfortunately, or fortunately, I was born a generation later - I have always been one generation too late- after the "historical" graffiti pioneers of NY - after those who first painted in Rome and after those who stormed the "heart of the state government" in the 1970s[8]. However, the desire to send a message or simply write my tag - again and again - is great. I do not miss an opportunity to write sentences, leave my thoughts on a certain topic or a certain injustice hoping that someone will understand it and see in me not only a vandal but also a rebel.

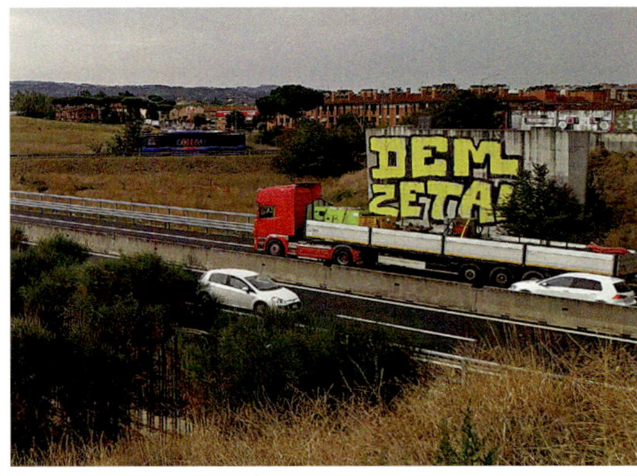

距离我们喷"我们的第一次，献给伟大的爱"在罗马环城路上已经过去很久了。在 DRES 开发了这一区域后，我们团队于2000年后开始陆续沿着环城线开始喷涂鸦。他曾对我说："地铁在晚上都会关门，但是这条环线从不关门。"不过我们有一段时间没再在那里喷东西了，但是我们有必要提醒其他罗马写手，在这儿，是谁对他的爱最真最深。

It has been a long time since we painted 'our first, great love': the *Grande Raccordo Anulare* (Rome ring road). We started painting around that road in 2000 after DRES realized its potential. He once told me: "The subway closes at night, the *Grande Raccordo Anulare* never closes". We have neglected it for a while, but sometimes we have to remind other Roman writers who loved it first and who loves it the most.

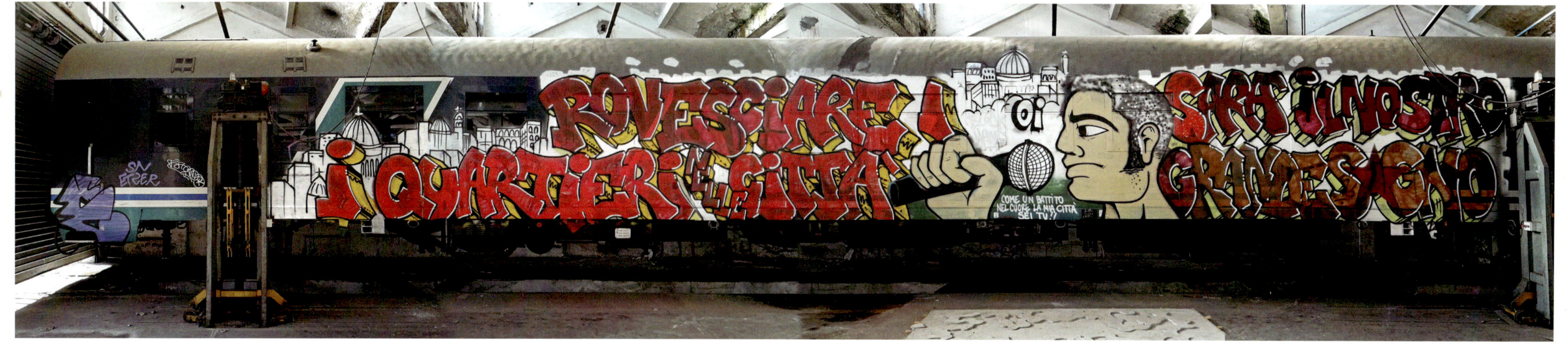

这截列车是我和 GIOEL 在卡萨尔·伯尔托内一同完成的，它是为了纪念 Angelo Conti，他的绰号是"雪茄"（Sigaro，意为"雪茄"），他是 Banda Bassotti* 历史的一份子。最近，他们整理了一些藏品，并在"雪茄"朋友的护送下把火车挂在一辆卡车上运到城市里展出。我相信涂鸦还必须传递一定的社会信息，向激励过你的人表示敬意，或者谴责不公正。

This car was done by me and GIOEL inside a squat in Casal Bertone, it is dedicated to the memory of Angelo Conti known as Sigaro (Cigar), the historical voice of the *Banda Bassotti**. Recently they cleared those deposits and hooked the train to a truck and took it away to the city escorted by Sigaro's friends who claimed ownership. I believe that graffiti must also send social messages, pay homage to people who have inspired you, or denounce injustices.

*Banda Bassotti 是 1987年在罗马成立的意大利 ska-punk 乐队。他们的歌曲通常是政治性的，关注共产主义和反法西斯问题。这篇文章写道："颠覆城市社区，这将是我们的伟大梦想"。

*Banda Bassotti is an Italian ska-punk band formed in 1987 in Rome. Their songs are generally political in nature, focusing on Communist and anti-Fascist issues. The piece reads: 'To subvert the city neighborhoods, this will be our great dream'.

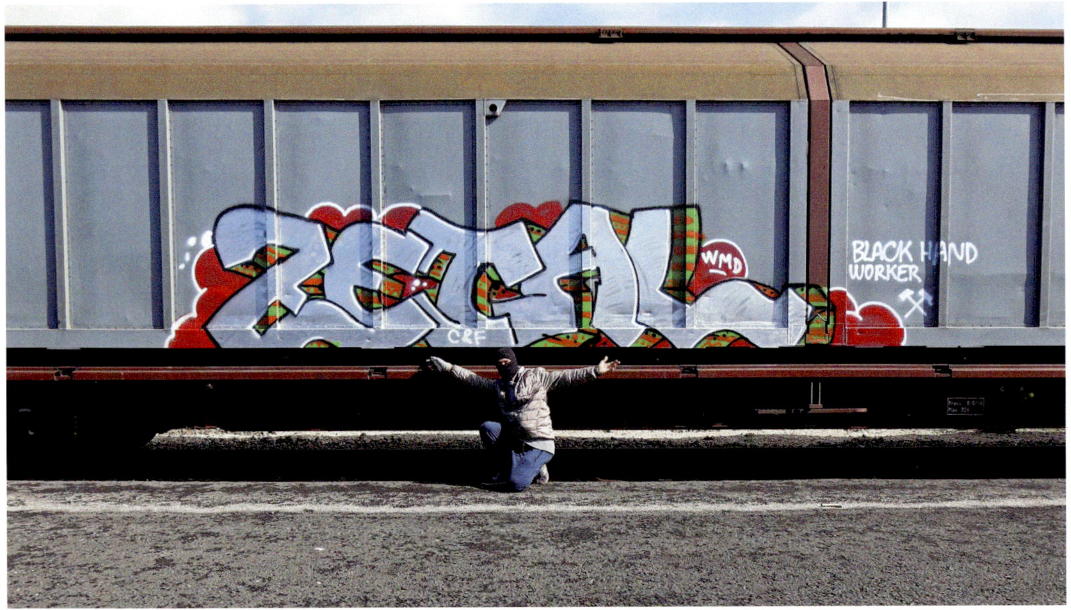

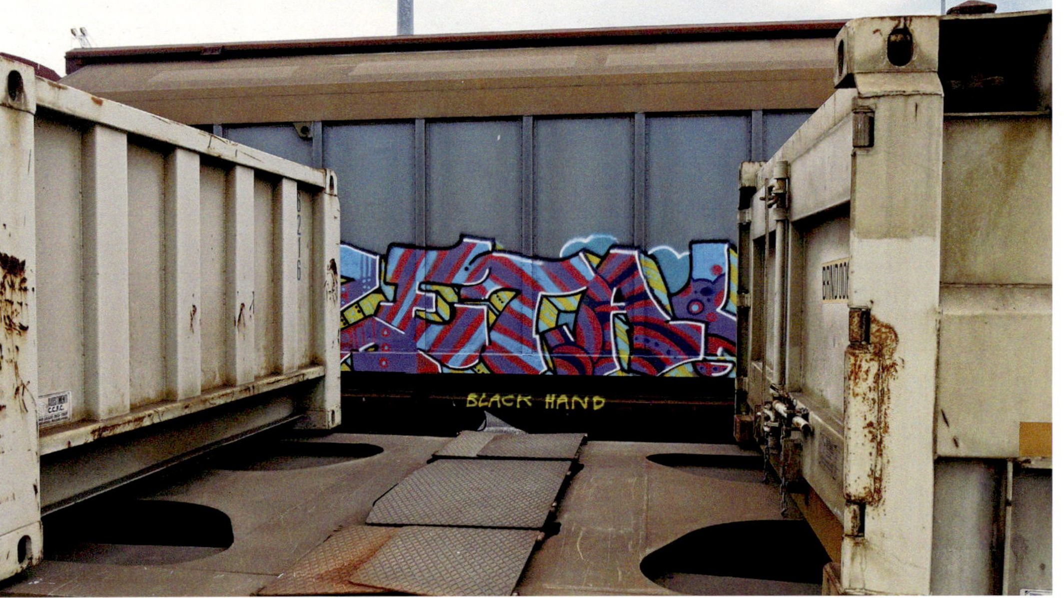
WMD
BLACK HAND
WORKER
CRF
BLACK HAND

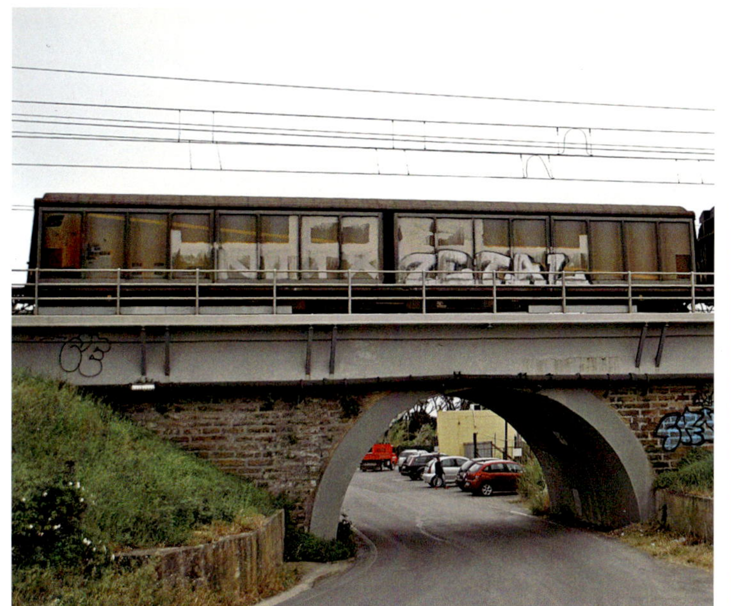

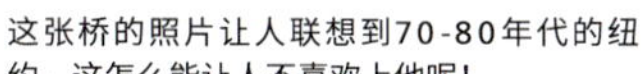

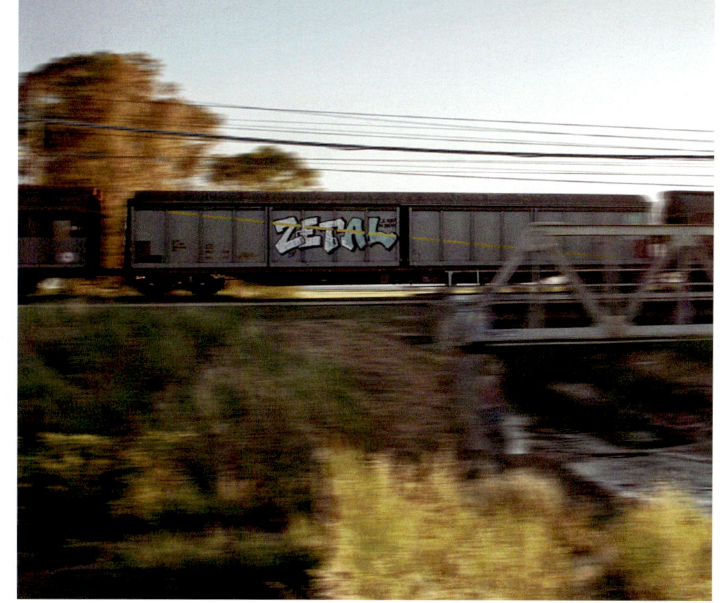

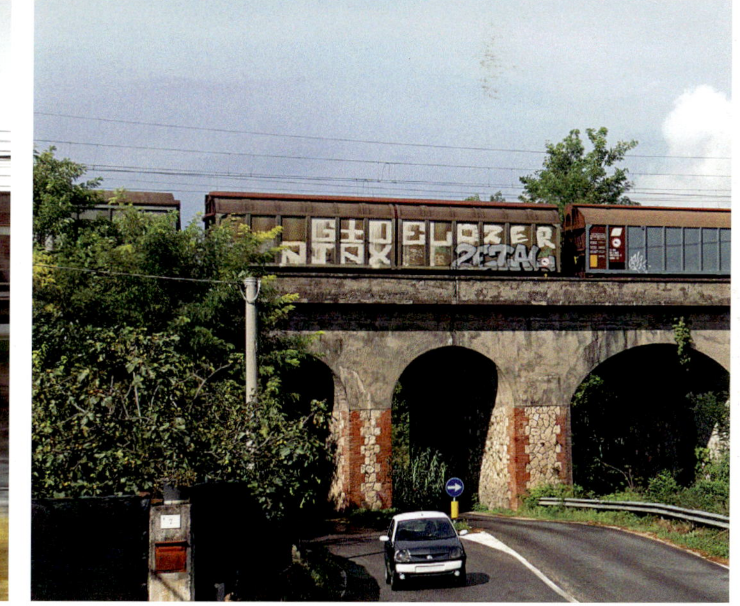

这张桥的照片让人联想到70-80年代的纽约，这怎么能让人不喜欢上他呢！

The photos of the bridges are reminiscent of the glorious NY photos of the 70s and 80s, how not to like it!

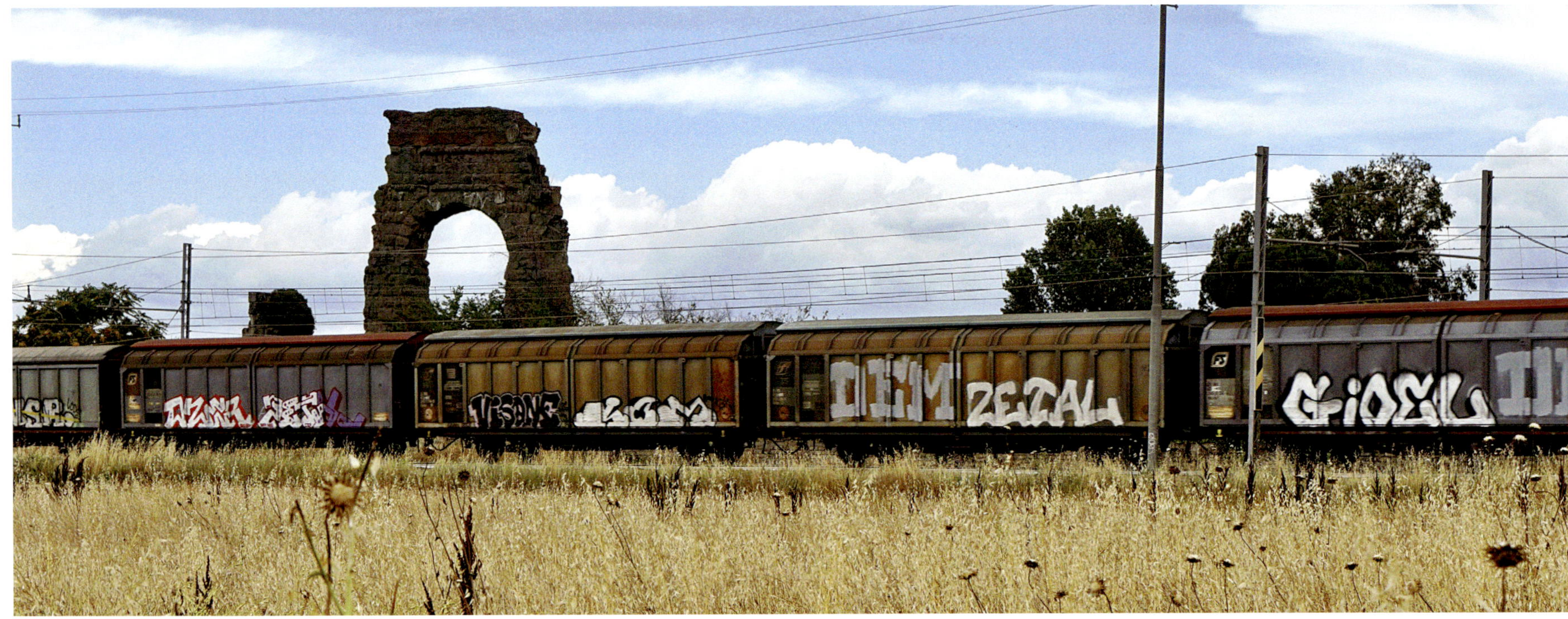

这是一处历史悠久的地方，可能也是最经典的罗马火车涂鸦点。我们很喜欢去那里拍摄货运火车的照片，尤其是全景照片。这些火车与周围的景观很好地融合在一起，特别是罗马的景观。

—

This place is a historic location, probably the most classic Roman trackside spot! We really like to go there to take pictures of freights, especially panoramic photos. That scrap metal blends very well with the landscape, especially with the Roman landscape.

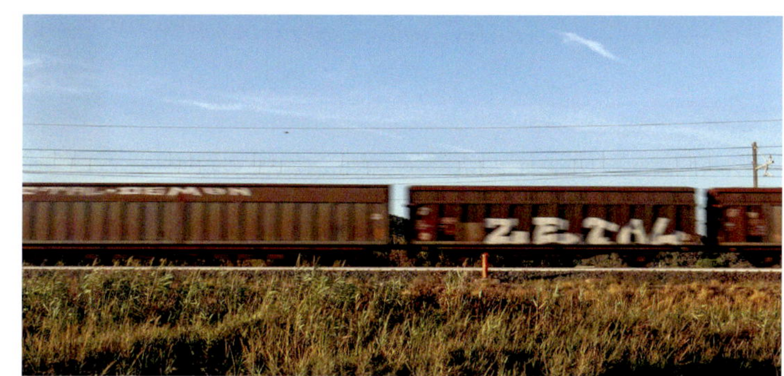
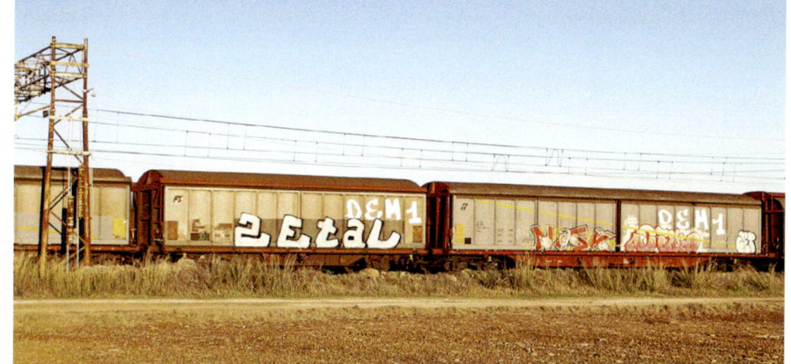
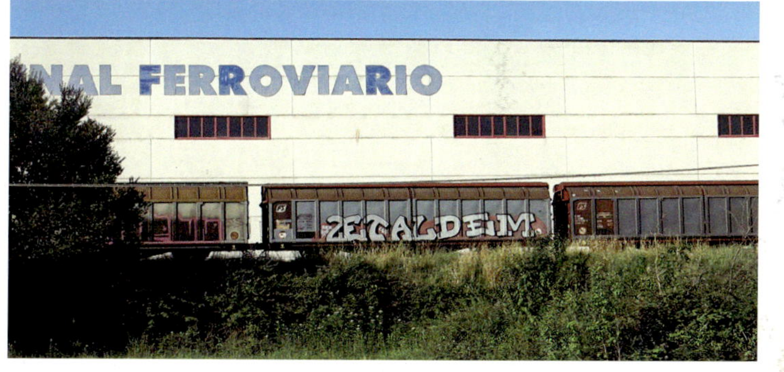

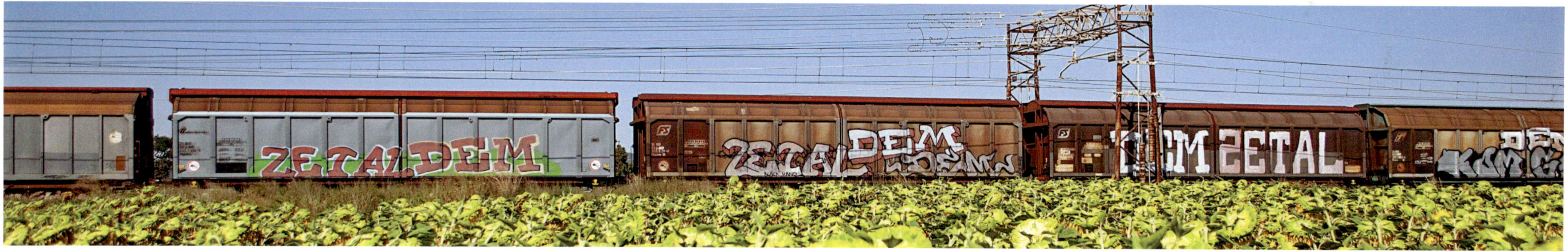

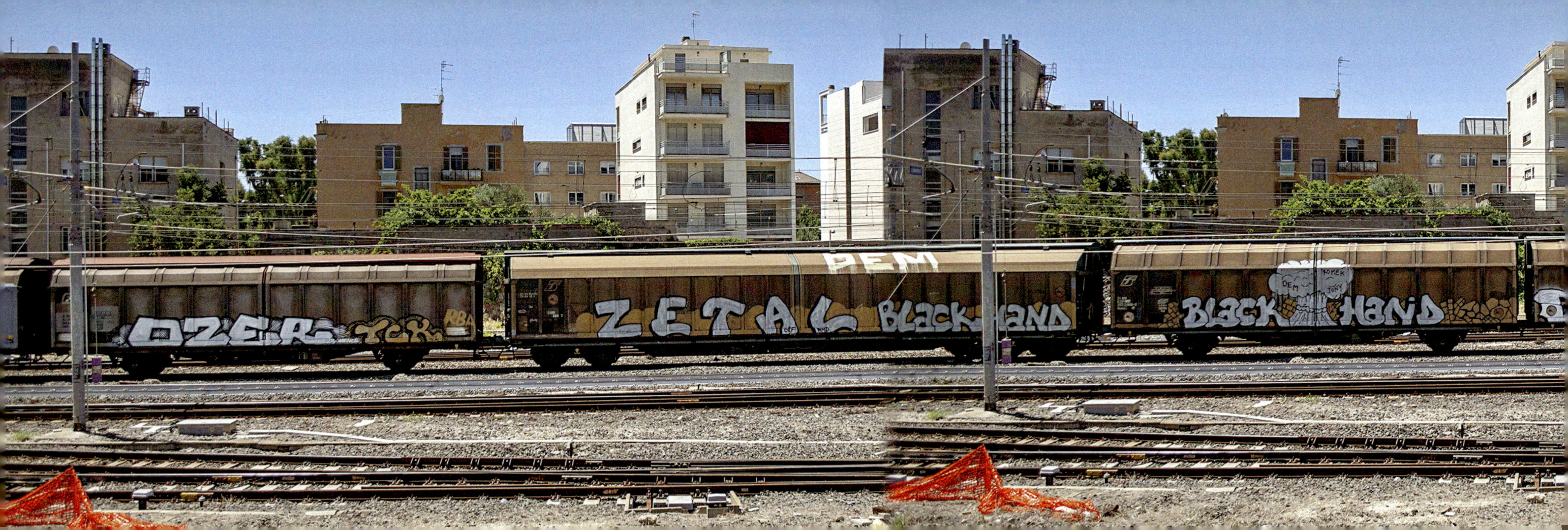

DEM
OZER
TCK
RBA
ZETA6
BLACK HAND
BLACK HAND
DEM

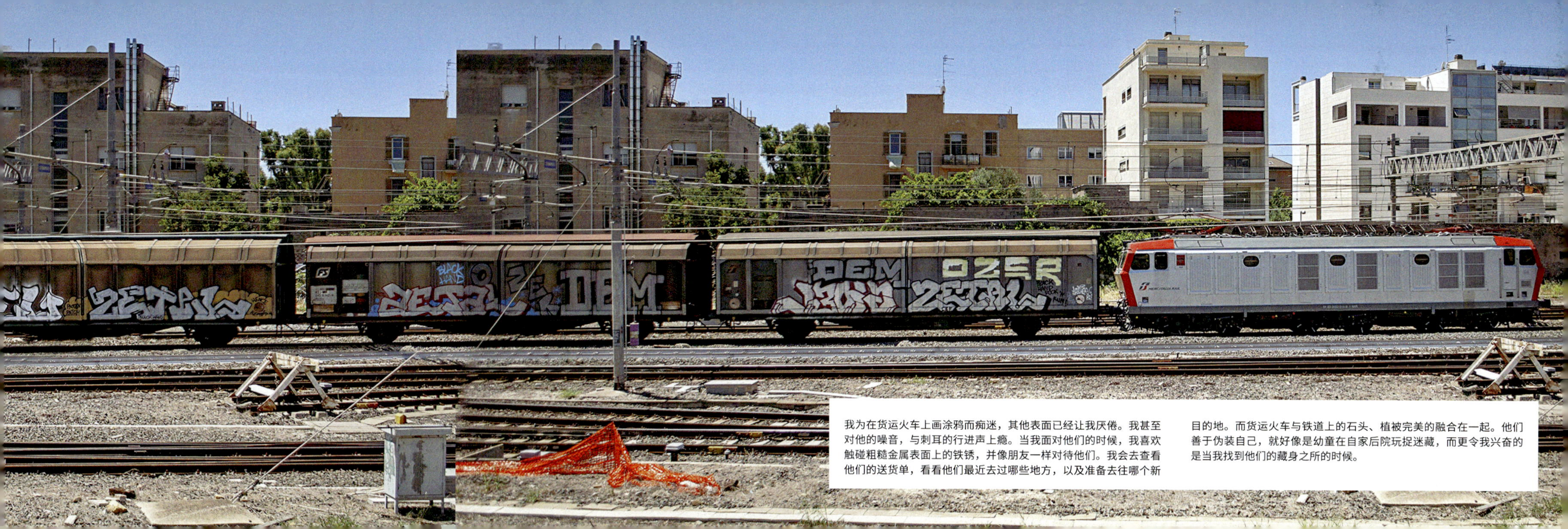
我为在货运火车上画涂鸦而痴迷，其他表面已经让我厌倦。我甚至对他的噪音，与刺耳的行进声上瘾。当我面对他们的时候，我喜欢触碰粗糙金属表面上的铁锈，并像朋友一样对待他们。我会去查看他们的送货单，看看他们最近去过哪些地方，以及准备去往哪个新目的地。而货运火车与铁道上的石头、植被完美的融合在一起。他们善于伪装自己，就好像是幼童在自家后院玩捉迷藏，而更令我兴奋的是当我找到他们的藏身之所的时候。

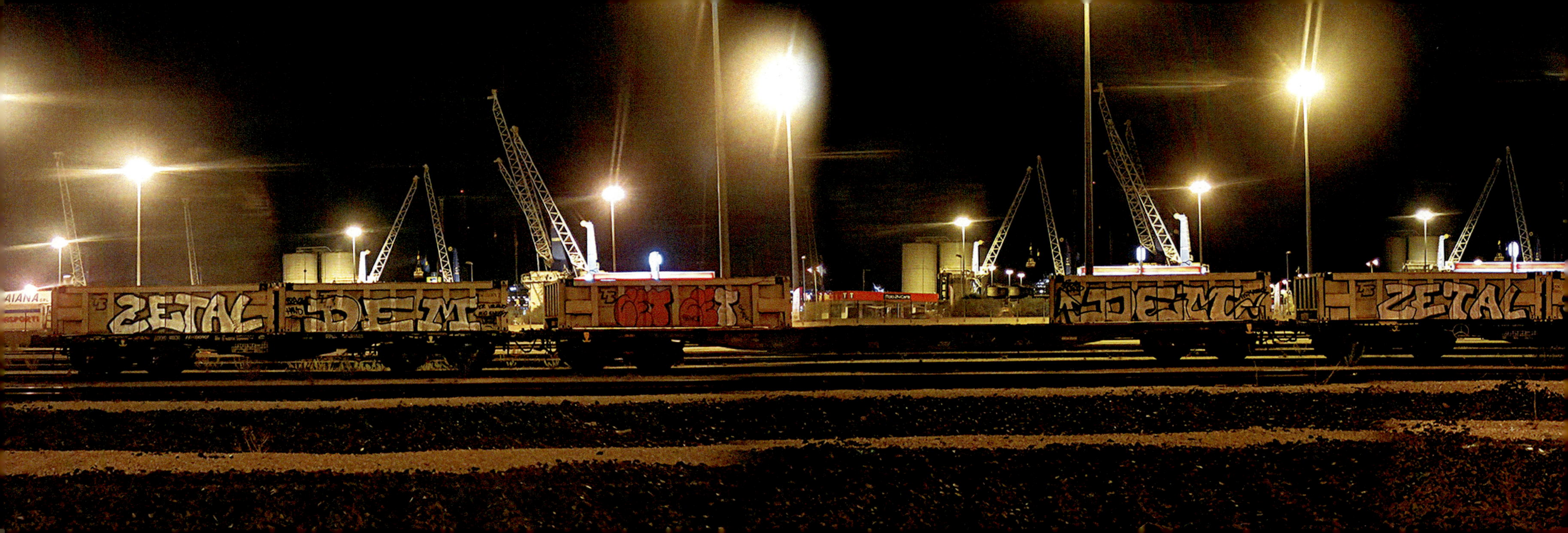

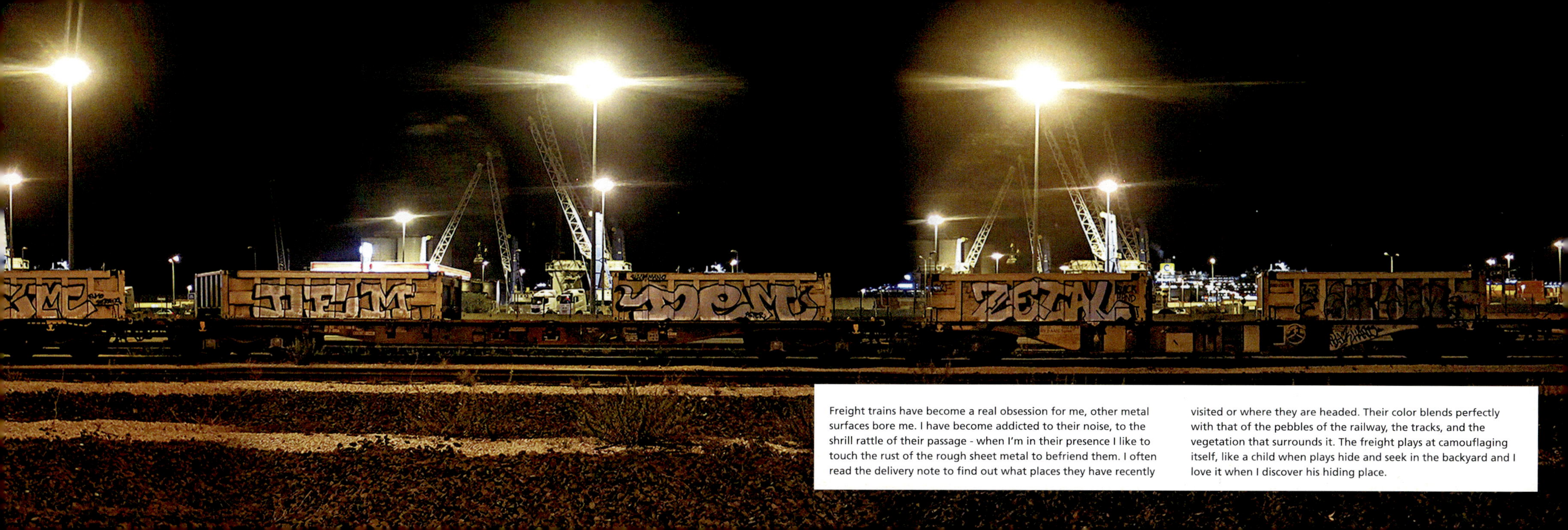

Freight trains have become a real obsession for me, other metal surfaces bore me. I have become addicted to their noise, to the shrill rattle of their passage - when I'm in their presence I like to touch the rust of the rough sheet metal to befriend them. I often read the delivery note to find out what places they have recently visited or where they are headed. Their color blends perfectly with that of the pebbles of the railway, the tracks, and the vegetation that surrounds it. The freight plays at camouflaging itself, like a child when plays hide and seek in the backyard and I love it when I discover his hiding place.

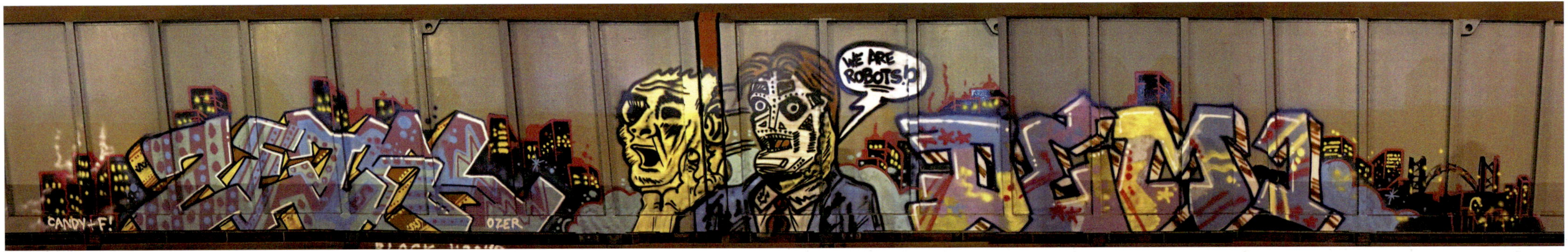

WE ARE ROBOTS!
CANDY + F!
OZER
BLACK HAND

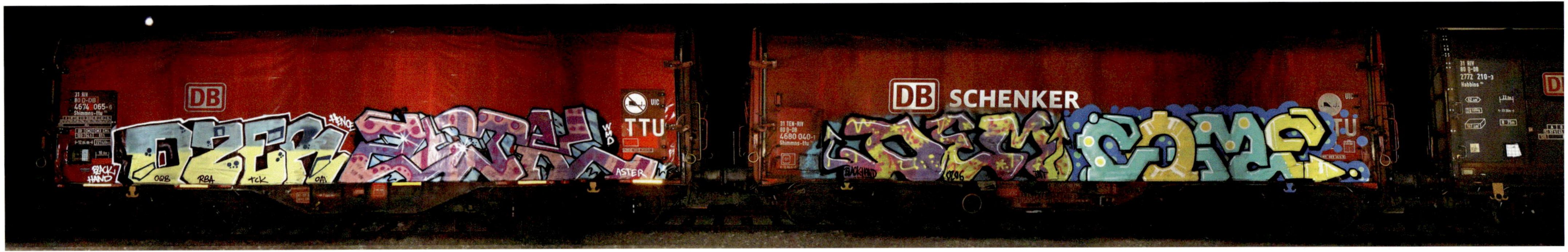

DB
TTU
UIC
BLACK HAND
OZB
RBA
TCK
OAV
ASTER
DB SCHENKER
UIC
TTU

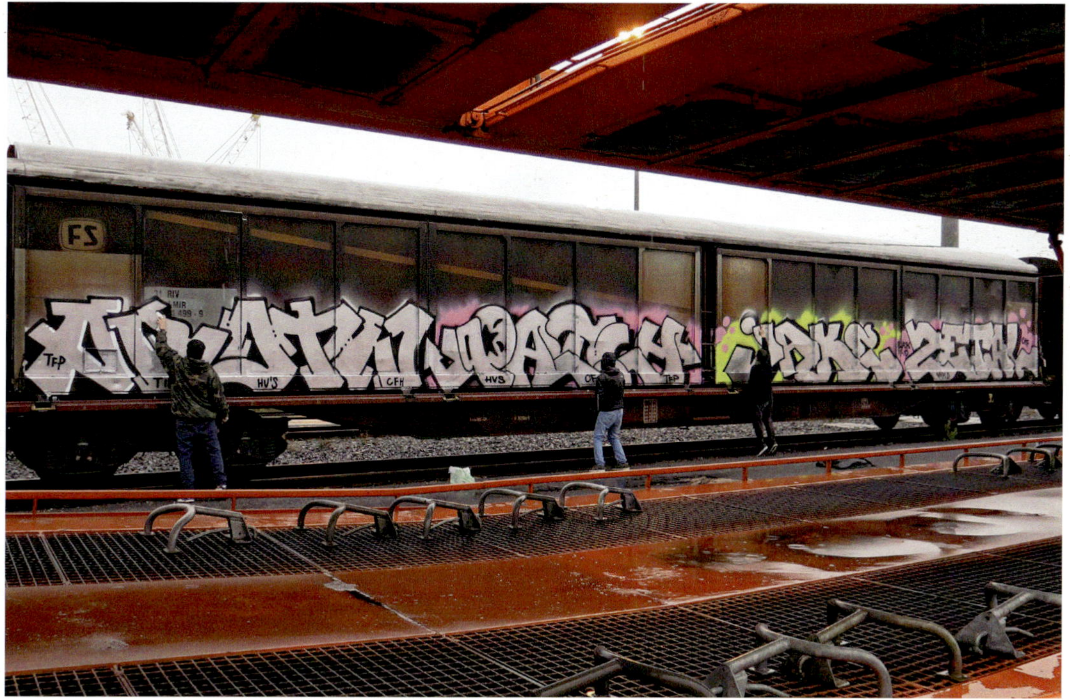

列车的左下角写着："冲向天空"，右边写着："向所有为理想而奋斗的同志致敬"。Assalto al cielo 是一部意大利电影的名字，这部电影讲述的是在 1967年到 1977年间，年轻人在议会外的政治斗争中活跃起来的故事。

—

The train at the bottom left reads: 'Assault to the sky', and on the right: 'A tribute to all the comrades who fought for an ideal'. *Assalto al cielo* is also the name of an italian movie about the youngsters who enlivened the extra-parliamentary political battles between 1967 and 1977.

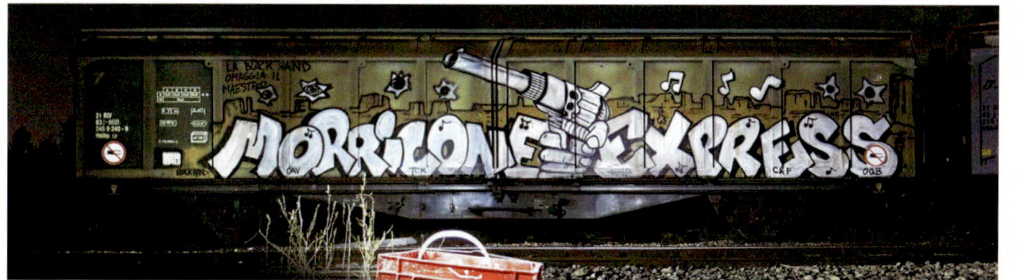

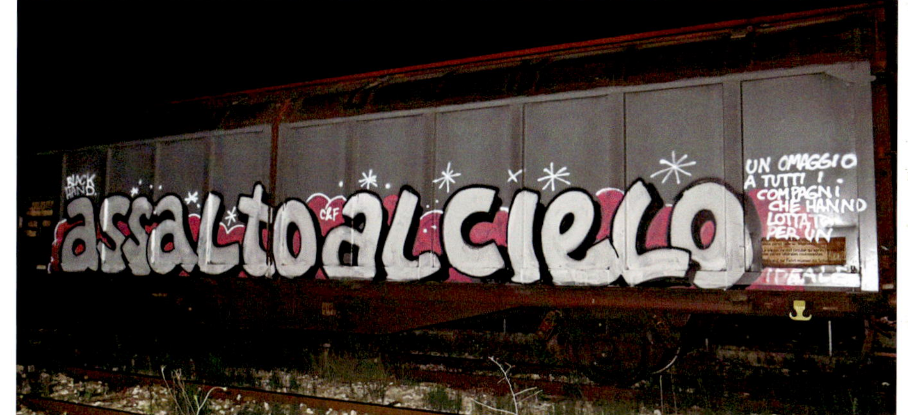

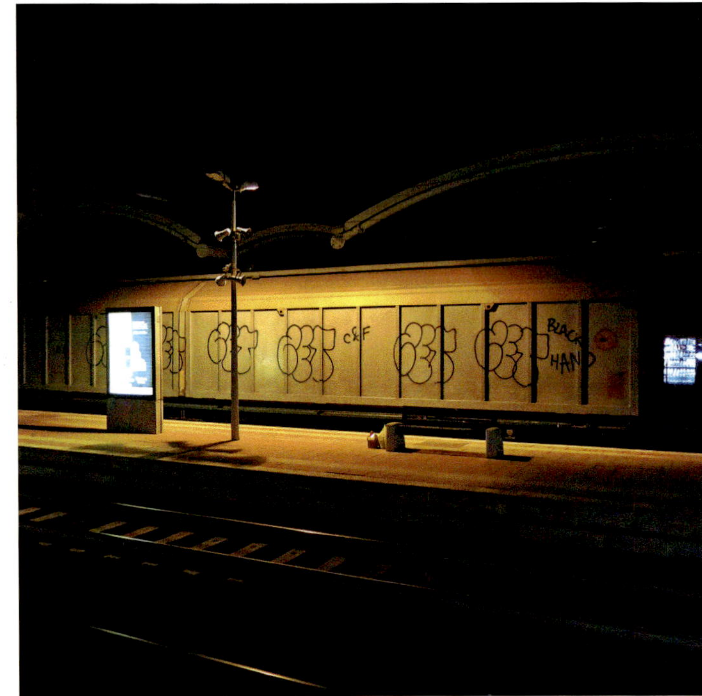

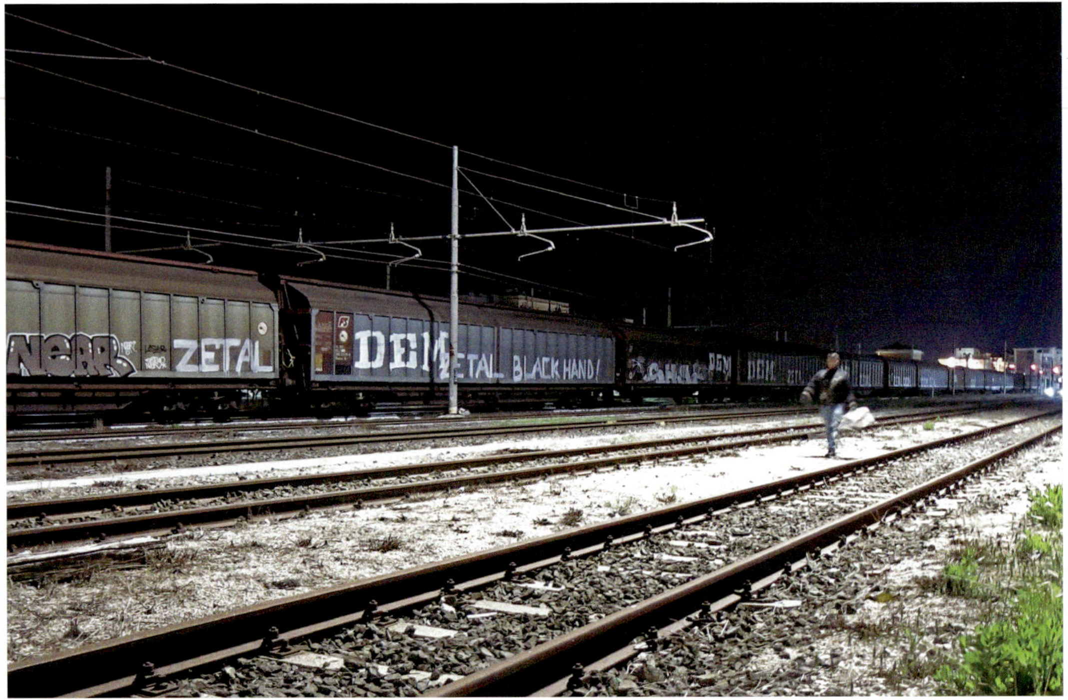

当我们站在货运列车的前面时，我们意识到这里数量庞大，如果只是画一截车厢那就像一滴水滴进大海里，所以当我们准备去喷涂涂鸦的时候，我们为自己配备一个大桶,里面装的不是水,但是满满的油漆。

—

When we stand in front of the freight trains we are aware that there is a huge amount of them, just painting a single car is like adding a drop to the sea, so when we go out on a mission we equip ourselves with a large bucket - not of water - but of paint.

货运列车停车区的氛围不同于其他停靠点，这里充满了更多的浪漫。这种巨大的宁静感会让你沉浸其中，你会立刻变得更能接受噪音、声音和气味。

—

The atmosphere in a freight yard is different from the other yards, there is more romance. That greater tranquility makes you appreciate it more and you immediately become more receptive to noises, sounds, and smells.

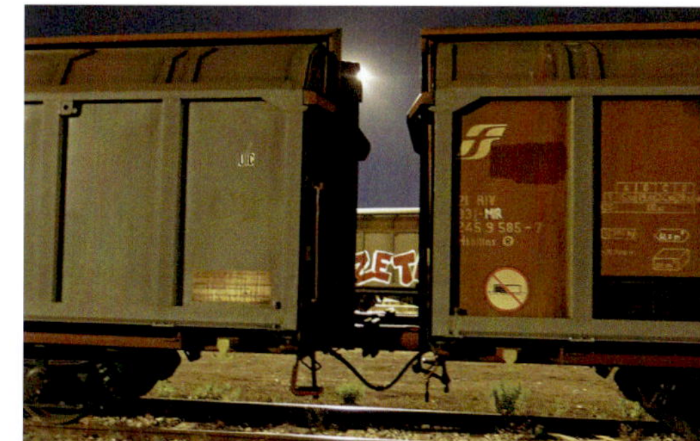
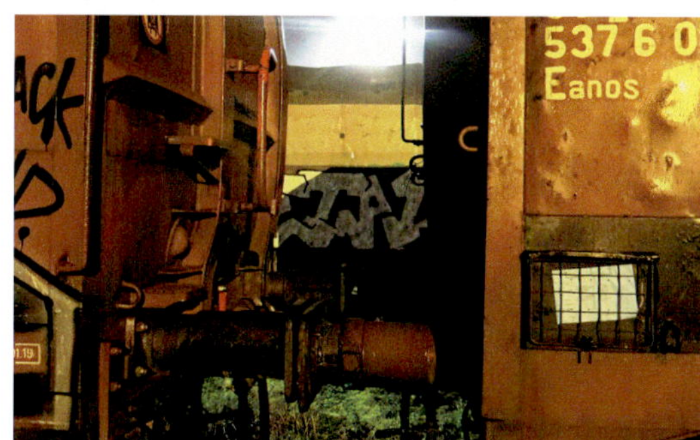
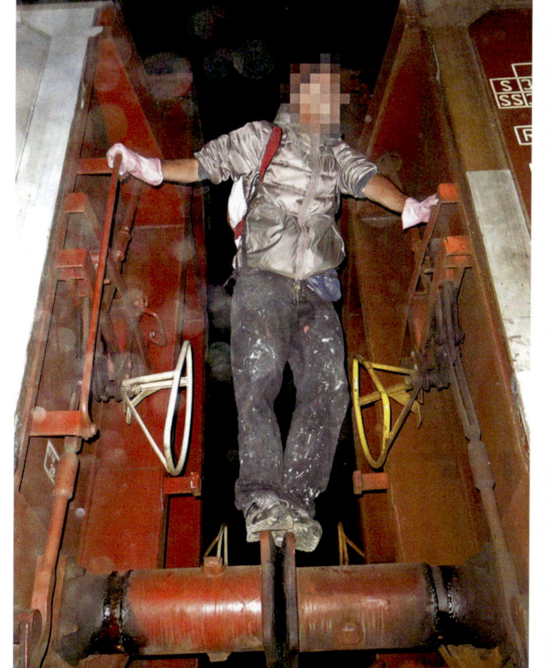
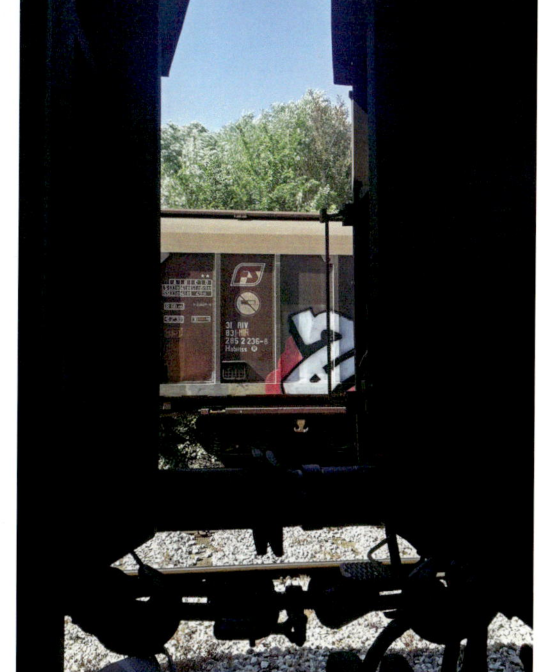
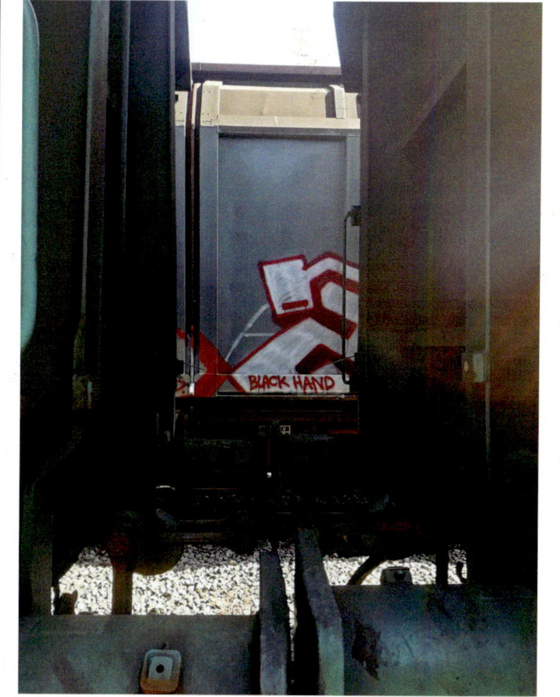

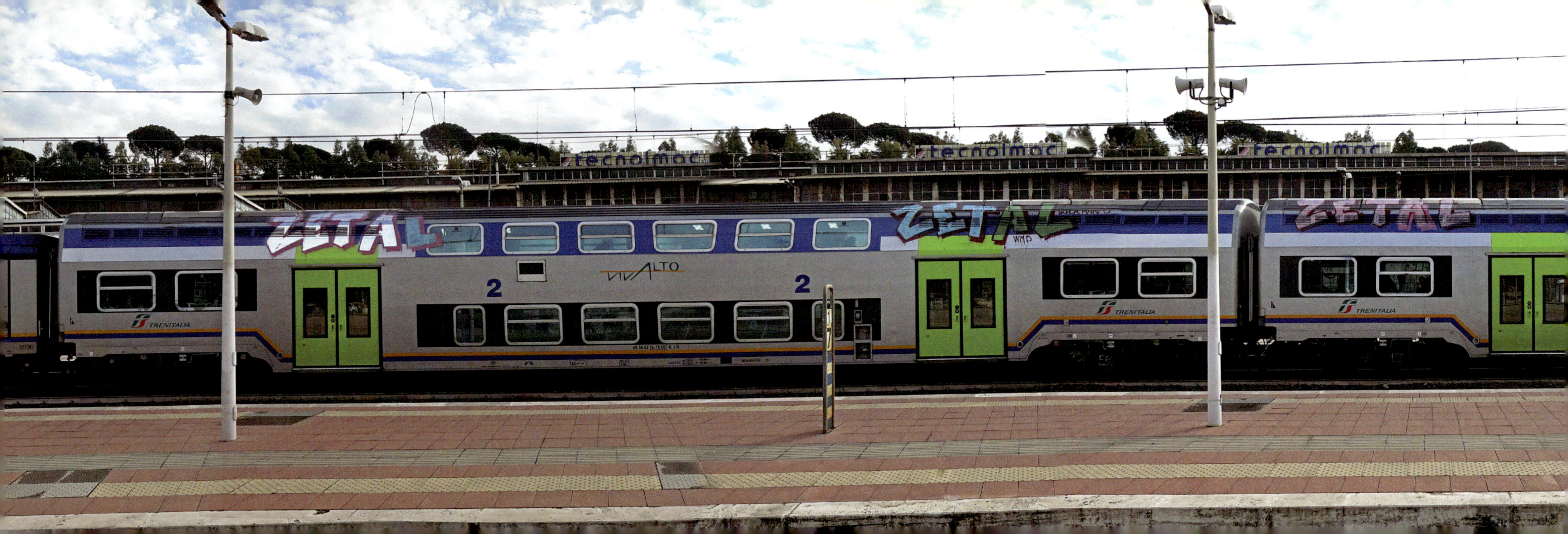

tecnolmac
2
vivALTO
2
TRENITALIA

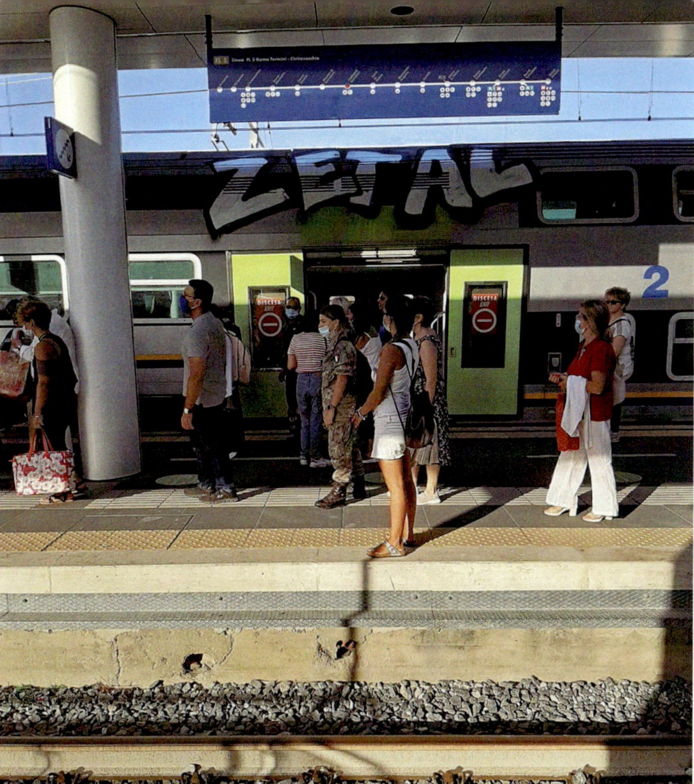

ZETA

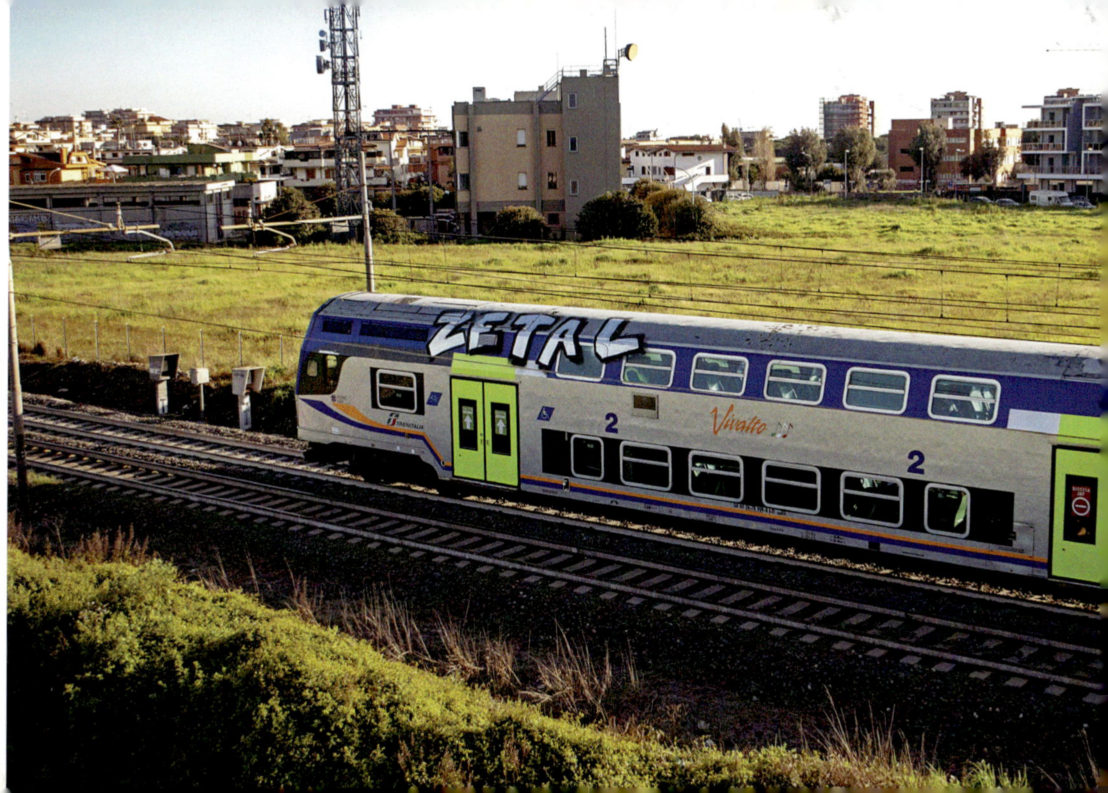

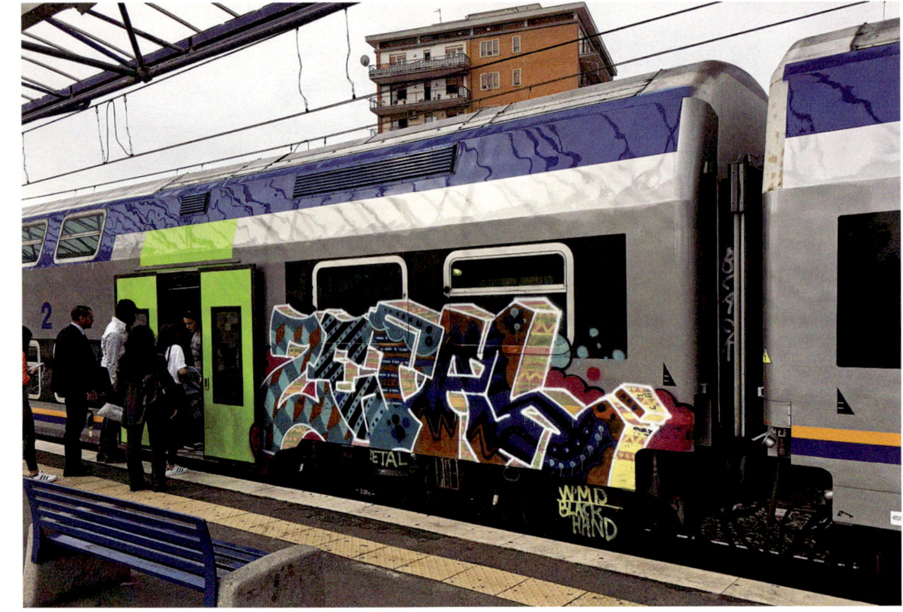

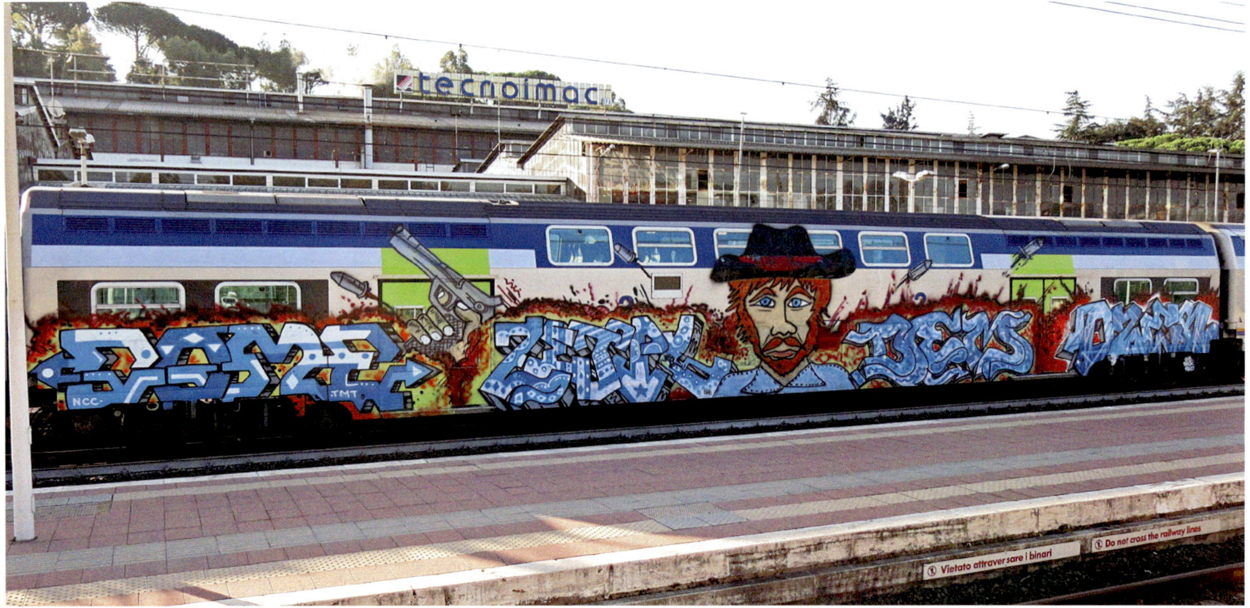

我住的地方离罗马火车停靠点很远，当我家附近出现了一处停靠点时，那是一种无法抗拒的力量，我们创作了一系列伟大的作品，我们时常进入停靠点画一整截火车，但是过了一段时候后我们就对这种货车感到倦怠，因为没过几天这些涂鸦就会被清理，这对我们来说是一种浪费。所以我们决定只喷火车顶部，这项计划持续了几个月。在这截首尾相连的货车中，我们写道："BELLI, SPORCHI E RIBELLI"（帅气、肮脏和叛逆）——这是一部来自斯科拉电影的标题[9]。这三个形容词完全包含了我们团队的想法。左边的傀儡代表着一种紧密的血缘关系，而右边的傀儡手握刀，准备攻击那些背叛和反对我们的人。
—

I have always lived far from the Roman yards, and when a layup showed up near my house we could not resist and for some time we made some great production, entire wagons with top2bottom puppets, but after some time we get tired that those wagons only run for a few days before being buffed, such a big effort wasted. So we decided to just paint roofs, those will go around for months. In this e2e we wrote: 'BELLI, SPORCHI E RIBELLI' (beautiful, dirty and rebellious) a pun on the title of Scola's film[9]. These three adjectives fully enclose the idea behind my crew. The puppet on the left represents a blood bond and on the right, a hand holding a knife is ready to attack those who betray and oppose us.

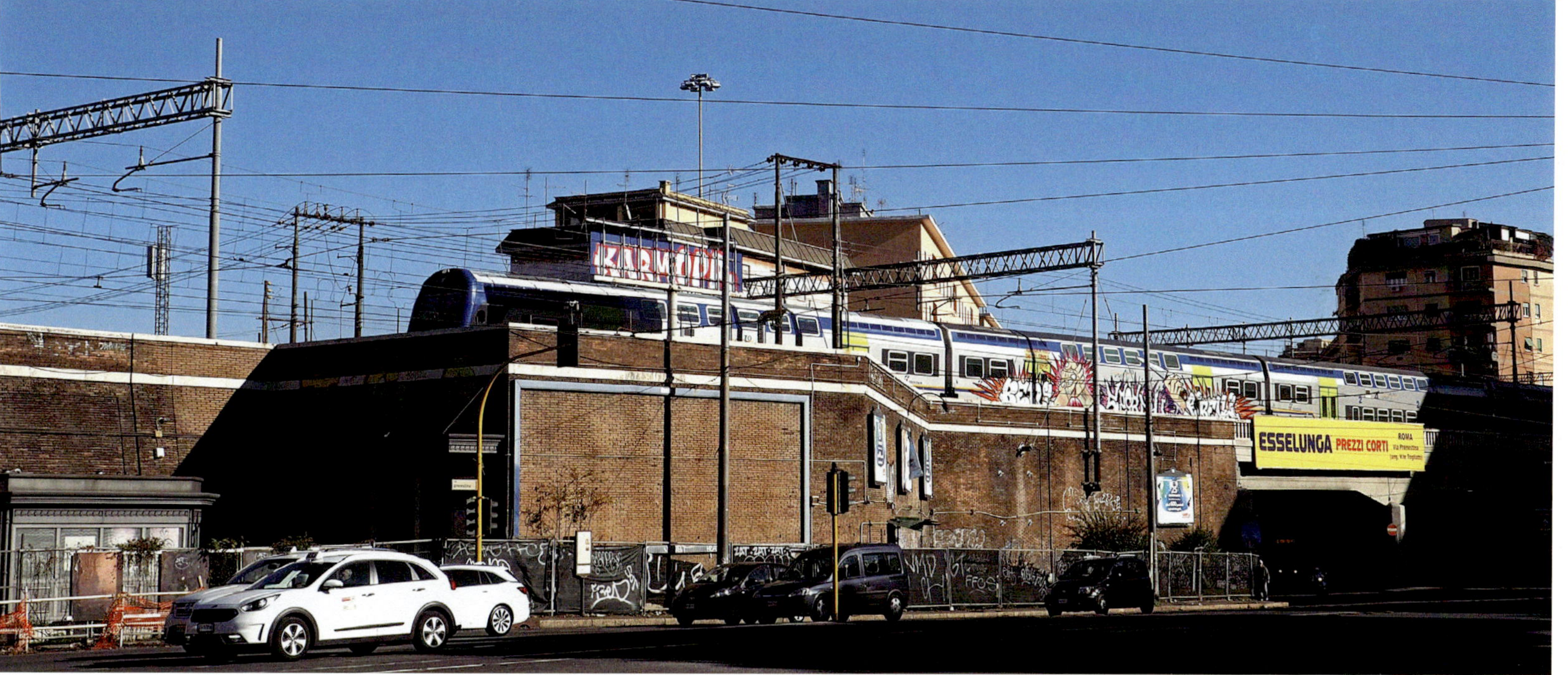

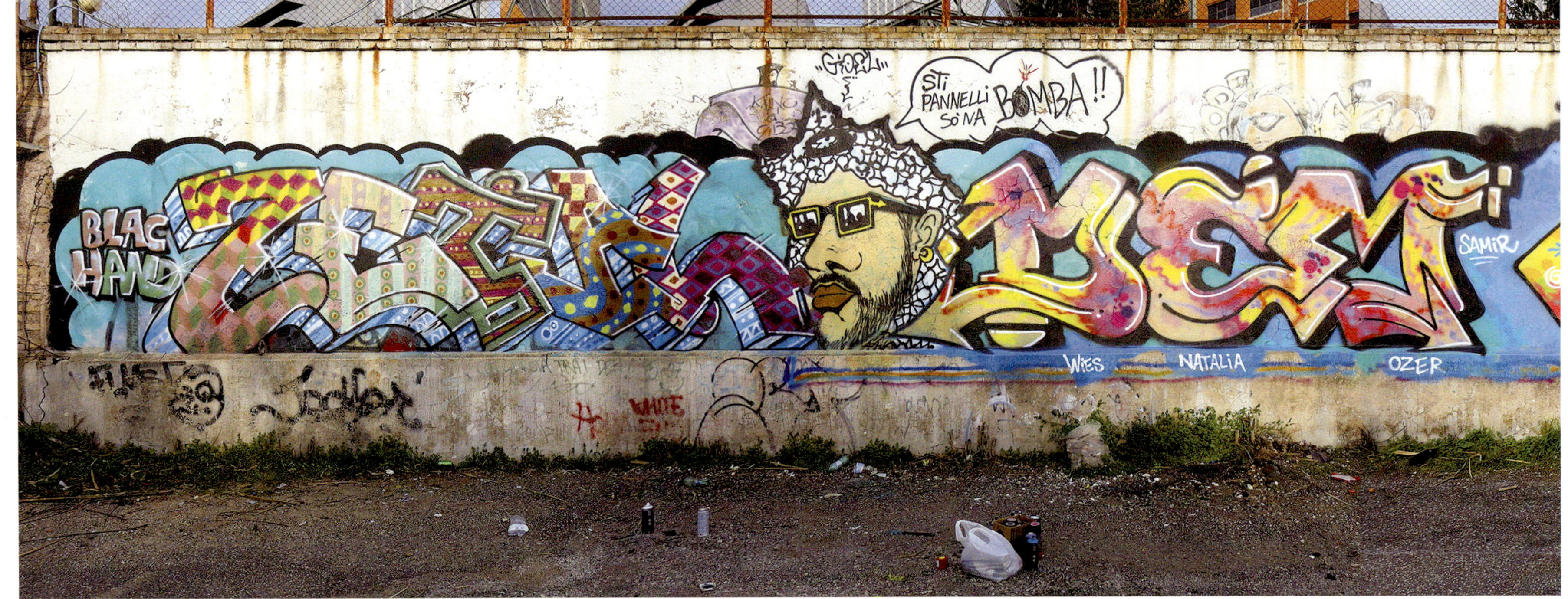

ZETAL 和 DEM 的上墙合作。 中间有一幅亚西尔·阿拉法特（Yasser Arafat）的肖像，上面写着："Sti pannelli so' na bomba!"（这些围挡都是炸弹!）。

—

ZETAL and DEM join forces on a wall. At the centre a portrait of Yasser Arafat that says: "Sti pannelli so' na bomba!" (These panels are a bomb!).

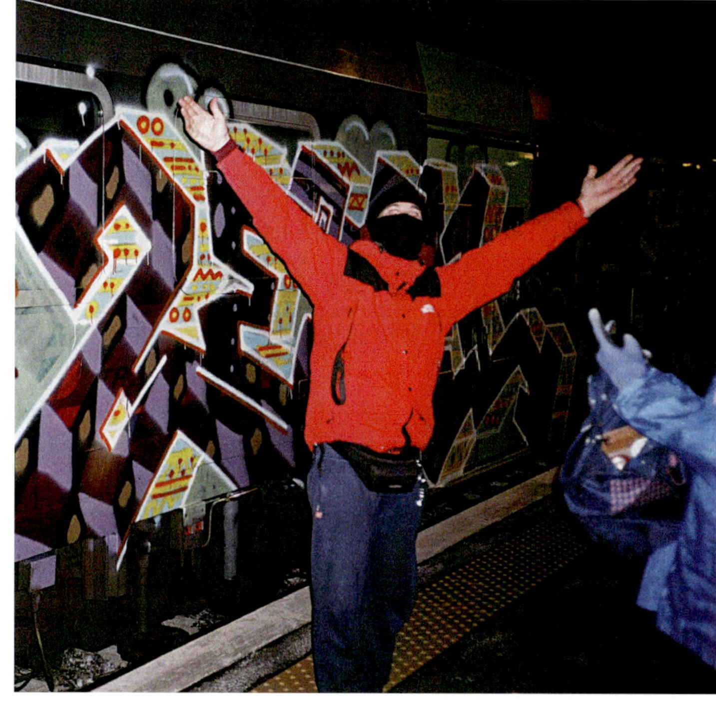

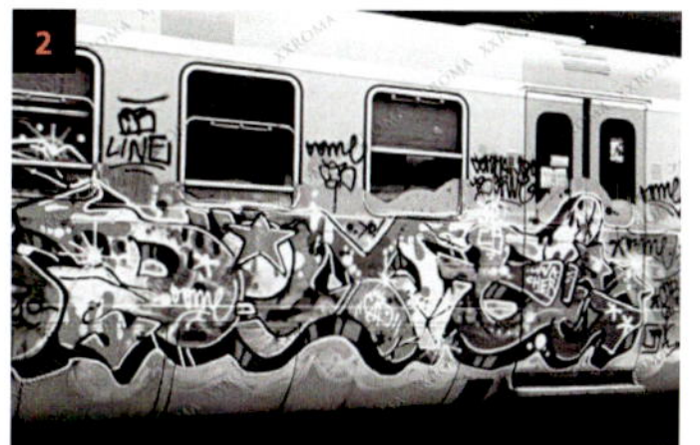

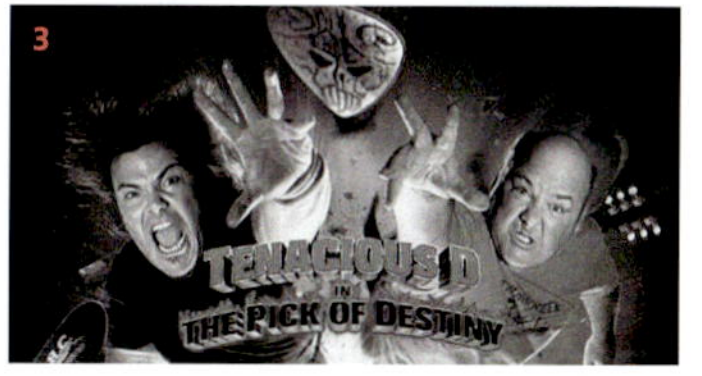

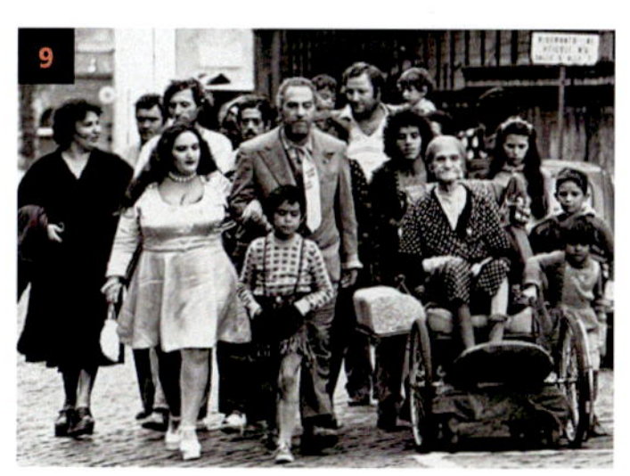

1. Bucchero 是一种前罗马时期产自意大利中部地区的伊特鲁里亚人生产的瓷器。陶器的装饰通常是使用齿轮或梳状工具来制造成排的点，并排列成扇形的图案。

2. DOME，CB，1999年

3. 《命运之选》是一部 2006年上映的美国音乐奇幻喜剧电影，讲述的是喜剧摇滚二人组《坚韧的D》的故事。

4. 这是一种传统的意大利面食酱料，主要成分是猪肉、阿马特里切干酪、番茄和洋葱制成的羊乳干酪。

5. 这是一种来自罗马的意大利面，由鸡蛋、硬奶酪、腌猪肉和黑胡椒制成。

6. 更多关于 BICER 的信息，请参考:无妥协方式 第二期，第 9-30页。

7. 意大利语中"货运火车"的意思。

8. ZETAL 这里指的是 Years of Lead (意大利语：Anni di piombo)，这是意大利从 60年代末持续到 80年代末的社会和政治的动荡时期，其标志是极左翼和极右翼政治恐怖主义事件的浪潮。

9. 《丑陋、肮脏和坏》（布鲁蒂、斯皮蒂）是一部意大利荒诞电影，由埃托雷·斯科拉执导，于 1976年上映。这部电影讲述了一个居住在罗马周遭一个极其贫穷的棚户区的阿普利亚大家庭的离奇故事。

1. *Bucchero* is a class of ceramics produced in central Italy by the region's pre-Roman Etruscan population. The pottery was often decorated by using a toothed wheel or a comb-like instrument to create rows of dots arranged in fan patterns.

2. DOME, CB, 1999

3. *Tenacious D in The Pick of Destiny* is a 2006 American musical fantasy comedy film about comedy rock duo Tenacious D.

4. A traditional Italian pasta sauce based on guanciale (cured pork cheek), pecorino cheese from Amatrice, tomato, and, in some variations, onion.

5. An Italian pasta dish from Rome made with egg, hard cheese, cured pork, and black pepper.

6. For more information about BICER: *No Apologies 2*, pg. 9-30.

7. Italian for 'freight train'.

8. Here ZETAL refers to the Years of Lead (Italian: *Anni di piombo*), a period of social and political turmoil in Italy that lasted from the late 1960s until the late 1980s, marked by a wave of both far-left and far-right incidents of political terrorism.

9. *Ugly, Dirty and Bad* (*Brutti, sporchi e cattivi*) is an Italian grotesque film directed by Ettore Scola and released in 1976. The film tells the grotesque story of a large Apulian family living in an extremely poor shantytown of the periphery of Rome.

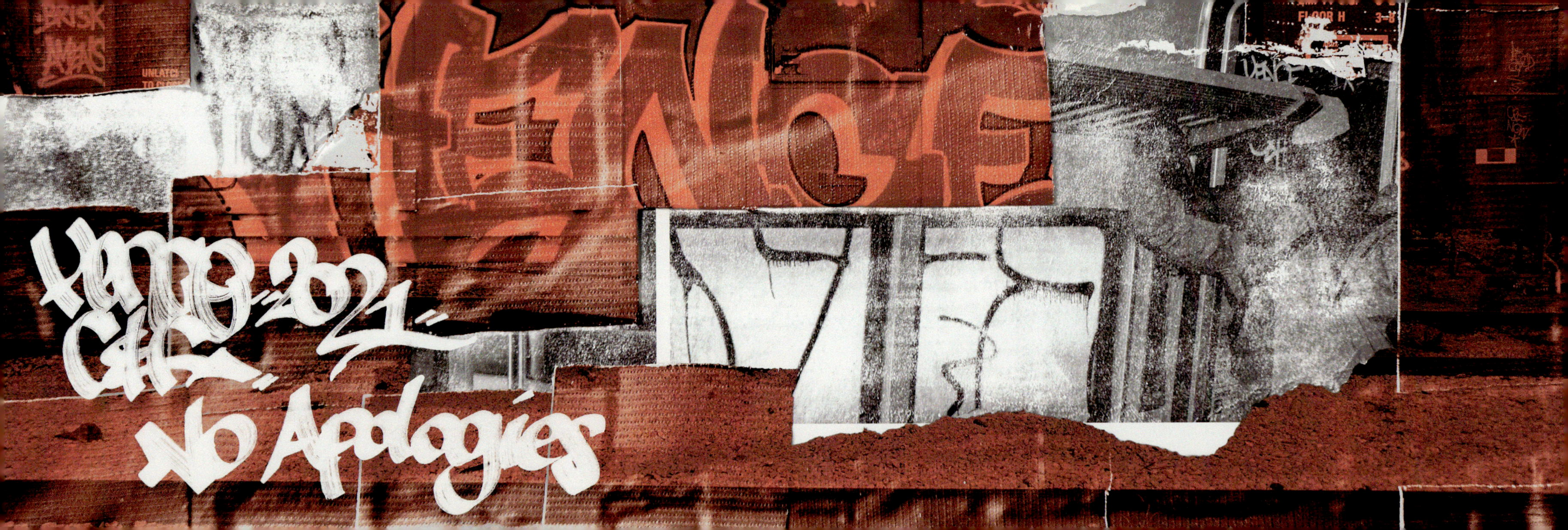
BRISK
2021
No Apologies

HENCE
纽约的传说

你是一位在纽约长大的写手，这座城市是一切涂鸦的起点，也是许多开拓者和传奇人物奋斗过的地方。能给我们讲讲你早年的一些故事吗？

我一直觉得自己与纽约的涂鸦历史有着某种强烈的羁绊。我的行为就像是他的一种召唤，无论我走到哪里，涂鸦几乎无所不在。在80年代末到90年代初我接触到涂鸦签名，以及存在于街头的艺术，这对我来说是一个巨大的启发。我生活的街区里"PERM"的签名从80年代一直留到了90年代。在我每天经过的街角邮箱上有一个"JONONE 85"的涂鸦签名。停车场里则留着一些80年代的涂鸦，在我小的时候，他们几乎没有更新过，时间似乎只在墙皮剥落与颜色退化上做文章，而这种历史感一直保持到90年代早期，直到我与其他几位写手在他边上签名后情况才有所改变。墙上还有一件以THOR（雷神）为主题的作品，是由SCRIBE, TEAM, WOLF, VFR, SEV 和 REAS, REVLON 合作完成的。这些以字体为主的涂鸦与理查德·汉布尔顿（Richard Hambleton）等艺术家的作品一同出现在墙上。

在接触涂鸦初期，我还遇到了一些对我影响很深的老写手和艺术家，他们的作品给我留下了深刻的印象。1987年，我所售卖的卡通画风格是受 Keith Haring 和 Kenny Scharf 的启发。还有一次，MESH（AOK）向我和我的朋友做了自我介绍，并问我们是否知道他的名字。并在我的一幅画的背面写下了签名，然后直截了当地告诉我们"不要做涂鸦。"我想他那时已经不是那么参与涂鸦了，但他还是很在意他的认知度。当时我并不知道 MESH（AOK），自从与他见面，并得到他的签名后，我才开始注意这个名字。

在我接触涂鸦的早期，能够上街喷漆涂鸦总是让我肾上腺素澎湃，但因为媒体总把涂鸦的行为描绘成负面，也一度让我褪去热情。在五金店里，喷漆售卖柜会被罩上金属笼子以防止偷窃，MTA（美国铁路）的站台上也都贴有反涂鸦的宣传。这座城市，总是将涂鸦与犯罪联系在一起。当我还是个孩子的时候，周遭都是反涂鸦的宣传，这潜移默化的影响差点让我放弃涂鸦。在进入四年级的学期，我的木工老师给了我人生第一罐喷漆，那是"Krylon"牌喷漆的哑光黑色。他还给我看了布鲁斯·戴维森的摄影书《地铁》。因为他看到我画的卡通与泡泡字，知道我对涂鸦感兴趣。几年后，当我上中学时，他们问我是否还在涂鸦，但我撒谎告诉他，我不再画了。因为我不想让学校里的其他老师知道我除去艺术之外的事情。我的小学生涯对我的影响很大，由于对城市景观，废弃建筑，交通工具和大众运输很感兴趣，我画了无数的素描。

那个时候，我朋友的哥哥 SENZ 正在积极涂鸦。他的房间就像一个小小的涂鸦博物馆。在 SENZ 的墙上有令人惊叹的涂鸦手稿和字体轮廓，桌上总是摆放着马克笔与手稿本。我在1988年和他弟弟一起玩的时候注意到了他的涂鸦，并在1990年成为了好朋友。那年秋天，SENZ 给了我一份名单，并用红色记号笔在一张横格纸上写下不同的名字，我于是选择了"HENCE"作为涂鸦的代号。对我来说，这个名字很酷，而且也还未被其他写手使用过。随即我们便出门炸街，那真是一次难忘的体验。

在涂鸦的早期阶段，我到处签名的目的是为了在涂鸦圈里出名，但同时我会画一些完整主题的涂鸦创作。在1992到1993年间，我与朋友们在纽约的不同"涂鸦名人堂"画涂鸦，比如自由隧道、组装工厂、僵尸货车和佩勒姆线。在那里，我们遇到过 HUSH, SMITH, REAS 和 OMNI 等人的伟大作品。

随着我在高中后期对涂鸦的深入了解，研究涂鸦历史的兴趣也越来越浓。历史与我携手并进，因为这座城市的独特历史，也拥有欣赏涂鸦的基因，这让我们与自己街区的涂鸦历史产生了更加深刻的联结。我的搭档 REBEL（LOB）在这方面的研究做得很深入，并且带我很快的上了手。我们是在1994年的冬天通过共同的朋友认识的，在第一次见面的晚上，我们就在布鲁克林街区制造了一场史诗般的街头涂鸦轰炸。在这段友谊中，发掘涂鸦历史一直是我们最着迷的东西，当我们在废弃的旧火车上发现了一些成旧的签名，那就像是时间胶囊里裹挟的宝石一般闪耀。在一节一节的旧车箱中穿梭，并用一卷又一卷的胶片不知疲倦的记录这些老签名，那种感觉真像是上了天堂一样开心。在1995年那段时间，我们深入发掘了纽约仍然存在的涂鸦历史。

自从90年代以来，你画了很多货运火车，是什么让你对它们这么感兴趣？谁是纽约货车文化的先驱？

CAVS、SENTO（TFP）、SIEN5（BFK）、HUSH（SPORTS）、STAK（TFP）、CES、IZ、SACH、SMITH、PINK、FREE5、MUZE 和 ZEPHYR 都是纽约货运火车的先驱。

1993年的夏天，我坐着7号线的火车准备去里尔河沿岸的铁路墙面画涂鸦，我向下望了一眼沿阳车库。在那里停满了表面平滑的货车，上面都是来自我上文提到的前辈们的涂鸦。在此之前，我只在涂鸦杂志上看到过货运火车的作品，那些作品让我印象深刻，但能够亲眼看到它们，即使是从远处看，也是一种完全不同的感觉。

我第一次喷货运火车是在 1994年与 SB 907 一块做的，我们只勾了一个字体外框在一节漏斗货车上，但我们仍然很高兴那天晚上做了这件事。我们在铁轨上走了好几英里，四处检查废弃的可涂鸦地点，偶然发现了那几节货车。1995年，我在当地画了另外一组货车，我很喜欢它，尽管我周围都覆盖着即膝的雪，货车最终的目的地也没开往多远，但我仍然感觉很好。1996年夏天，我和 SYSMIC 去了一个大型的货车停车库，那是 SYSMIC 第一次主动邀请我。那次去货运站的经历将我的涂鸦提升到另外一个水平，也成为我毕生涂鸦的动力，它让我努力将自己的涂鸦变得更好，因为我知道这些货车会去往很多地方，被更多的人看到。而我也常常在不同的区域为人画壁画。离开院子的第二天，我正在小区停车场的一大块墙上打草稿。到了第二年，我开始画各种类型的货车。在美国铁路上有各式各样的货车型号，有贡多拉敞篷货车、集装箱货车、漏斗货车、平底货车、油罐货车、汽车载运车和双层连载车。这些我都喜欢。

你在不同介质上都呈现了精美的字体，以及体量庞大的作品，他们从签名到简单字体不胜枚举。那你对优秀写手的定义是什么？

我喜欢所有的涂鸦形式，从签名到简单的字体，半狂野和狂野的风格都是我所爱。这大概是因为我被周围伟大的签名潜移默化的影响，要先把签名写好，而且尽可能的到处签名是非常重要的，我对这些奠基者表示莫大的尊敬，而我所做的只是把这种精神带回最本质的层面。让我最感敬佩的是那些能驾驭所有风格的涂鸦写手。他们的作品映射出生活中丰富的经历，这也使他们的作品经久不衰。

你曾经数次拜访过欧洲，并在当地创作涂鸦。你觉得那里的涂鸦如何？

欧洲之旅真的是一段美妙的经历。每一次的旅行更加佐证了这一看法。我很幸运能在那里遇到很棒的人，并拥有最棒的体验。欧洲与美国的涂鸦氛围最主要是在态度和文化环境上的不同。我的第一次荷兰之旅就让我深受启发。TKR 227（MH）带我领略了当地的涂鸦。那一次旅程真的令我非常难忘，而且行程满满。TKR 对他所在的城市与欧洲的旅行路线都很熟悉。我们在阿姆斯特丹喷了几个点，还顺道去了哥本哈根玩了几天。通过那次旅行经历，我便与当地写手搭上线了，斯堪的纳维亚（半岛）的写手们比起纽约的硬派写手更悠闲友好。我也很幸运在1999年访问了意大利，并在巴黎与 TROTA（THE），SMART，ENS 和 KEIN，以及 OPAK 和 SDK 一起涂鸦，那都是很酷的经历。

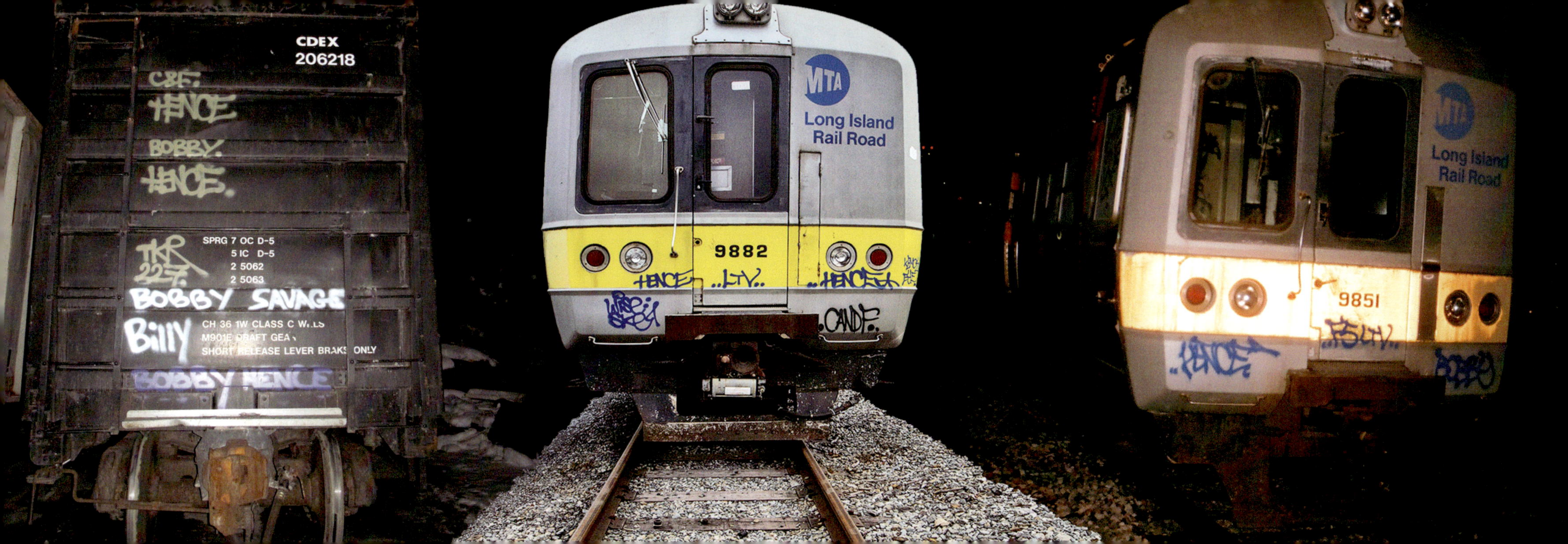

CDEX
206218
CBF.
HENCE
BOBBY.
HENCE.
TKR
227
SPRG 7 OC D-5
5 IC D-5
2 5062
2 5063
BOBBY SAVAGE
Billy
CH 36 1W CLASS C WHLS
M901E DRAFT GEA
SHORT RELEASE LEVER BRAKS ONLY
BOBBY HENCE
MTA
Long Island
Rail Road
9882
HENCE ..LTV.. HENCE
CANDF.
Long Island
Rail Road
9851
HENCE
BOBBY

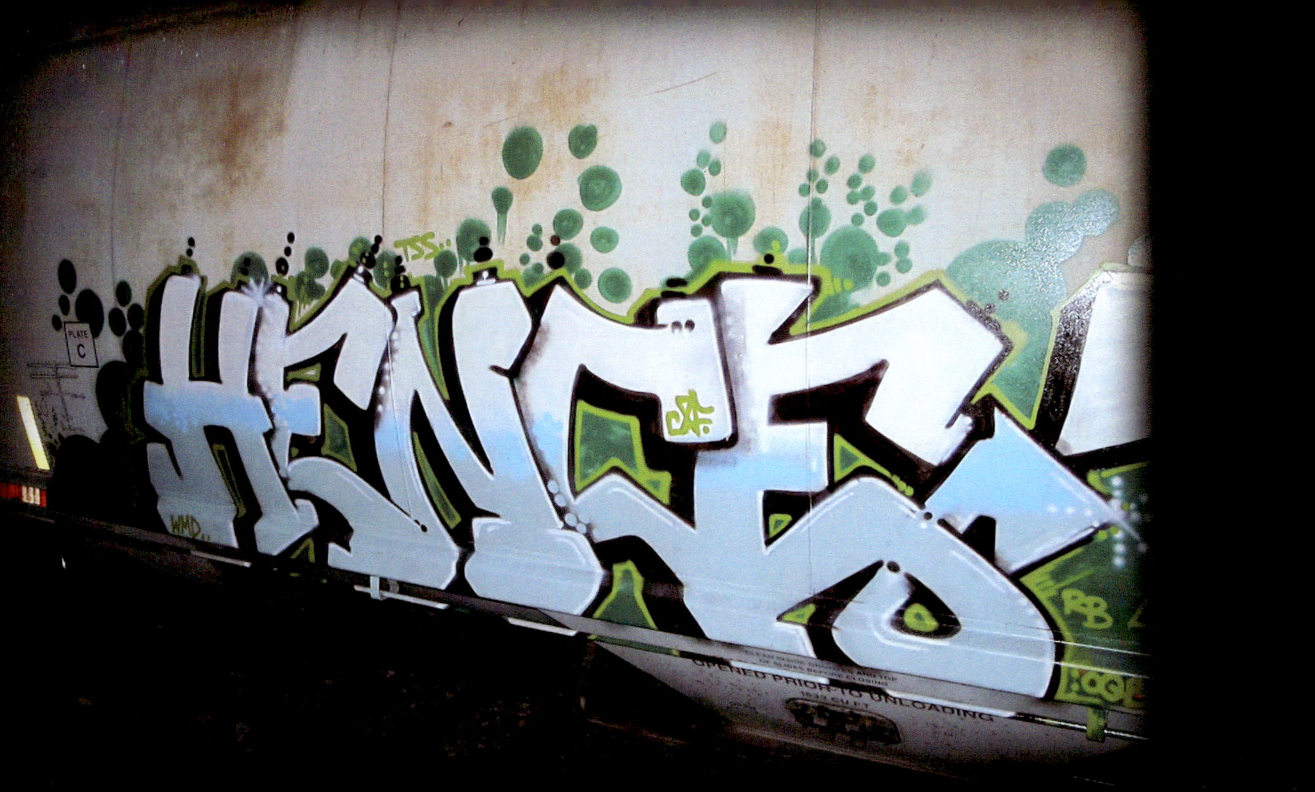

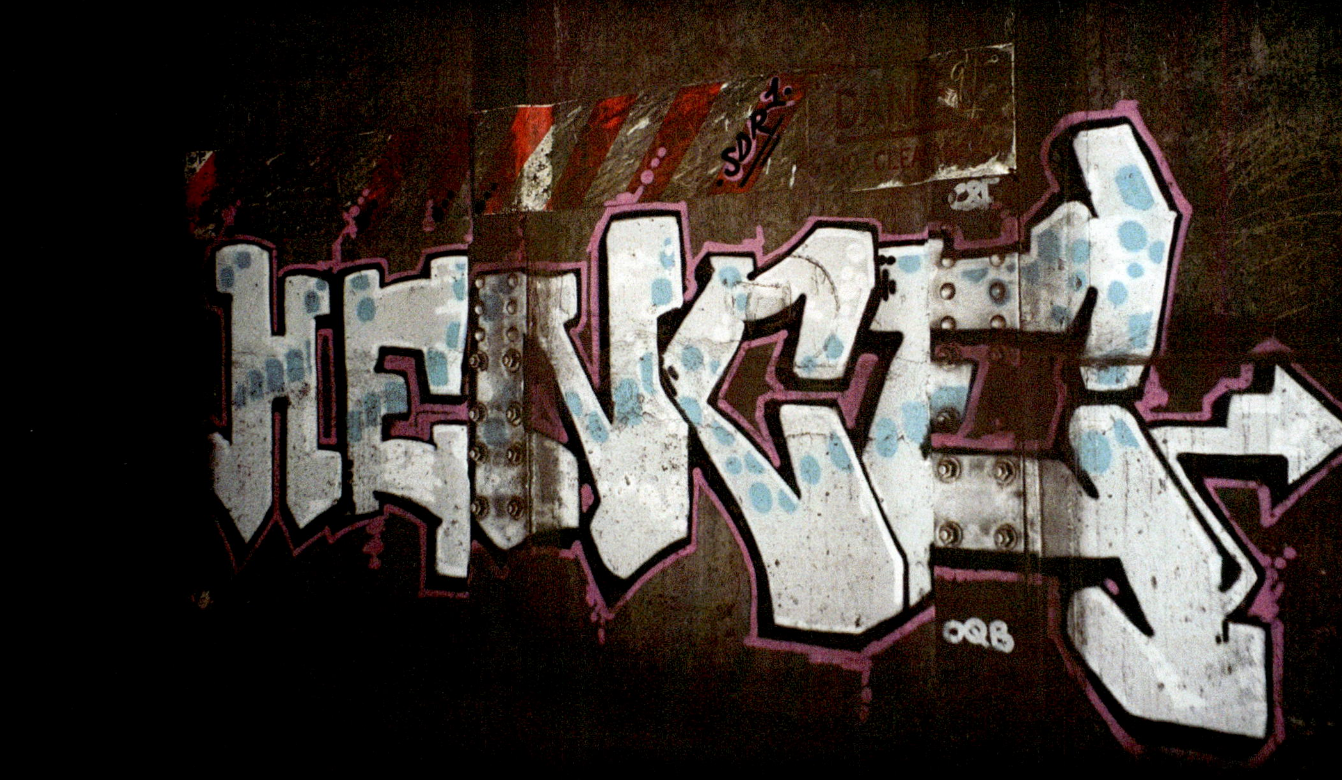

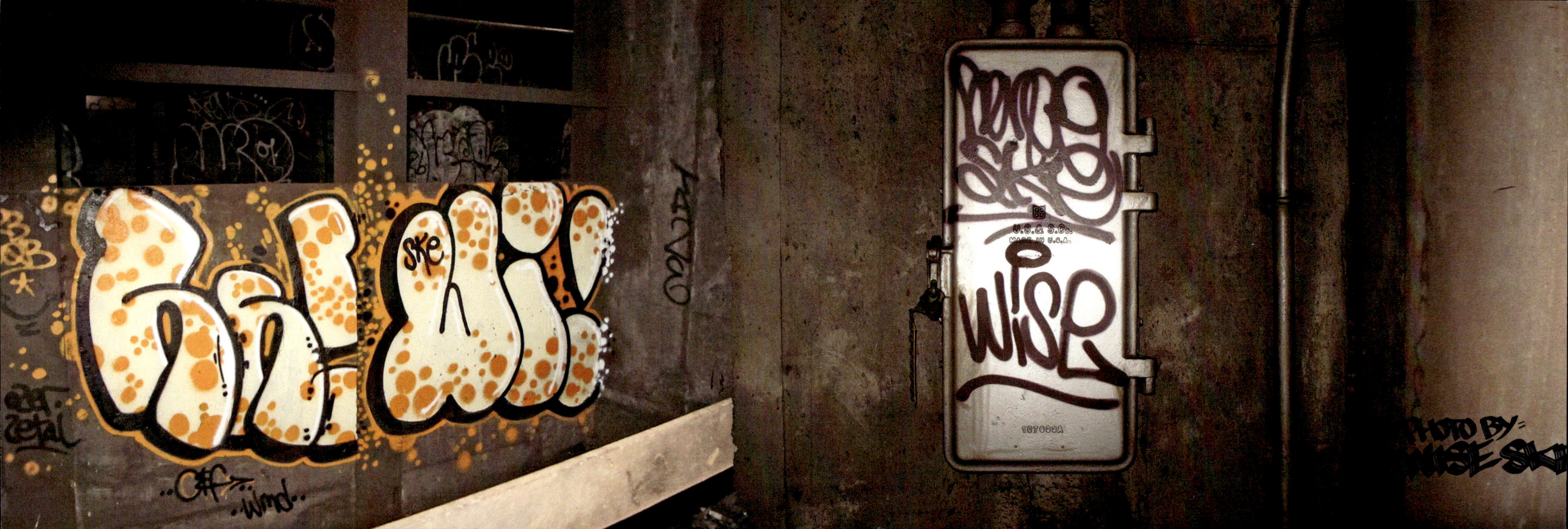

SKE
WISE
PHOTO BY :
WISE SK

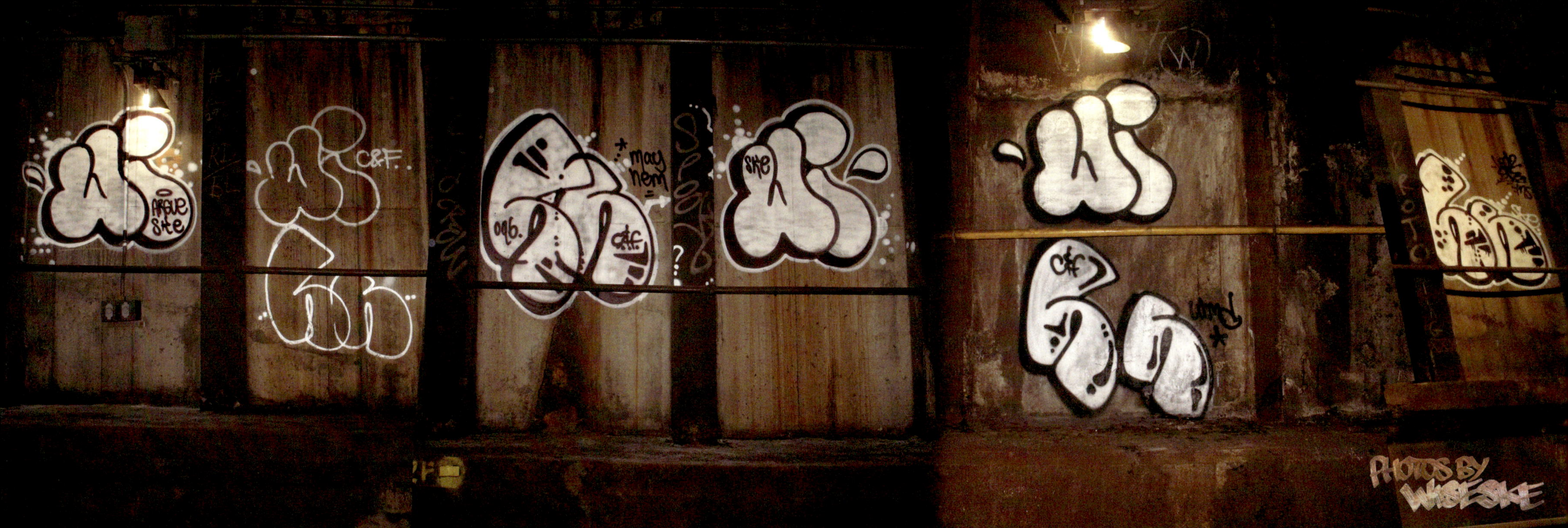

PHOTOS BY
WISESKE

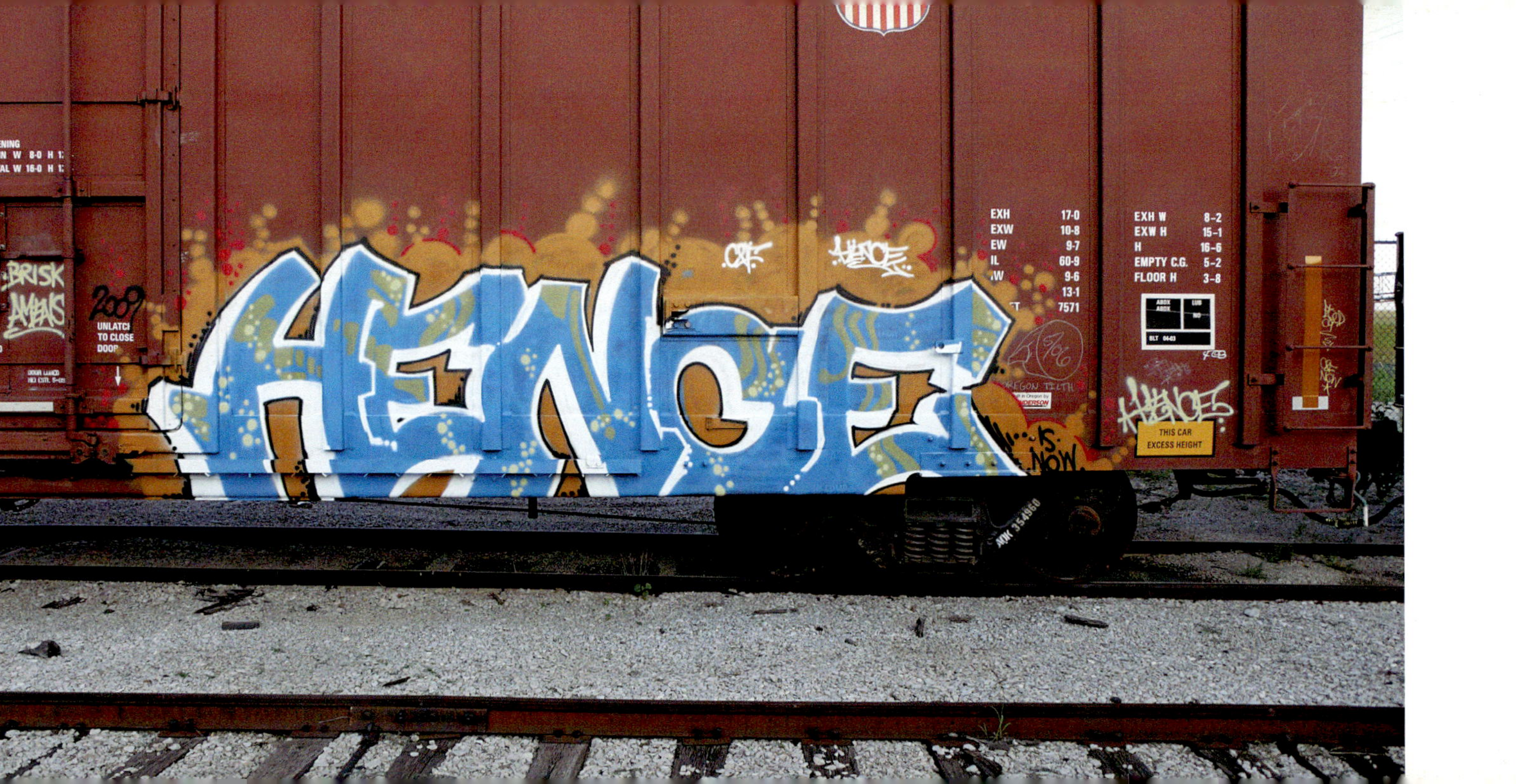

OPENING
MAIN W 8-0 H
TOTAL W 16-0 H
CLOSE
BRISK
AMENS
SD
UNLATCH
TO CLOSE
DOOR
EXH   17-0
EXW   10-8
EW   9-7
IL   60-9
W   9-6
           13-1
           7571
EXH W   8-2
EXW H   15-1
H   16-6
EMPTY C.G. 5-2
FLOOR H   3-8
BLT 04-03
THIS CAR
EXCESS HEIGHT
IS
NOW

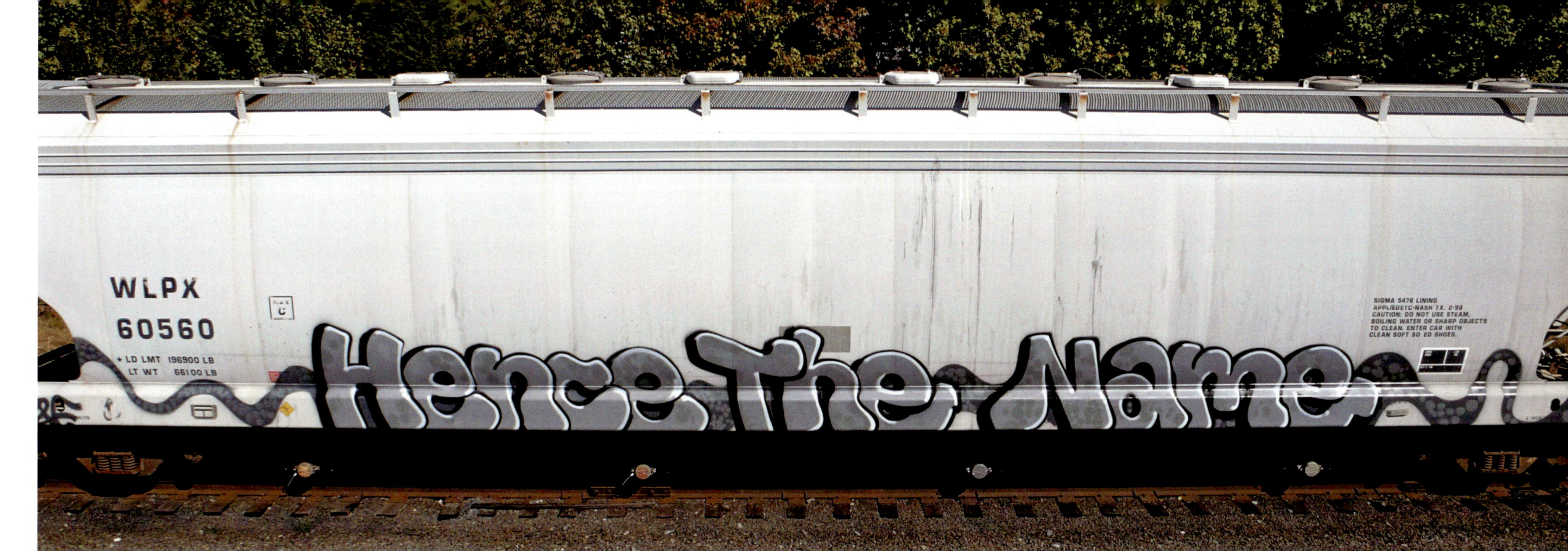

WLPX
60560
★ LD LMT 196900 LB
LT WT 66100 LB
SIGMA 5476 LINING
APPLIEDTC·NASH TX. 2-98
CAUTION: DO NOT USE STEAM,
BOILING WATER OR SHARP OBJECTS
TO CLEAN. ENTER CAR WITH
CLEAN SOFT SOLED SHOES.
Hence The Name

HENCE
The lore of NYC

I always felt a strong connection to the history of NYC. Graf was everywhere I went and it felt almost like a calling. The tags I saw in the late '80s and '90s as well as art on the street, were a huge inspiration for me. There were still old 'perm' tags from the '80s in my neighborhood that lasted until the late '90s. There was a JONONE 85 on my corner mailbox that I passed every day. Parking lots were running with some '80s stuff that did not change much during my early years of looking at it, it just faded into the wall or chipped away, until a few of us early '90s guys tagged next to it. There was a THOR piece, tags by SCRIBE, TEAM, VFR, SEV, REAS and WOLF. REVLON had old pieces. This name-based graf shared the walls with pictures by artists such as Richard Hambleton.

"There were metal cages on spray cans in city hardware stores and anti-graffiti propaganda by the MTA. Graffiti was associated with crime and a problem in the city. As a young kid, I was surrounded by anti- graffiti hype and I was actually in the mindset that I could give it up"

During my early pre-graffiti writing days the idea of writing was inspiring and forbidden at the same time because the media painted it negatively. There were metal cages on spray cans in city hardware stores and anti-graffiti propaganda by the MTA.

Graffiti was associated with crime and a problem in the city. As a young kid, I was surrounded by anti-graffiti hype and I was actually in the mindset that I could give it up. My woodshop teacher gave me one of my first spray cans in 4th grade, a flat black Krylon. He also showed me Bruce Davidson's photography book Subway. He knew I was interested in graf because of my cartoon and bubble letter drawings. Years later when I was in middle school and I actually started to write he asked me if I was still doing graffiti but I told him I quit. I didn't want other teachers in my school knowing my business beyond my regular art. During my early grade school years, I was interested in the cityscape, abandoned buildings, vehicles, and modes of transportation, which I made countless drawings of.

Before I wrote and when I started out, I met a few important older writers and artists who made a lasting impression on me. In 1987 I was selling my cartoon drawings that were inspired by Keith Haring and Kenny Scharf. MESH (AOK) introduced himself to my friend and me and asked if we knew his name. He wrote a tag on the back of one of my drawings and then told us point-blank "Don't do graffiti." I think he was getting out of it by then, but he still wanted us to know who he was. At the time I did not know, but after meeting him and seeing him write his tag I started to notice his name around.

Around this time, my friend's older brother SENZ was actively writing. His room was like a small graf museum. SENZ had amazing drawings and outlines on his walls, black books, design marker sets on a desk. I took notice of his stuff while hanging with his brother in '88 and became cool with him in 1990. In the fall of that year, SENZ gave me a list of names he wrote in red Design marker on a ruled sheet of paper and I chose HENCE. To me, it looked and sounded cool and it was not taken already. We went on a street bomb and it was the ultimate experience.

I mainly tagged during these early years as getting up and fame was the main goal, but I also started painting some pieces. By '92 and '93, my friends and I were traveling around to the different 'halls of fame' in the city such as the Freedom Tunnel. The Piecing Factories, the Dead Tracks, and the Pelham Tracks. We saw great pieces by HUSH, SMITH, REAS and OMNI to name a few.

As I got deeper into writing later in high school I got more into history. The two went hand and hand. The more serious partners I wrote with had deeper connections to graf in their neighborhoods, thus unique histories, and true appreciation for the history of NYC. My partner REBEL (LOB) was deep into it and schooled me on this pretty quickly. We met in the winter of '94 through friends in common and went on an epic street bomb in Brooklyn the first night we met. Throughout the friendship, history was always the thing that we went crazy about the most, finding old tags like time-capsuled gems in old trains at the Ghost Yard and the Scrap Yard. We were in heaven going through old trains and shooting rolls of film of old signatures. In 95 we were very deep into discovering the history that was still living.

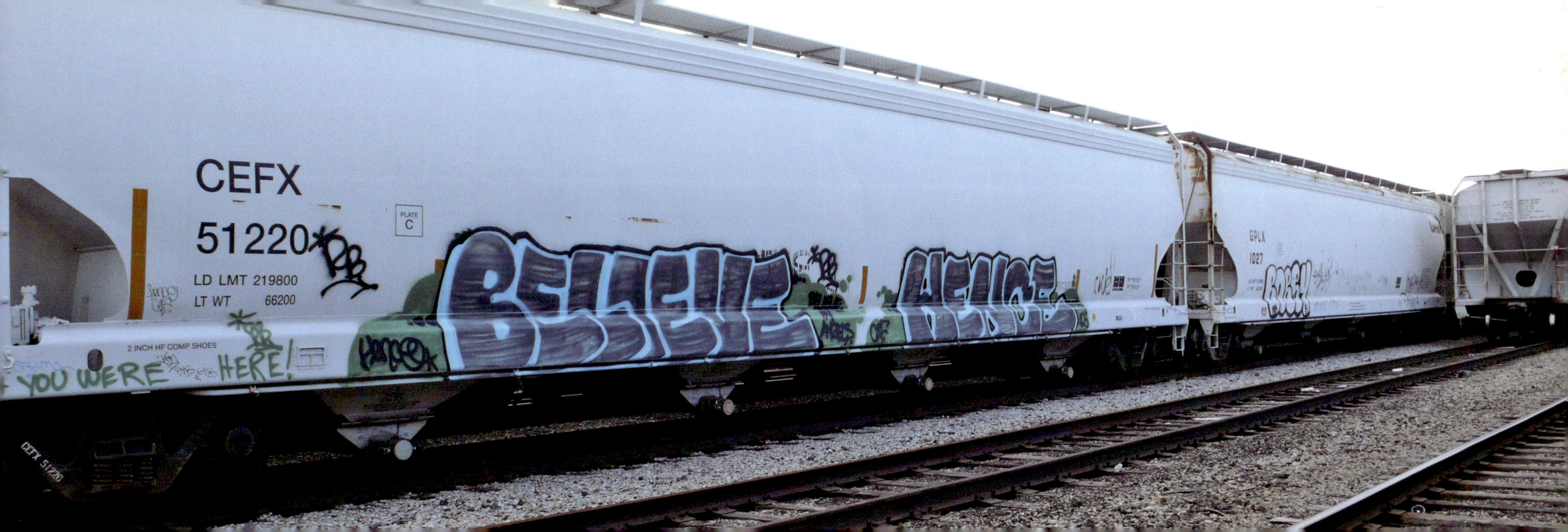

CEFX
51220
PLATE C
LD LMT 219800
LT WT 66200
2 INCH HF COMP SHOES
YOU WERE HERE!
GPLX 1027
CEFX 51220

"I went to a big yard for the first time in summer '96 with SYSMIC who invited me. This experience of going to a freight yard was a whole new level and fuel to my writing career, it made me want to get much better because I knew the freights would travel and be seen by a whole different audience"

You have painted a lot of freights since the '90s, What got you interested in painting them? Who are the pioneers of the freight culture in New York?

Some pioneers of the freight movement in NYC are CAVS, SENTO (TFP), SIEN5 (BFK), HUSH (SPORTS), STAK (TFP), CES, IZ, SACH, SMITH, PINK, FREE5, MUZE, and ZEPHYR.

In the summer of '93, I was riding the 7 train elevated on my way to paint a trackside spot along the LIRR and looked down at the Sunny Side yard. I stared out the window and saw that the yard was full of flat cars with colorful pieces by some of the pioneers I mentioned earlier. Until this moment I had only seen freight pieces in graf magazines, which was impressive, but seeing them live, even from a distance was a whole different feeling.

I hit my first freight in '94 with SB 907, we only did outlines on a hopper but I was still very happy to do it that night. We walked for miles on tracks and checked out abandoned spots and casually came across a small siding of cars. I got to paint a local set of cars in '95 and loved it even though I was knee-deep in snow and the cars didn't travel too far, it still felt right. I went to a big yard for the first time in summer '96 with SYSMIC who invited me. This experience of going to a freight yard was a whole new level and fuel to my writing career, it made me want to get much better because I knew the freights would travel and be seen by a whole different audience. I was accustomed to painting for people in the boroughs. The day after going to the yard I was drawing sketches for a big wall piece for my neighborhood parking lot. By the following year, I was beginning to paint all types of freight cars. There are a great variety of car models in the US railroad, gondolas, boxes, hoppers, spine cars, tankers, racks, and intermodals. I'm into all of them.

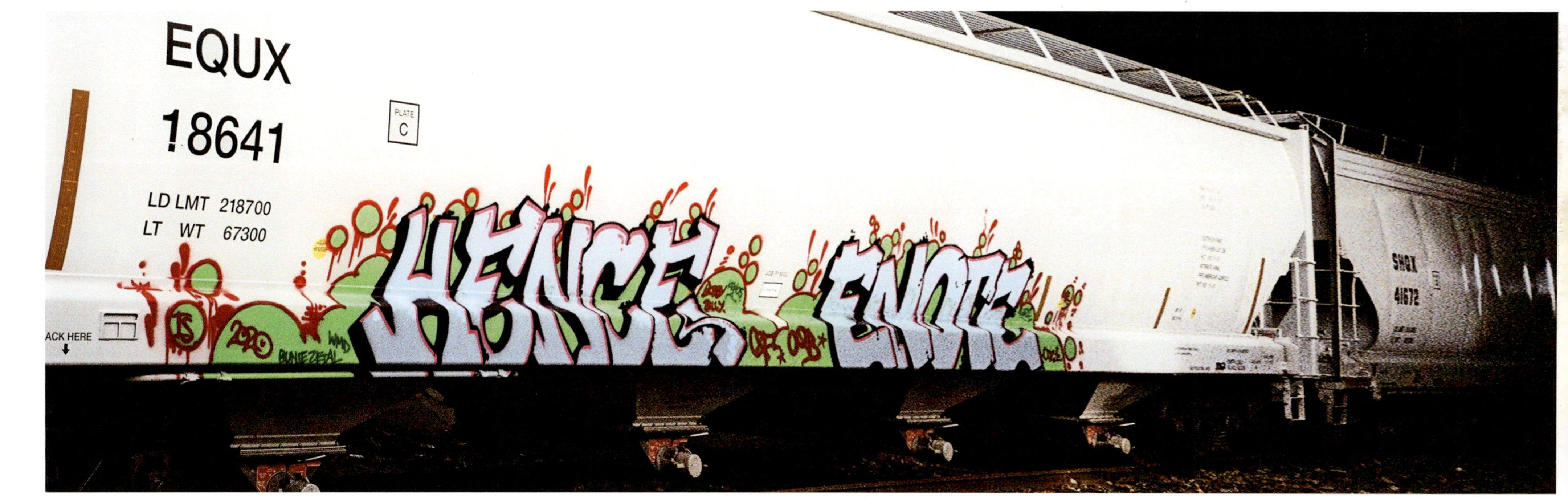

EQUX
18641
PLATE
C
LD LMT 218700
LT WT 67300

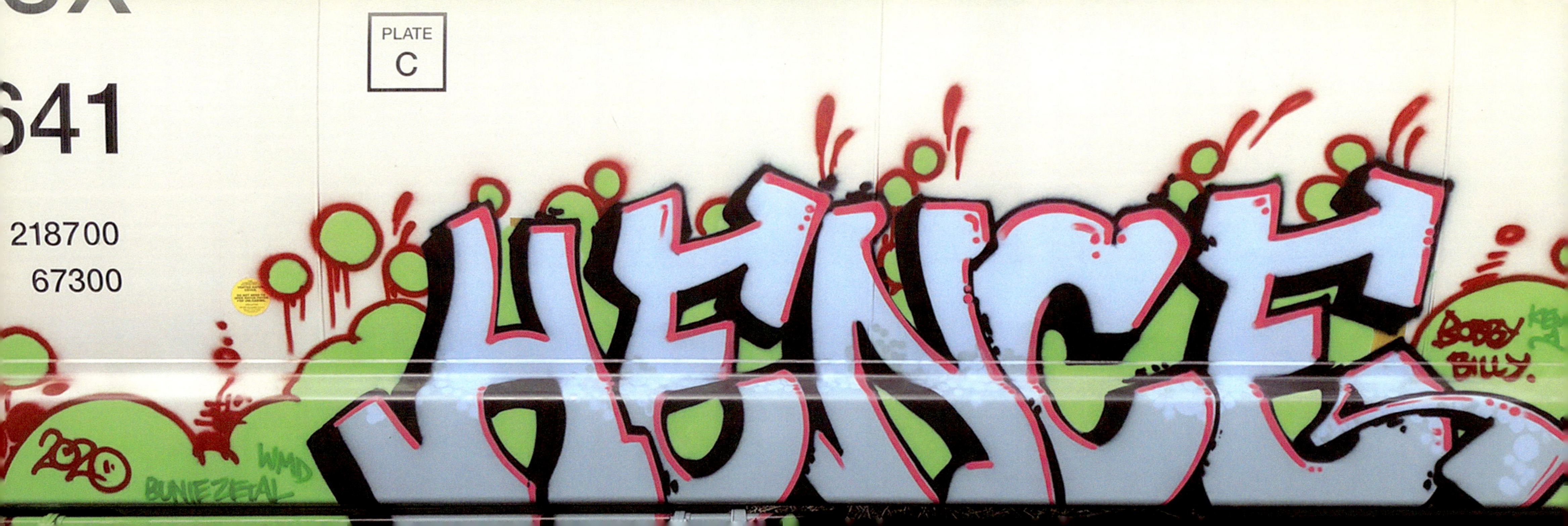
641
PLATE
C
218700
67300
HENCE
2020
BUNIEZETAL
WMD
BOBBY
BILLY

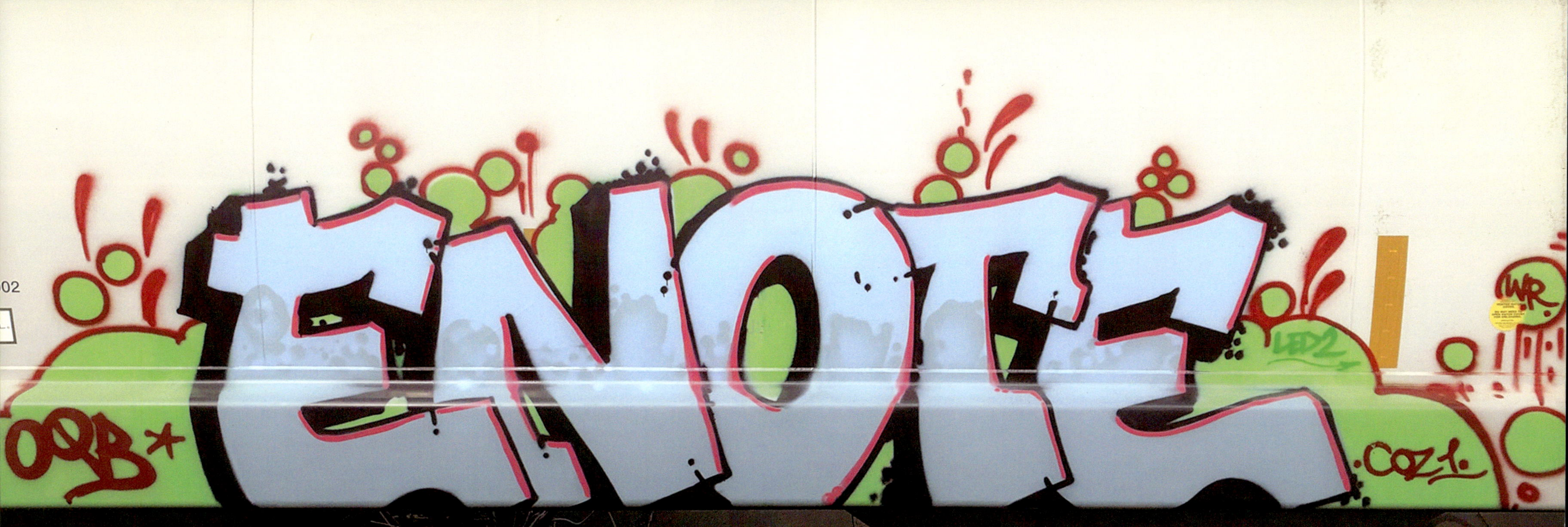

ENOTE
LED 2
OQB *
COZ1

You have painted on every surface with the finest letters and produced a huge body of work that ranges from tags to burners. What is your definition of a good writer?

I enjoy all the forms from signatures to simple styles, semi-wild and wild styles. I think because I grew up around the great tags and, getting that part down first and getting up with tags was essential. I truly appreciate this foundation and always come back to it. The writers who are the most well-rounded and versatile are the most interesting to me. The greats have seen and experienced a lot in their lives and painted powerful pieces that are timeless.

You have been to Europe a few times and had the chance of painting there. How was it?

It was the most amazing experience to travel in Europe. I can say this more certainly every time I go. I've been fortunate to meet great people and have great experiences there. The scenes mainly differed in attitudes and cultural approaches. When I went to Holland for the first time I was very inspired. My friend TKR 227 MH'S showed me amazing things. My first trip was very memorable and action-packed. TKR was in tune with his city and with traveling in Europe. We did some cool hits around town in Amsterdam and went to Copenhagen briefly for a few days. From those experiences, I was hooked. The writers in Scandinavia were more laidback and friendly than NYC toughness I was accustomed to. I was also fortunate to visit Italy in '99 and paint with TROTA (THE), SMART, ENS, and KEIN, as well as OPAK and SDK in Paris at a very cool time.

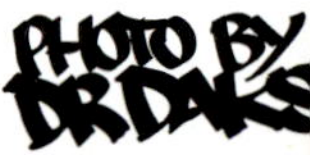

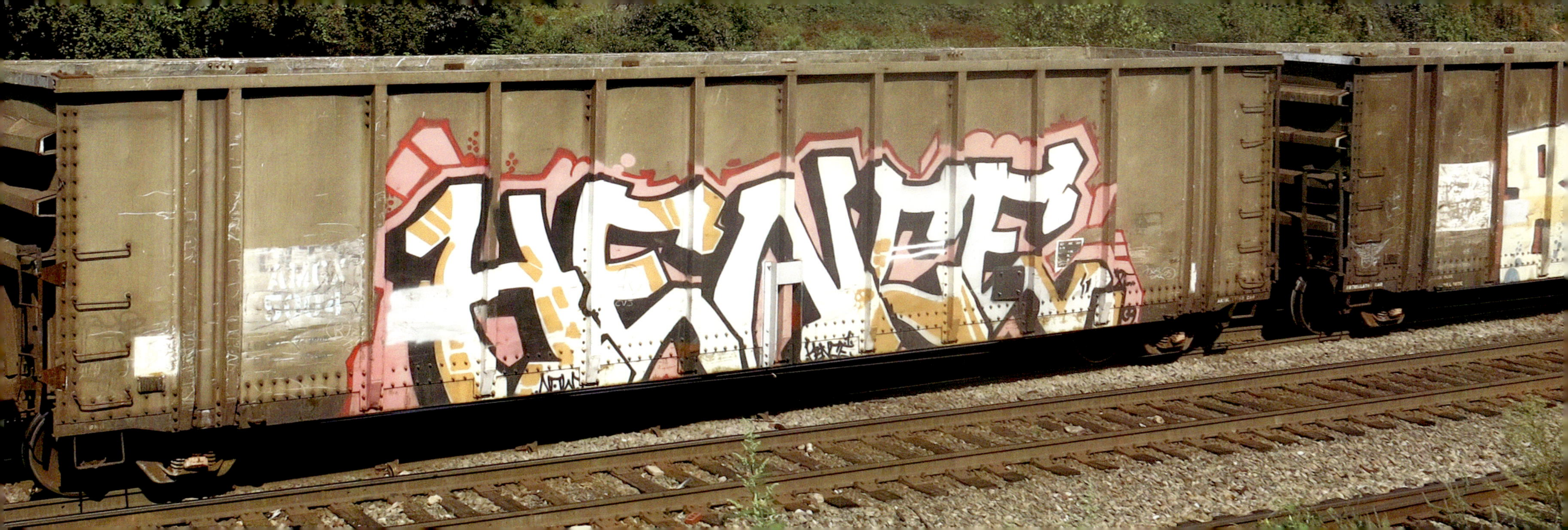

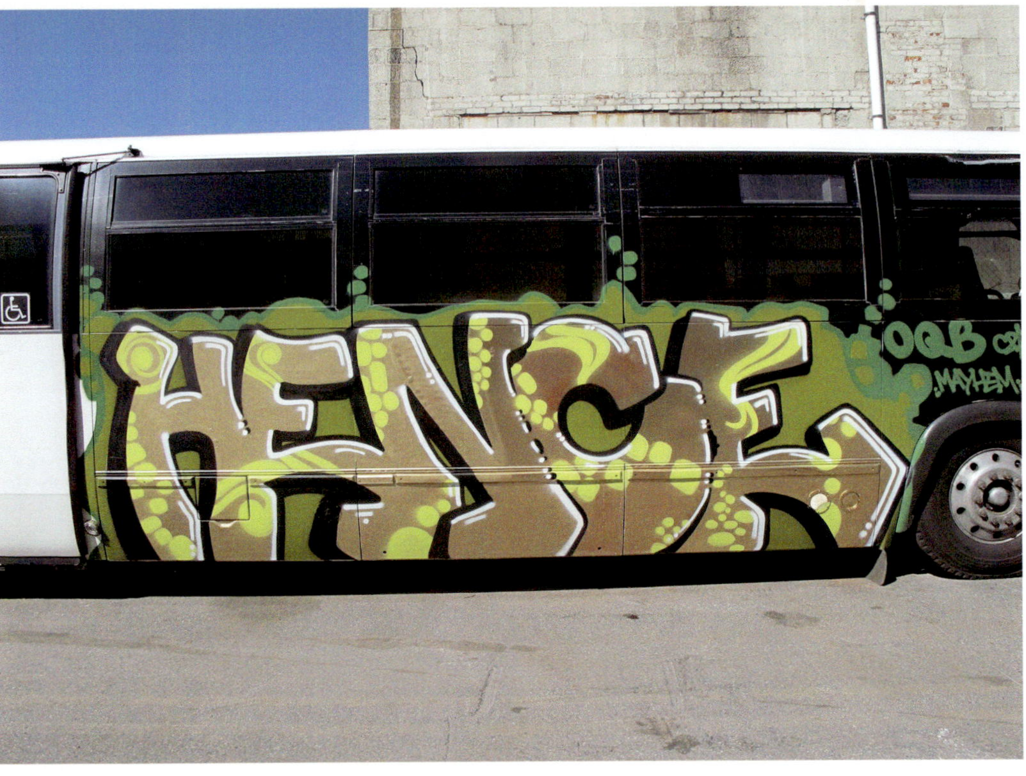

HENCE
OQB
.MAYHEM.

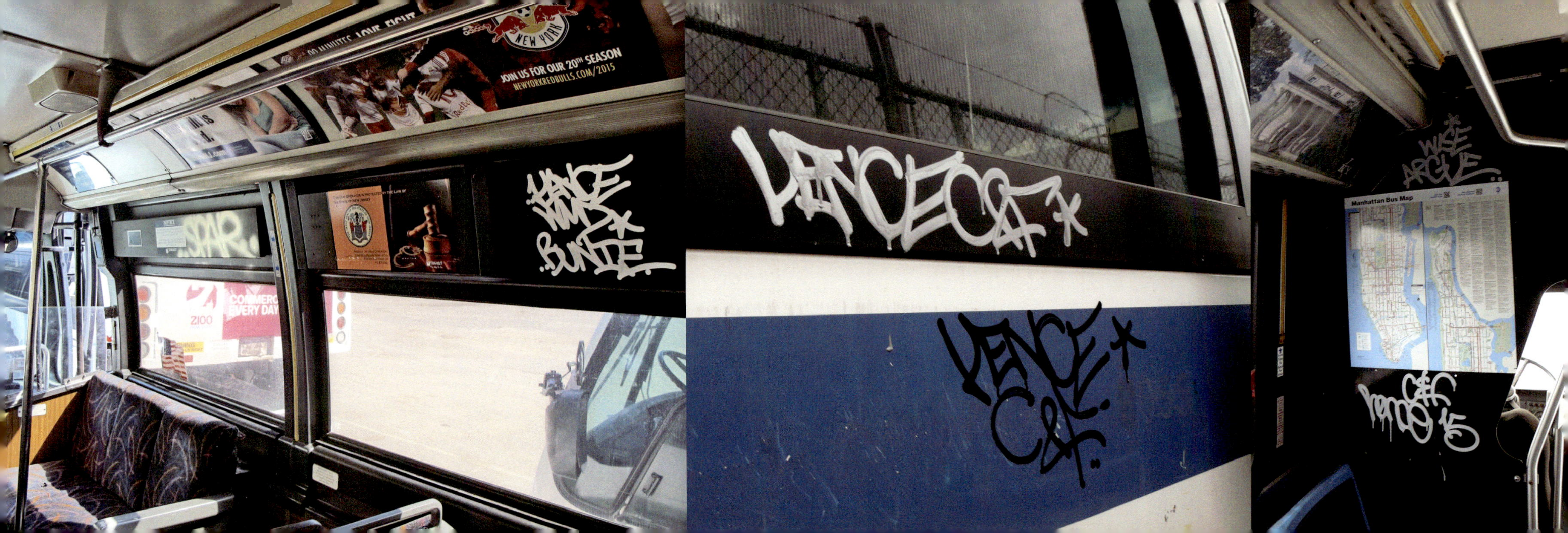

NEW YORK
JOIN US FOR OUR 20TH SEASON
NEWYORKREDBULLS.COM/2015
Manhattan Bus Map

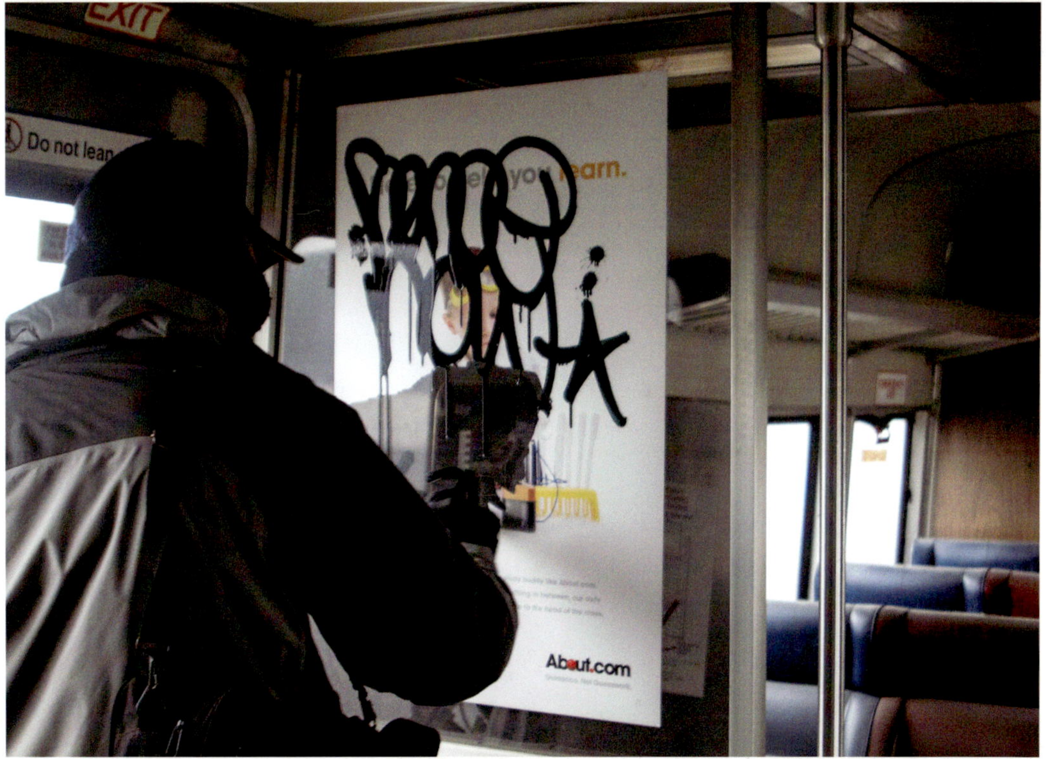

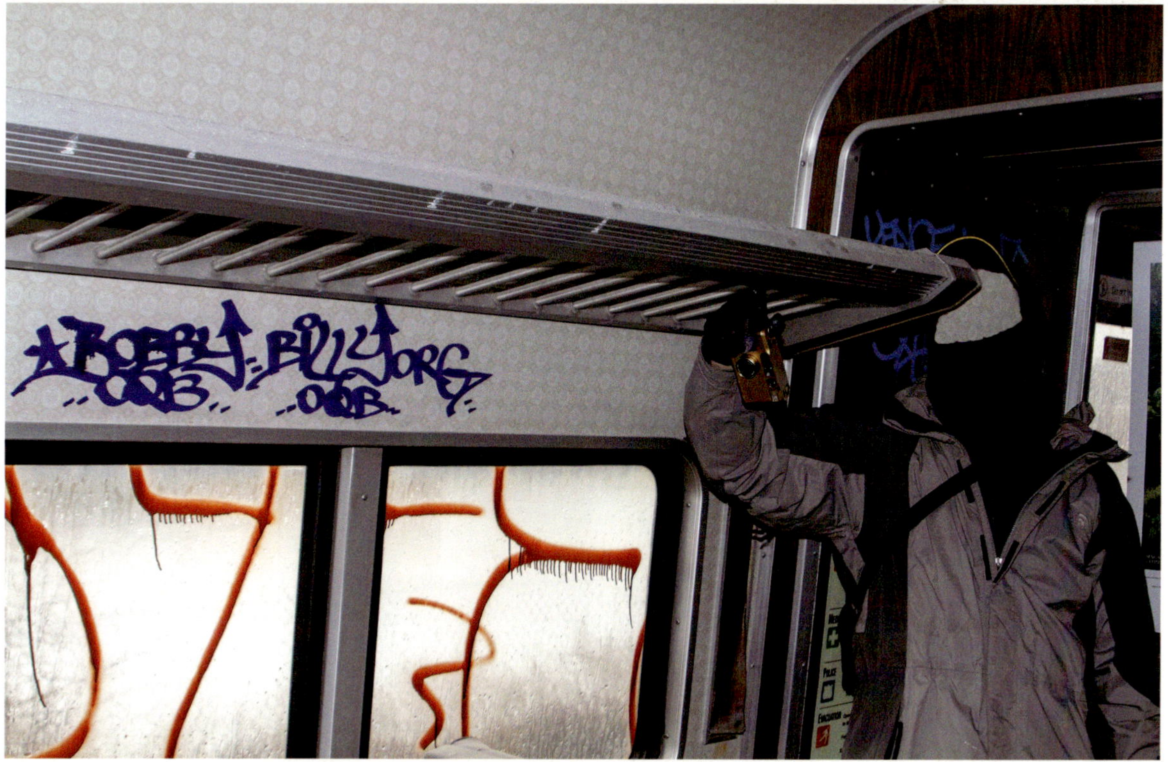

PHOTOS BY BAD GUY JOE

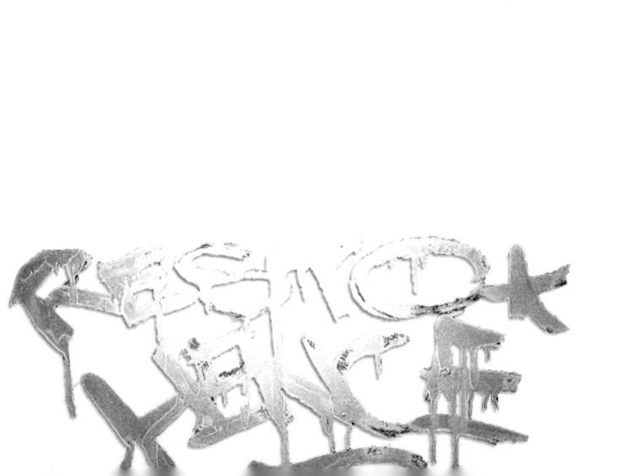

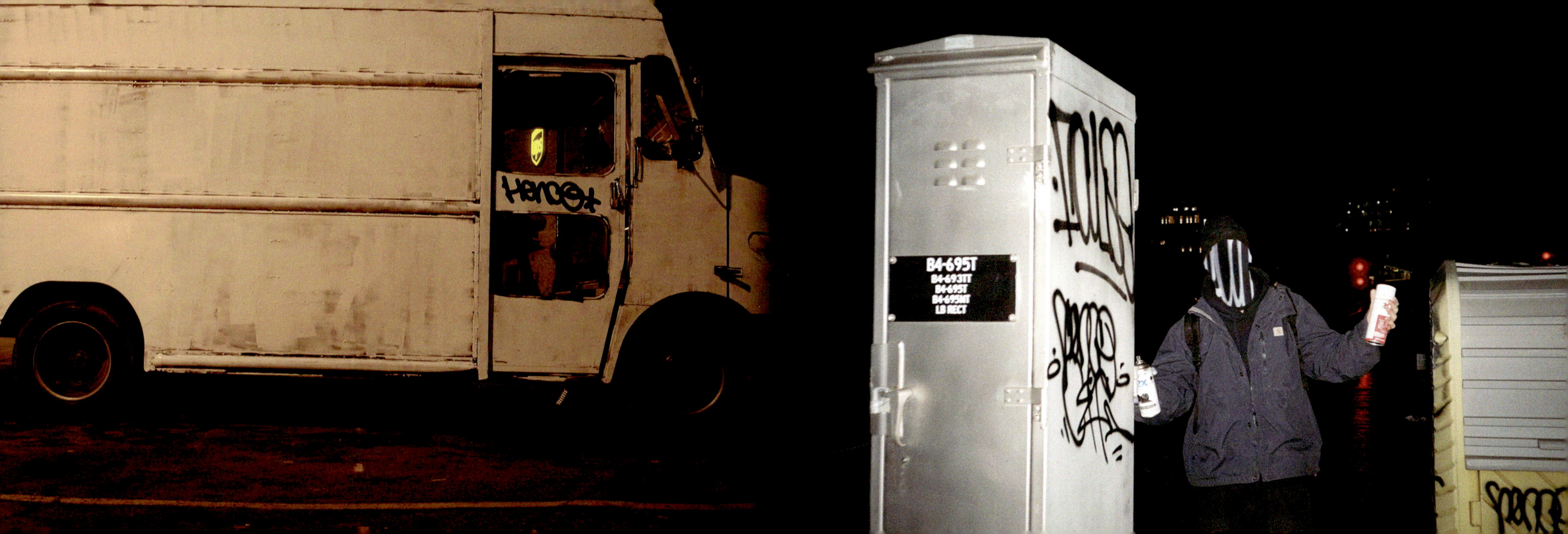

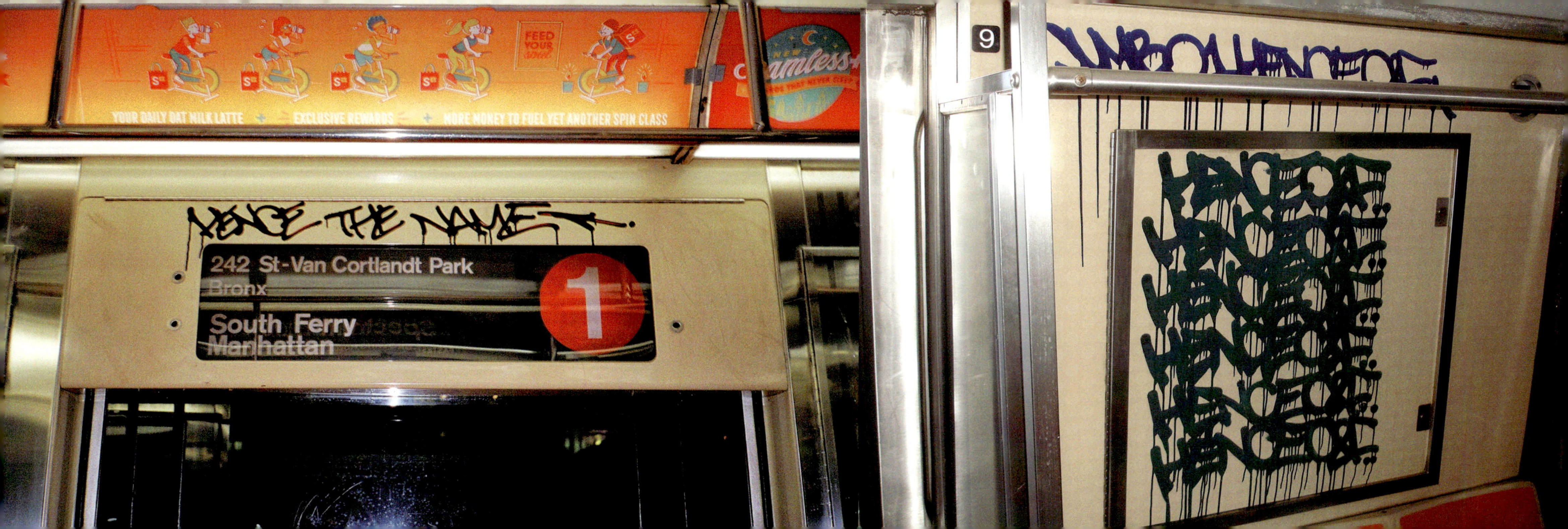

FEED YOUR
New
Seamless
YOUR DAILY OAT MILK LATTE + EXCLUSIVE REWARDS + MORE MONEY TO FUEL YET ANOTHER SPIN CLASS
HENCE THE NAME
242 St-Van Cortlandt Park
Bronx
South Ferry
Manhattan
1
9

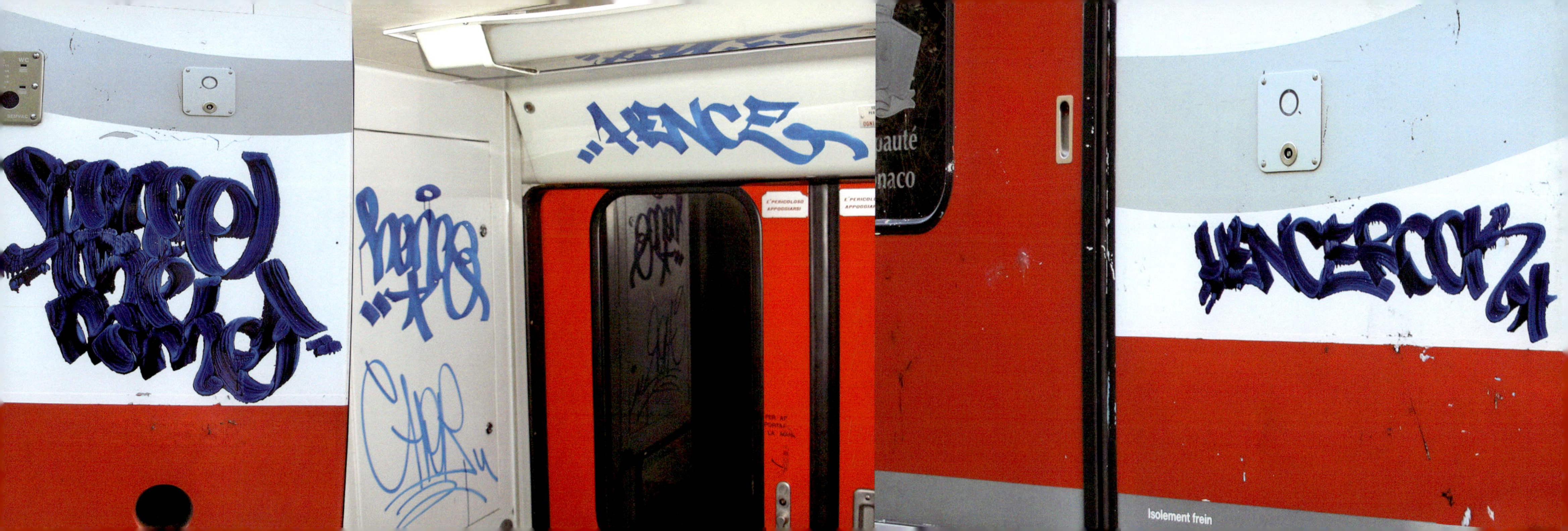

Isolement frein

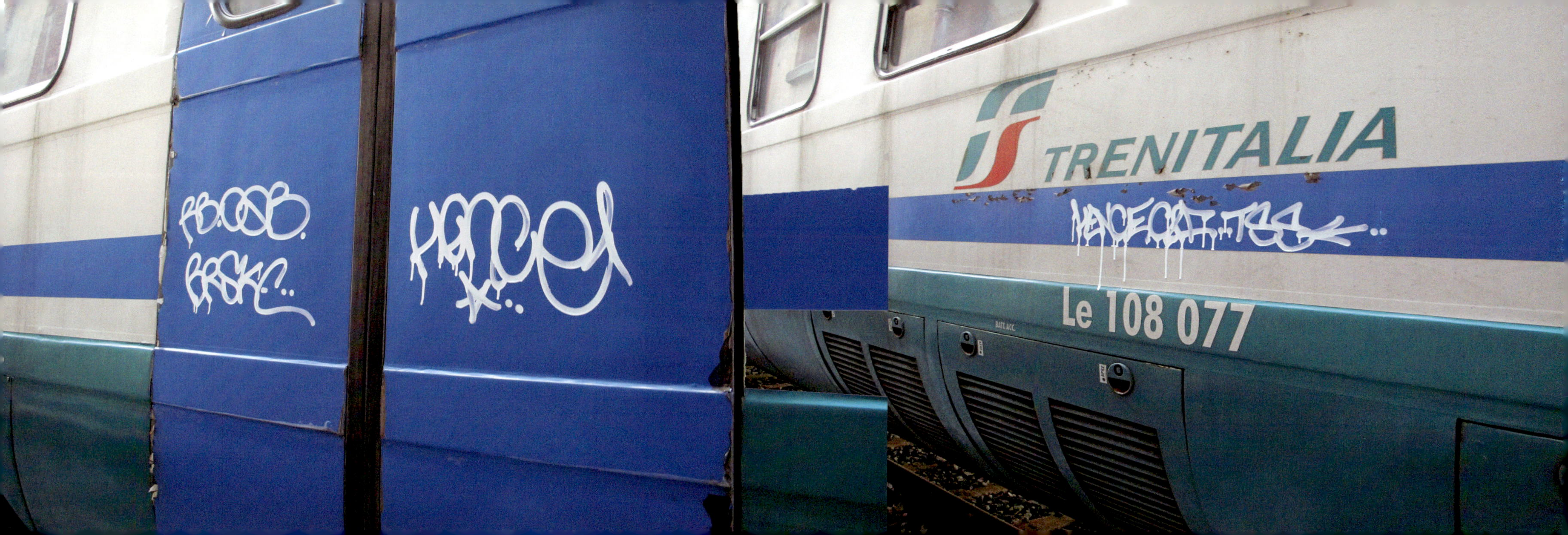
TRENITALIA
Le 108 077

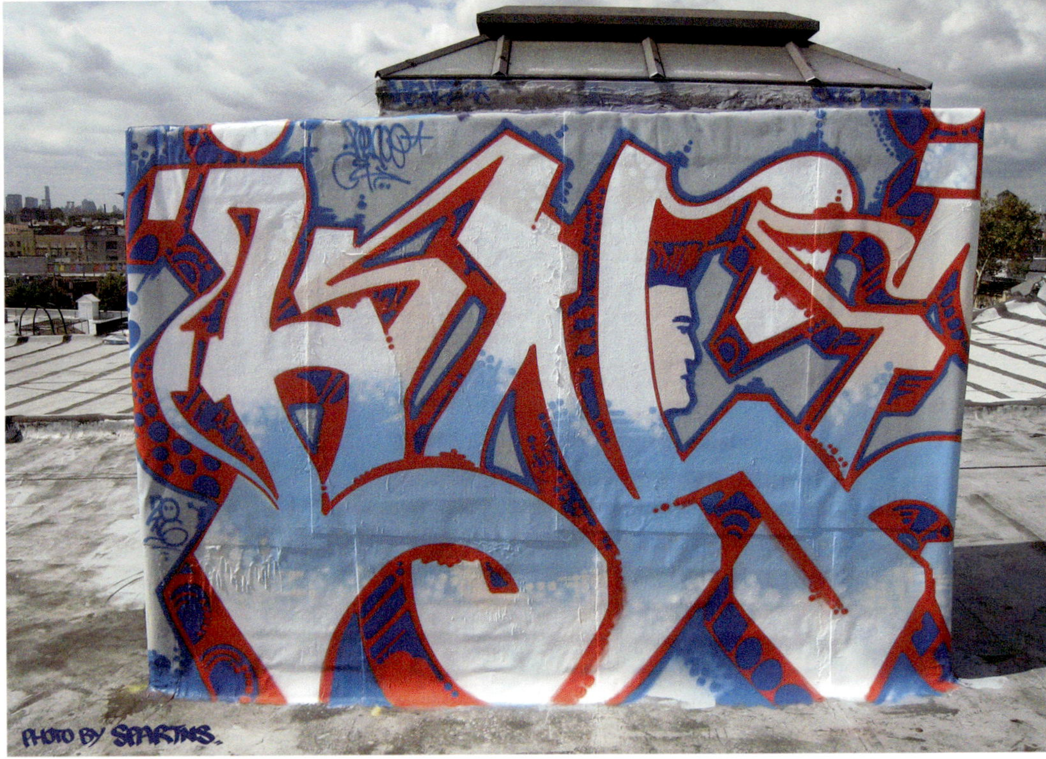

PHOTO BY SPARTNS.

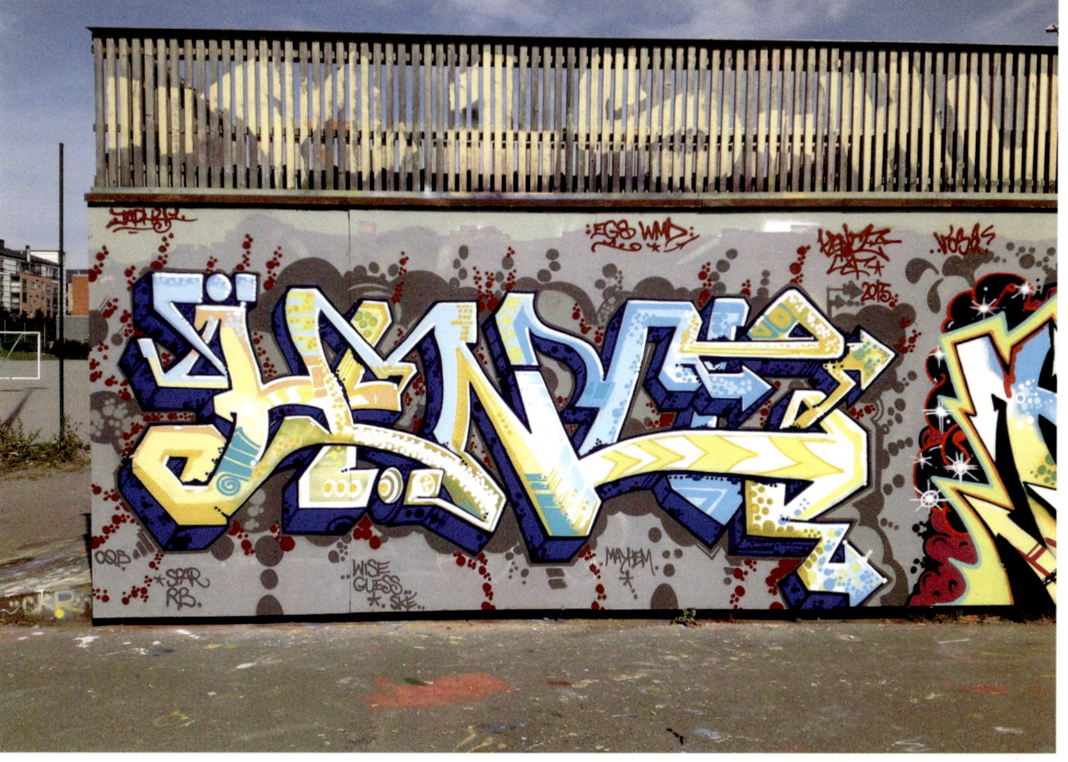

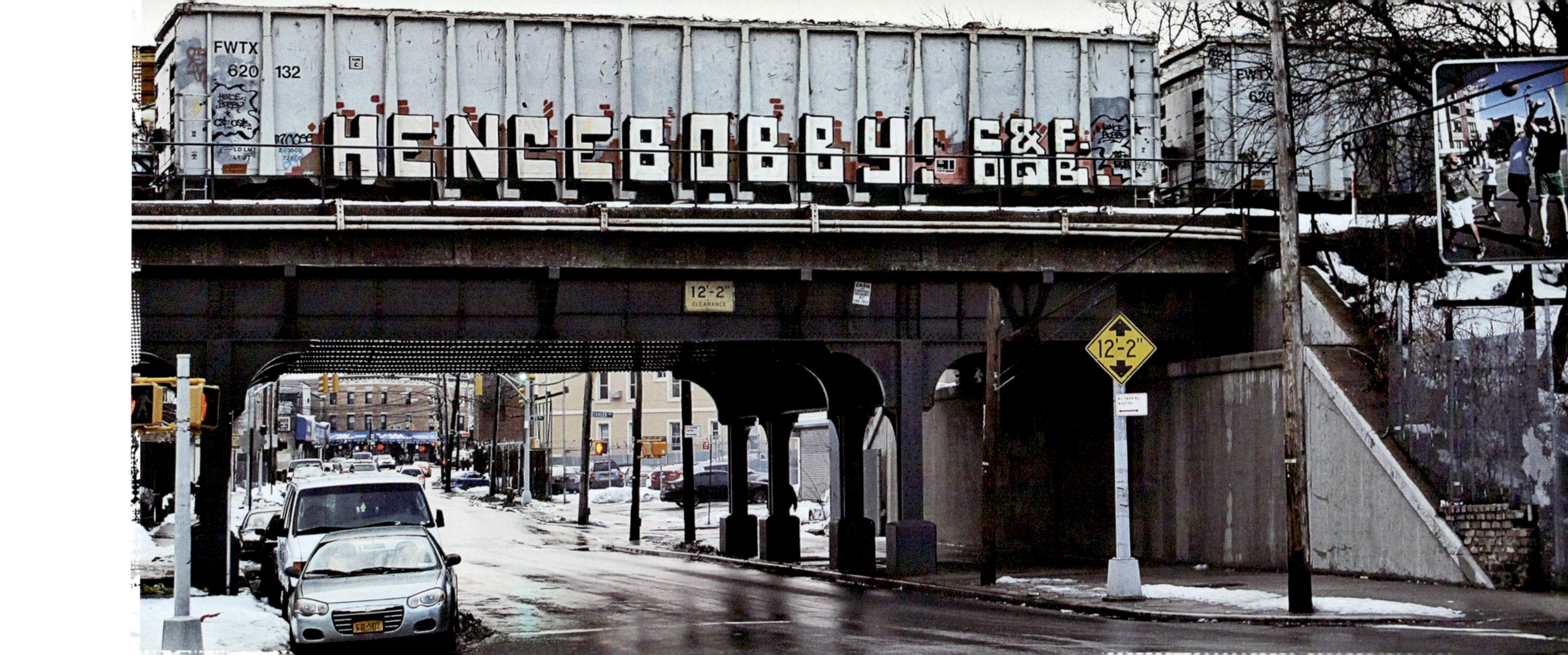

FWTX
620 132
HENCE BOBBY C&F
12'-2" CLEARANCE
12'-2"
FWTX
620

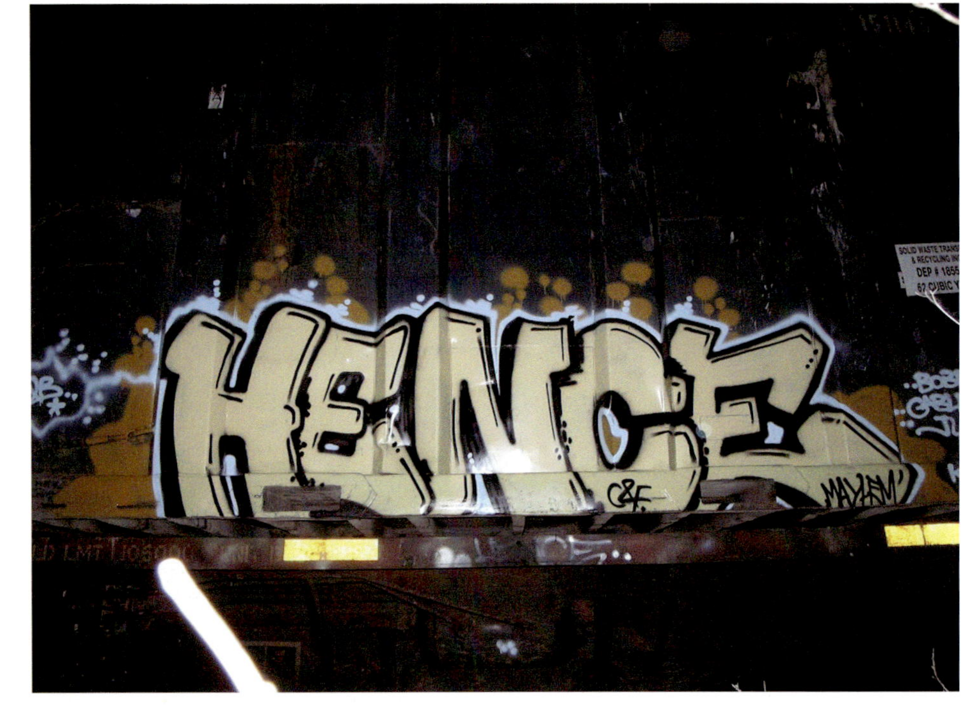

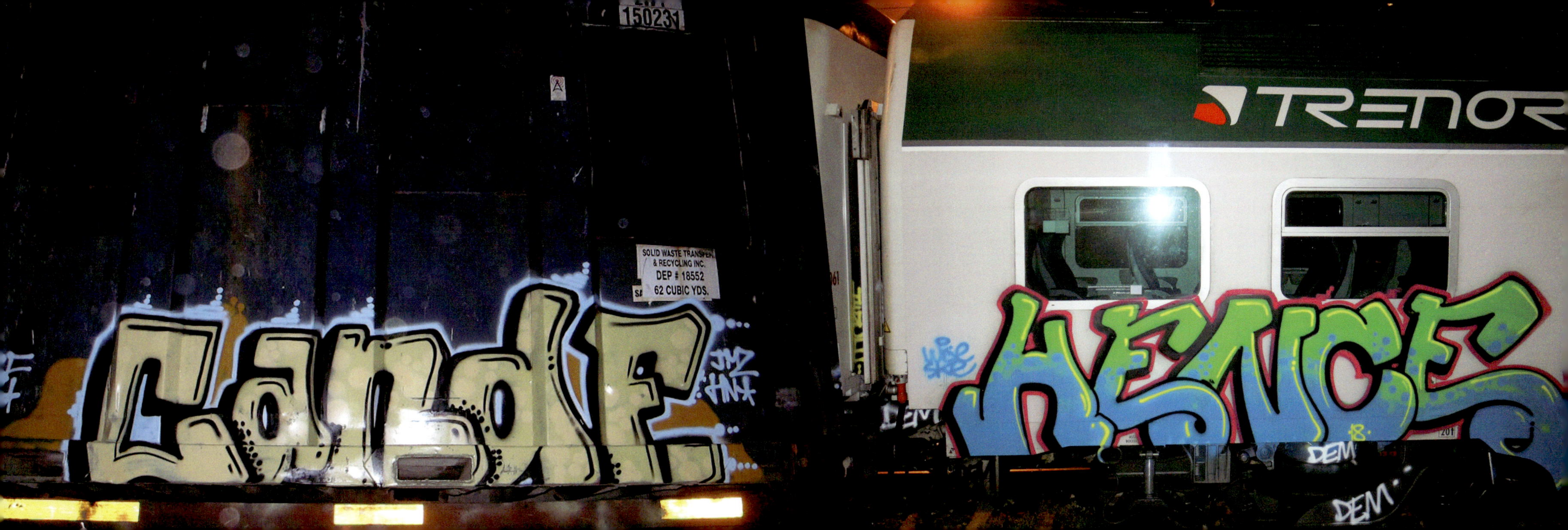

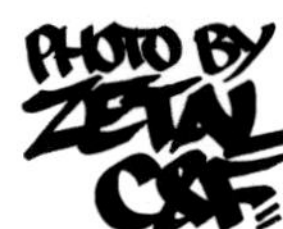

PHOTO BY
ZETA/
CRF

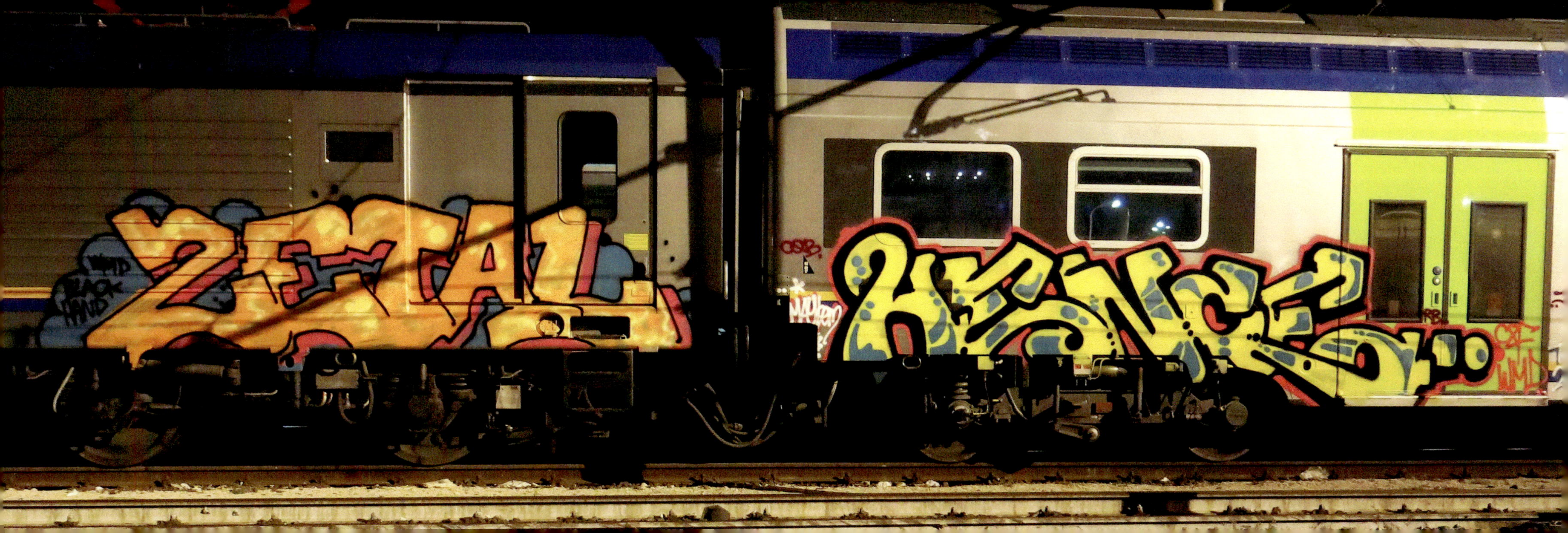

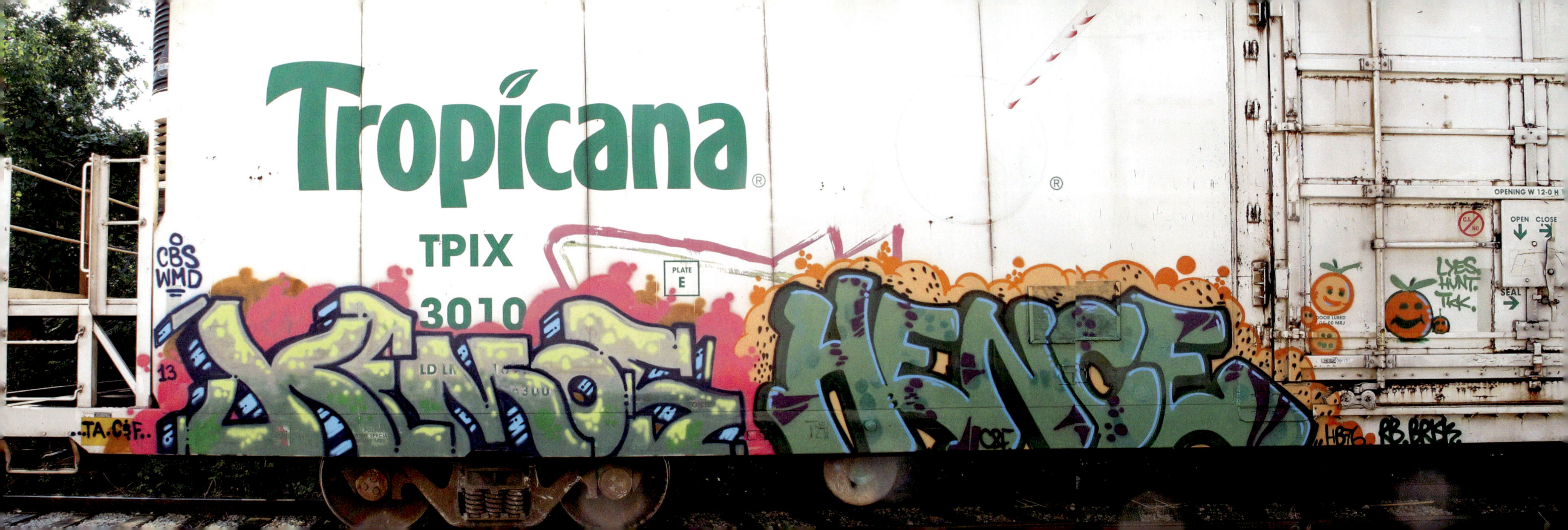

Tropicana
TPIX
3010
CBS
WMD
PLATE
E

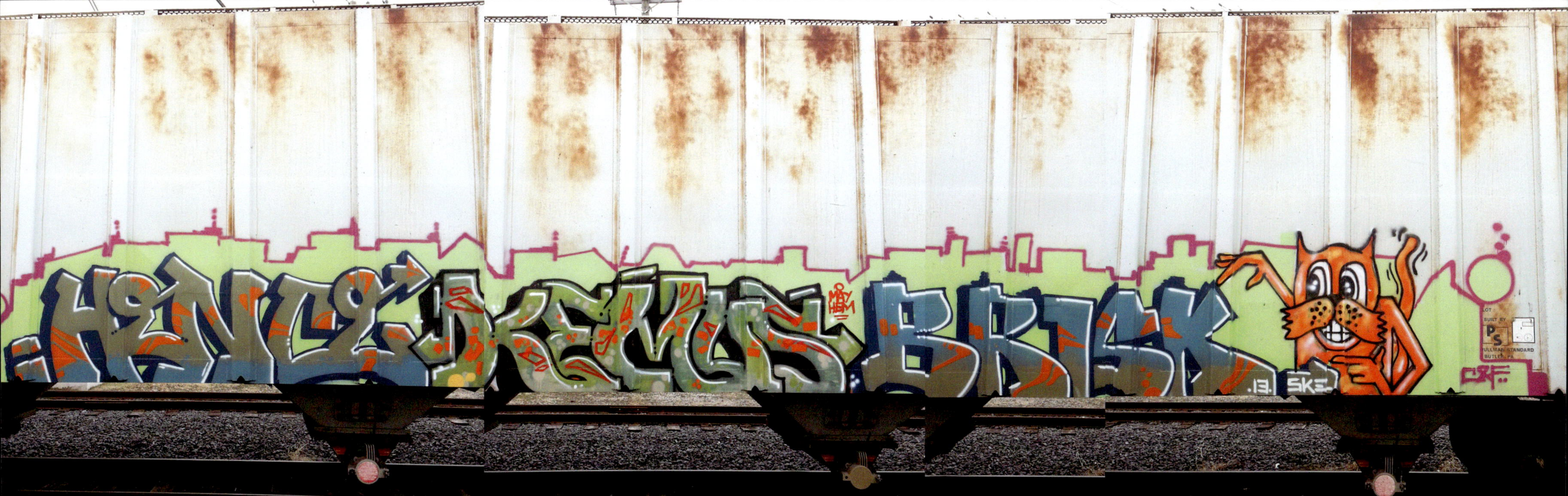

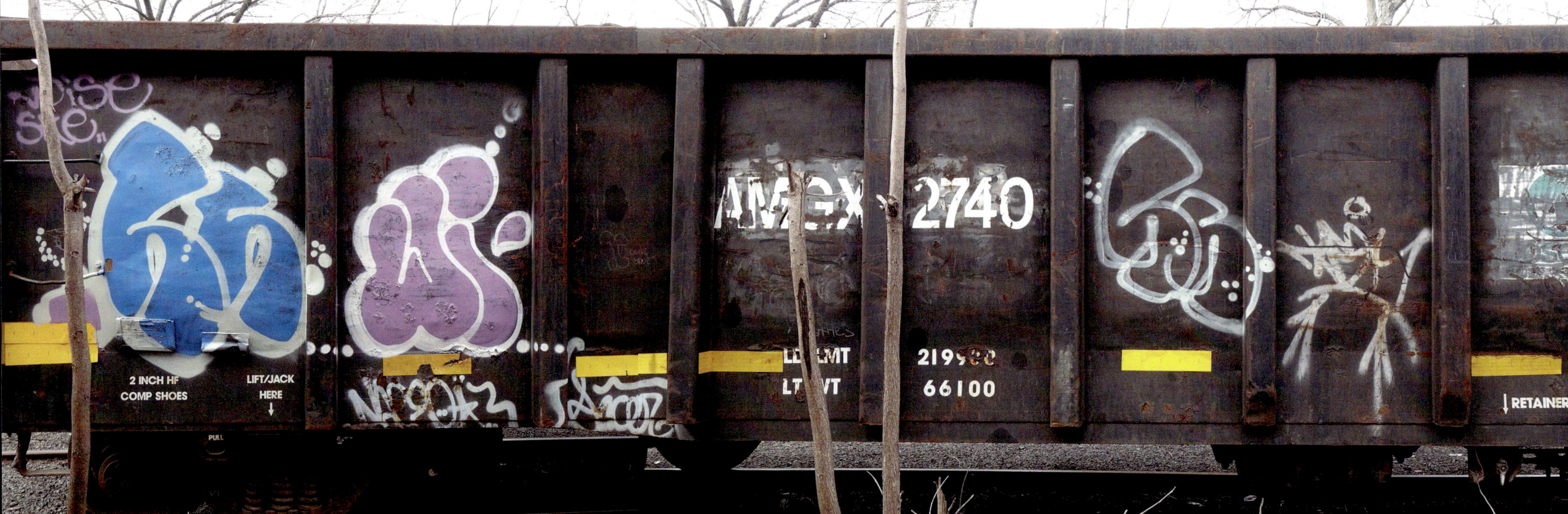

2 INCH HF
COMP SHOES
LIFT/JACK
HERE
AMGX 2740
LD LMT 219500
LT WT 66100
PULL
RETAINER

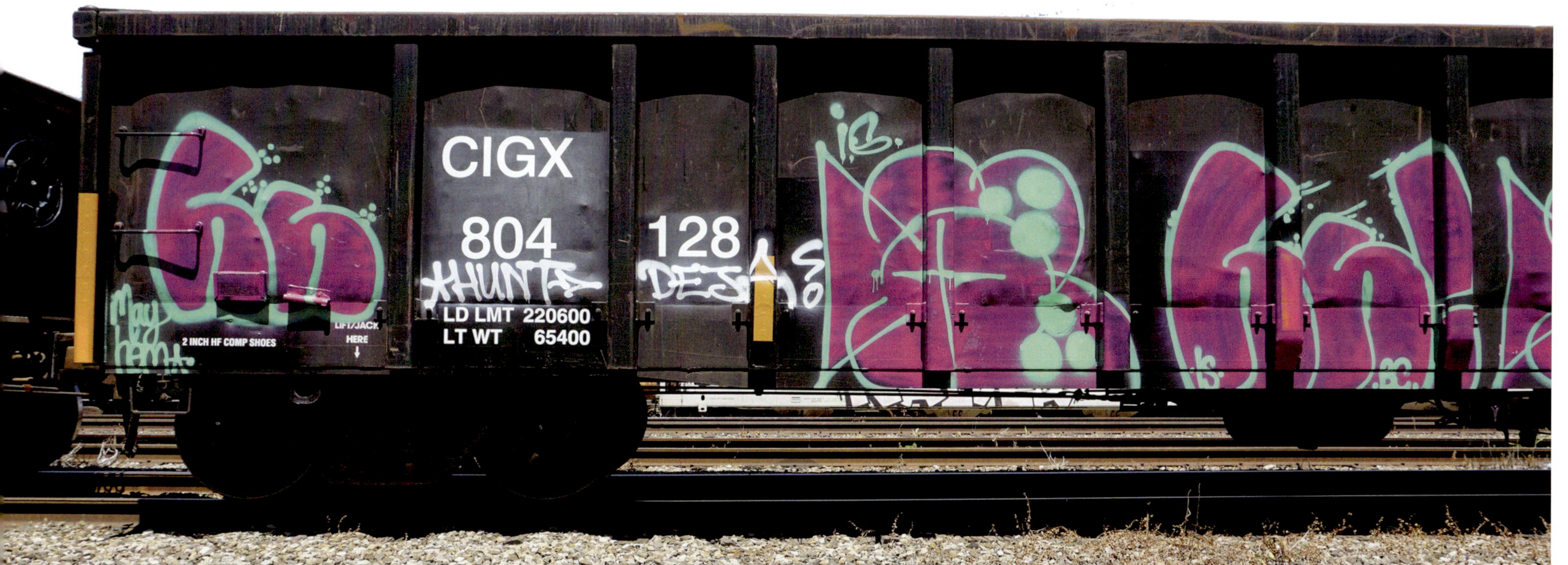
CIGX
804   128
LD LMT 220600
LT WT   65400
2 INCH HF COMP SHOES
LIFT/JACK
HERE

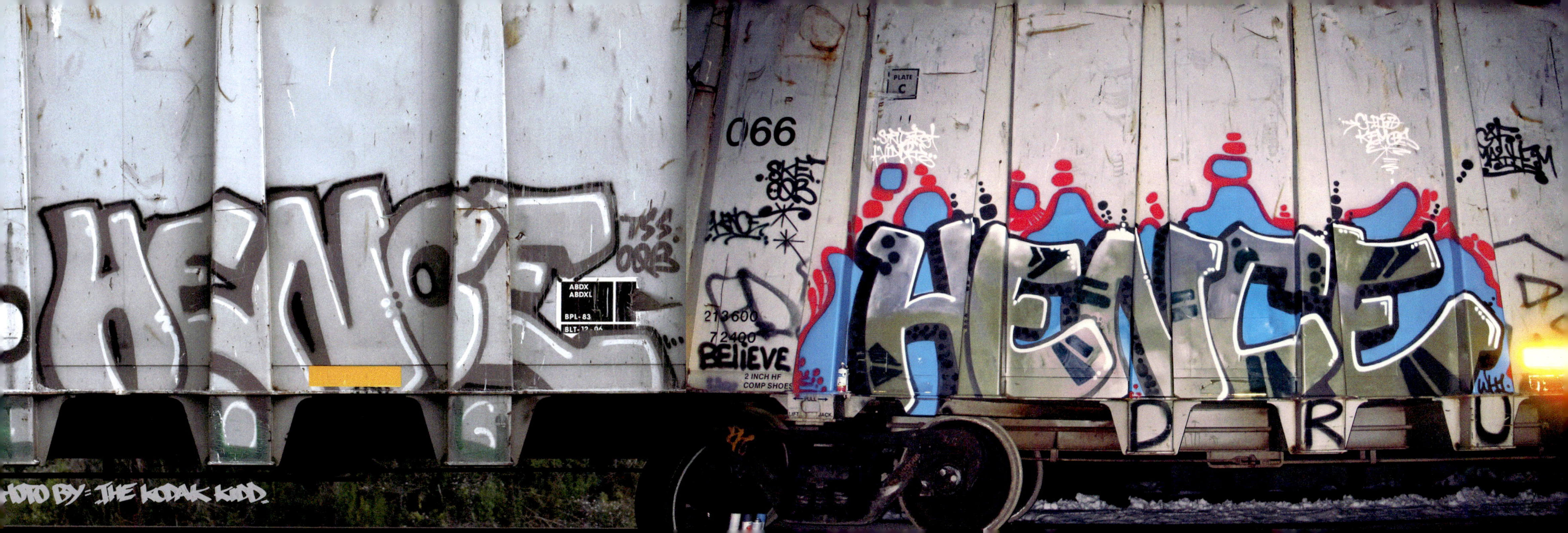
066
PLATE C
213600
7 2400
BELIEVE
2 INCH HF
COMP SHOES
PULL
LIFT JACK
ABDX
ABDXL
BPL-83
BLT-12-06
HOTO BY= THE KODAK KIDD

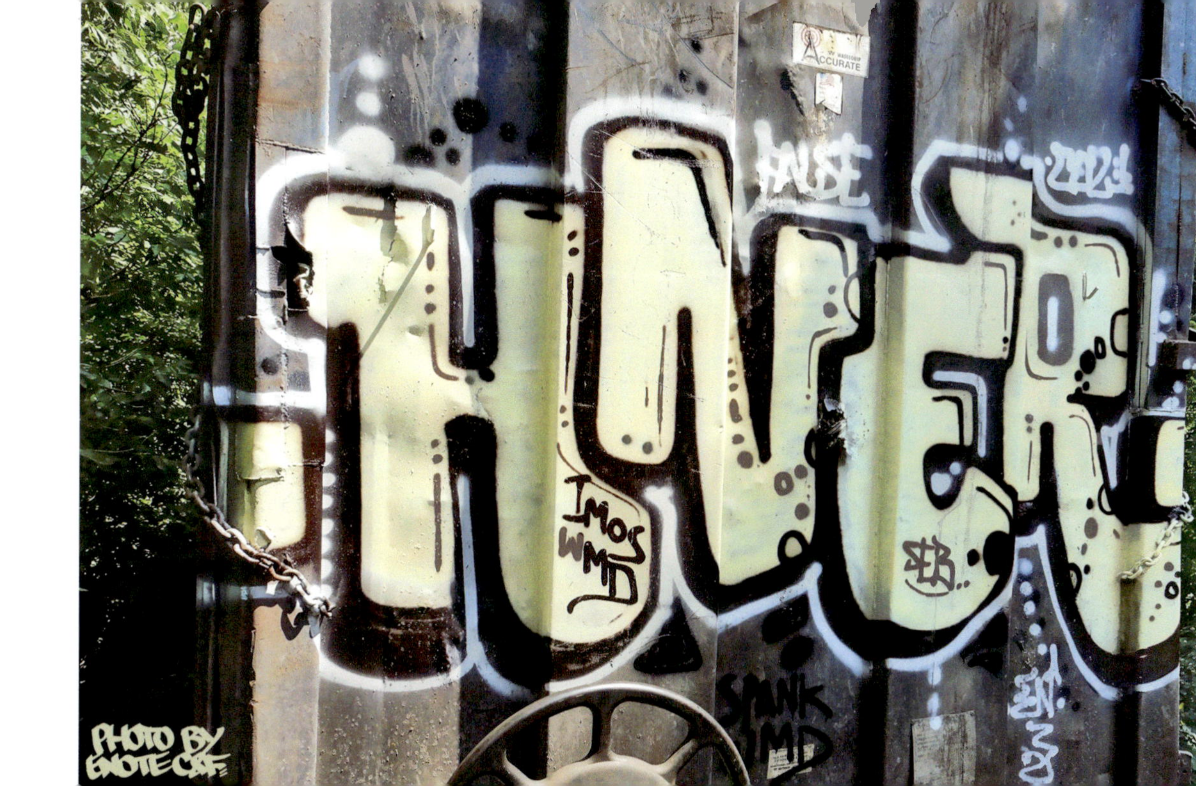

ACCURATE
PAUSE
2024
IMOS
WMD
SEB
SPANK
WMD
PHOTO BY
GNOTE CRE

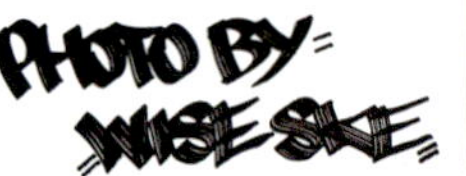
PHOTO BY
WISE SKE

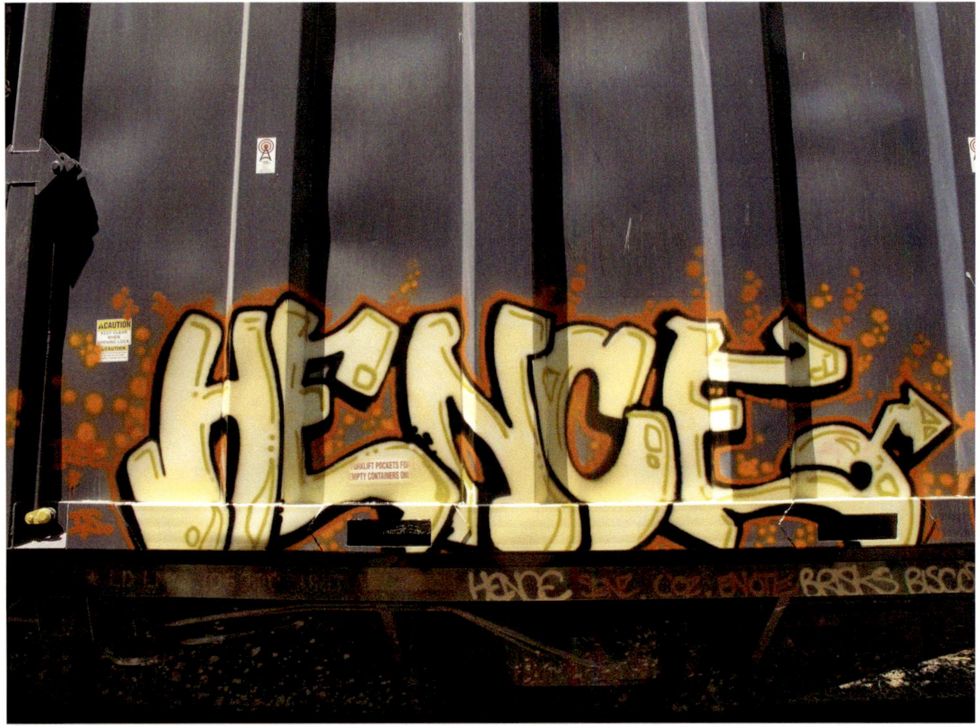

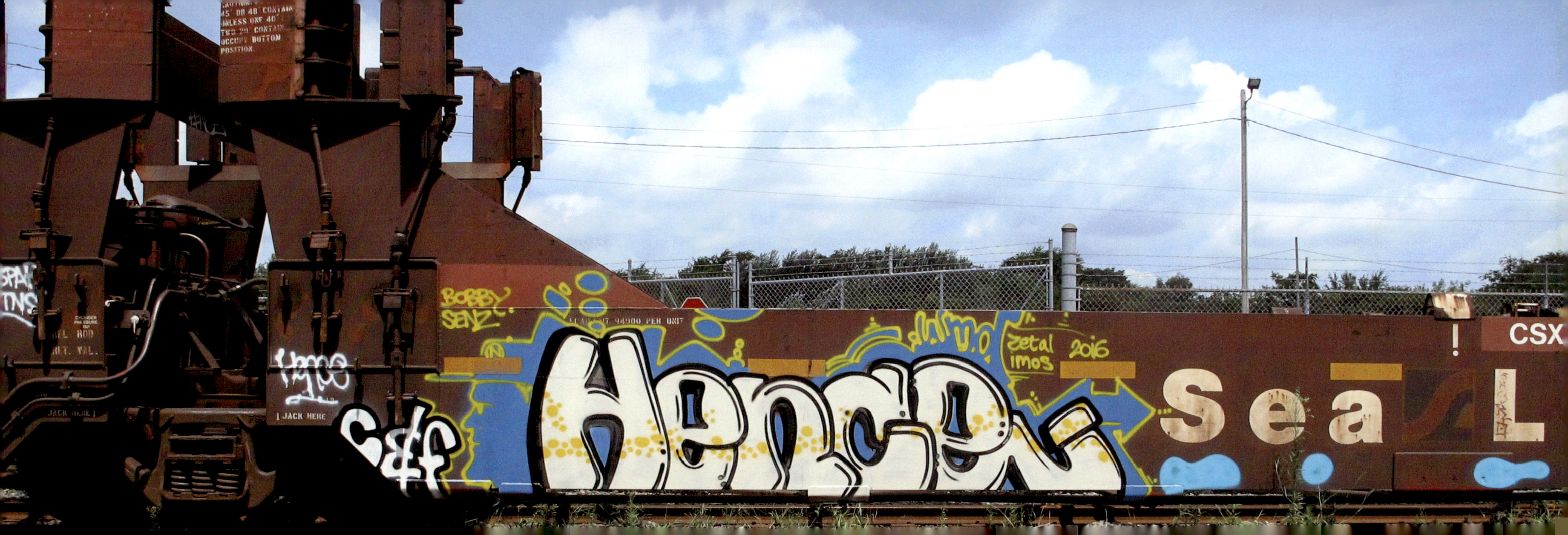
BOBBY
SENZ
Hence
zetal
imos 2016
CSX
Sea L

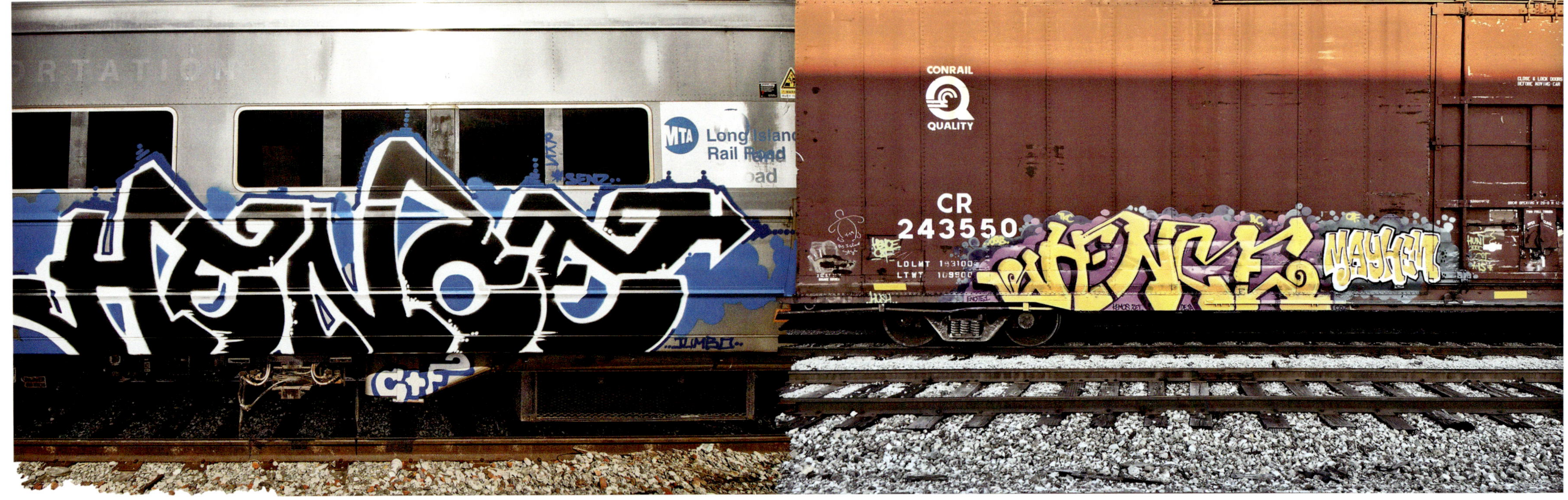

ORTATION
MTA
Long Island
Rail Road
SENZ
CONRAIL
QUALITY
CR
243550

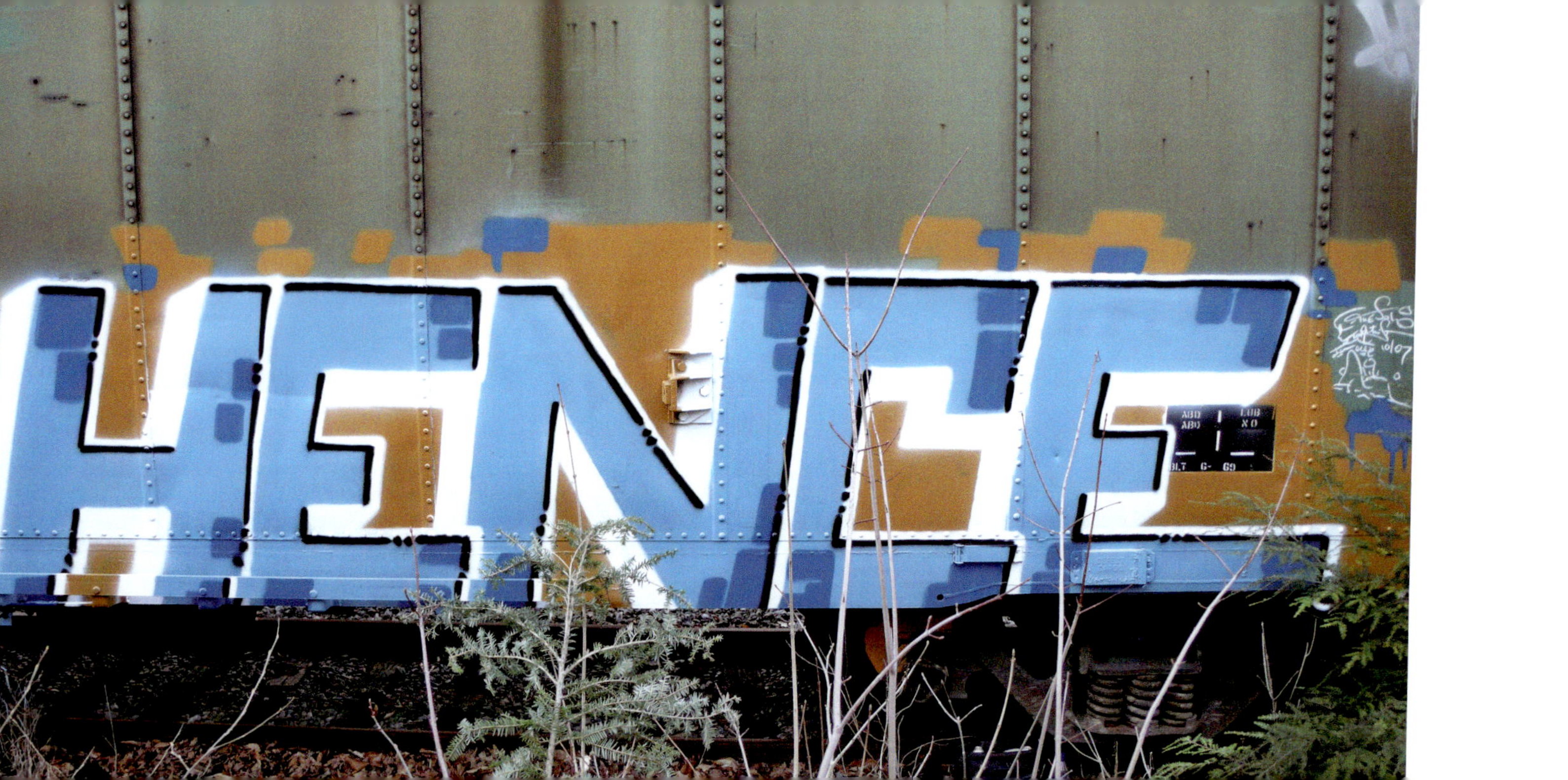
HENCE
ABD
ABD
LUB
X 0
BLT   G-   G9

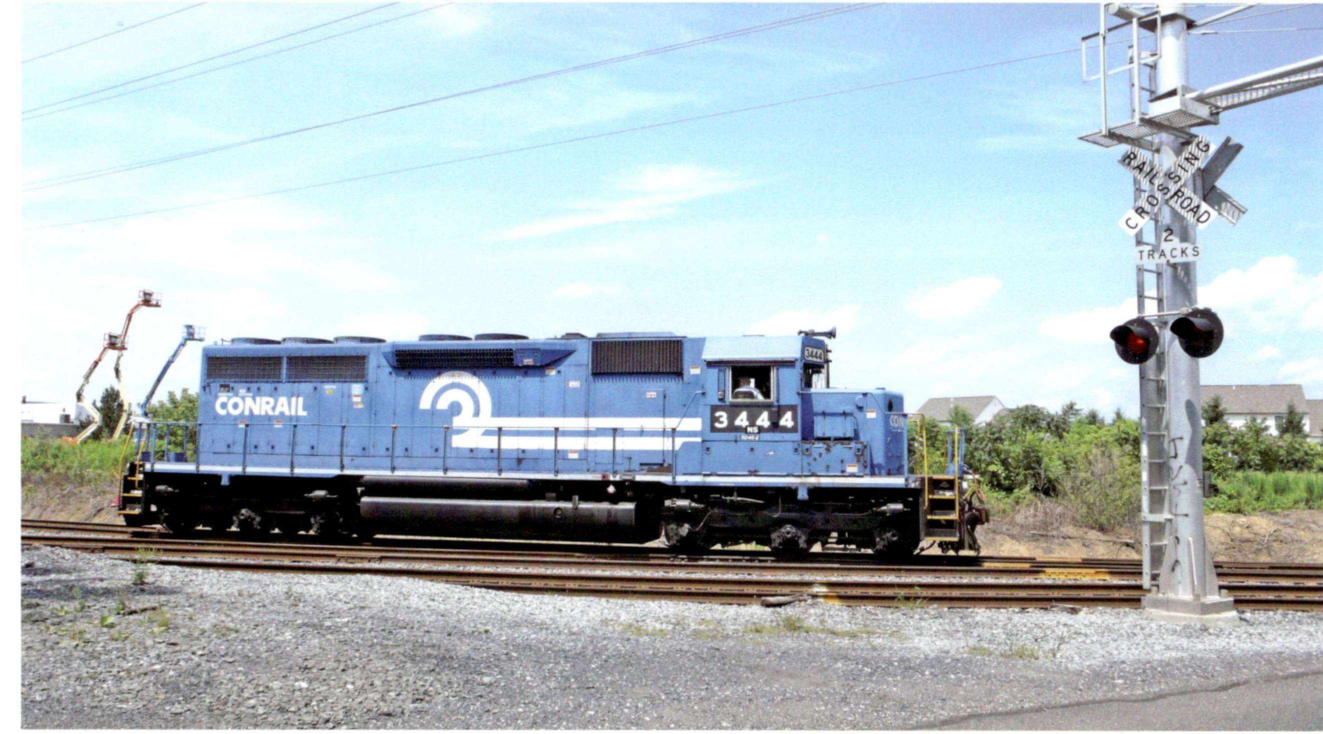
CONRAIL
3444
RAILROAD CROSSING
2 TRACKS

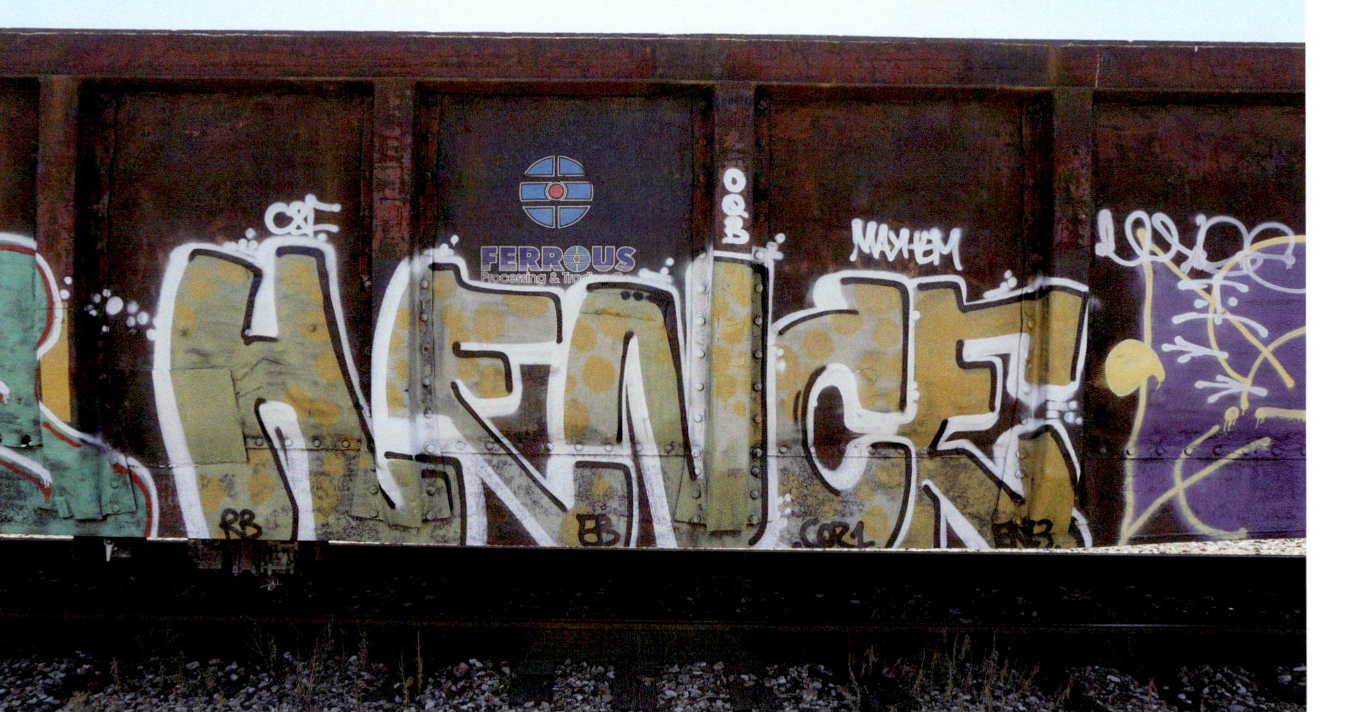

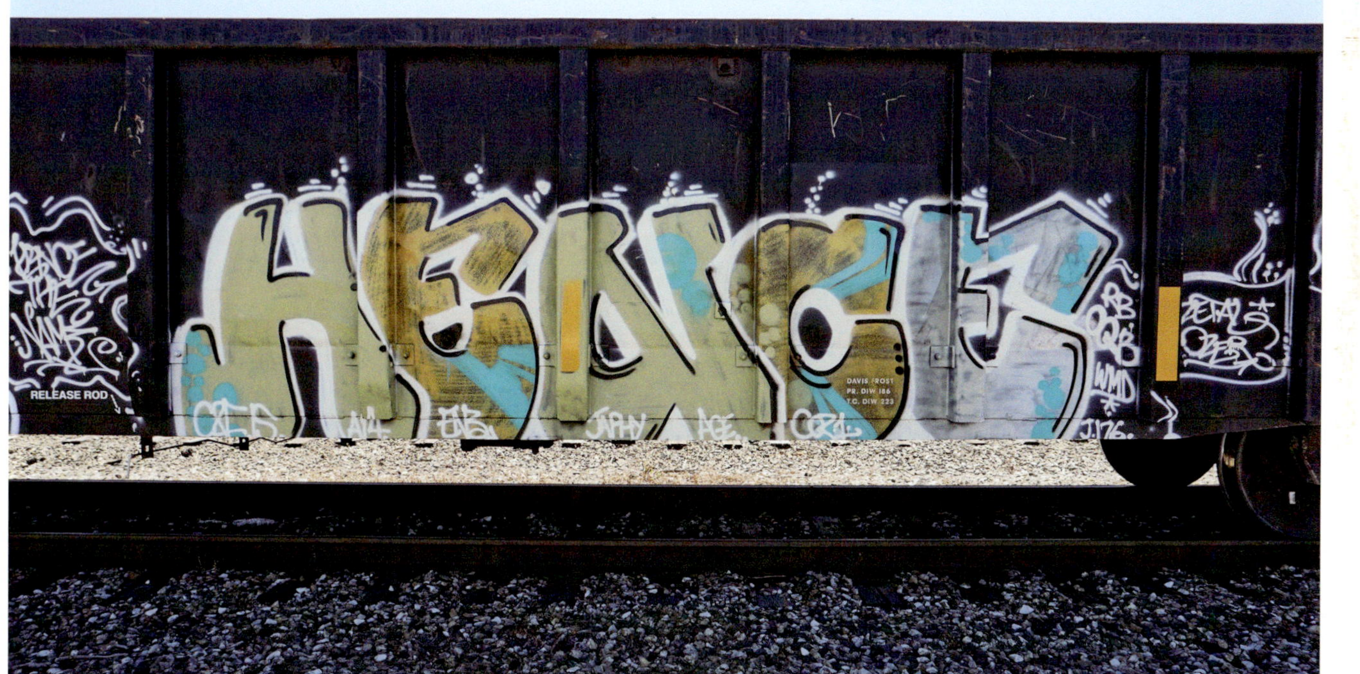

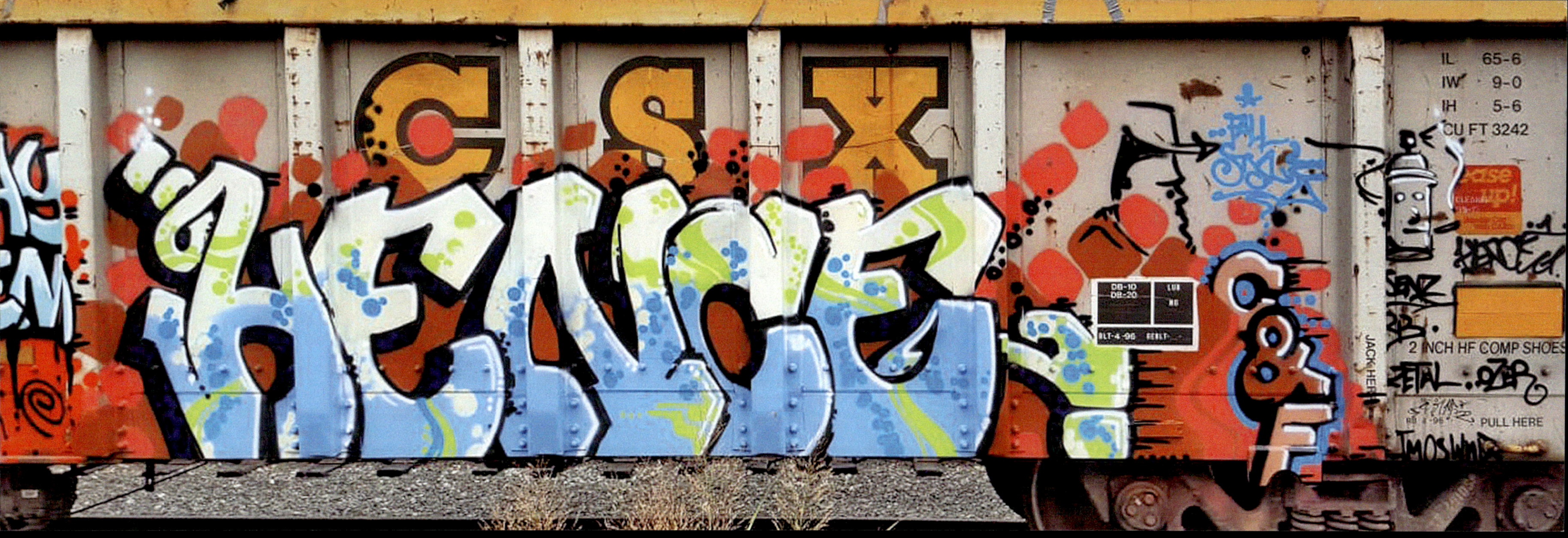

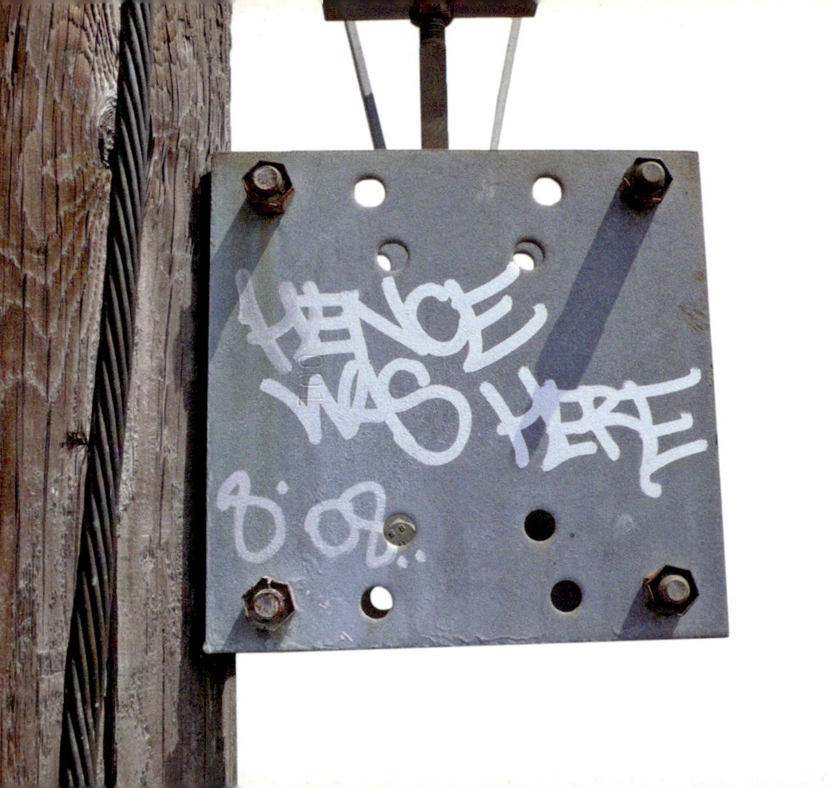

HENCE
WAS HERE
8·08

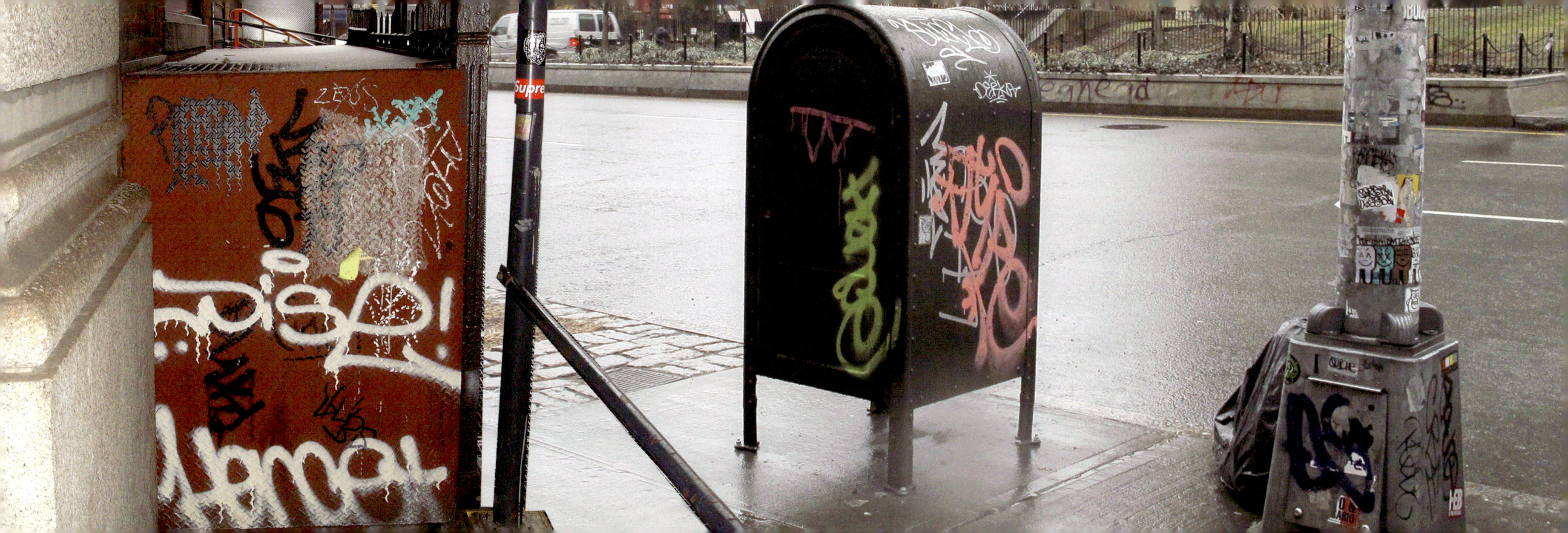

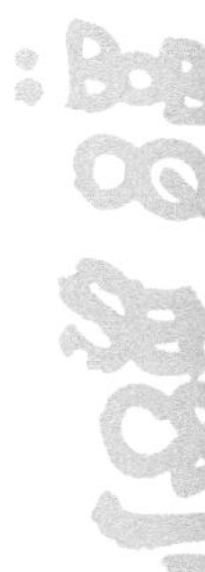

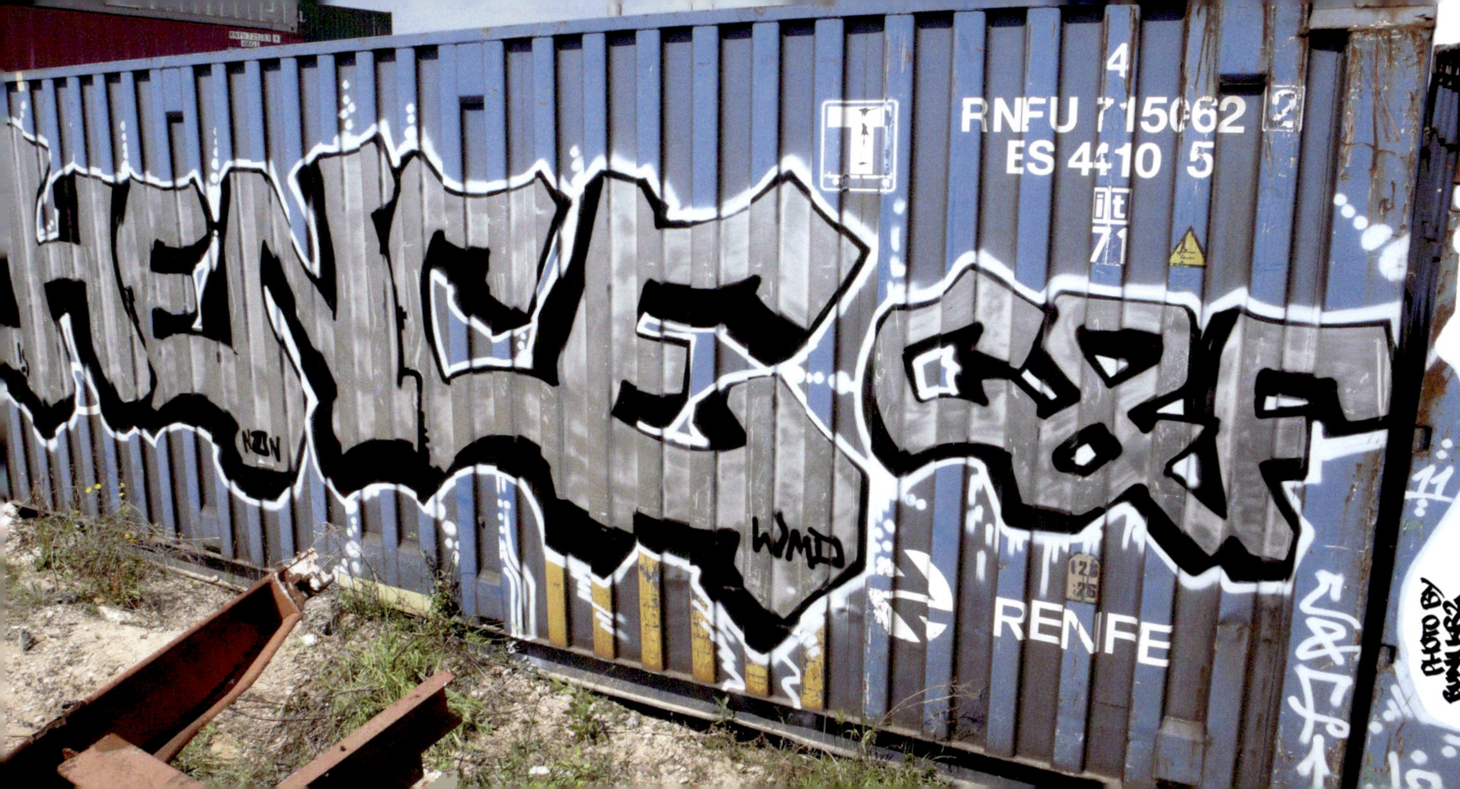
4
RNFU 715062
ES 4410 5
RENFE
PHOTO BY
FUNKER

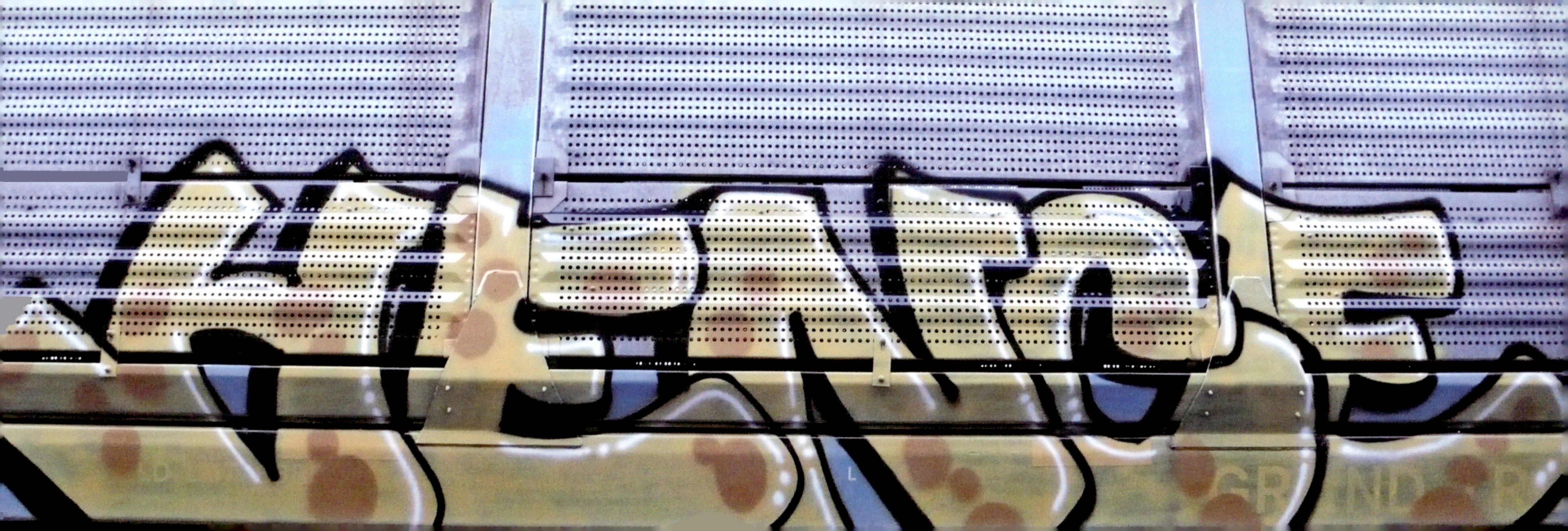

PHOTO BY KEMO

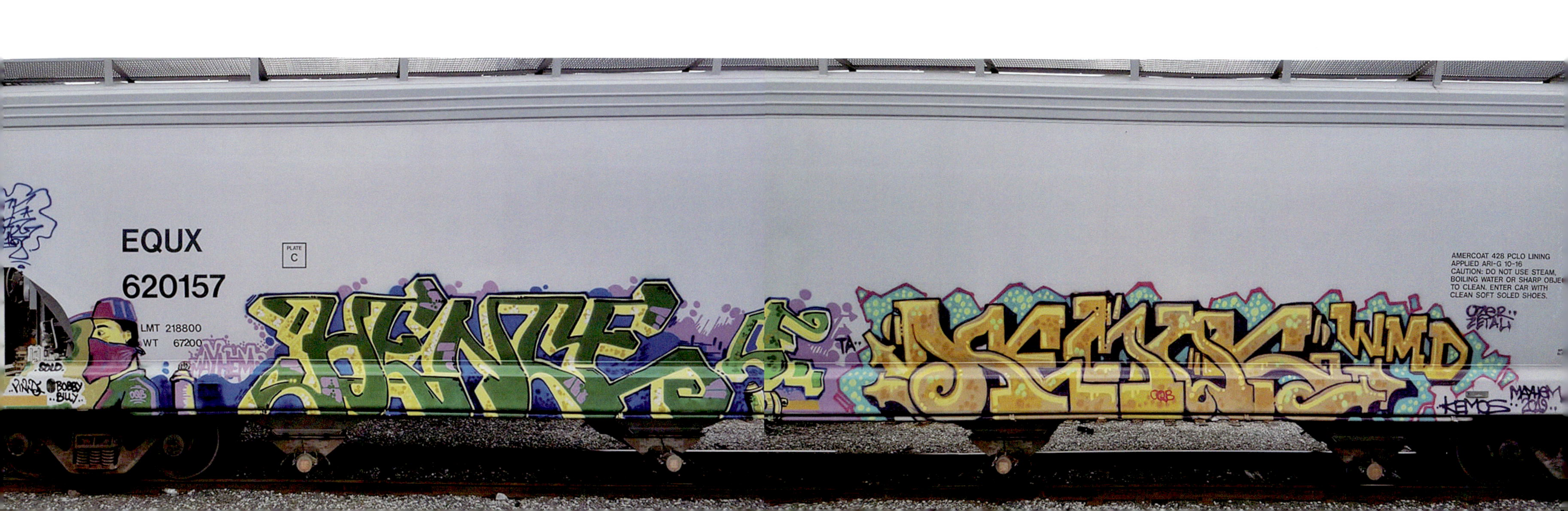

EQUX
620157
PLATE
C
LMT 218800
WT 67200
AMERCOAT 428 PCLO LINING
APPLIED ARI-G 10-16
CAUTION: DO NOT USE STEAM,
BOILING WATER OR SHARP OBJE
TO CLEAN. ENTER CAR WITH
CLEAN SOFT SOLED SHOES.
WMD

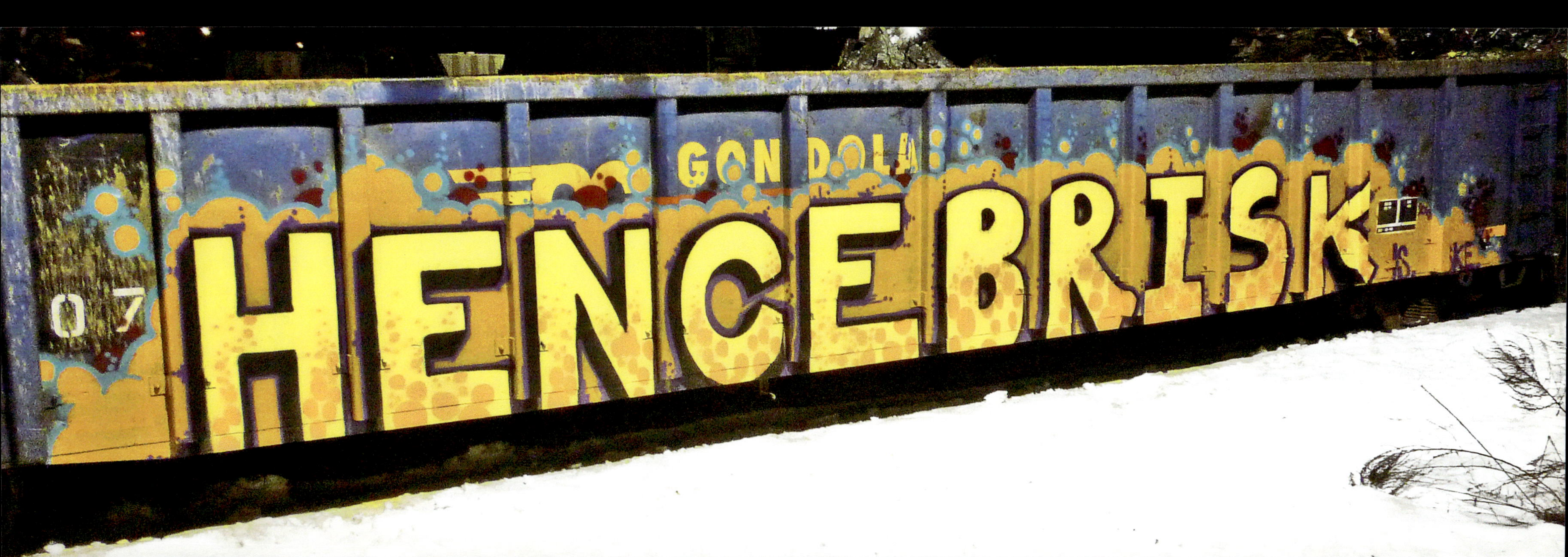
GON DOLA
07
HENCE BRISK

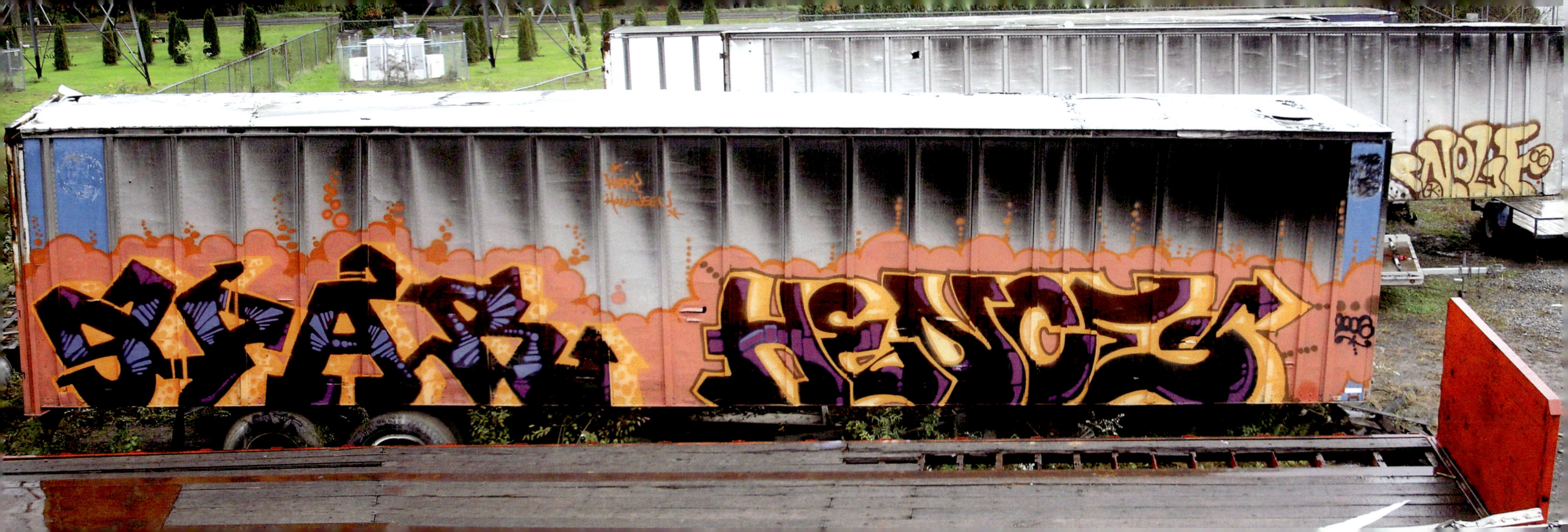

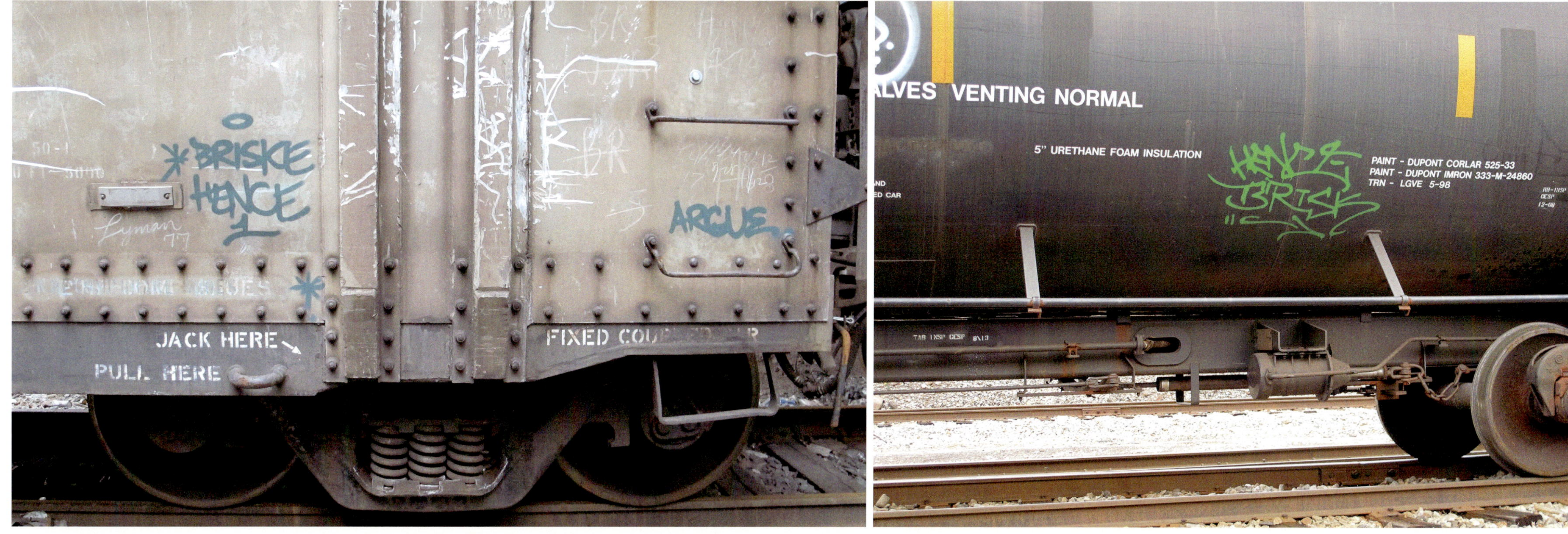
BRISKE
HENCE
ARGUE
JACK HERE
PULL HERE
FIXED COUPLED CAR
VALVES VENTING NORMAL
5" URETHANE FOAM INSULATION
PAINT - DUPONT CORLAR 525-33
PAINT - DUPONT IMRON 333-M-24860
TRN - LGVE 5-98

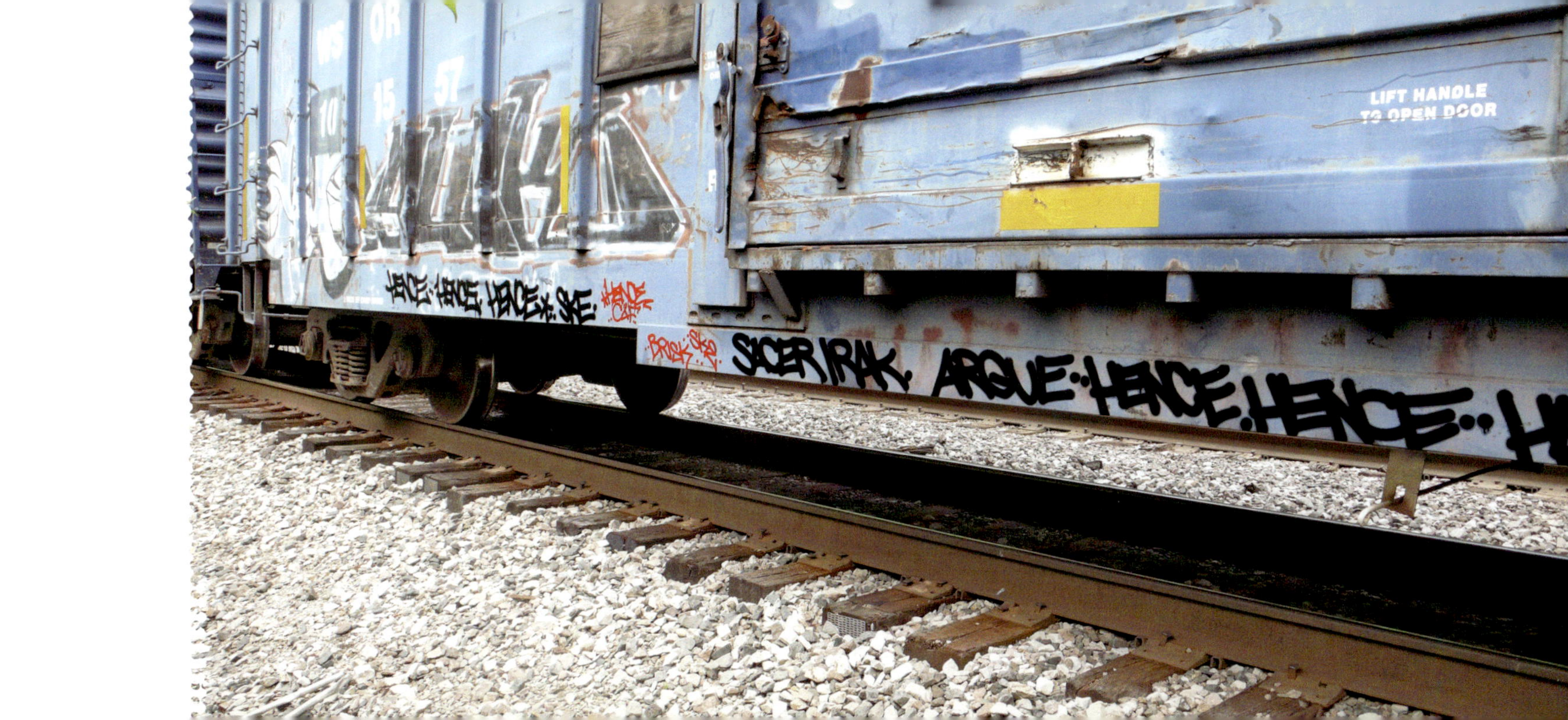
OR
57
15
10
LIFT HANDLE
TO OPEN DOOR

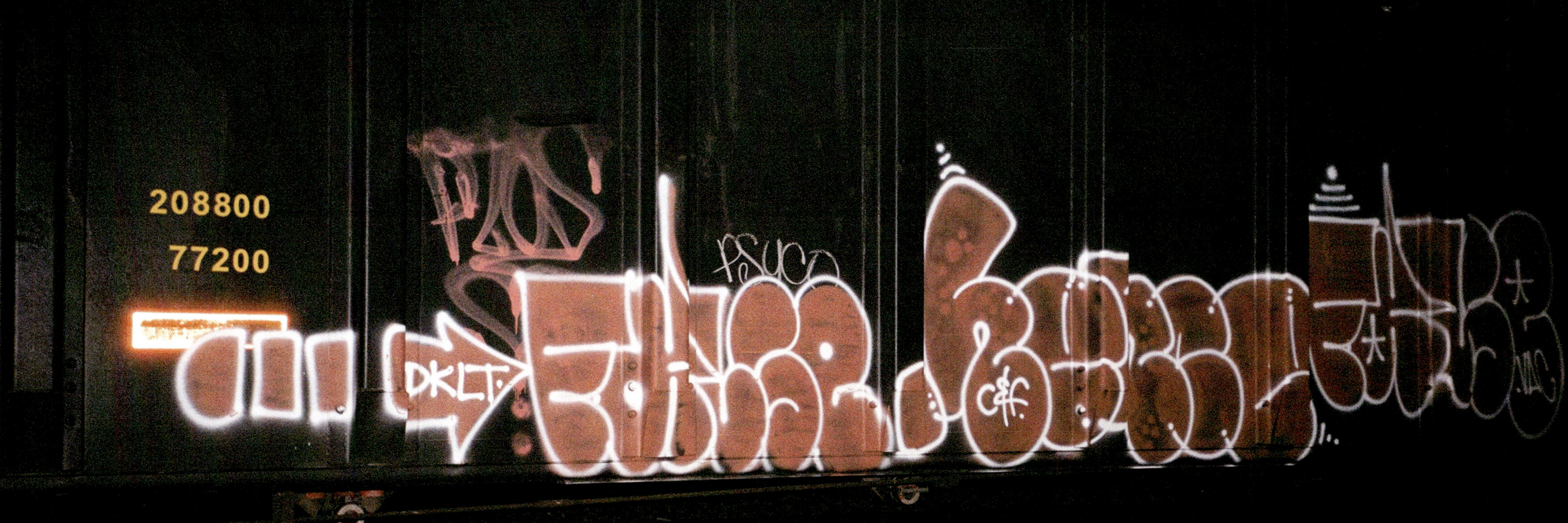

208800
77200

你认为分享这种经历会在写手之间建立一种特殊的联结纽带吗?

感谢这些年来和我一起涂鸦的所有写手。我们所经历的所有涂鸦背后都一定充满故事和冒险。纽约的前行者和早期的涂鸦永远不会过时。而每当我们讨论它们时,这些宝藏使这座城市变得更有趣。当我们发掘城市的切入点与一般民众不同的时候,或者说那些被遗忘的角落,我们与这座城市之间产生了某种特殊的连接。屋顶、火车轨道与隧道中我们所看到的城市,通常只有城市施工人员及探索公共交通的粉丝才能够欣赏得到。我们不断地上街涂鸦,磨合团队,经过长期相处并互相激励,不断的涂鸦、合作、分享和鼓励彼此让我们之间产生的羁绊更加坚固。

在这里我想感谢我的伙伴 SENZ,A14,IO69(IS),SPAR(TNS),WISE,STES & BRISK(SKE),KEMOS,CENSE,EYE,HUNT,FALSE,CHIP7 (MAYHEM Crew),COZ,ENOTE(C&F),KNJ,RB(OQB),BILLY(ORG,OQB),SOLO,STRIDER(BC),VINNY(3YB),SMITH,WHISPER,KB(TSS),F5(LTV),EGS,JAPHY,TRAMA(FTC),ZIPIT(WMD),BUNI(KR2),SEB(NCC),ZETAL,OZER,DEM & GIOEL(Black Hand crew),IMOS(WMD),DES(WMD),TKR 227(MH's),SWA,SMART(RIS),O'CLOCK,DIEGO(FMK),OPAK(SDK),TROTA(THE),HAKER,TL.ONE,FETISH,REBEL(SC),JUMBO,RESTO & TERNS,4SKOR,SECR,AMENS,HOACS(LD),OBCES(LD),IREE(FS),EBEE(TKC),VILE8,WYSE(D30),LYES(NETWORK),BOE(WOW),BOOTS 119(MG),PURE & MASON(TFP)。

谢谢你,无妥协方式!!

HENCE 1,C&F,2021

Can you tell us something about your crews and the writers that have been with you during these decades of activity? Do you think that sharing this kind of experience creates a special bond between people?

Thanks to all my partners I have written with through the years. There are stories and adventures that correspond with every signature, piece, and throw-up. There is the lore of old NYC and writing in the early years that never gets old. It only gets more interesting as we discuss it often. There is a special bond as we see the city from a different perspective than the average person doesn't know or care to look deeply at. The things we see from a rooftop, train tracks, or tunnel, coupled with a true appreciation for the city, the architecture, secret places, and the detail that usually only the workers and transit fans care about. We go on missions constantly and know our partner's strengths and what motivates each other, how to work together and collaborate, share and push one another.

Thank you SENZ, A14, IO69 (IS), SPAR (TNS), WISE, STES & BRISK (SKE), KEMOS, CENSE, EYE, HUNT, FALSE, CHIP 7 (MAYHEM Crew), COZ, ENOTE (C&F), KNJ, RB (OQB), BILLY (ORG, OQB), SOLO, STRIDER (BC), VINNY (3YB), SMITH, WHISPER, KB (TSS), F5 (LTV), EGS, JAPHY, TRAMA (FTC), ZIPIT (WMD), BUNI (KR2), SEB (NCC), ZETAL, OZER, DEM & GIOEL (Black Hand crew), IMOS (WMD), DES (WMD), TKR 227 (MH's), SWA, SMART (RIS), O'CLOCK, DIEGO (FMK), OPAK (SDK), TROTA (THE), HAKER, TL.ONE, FETISH, REBEL (SC), JUMBO, RESTO and TERNS, 4SKOR, SECR, AMENS, HOACS (LD), OBCES (LD), IREE (FS), EBEE (TKC), VILE8, WYSE (D30), LYES (NETWORK), BOE (WOW), BOOTS 119 (MG), PURE and MASON (TFP).

Thank you No Apologies!!

HENCE 1 (C&F) 2021

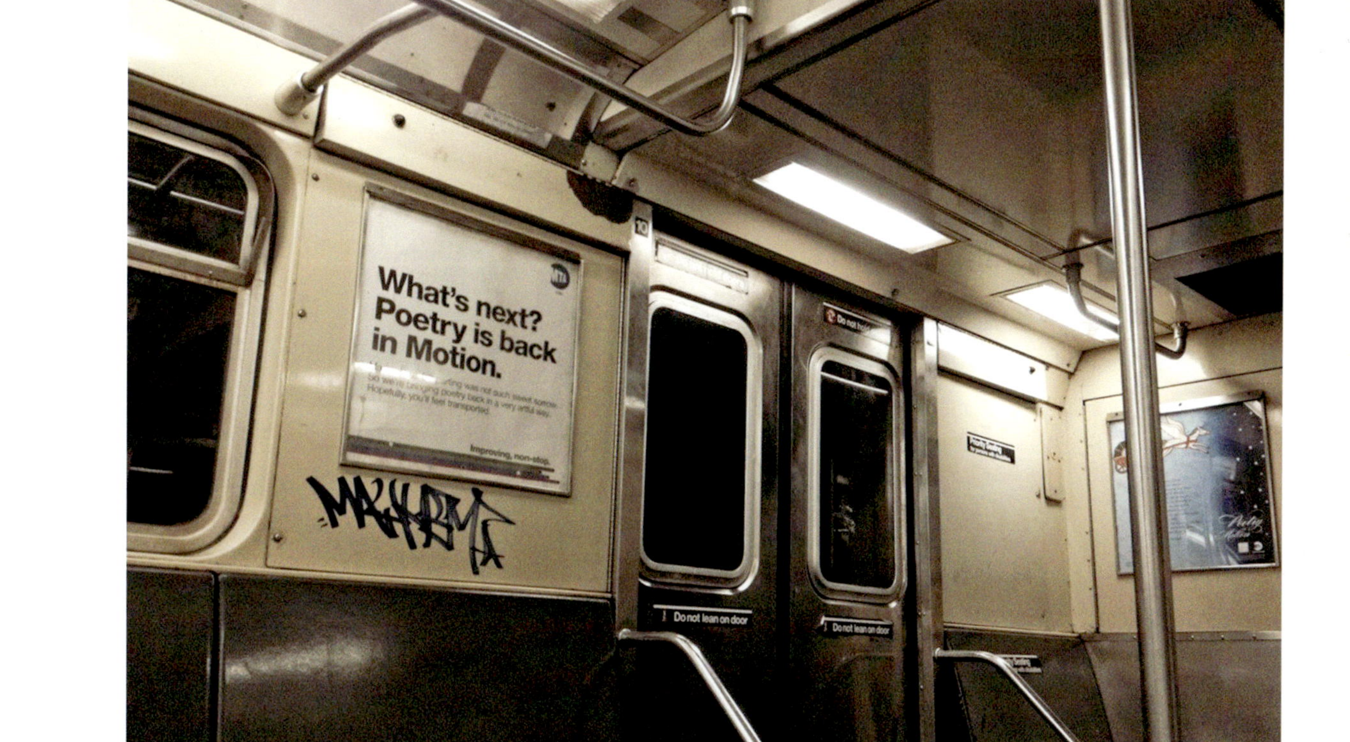

What's next?
Poetry is back
in Motion.
Improving, non-stop.
Do not lean on door
Do not lean on door

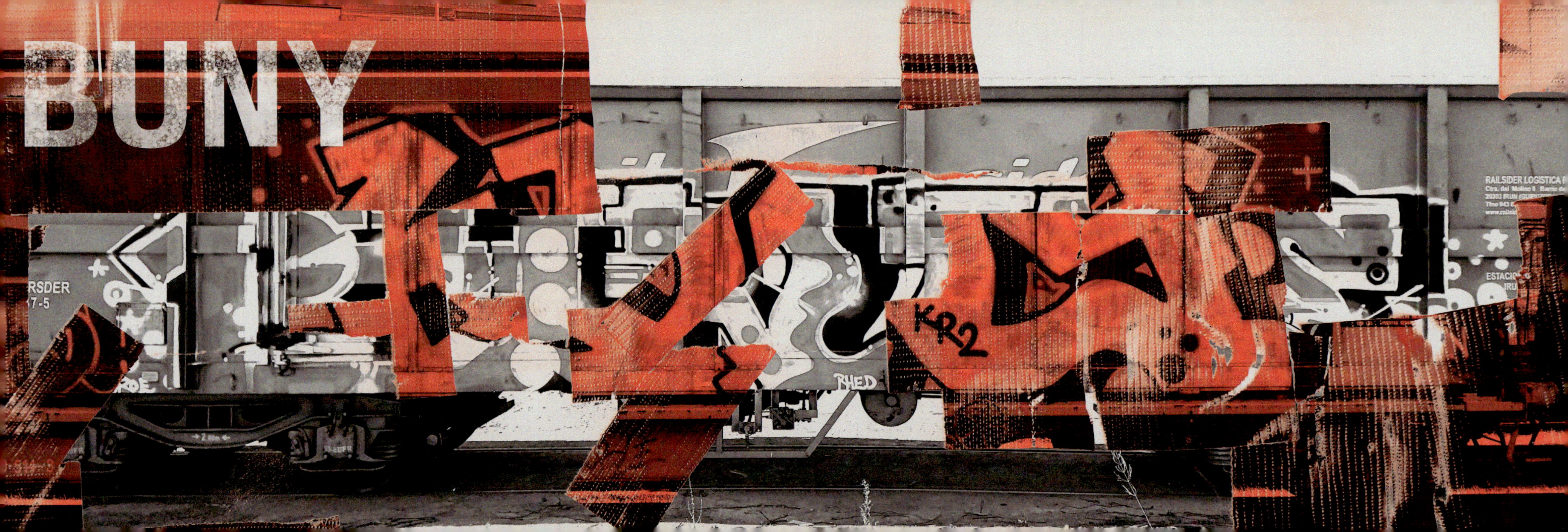

BUNY
RSDER
7-5
KR2
RHED
RAILSIDER LOGISTICA
Ctra. del Molino 8 Barrio
20303 IRUN (GUIP
Tino 943
www.railsi
ESTACIO
IRU

BUNY
年轻不放弃

众所周知 BUNY 是一个涂鸦的名字，但你能告诉我们一些关于你成为涂鸦写手的经历吗？

从 1989 年开始，因为受到老朋克风格 MADrizzz 签名里的箭头启发，诞生了我的第一个涂鸦签名。

> **"十年后，我和团队成员 SHA 在马德里地铁的一节红色车厢上重新喷上了这个主题"**

当安东尼奥决定和我一起画第一幅涂鸦时。我们合作了一幅含有 "DUO" 字母的作品，而其中的含义就是俩人的结盟。这也是我这辈子做的第一件涂鸦作品。我们使用粉色、奶油色和红色作为填充，黑色作为字体外框。但是我们并没有为他留下完整的照片，图片中只囊括了一个字母 D。十年后，我和团队成员 SHA 在马德里地铁的一节红色车厢上重新喷上了这个主题。

哪些写手对你的影响最大？

MUELLE，GLUB，BLECK（la rata），BIX，还有一个以字母 B 开头，并以字母 Y 甩出的箭头做结尾的写手。我真的很喜欢这些写手的作品。

谁会跟你一块画涂鸦？

HIGOS，YHEN，RHED，还有每一次行动中的朋友。

作为一名写手，你经历过哪些不同阶段？

当然，我所经历的每个阶段，其他写手也都有体会。从签名，到单线涂鸦，以及完整作品都必须是新鲜的并且不重复…现在许多涂鸦的地点以及表面都被政府有计划的破坏，周遭的环境在不断变化。但是这也强迫我变得更加强大。

我喜欢带着不同的材料炸街。每个真正的涂鸦人都有自己得心应手的工具与颜色。

> **"在街上画涂鸦当然一年比一年艰难，也一年比一年激烈。将自己的风格进化提升是必须的，这也是我无法逃避的问题"**

30 多年来，你一直都在不同的立面上创作。而马德里这里的涂鸦氛围在这段时间里发生了怎样的变化呢？

马德里的涂鸦氛围确实在不断变化。城市中的"豺狼"每天都在成长，所以你需要时刻关注着周遭的动向。在街上画涂鸦当然一年比一年艰难，也一年比一年激烈。将自己的风格进化提升是必须的，这也是我无法逃避的问题。

> **"一个成熟的写手应该擅长签名、单线涂鸦，以及一定量的火车作品。因为那不只是在家里画手稿或单纯画合法墙能得到的成就"**

在许多方面，你的作品代表了最真实的涂鸦精神，对你来说，定义一个好的写手需要什么条件？

我喜欢文字书写的所有范畴。一个成熟的写手应该擅长签名、单线涂鸦，以及一定量的火车作品。因为那不只是在家里画手稿或单纯画合法墙能得到的成就，但我也明白并不是每个人都有时间或精力去做这些真正涂鸦精神的创作。这也就是为什么只有真正强大的人才能在这场竞赛中生存下来。同时印证了让自己名字不断出现在街头的重要性，涂鸦贴纸自然而然地也成为了我占领街头的必需品。

在过去的 20 年里，涂鸦已经被许多不同的和不相关的因素污染了（像互联网，街头艺术，商业化…）但是你总是在作品中保持一种明确的态度。能和我们分享一下你对涂鸦的见解吗？

我只是努力按着街头的规则，追随我的情感，以及我的内心在做涂鸦。年复一年，涂鸦作为一种艺术形式越来越时髦，也越来越受欢迎，所以没有必要为了成就一件伟大的事情试图去追逐顶峰。如果你拥有一个良好的基础，建筑就完成了，而它也将像岩石一样屹立不倒。

在你的作品中，有许多画在货运列车上。你是什么时候开始，以及为什么热衷于画在货运列车上的呢？

那是在 2003 年初我开始选择货运列车做创作。因为涂鸦能在他们表面保留很久，并且跟随列车穿越很多地方，所以它成为一个完美的涂鸦目标也就不足为奇了。

现在喷货运列车的难度大吗？

当人们注意到它的作用时，很多停靠点被画满了涂鸦，因此对货车的安全措施就变得更加严格。而且有一些旧货车样式已经被淘汰，现在大部分货物会被存放在货车里而难以被喷绘。

一般货运列车上的涂鸦能保留多久？

这不好说…有时候可以长达十年，但有时候只能留一个月的时间，这你根本没法预估。

你最喜欢的货运列车的型号是什么？

那是一种白色冷藏车厢[1]。

在所有你画的货运列车里，到达的最远距离是哪里？

日本，新西兰，智利，加拿大，洛杉矶…

你也经常在隧道里画涂鸦，而政府通常不会清理那，一件作品可能会永远保存下去。有什么想法或故事可以和大家分享吗？

您的杂志中都会附带一句"集装箱，一次环游世界的旅行[2]"，证明了你的名字已经传播到世界的每一个角落，但你仍旧没有停止书写。哪些旅行给你留下了深刻的印象？

赫尔辛基，斯德哥尔摩，东京，首尔…

哪个地点将是你未来计划前往的呢？

非洲。

"那些地方虽然好画但是也肮脏。到处都是灰尘和脏水。但是我喜欢和朋友一起在那喝啤酒。隧道是个多么赞的地点，每个夜晚都是难忘的"

对于一个写手来说，涂鸦带给他的并不全是金钱、荣耀和赞许。但是涂鸦带给你的是利大于弊还是弊大于利呢？

我虽然物质上贫穷，但是精神上快乐着，因为每一次当我将名字写上街头，我会遇到越来越多志同道合的朋友，旅行到这个星球上之前从未到过的幻想之地。我不指望自己能成为一名收入丰厚的艺术家。但是最后我会心满意足的死去，所以我不奢求能从涂鸦中带来什么或得到什么。

几乎每一次的旅行都是快乐的……对发生的任何事情都不后悔，每一段经历也都是美好的回忆。我只是在等待那个能够炸街的时间点到来。在涂鸦这场游戏中，不断炸街才是最重要的。我只是跟着大浪潮走。虽然我已经太老了，不能走在这些波浪的最前端，但我的心态还是依旧年轻，也从不放弃。

对所有的轰炸选手们致以和平与尊重。

只有你知道自己是谁！

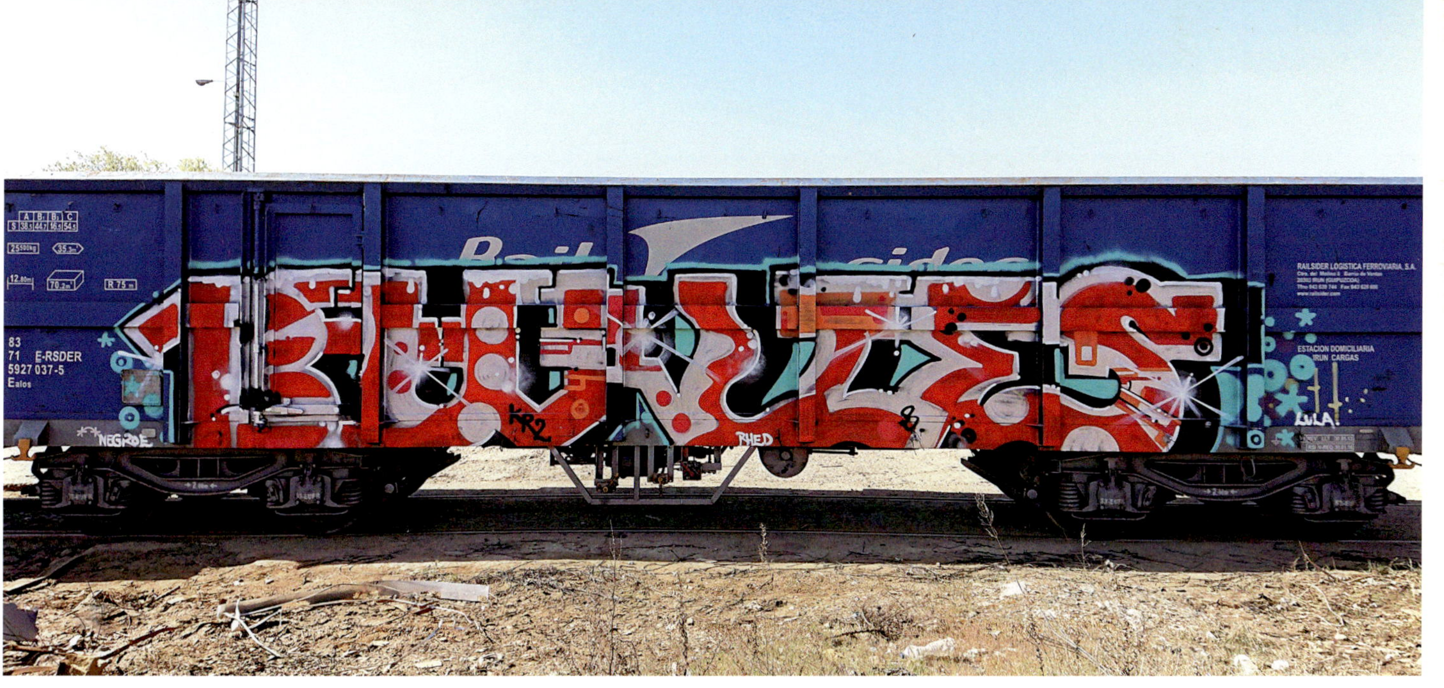

BUNY
Too young to quit

BUNY is a name that doesn't need any introduction but can you tell us something about your journey as a writer?

I started in 1989 catching my first spray can tag with arrow style inspired by MADrizzz old punk original flavor writing.

Everything was new when my partner Antonio decided to write the first piece together with me. We did a 'DUO' piece, which means the union of two persons. This was the first piece I did in my life. We used Novelty pink, cream, and red for the fill-in and black for the outline. We don't have a picture of it, just a bit of the letter D. Ten years later I was putting this name again on a subway red car in Madrid with my crew partner SHA.

Which are the writers that influenced you the most?

MUELLE, GLUB, BLECK (la rata), BIX, and one other who starts with the letter B and ends with an arrow on the 'Y'. I really love those letters.

Who are your partners in crime?

HIGOS, YHEN, RHED, and the ones you can see in our missions.

As a writer did you went through different phases?

Of course. It's part of the evolution of a writer. Tags, Throws, Pieces must be always fresh and new... Also, spots and surfaces are moving or being destroyed by the government nowadays, the context is constantly changing. All this brings about a strong development in everything.

I love to bomb with different kinds of tools. Every target needs the correct weapon and color.

You have been active on every surface for more than 20 years, a life spent writing. How do Madrid and its graffiti scene have changed during this time?

Madrid is constantly changing. *Chacals* (jackals) are growing day by day, on and on, so you need to be ready anytime for any kind of action. Things are getting harder and more aggressive every year. Evolution is a must, it can't be avoided.

In many ways, your work represents the most genuine spirit of graffiti. What defines a good writer for you?

I like to touch on all aspects of writing. A dope writer should be able to do tags, throws, and trains. Not just walls or sketches at home but I understand not everyone has the time or energy to do real things. That's why only the real, strong ones survive in this race. The most important thing is to get up. That's why I love to put stickers too.

In the last 20 years, a big part of the scene has been contaminated by many different and unrelated factors (like the internet, the street-art, the commercialization...) but you always maintained a well-defined attitude in your work. Can you share with us what is your idea of writing?

I just try to follow the rules, my feelings, and my heart. Year by year graffiti, as art, are more popular and fashionable so it's not necessary to do great things to be under the spotlight. If you have a good base, the building is done and it's solid as a rock.

Among your production, there are many freight trains. How did you start to dedicate yourself to this kind of surface?

It was around the beginning of 2003. It's easy to understand that it has durability and travels a lot so no mystery why it's a perfect target.

How hard is it at the moment to paint freights?

As people noticed that it works, yards got burned and the security is harder on these cars. Also, some models have disappeared so most of the stuff is loaded in containers nowadays.

How long a piece lasts usually?

It depends... Sometimes ten years sometimes one month. You never know.

Do you have a favorite freight model?

Yes. White flat reefer containers[1].

What is the most faraway place where your freights have been seen?

Japan, New Zealand, Chile, Canada, LA...

You also paint regularly in the tunnels, where the buff often does not arrive and where a piece can potentially last forever. Any thoughts or stories you feel like sharing?

"Yes. That shit is dirty. Full of dust and water. I love to be there with beers and friends. Lovely spots. Unforgettable nights"

Your project, *Container World, A journey around the globe*[2], proves that your name has traveled to every corner of the world but you also have wandered around to spray your tag. Which are the trips that left a mark on you?

Helsinki, Stockholm, Tokyo, Seoul...

And which is the place you would like to visit in the future?

Africa.

Probably as a writer it has not been all money, glory, and pats on the back. Graffiti pays or it takes more than it gives?

I'm still poor but really happy because, while trying to get up, I met people and visited parts of this planet that I've never thought of or imagined before. Not expecting to be a well-paid artist at the moment. I will die totally satisfied soon so I am not worried about what graffiti gives or takes.

It always has been a nice trip... No remorse about anything, experiences are always the best. I am just waiting for the ones that will come and I will be always ready to go bombing. Actions are the real deal in this game. I just follow the wave. Too old to be ahead of this scene but still too young to quit.

Peace and respect to all the real bombers out there.

YOU KNOW WHO YOU ARE!

1. 冷藏集装箱列车（也被称为冷藏箱）通常涂成白色，列车表面几乎是平坦的。

   Refrigerated containers (also known as *reefers*) are usually painted white and have almost flat surfaces.

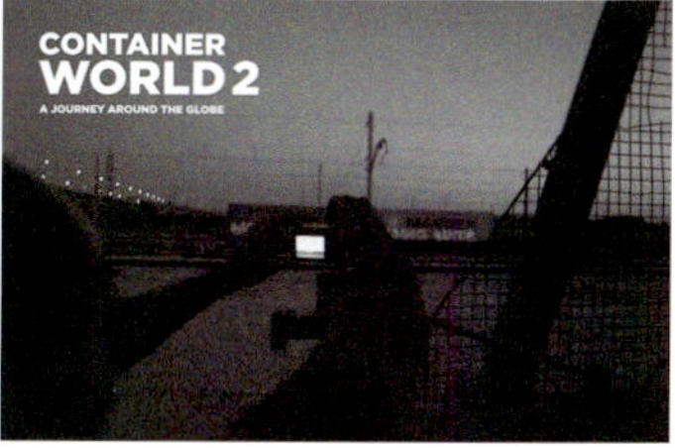

2. 经过 30 年的涂鸦创作，BUNY 推出了一本杂志，内容是他的集装箱涂鸦照片，而这些集装箱出现在地球上最偏远的地方。

   After 30 years of graffiti BUNY has launched a zine that is a photographic collection of the shipping containers tagged by him, popping up in the most remote places on the planet.

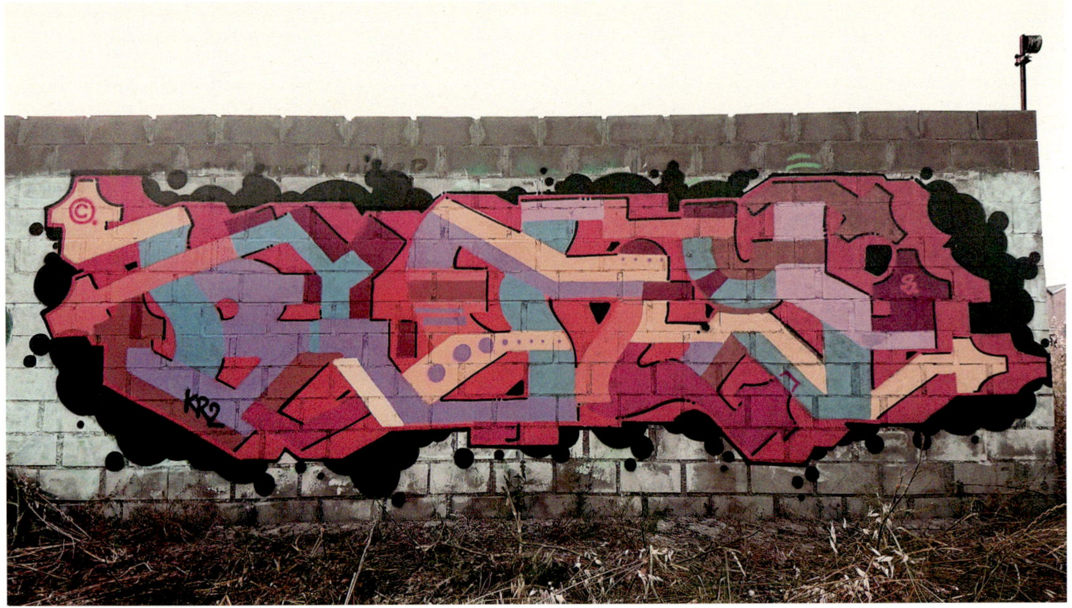
KR2

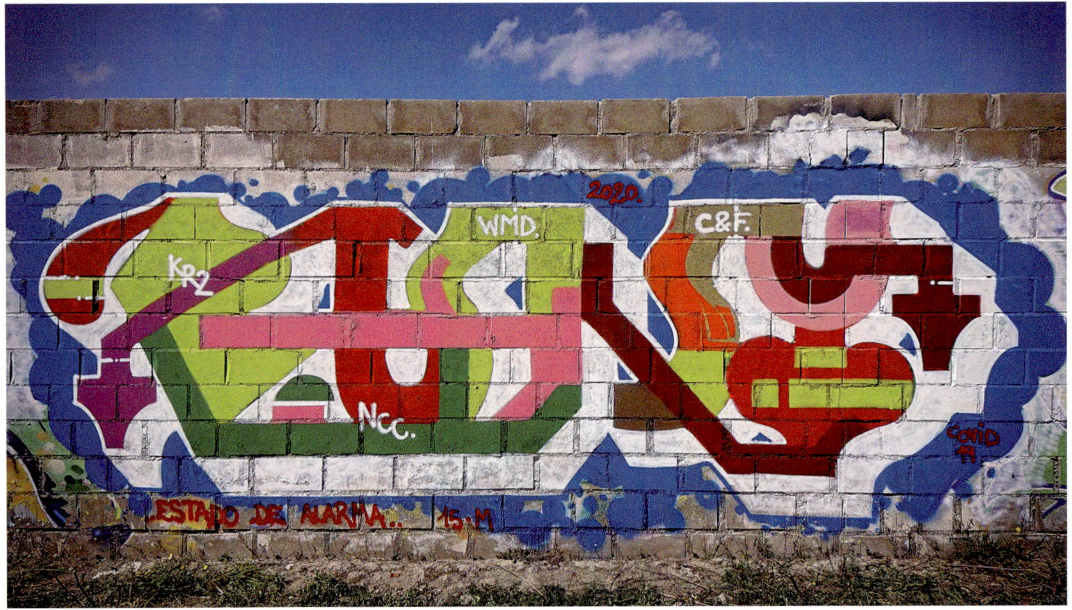
2020.
WMD.
C&F.
KR2
NCC.
ESTADO DE ALARMA.. 15-M

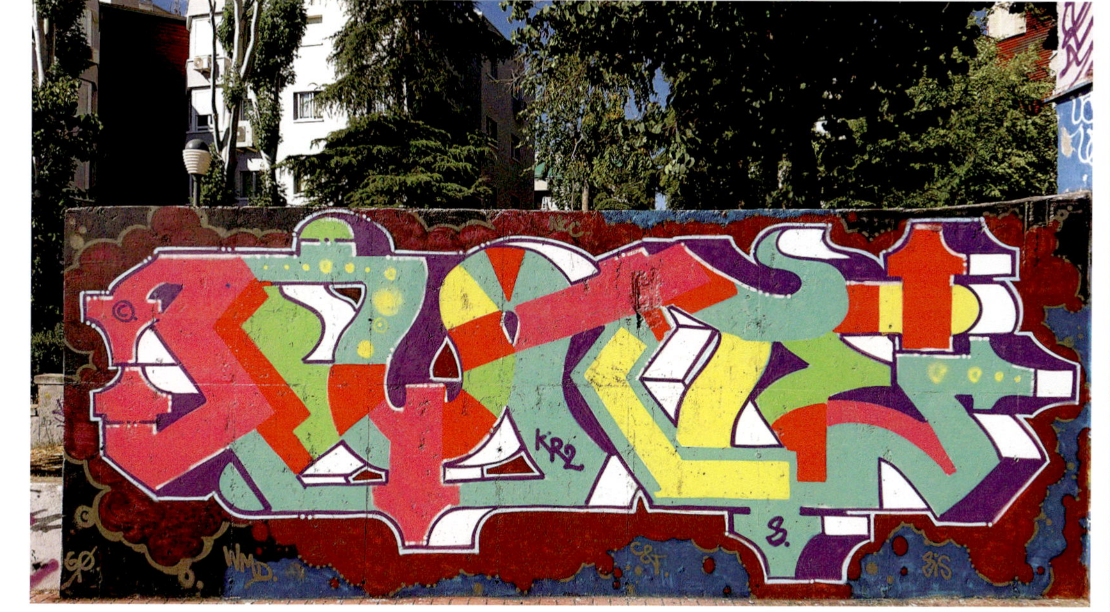

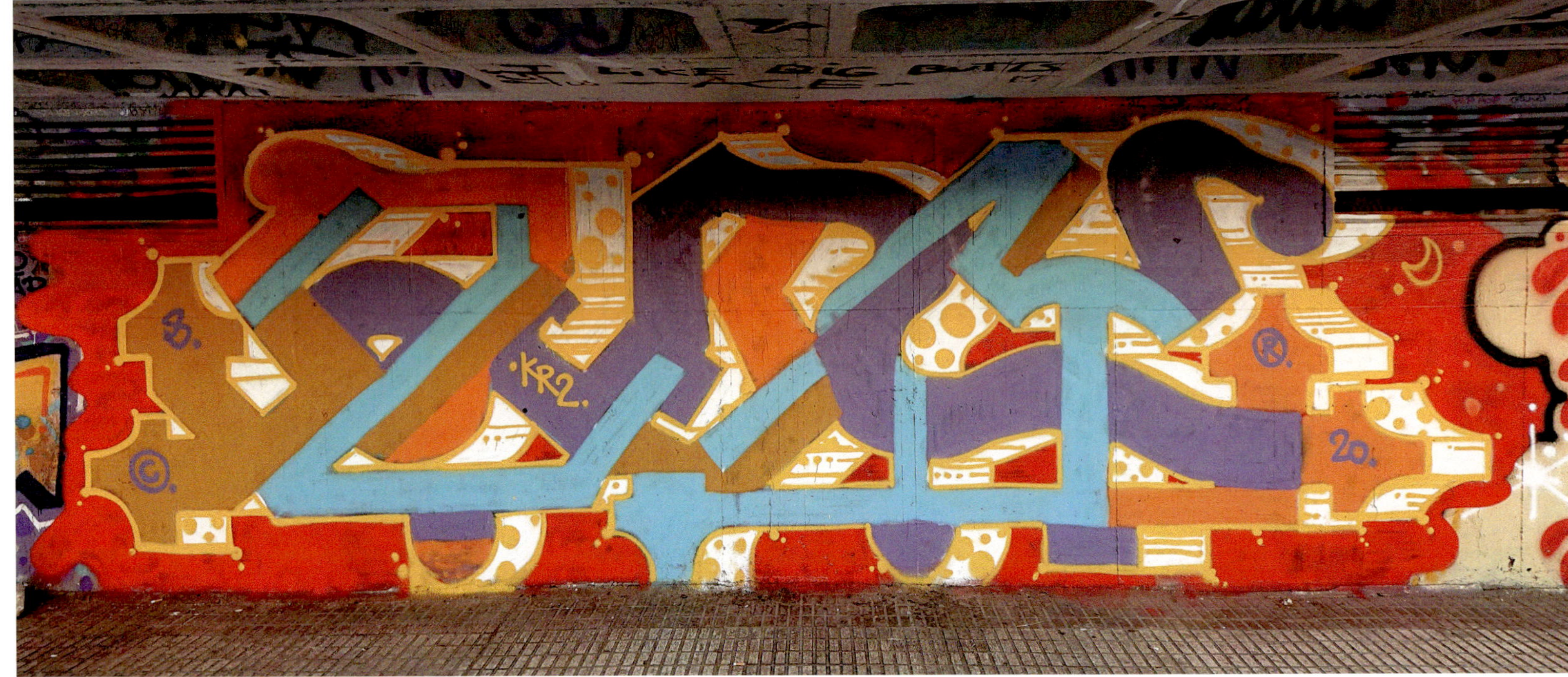

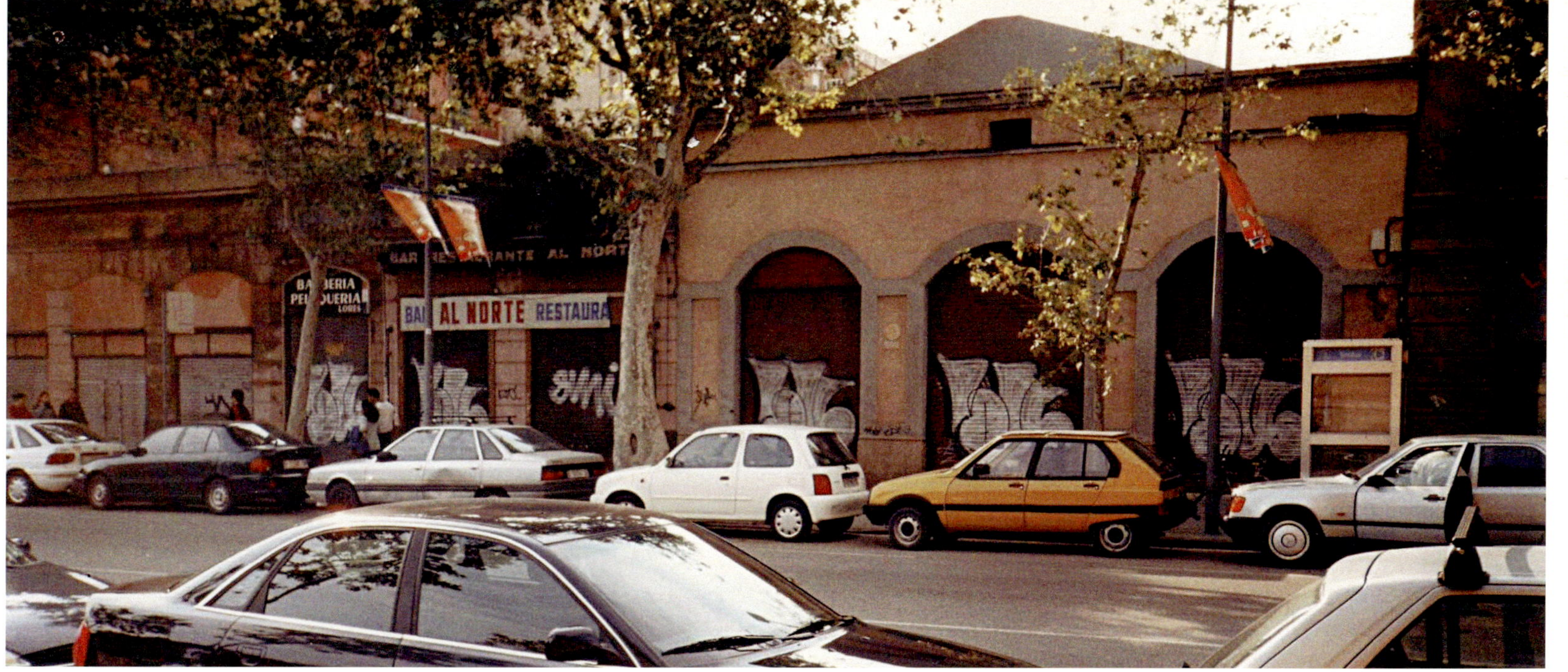

BARBERIA PELUQUERIA
BAR RESTAURANTE AL NORTE
BAR AL NORTE RESTAURA

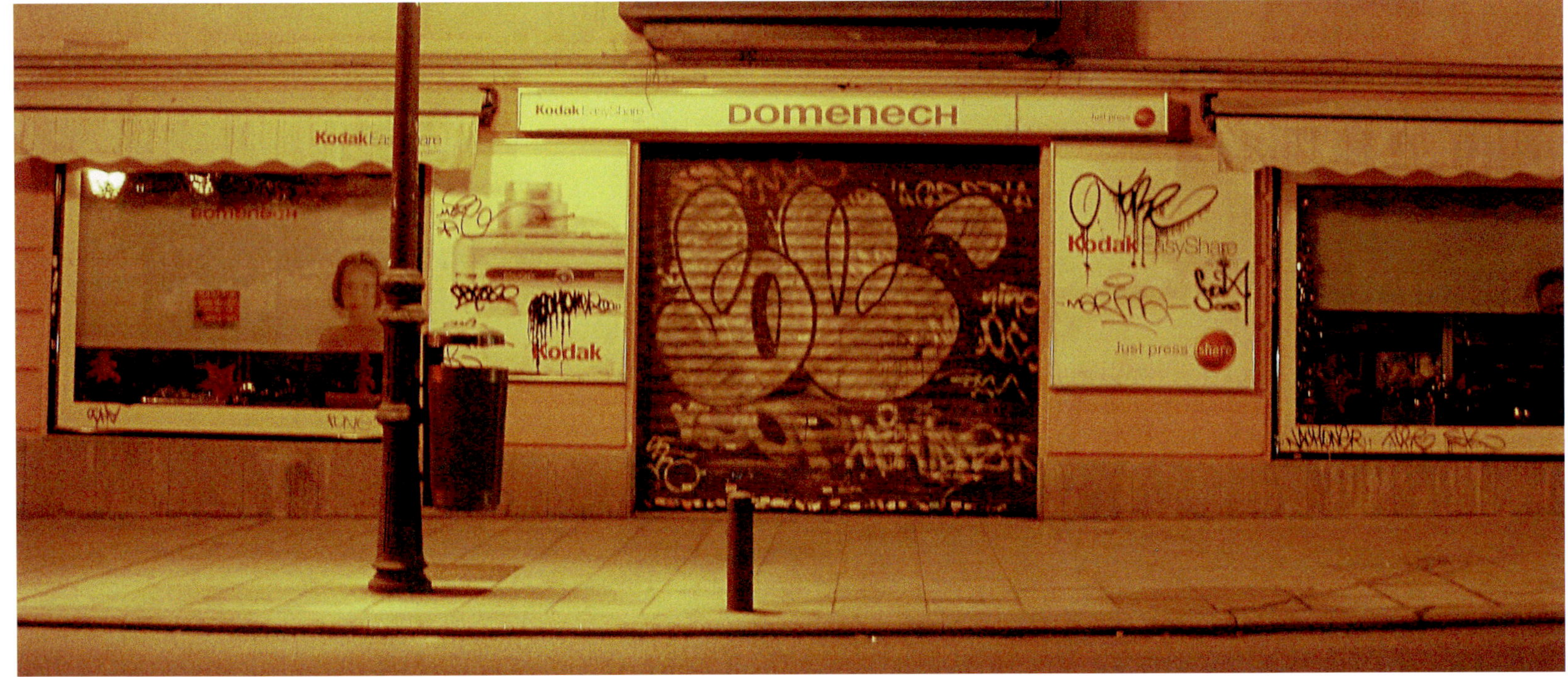

Kodak EasyShare
DOMENECH
Kodak EasyShare
Kodak
Kodak EasyShare
Just press share

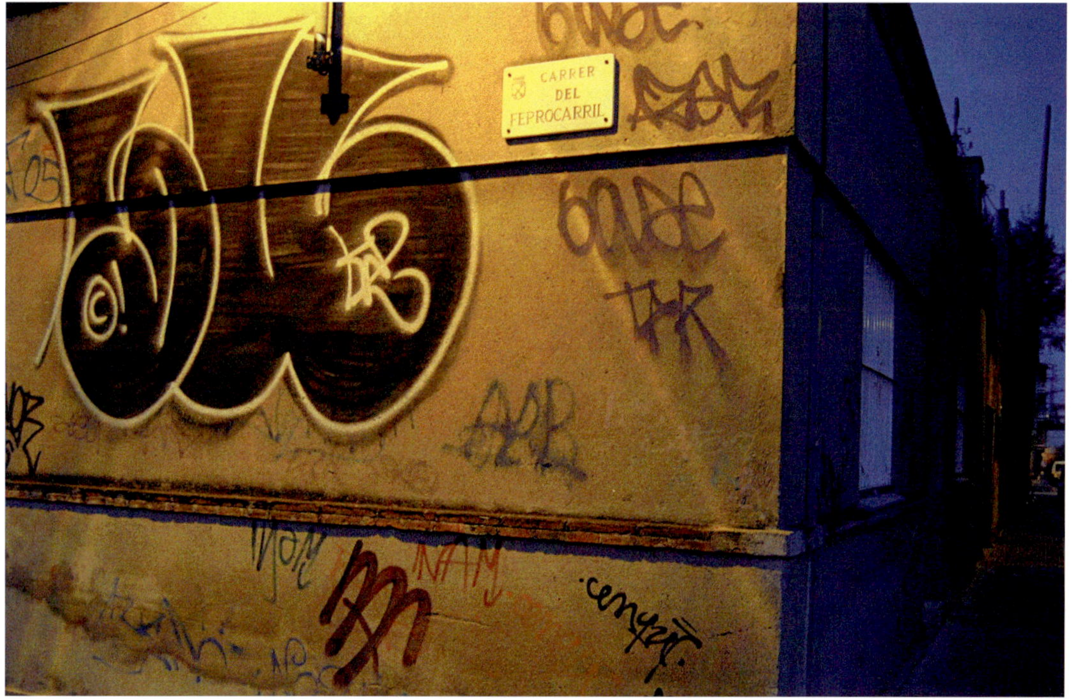

CARRER
DEL
FERROCARRIL

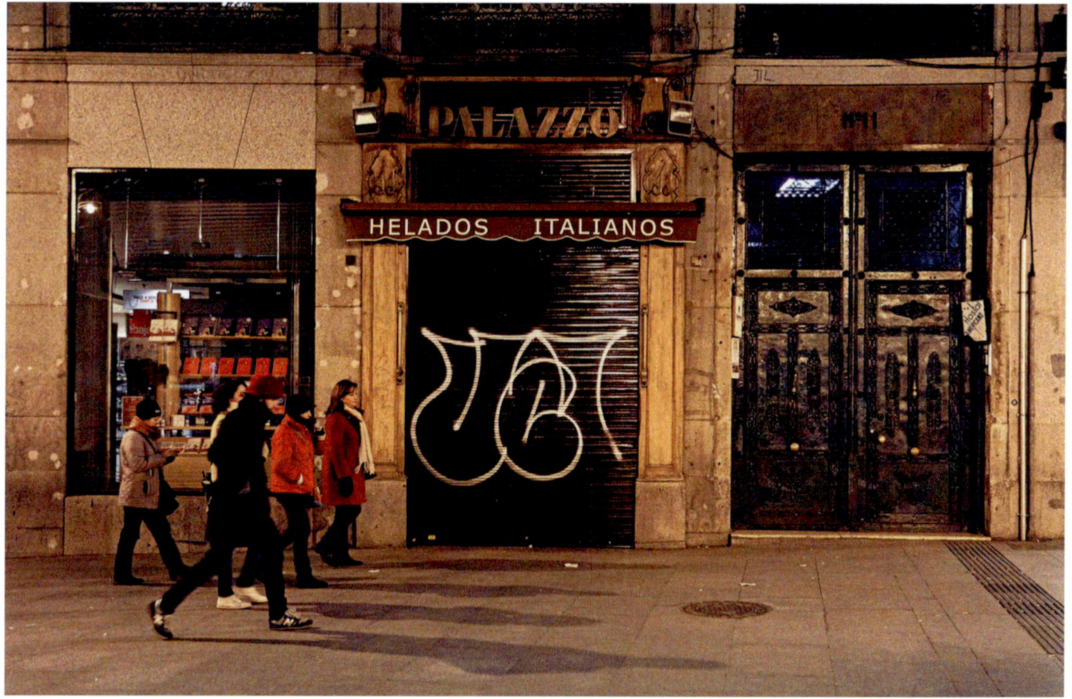

PALAZZO
HELADOS   ITALIANOS

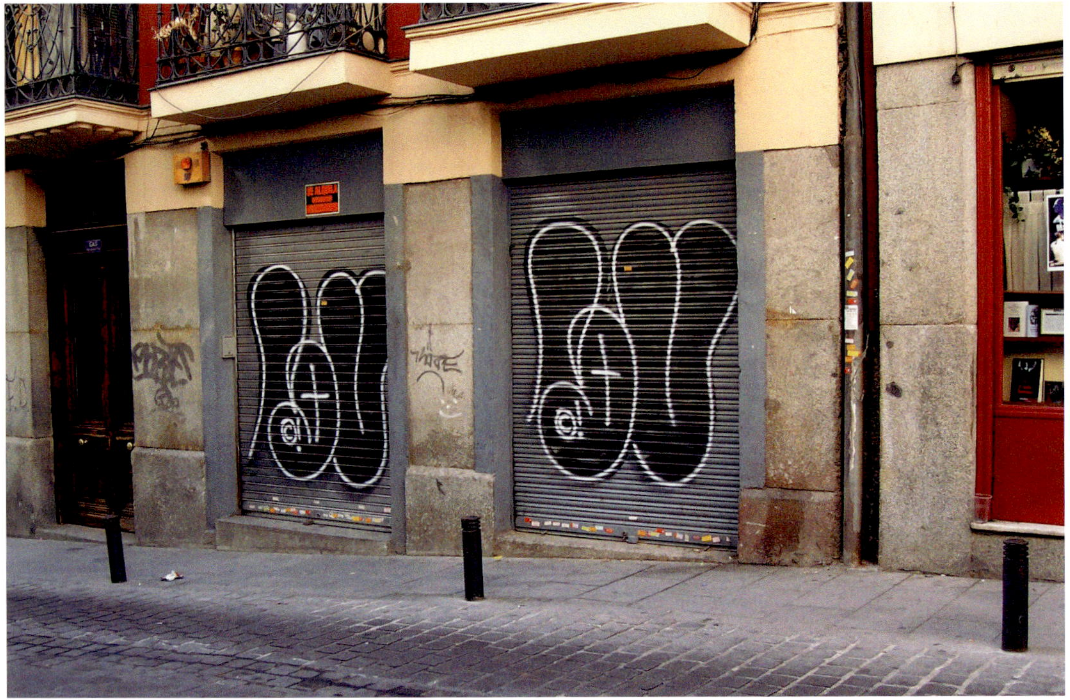

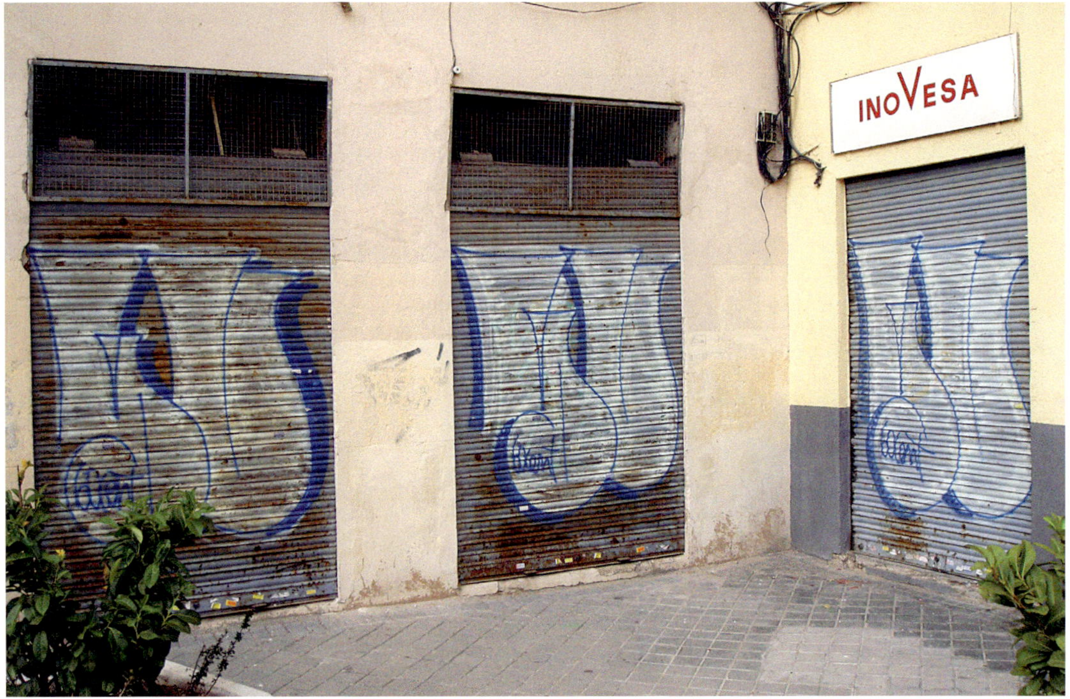

INOVESA

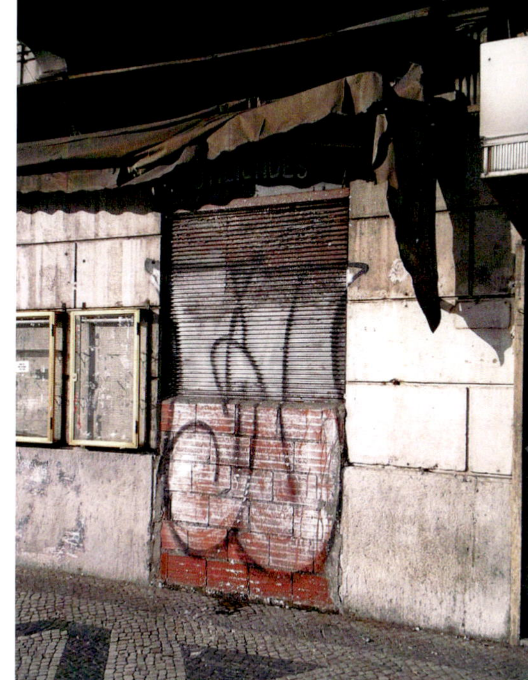

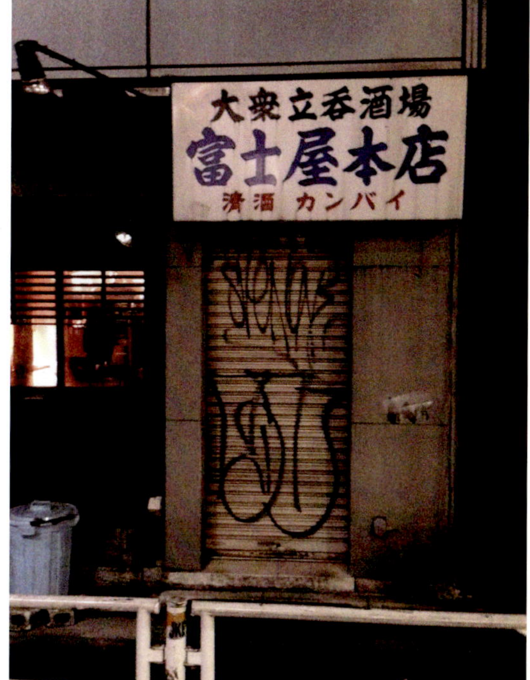

大衆立呑酒場
富士屋本店
清酒 カンバイ

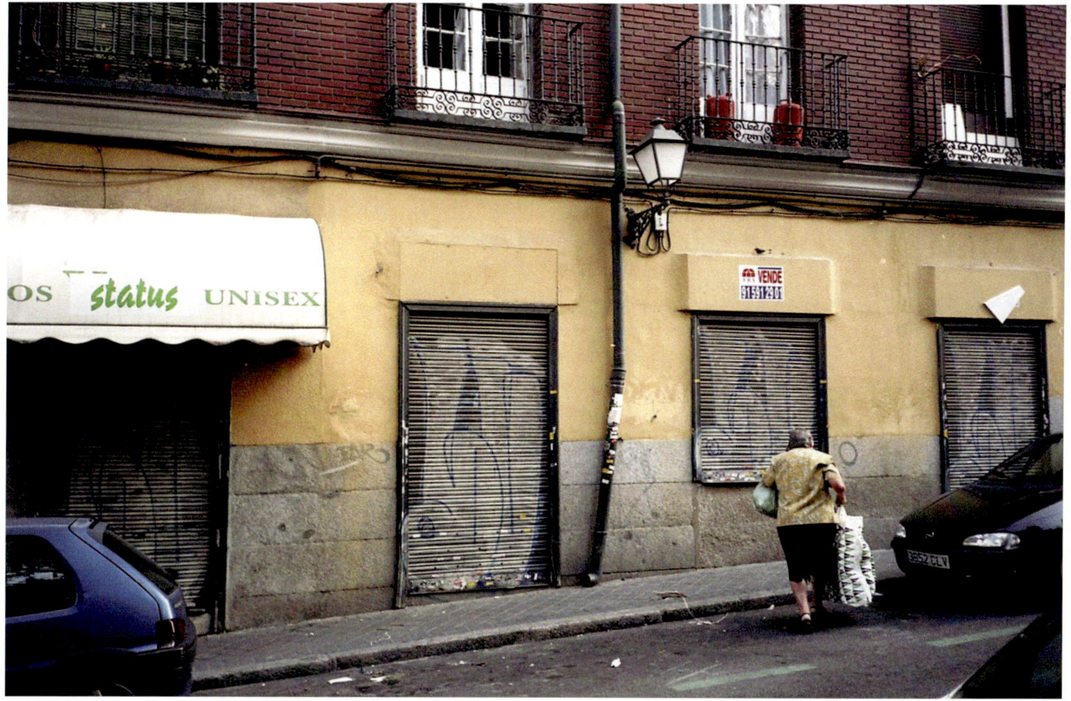

status UNISEX
VENDE

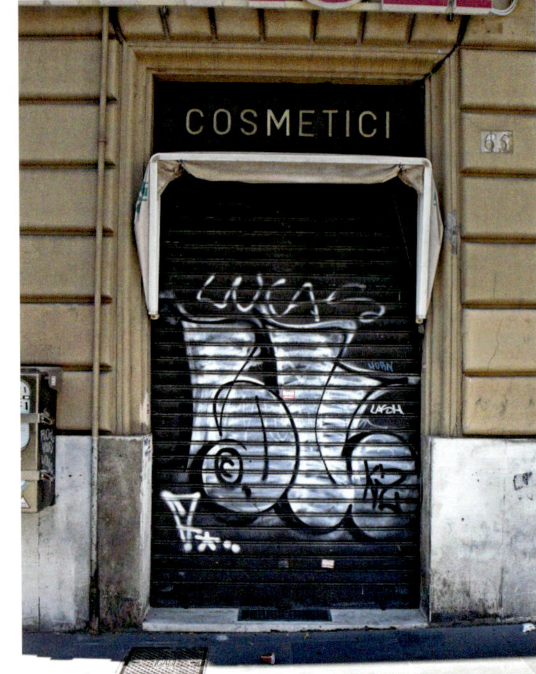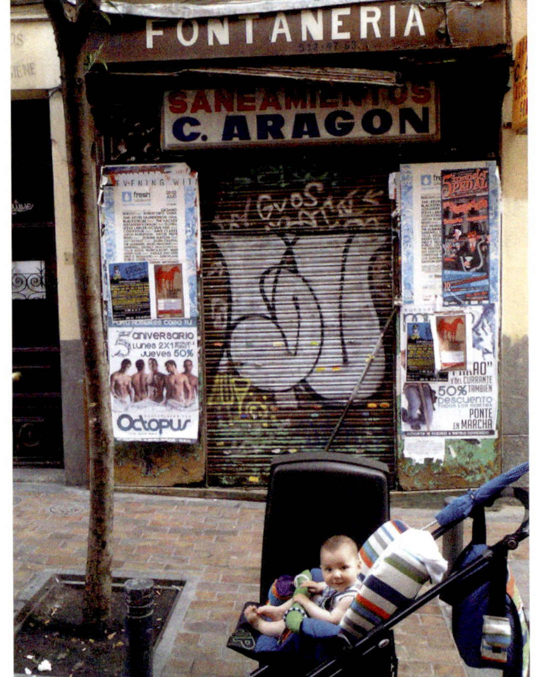

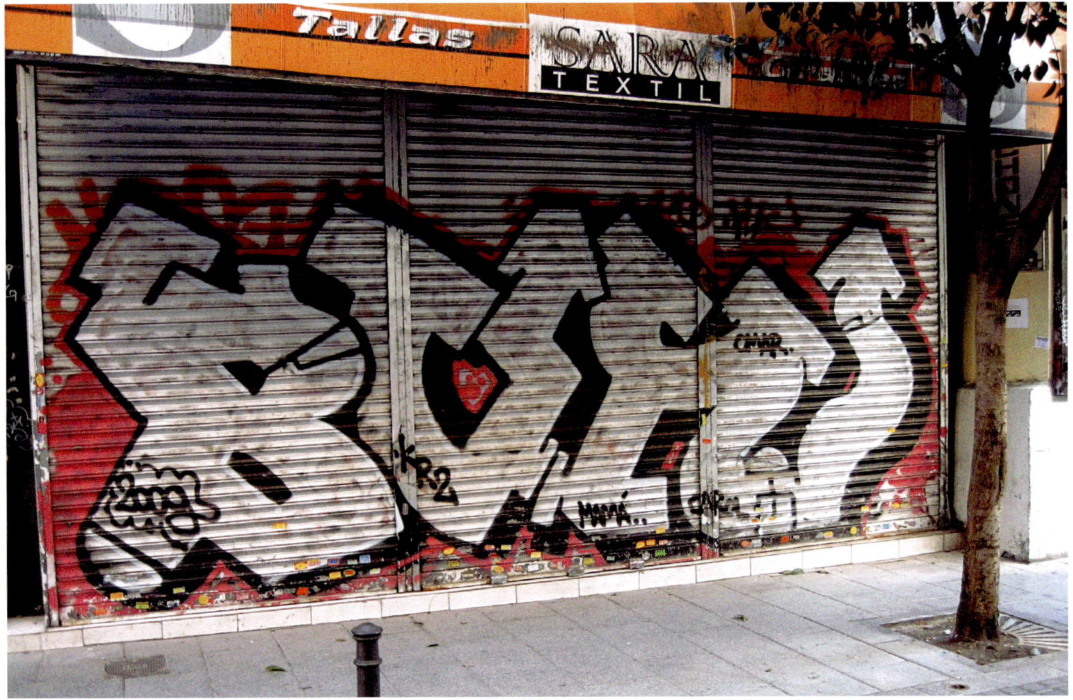

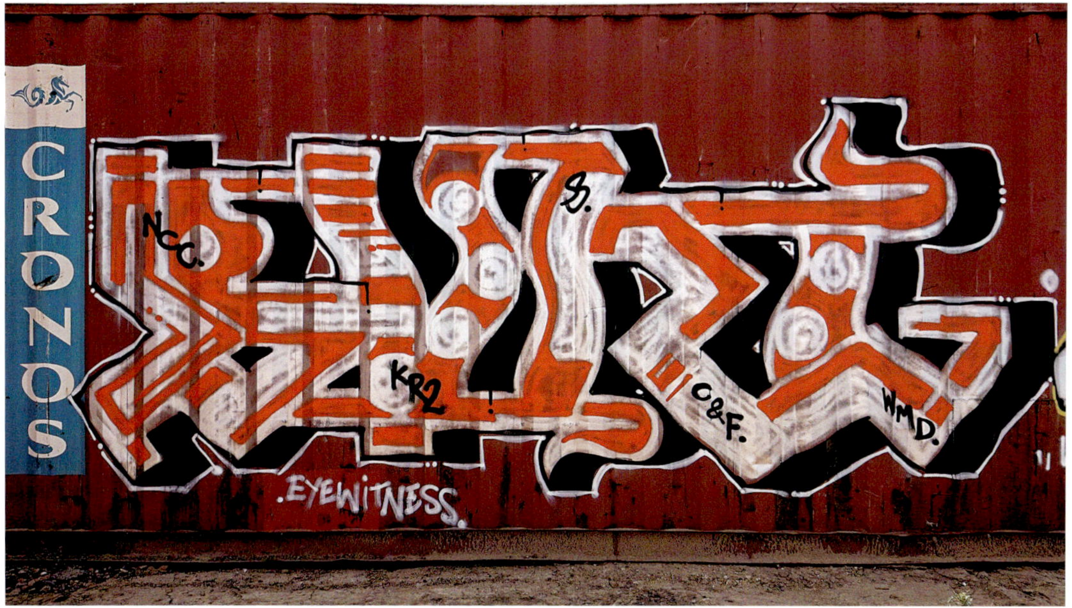

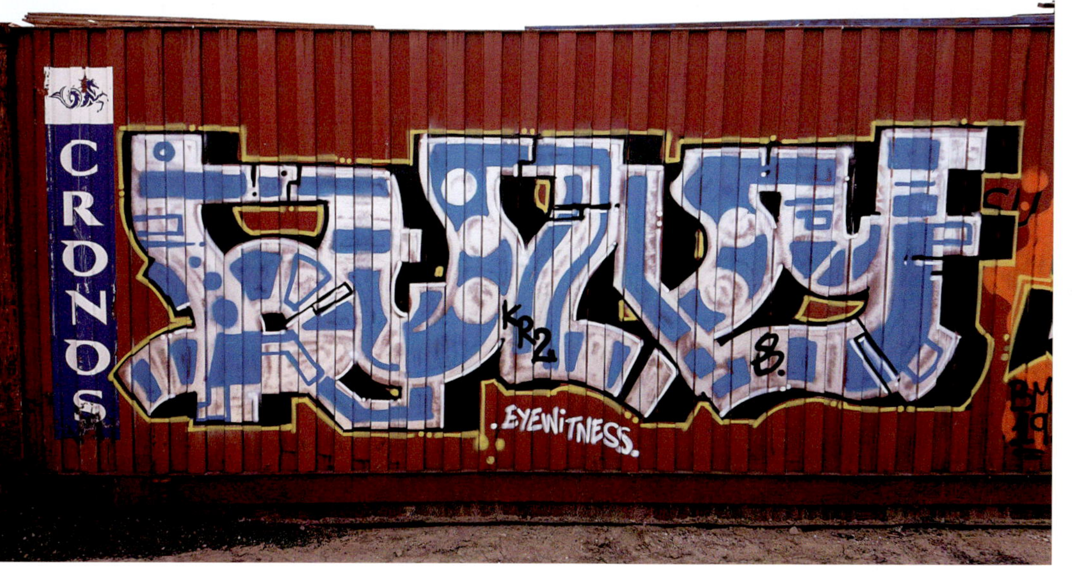

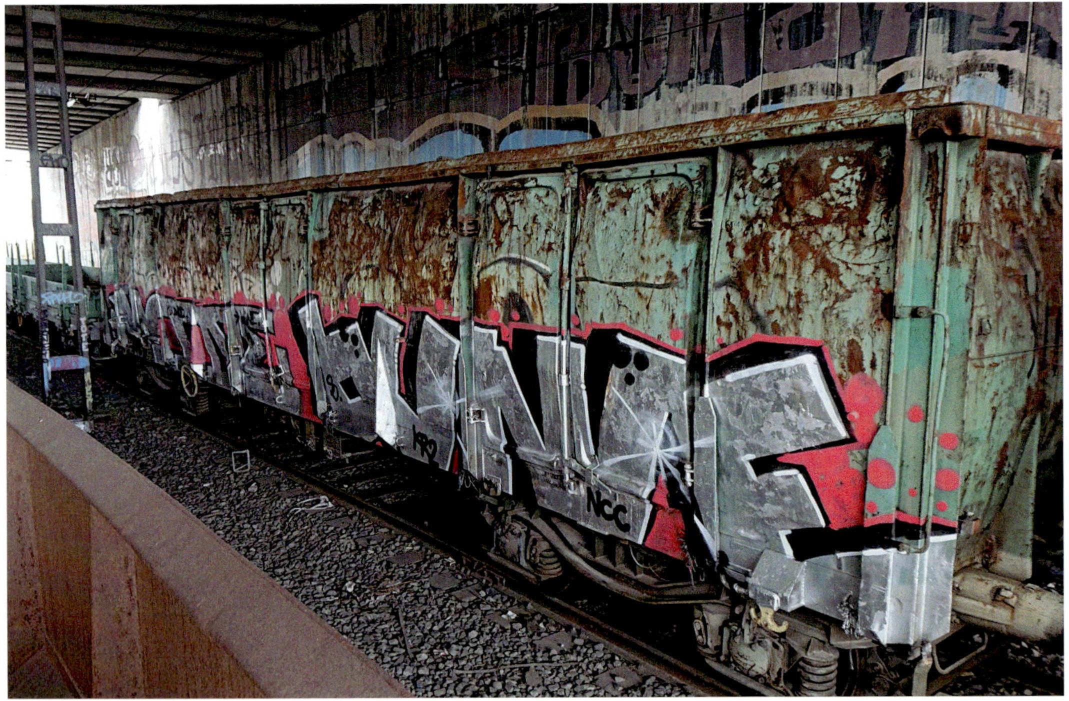

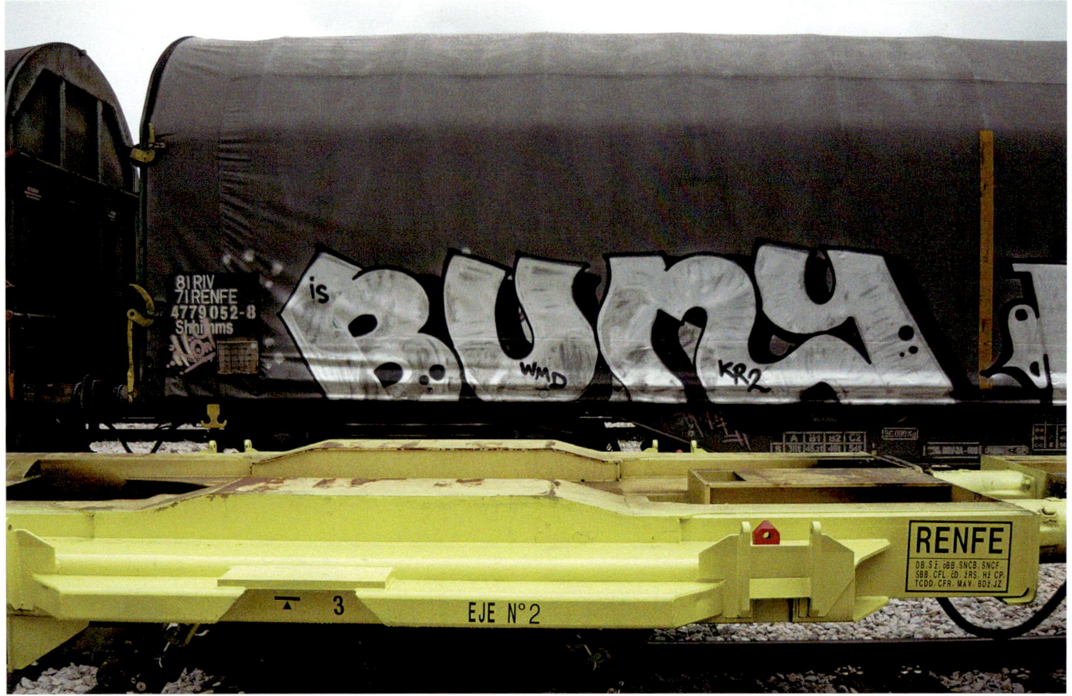
81 RIV
71 RENFE
4779 052-8
RENFE
EJE N°2

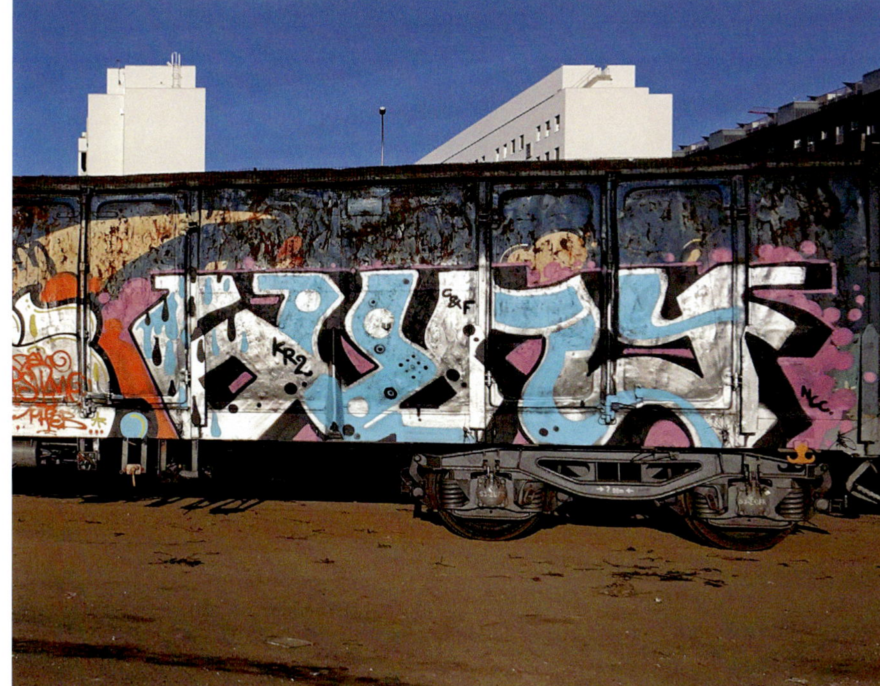

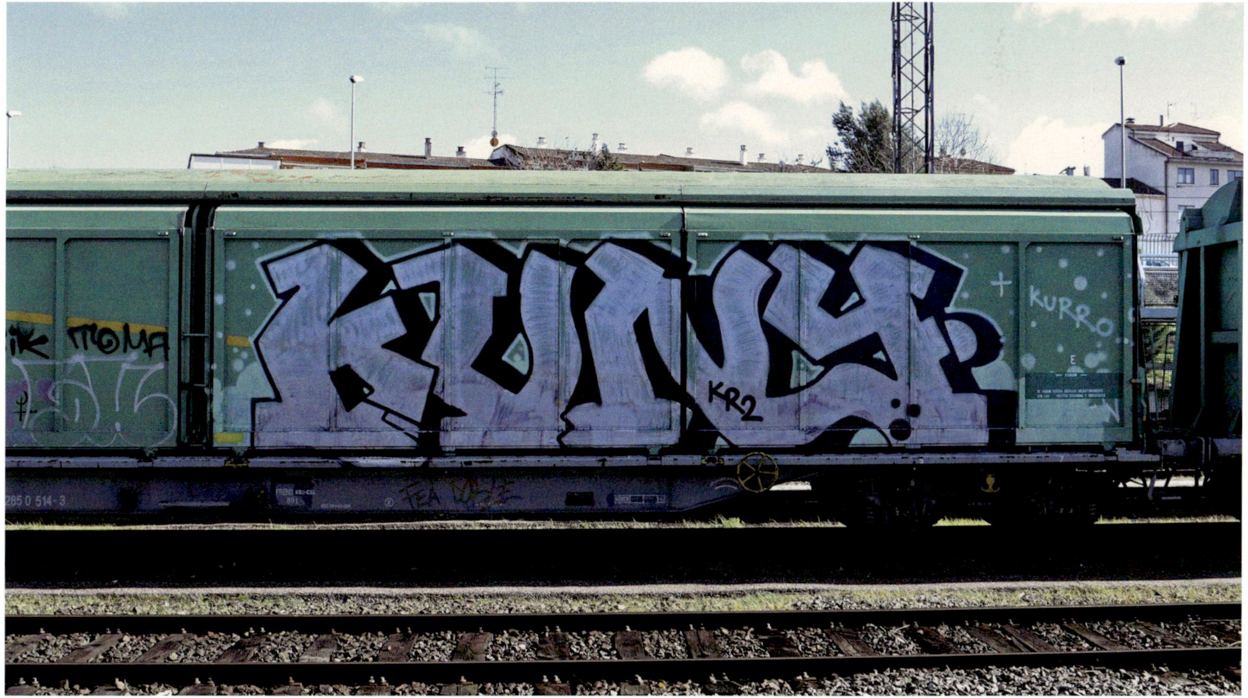

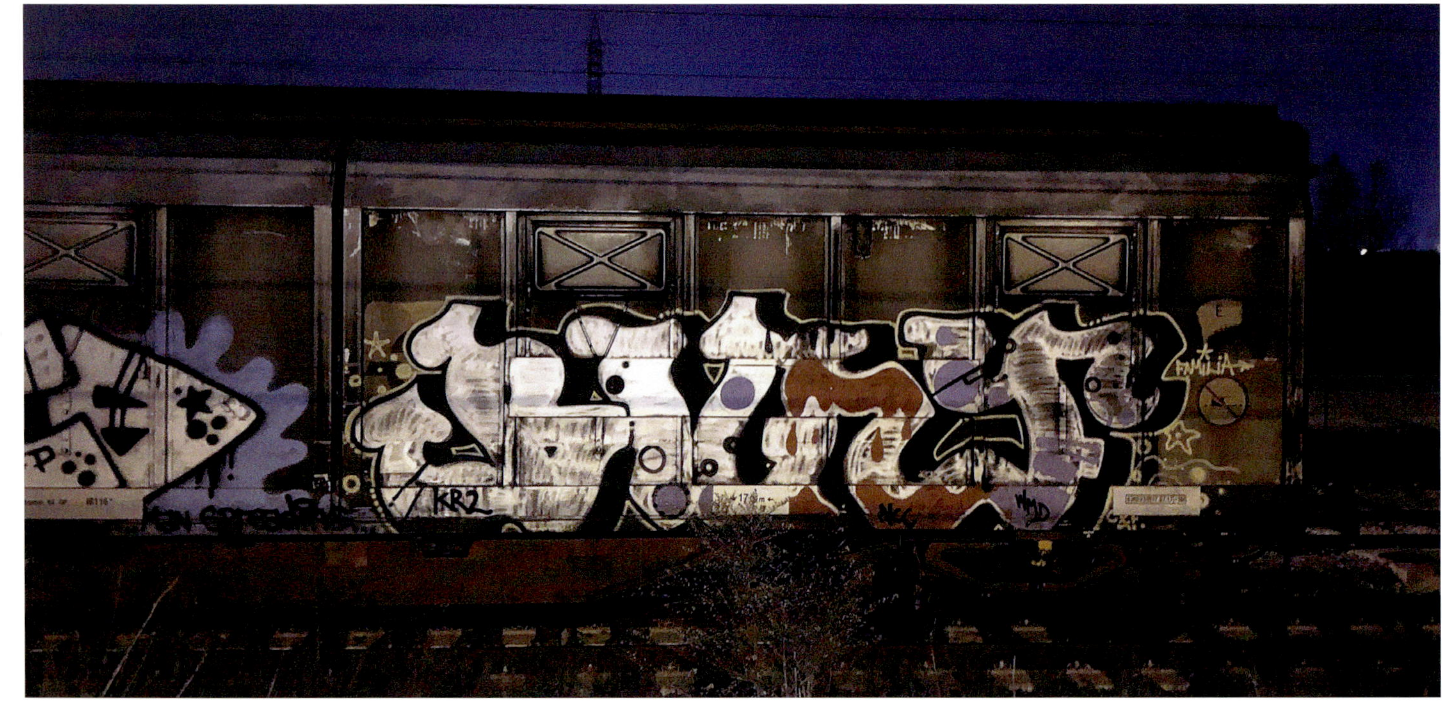

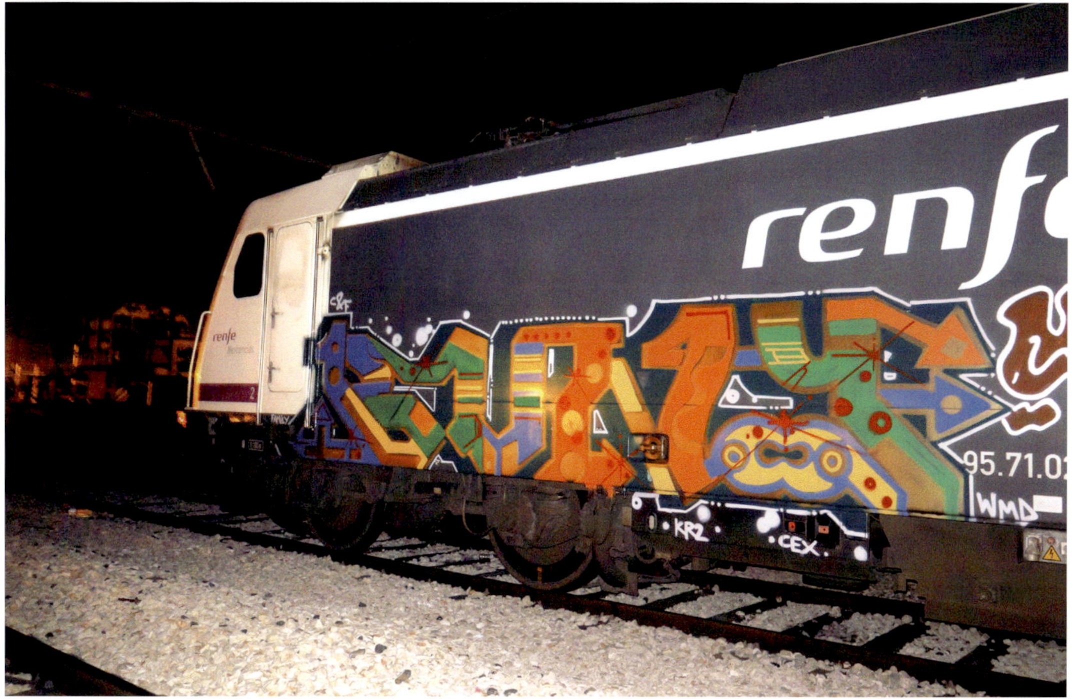
renf
95.71.02
WMD
KR2
CEX

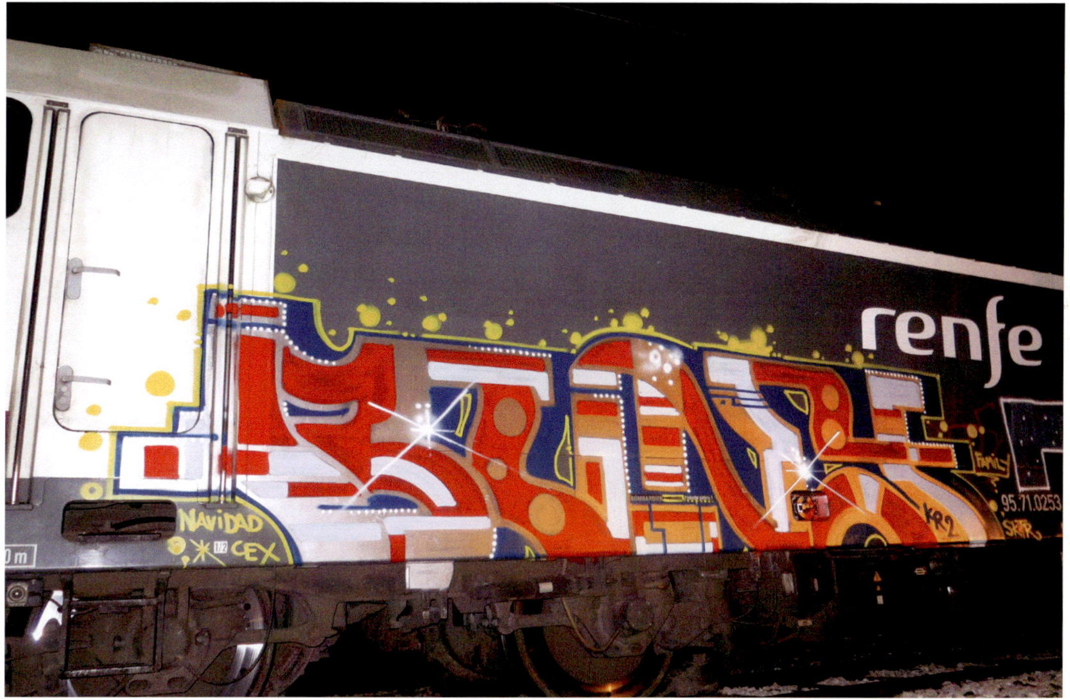
renfe
NAVIDAD
CEX
FAMILY
95.71.0253
KR2

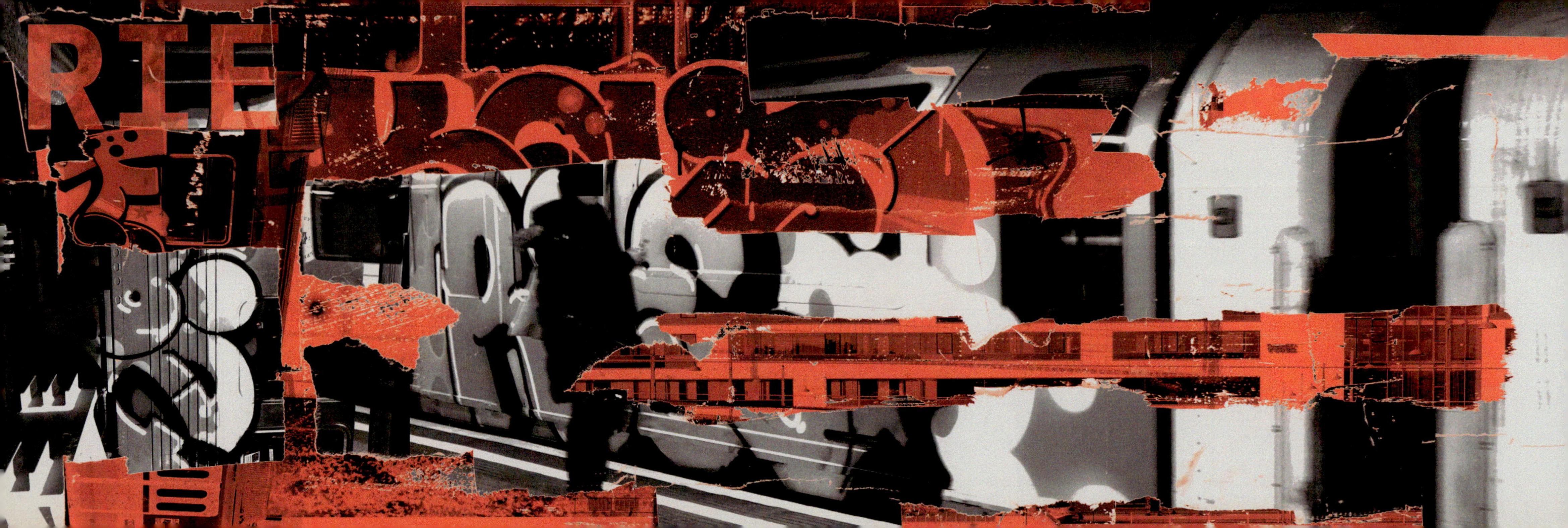

RIE
无故破坏

提到涂鸦，我们首先想到的不是芬兰，但她却有着悠久的涂鸦历史，对世界各地都都产生过很大影响。那么有哪位芬兰的写手对你的影响最大呢？

我在赫尔辛基长大，这是一个充斥着涂鸦的城市。从 90 年代早期到中期几乎覆盖整座城市。我从 90 年代中期开始画涂鸦，感觉那时候每个孩子都拥有自己的"代号"。随处可见HIV的名字和他的银色涂鸦，而TRAMA 有很多很酷的作品，并拥有不同的代号。有轨电车也是芬兰涂鸦的重要组成部分，那也是我非常想念的一段时光。车身上有很多很棒的手写体，比如 PYRO。而 MER、MIRO 和 MAIN 标新立异的风格在某种程度上影响了我很多。

芬兰也以其疯狂漫长的冬天和反对涂鸦的强硬立场而闻名。在"零容忍"政策实施的时代，画涂鸦是一件怎样的事情？你能否和我们分享一些故事，帮助我们了解在这个世界的角落里成为一名写手意味着什么吗？

由于全球变暖，赫尔辛基的严冬似乎已经成为过去，但它的寒冷却依旧令人感到煎熬。就我个人而言，我真的不太介意寒冷，但是喷漆却很介意。想在寒冷的冬天，手持冰冻的喷罐画出快速的涂鸦是一件并不容易的事情。而留在雪地上的脚印也是一件很烦人的事情。

"零容忍"时期始于 90 年代末。这座城市基本上把你能看到的涂鸦都清除了。许多经典的老学校作品在这个过程中消失了，存在的涂鸦作品质量也随之下降。政府还成立了一支专门针对涂鸦的秘密安保小组。我第一次碰到这个组织是在 99年的一次追捕中，但庆幸的是我们逃走了，那时候我们甚至都不知道他们是谁。2000-2008年，在城市里可以发现他们的踪迹。你也必须时刻注意跟踪你的路人，而不仅仅只是担心在火车站附近的便衣。在这期间，媒体也只关注涂鸦带给社会负面的内容，很多严厉的言辞都是在没有任何真实证据的情况下给出的。

"随身携带喷漆以及马克笔似乎成为非法的代言词，指纹和 DNA 的监控成了控制犯罪的重要标准"

有时候为了拍到火车上的作品，反而会比喷火车来的棘手。不记得从什么时候开始，我会刻意的避开火车站因为那里有一堆烦人的安保人员，他们会时不时来骚扰你。

虽然我们提到了你在芬兰的涂鸦创作，但其实你已经声名远扬，同时你也去过很多地方旅行。有没有哪些国家或人民对你的影响最深？

旅行对我来说非常重要，在新的地方画涂鸦会给我很多灵感，但我旅行不只是为了在特定火车或者地铁系统喷涂鸦。

斯德哥尔摩是我第一次在火车上涂鸦的外国城市，还与相识的当地人做了很多有趣的事情。我在他们身上学到了很多。在 2000年初我经常去那里，但自从 2003年以后，我就没有再去那里画涂鸦了。

荷兰和罗马是我最喜欢的目的地，那是一个跟好朋友画涂鸦和喝啤酒的好去处。

"我曾经花了无数个小时在罗马的地铁站台上拍照，享受那些被涂鸦轰炸过的火车"

这个城市引人入胜的地方，还有那些在街上与火车车身出现的相同的涂鸦名字，我真的很喜欢 90年代末到 2000年左右的风格。这与当时赫尔辛基的涂鸦形成了巨大的反差。

在这个写手把自己作为商业品牌的营销时代，其实很难找到一些关于你的信息，你一直保持低调。能说说你与涂鸦圈的关系，以及追逐名声之间有什么联系吗？

除了那些显而易见的原因之外，我生活中其实不是一个喜欢被关注的人。而对涂鸦圈的事情也默不关心，我几乎很少认识新的写手，只是跟一些老朋友一块喷涂鸦，或者成为独行侠。

"因为我对涂鸦几乎别无所求，他让我继续坚持的原因大概就是因为可以旅行和创作吧"

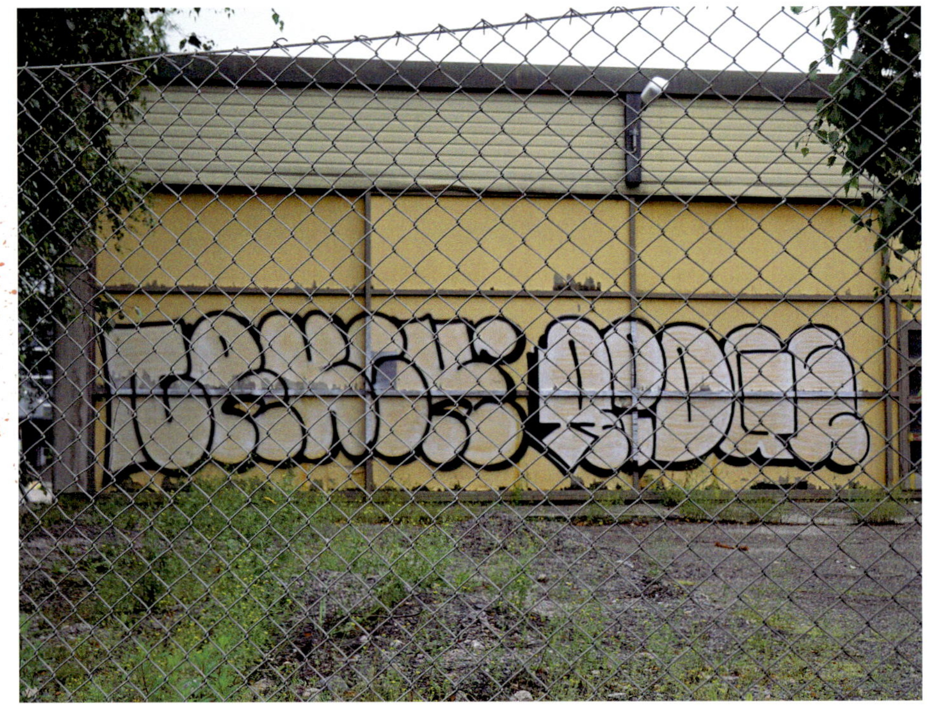

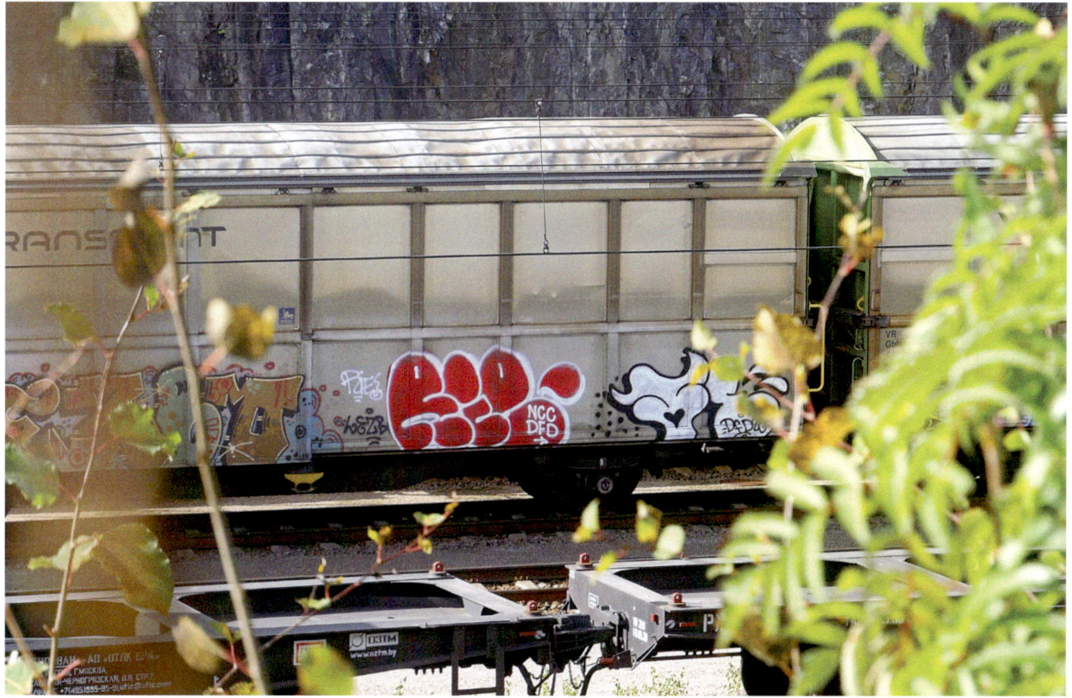
NCC
DFD

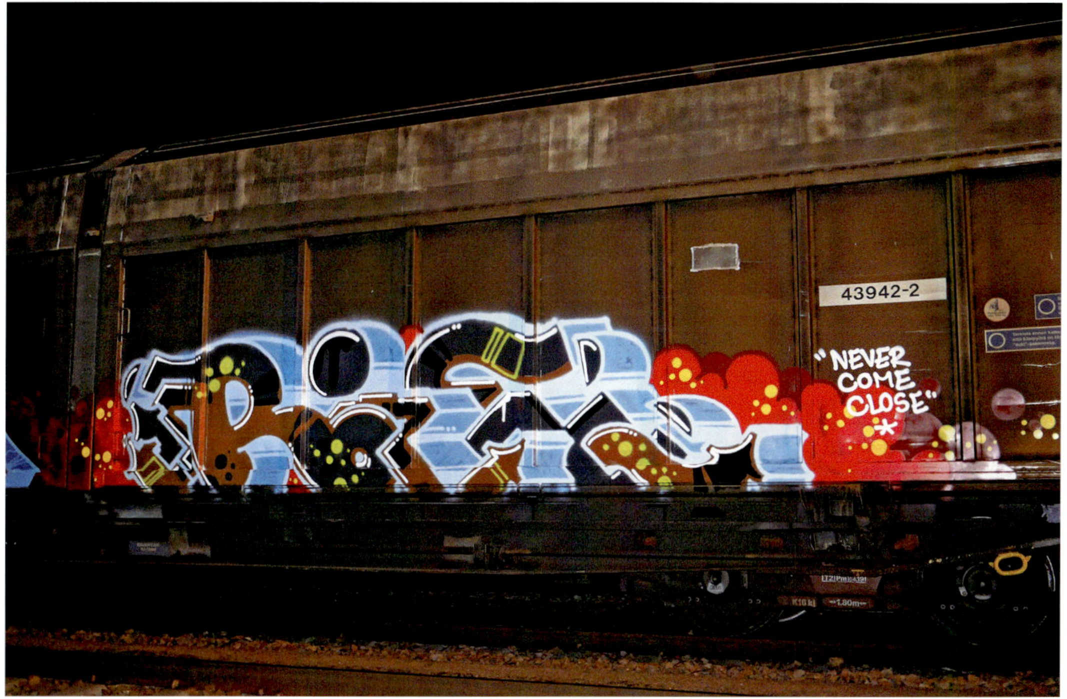
43942-2
"NEVER
COME
CLOSE"

RIE
Vandal without a cause

Finland is not the first place that comes to mind when thinking about graffiti but yet its scene has a long history and a great influence all around the world. Which is your relationship with your homeland and which are the Finnish writers that influenced you the most?

I grew up in Helsinki surrounded by graffiti. In the early to mid 90's it was everywhere. When I started writing in the mid-'90s, it felt like every other kid "had a tag." I remember HIV having tags and simple silvers all over and also TRAMA had a lot of cool stuff with various names. The trams were also a big part of graffiti and a part that I really miss. There were a lot of really good hand styles like PYRO and many others. MER, MIRO, and MAIN had some of the freshest styles that influenced me in some way or another.

Finland is also famous for its crazy long winters and its tough stance against graffiti. How was it to paint during the years of the Stop töhryille* (zero tolerance)? Can you share with us some stories that will help us to understand what it means to be a writer in this corner of the world?

The harsh winters seem to be a thing of the past in Helsinki thanks to global warming, but it still gets pretty nasty at times. Personally, I don't really mind the cold that much but the cans do! Trying to do a decent piece with frozen cans and fingers and do it fast isn't always easy. Footprints in the snow are also annoying.

The zero-tolerance period started at the end of the '90s. The city basically buffed almost everything you could think of. A lot of old styles disappeared and there was a huge drop in quality. A kind of vandal squad of undercover security guards only concentrating on graffiti was also formed. My first experience of them was a chase in '99, but we got away and didn't even know who they were. By 2000-2008 they were always around. You always had to look for anyone following you and not only near train yards but anywhere. During this period the media also started to write only negative things about writers and a lot of harsh sentences were given without any real evidence.

> **"Having spray paint or markers on you became illegal and fingerprints and DNA controls became standard"**

Getting flicks of trains was sometimes trickier than the actual painting. At some point, I started avoiding the stations altogether cause of the harassment by security.

We mentioned your country a lot but your fame reached further places and you have traveled quite extensively. Which are the countries or the people that had the most profound impact on you?

Traveling has been very important to me and it is very inspiring to see and paint new places, but I don't travel just to paint a certain model or train system.

Stockholm was the first foreign city where I painted trains and got to know locals and do a lot of funny shit. I learned a lot by seeing what they were doing. I used to go there a lot in the early 2000s but I haven't been back there to paint since 2003.

Holland and Rome are my favorite places to go to painting and drink beer with good friends.

> **"I've spent countless hours on the subway platforms in Rome taking flicks and just enjoying the totally trashed trains"**

I also liked the fact that the city streets were full of the same names as the trains and I really liked the style from the late '90s and early 2000s. Such a huge contrast to Helsinki during that period.

In a time when writers are promoting themselves like commercial brands, it is quite hard to find pieces of information about you, you keep a very low profile. Can you tell us what is your relationship with the graffiti scene and its quest for fame?

In addition to the obvious reasons for keeping a low profile, I don't enjoy attention in normal life either. I'm not very connected to the scene these days. I rarely meet new writers and I usually just paint with old friends or alone..

"I don't really have any agenda in graffiti other than continue doing it and traveling when possible".

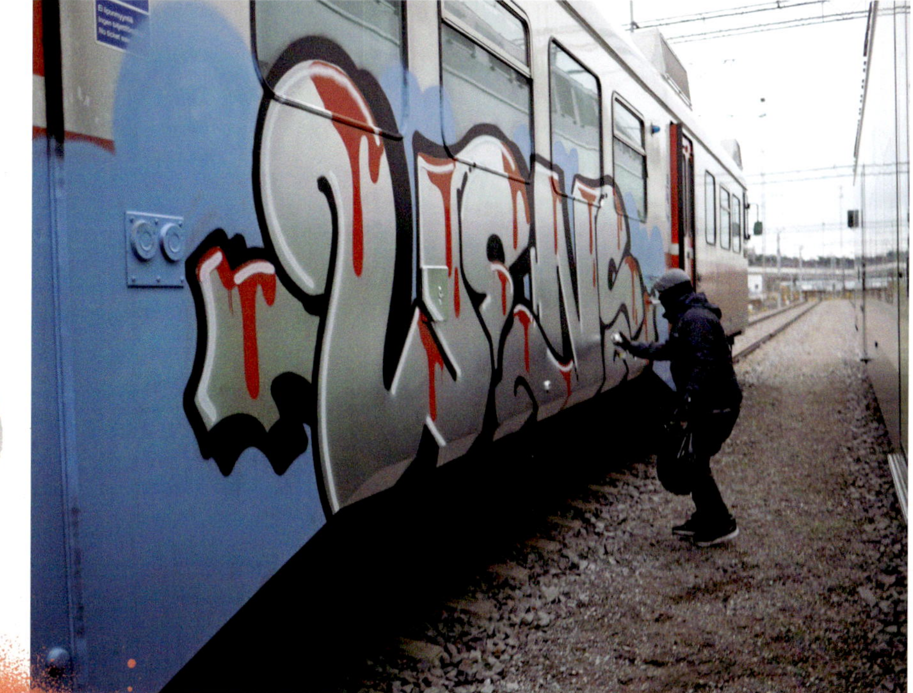

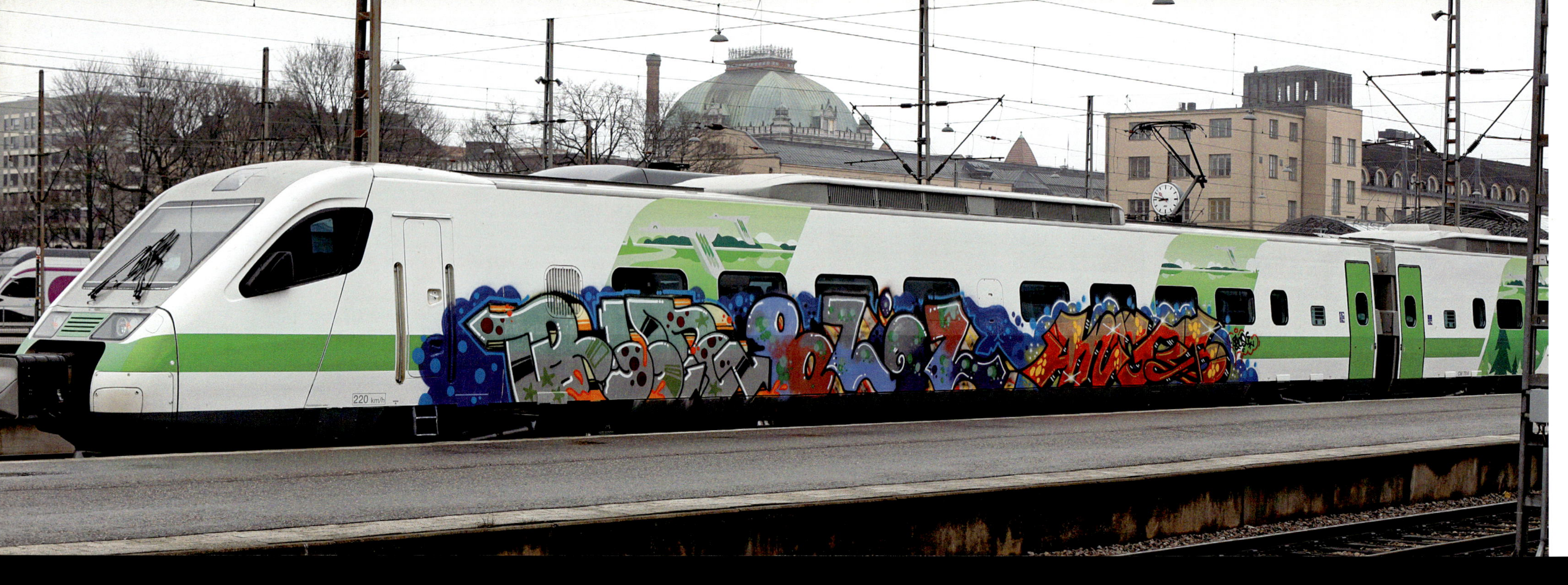

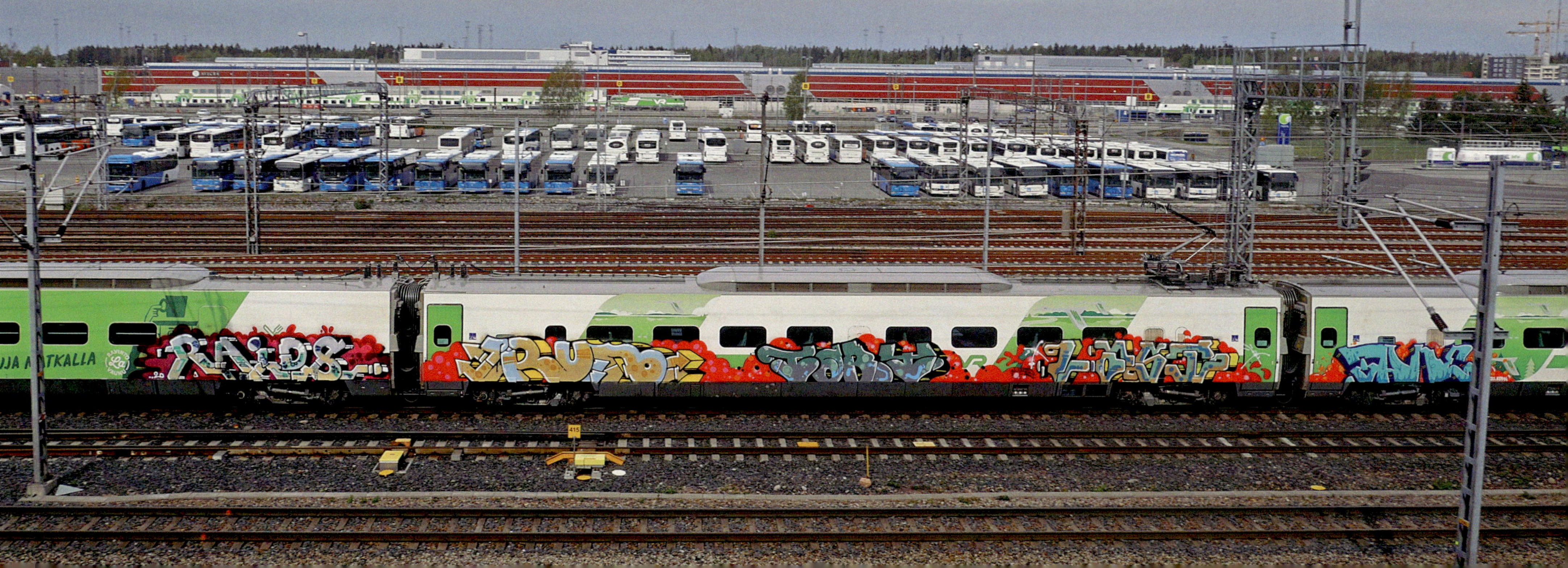

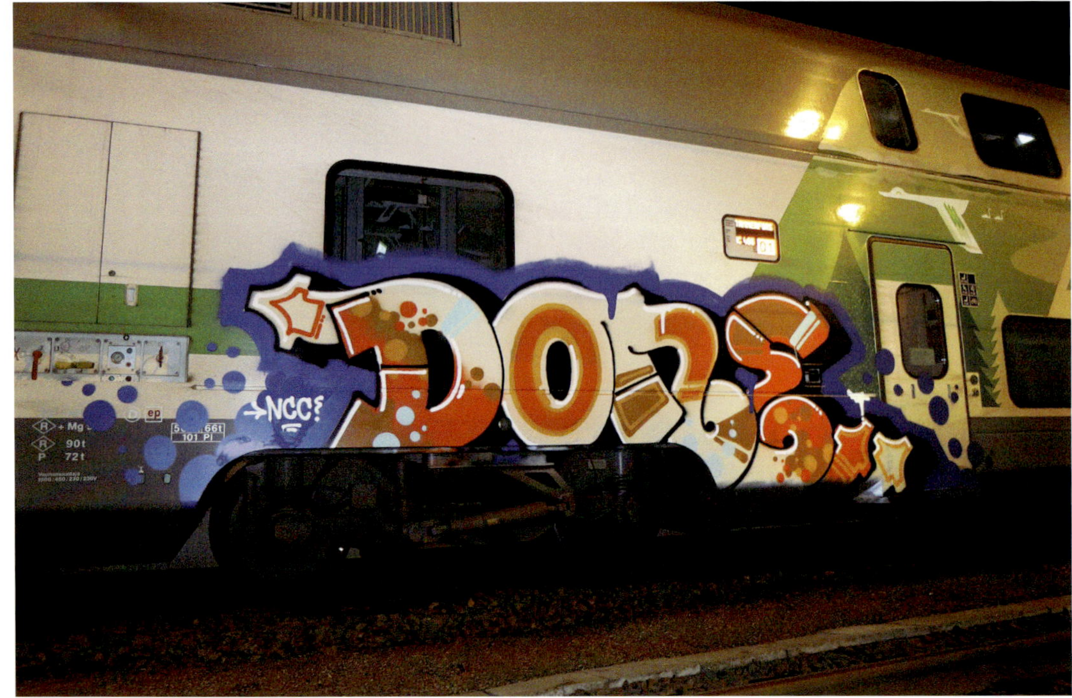

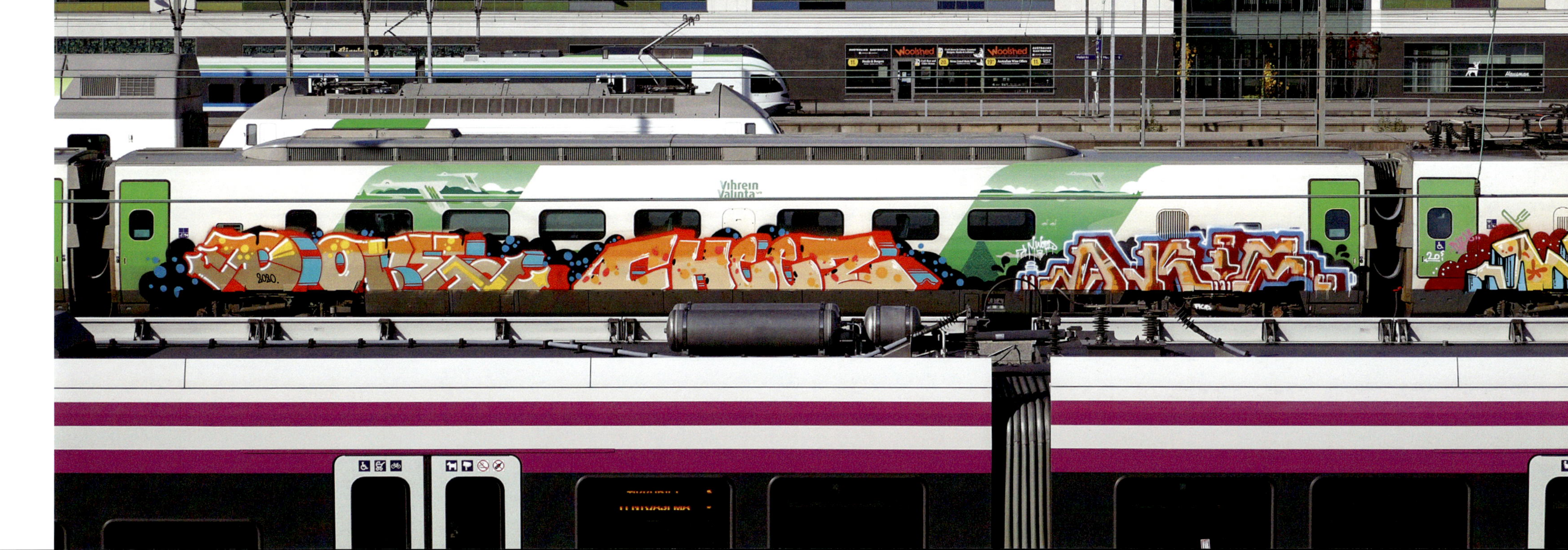

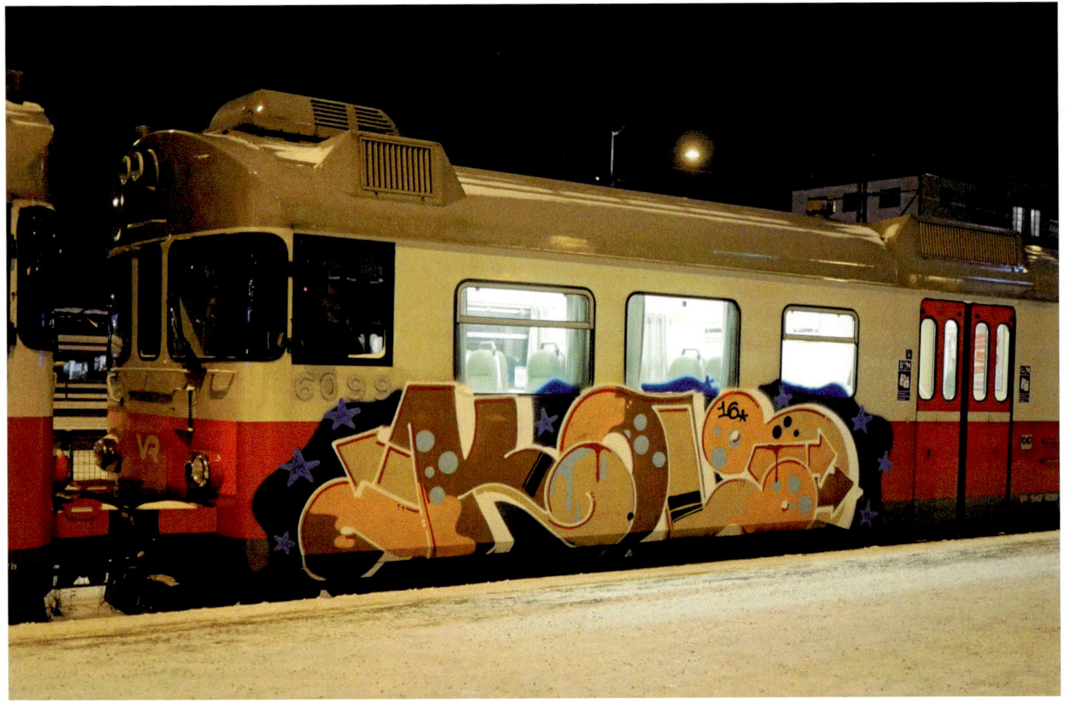

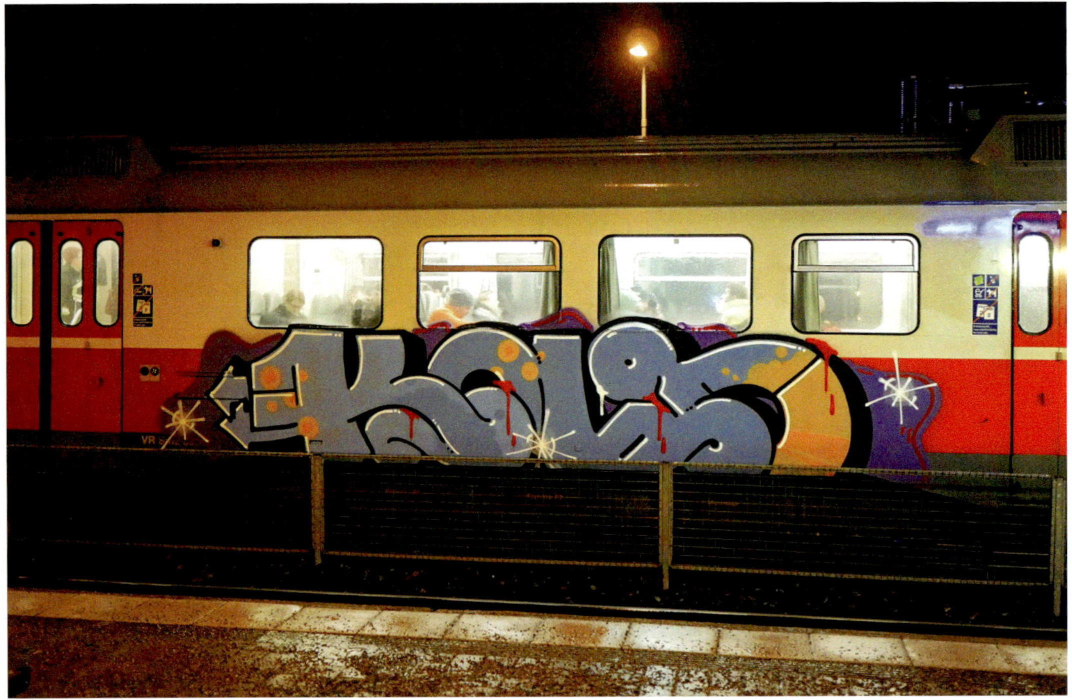

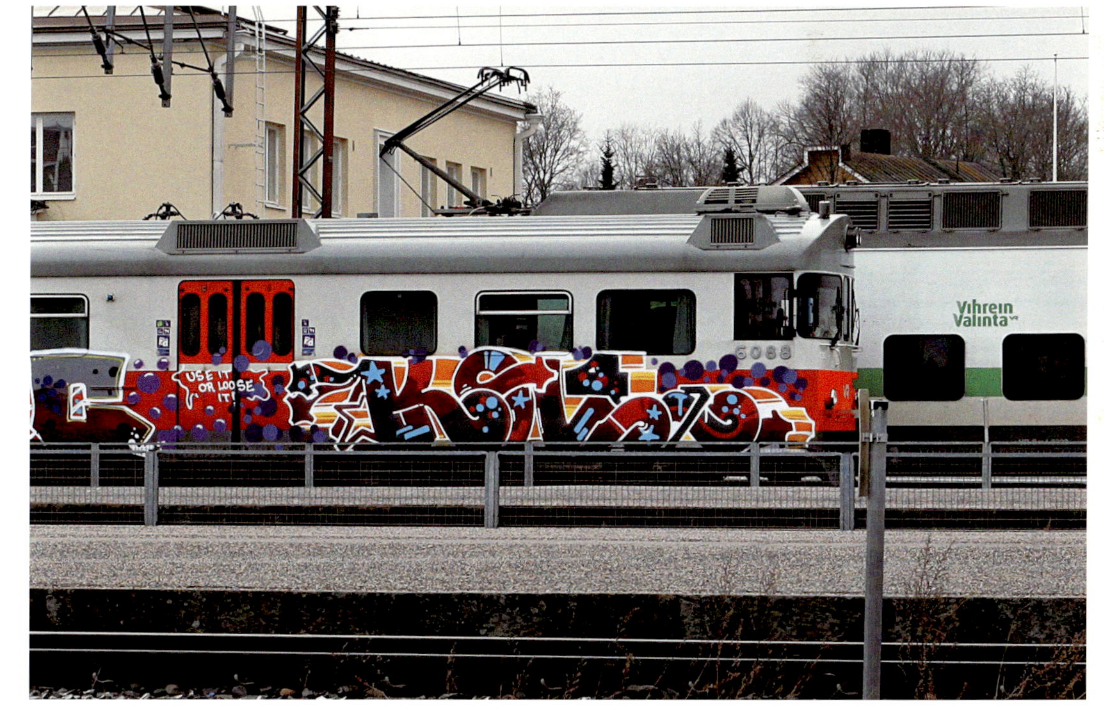
USE IT
OR LOOSE
IT
Vihreın
Valınta

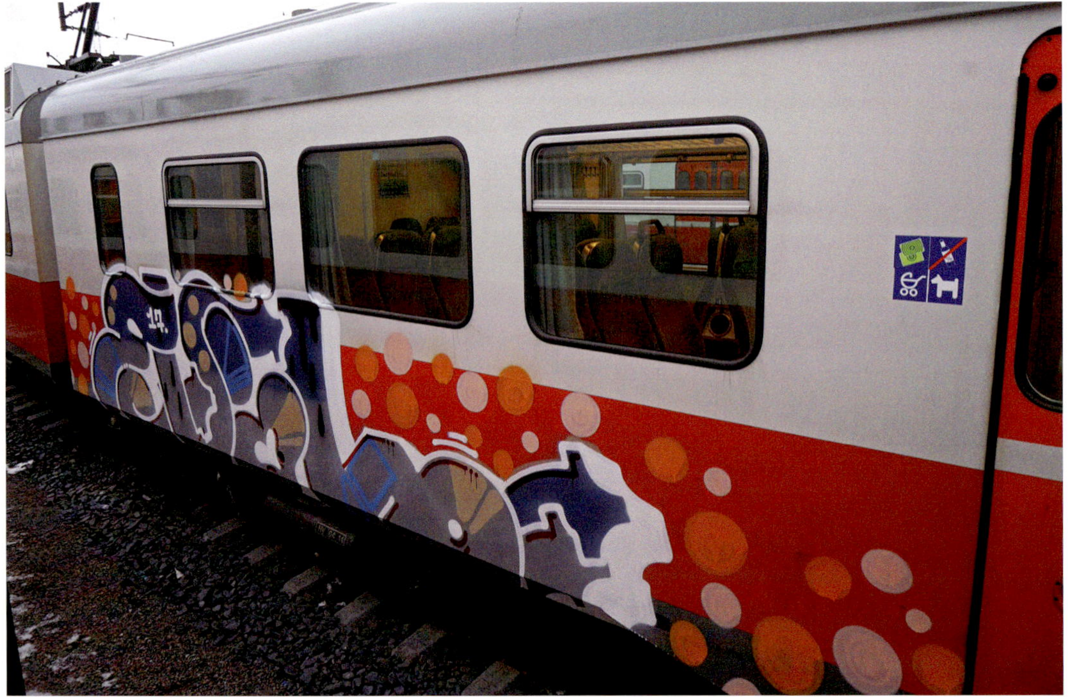

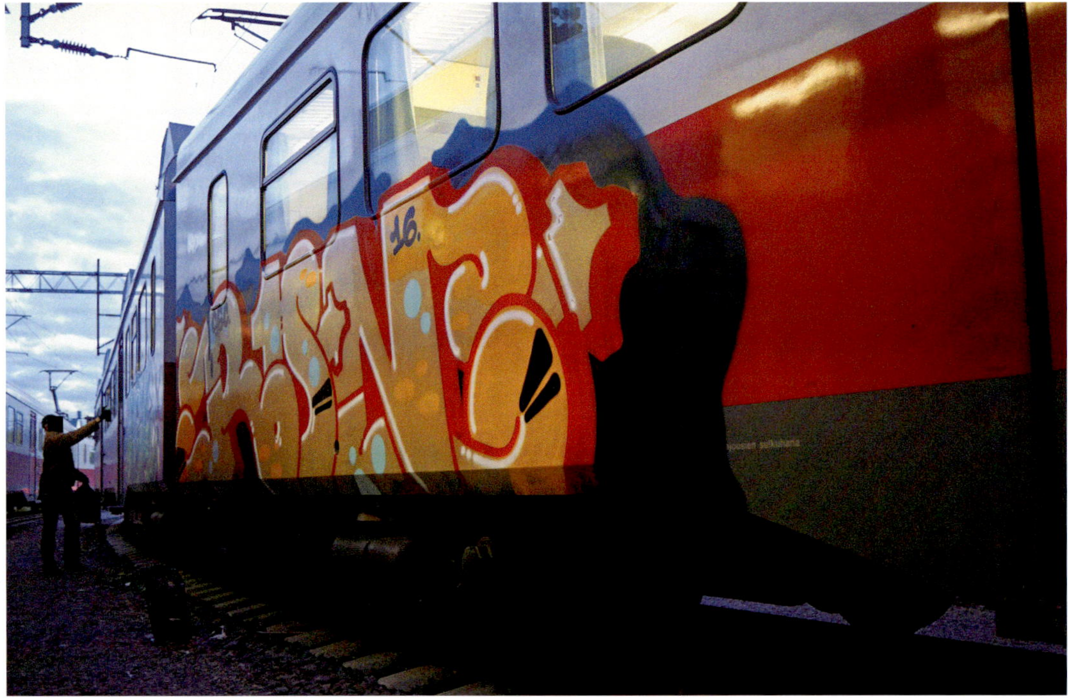

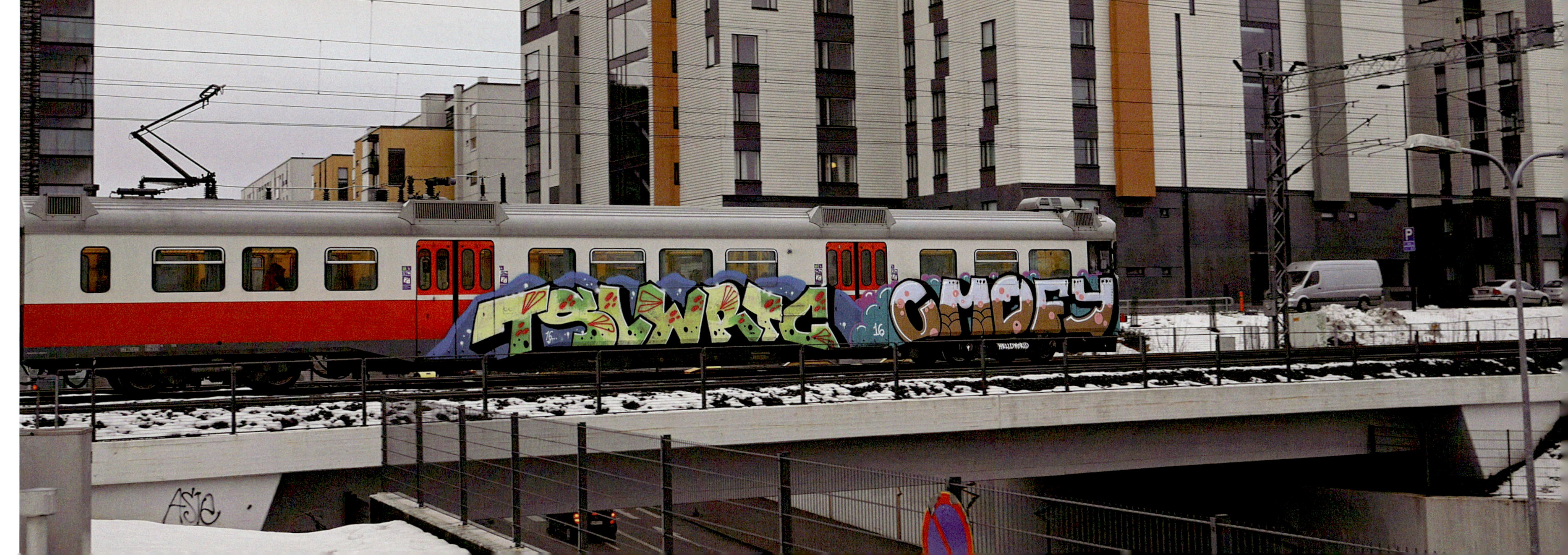

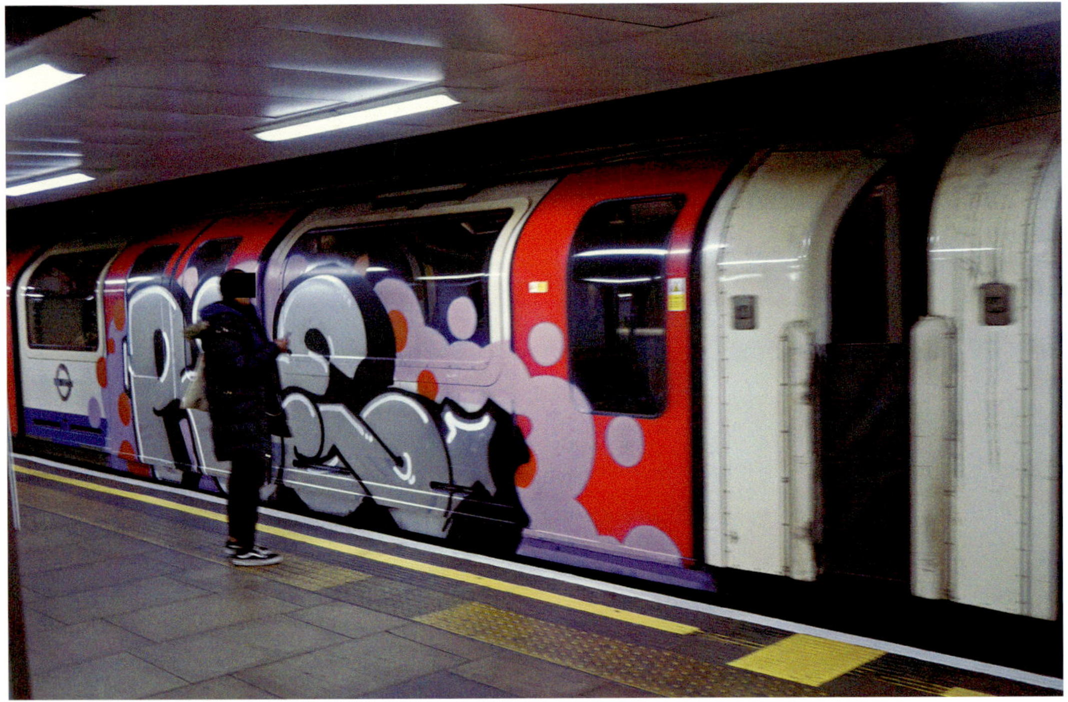

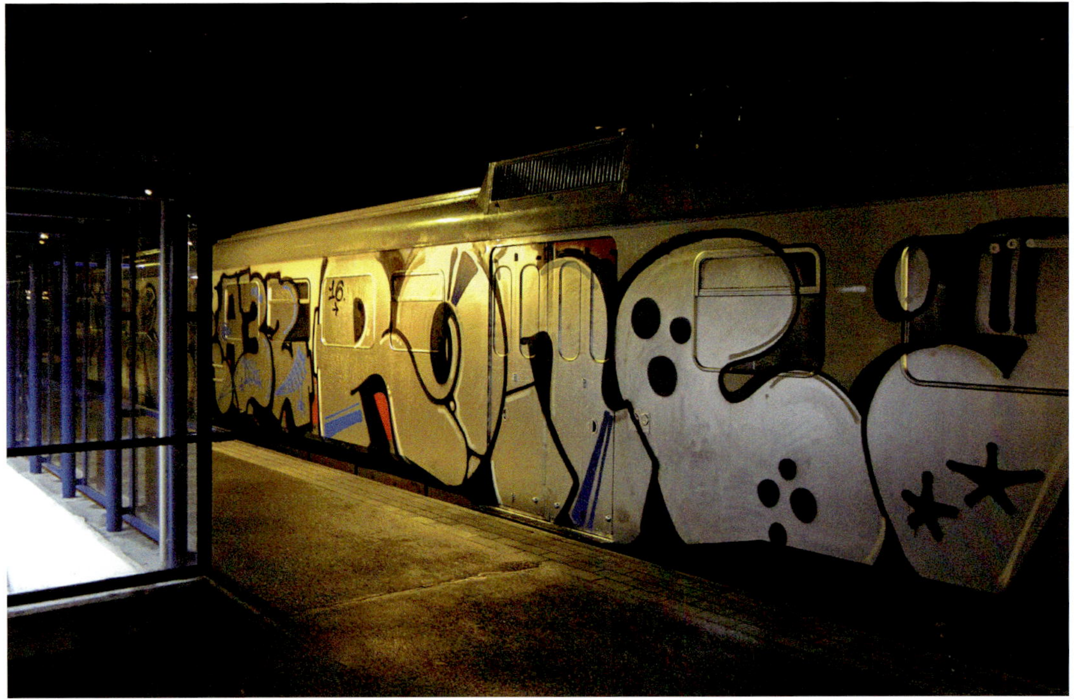

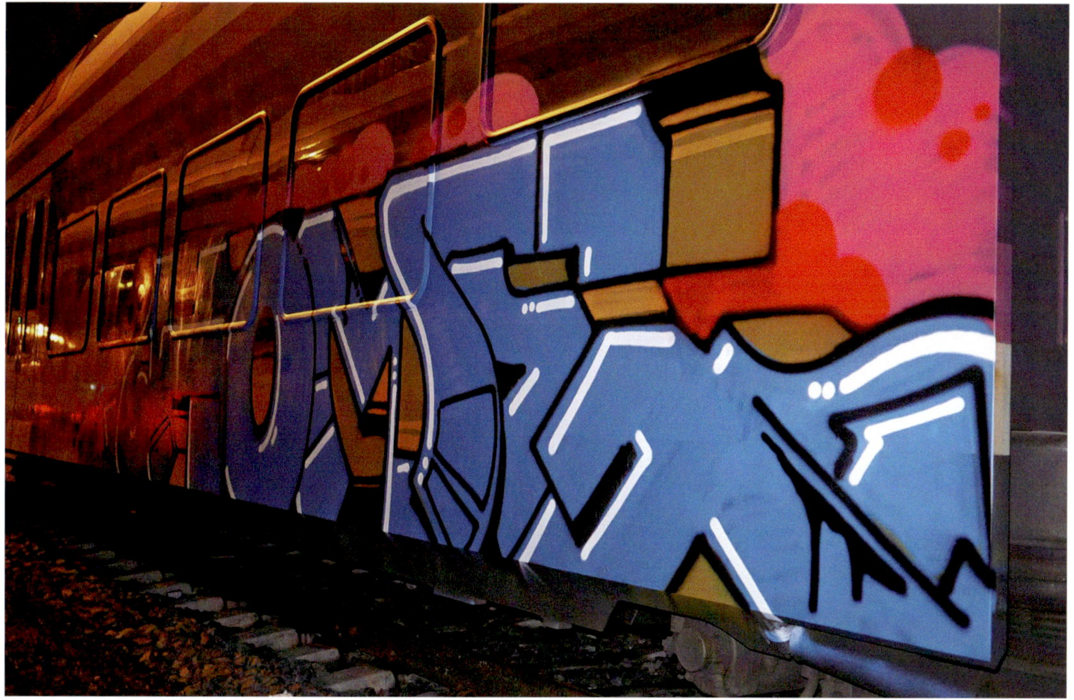

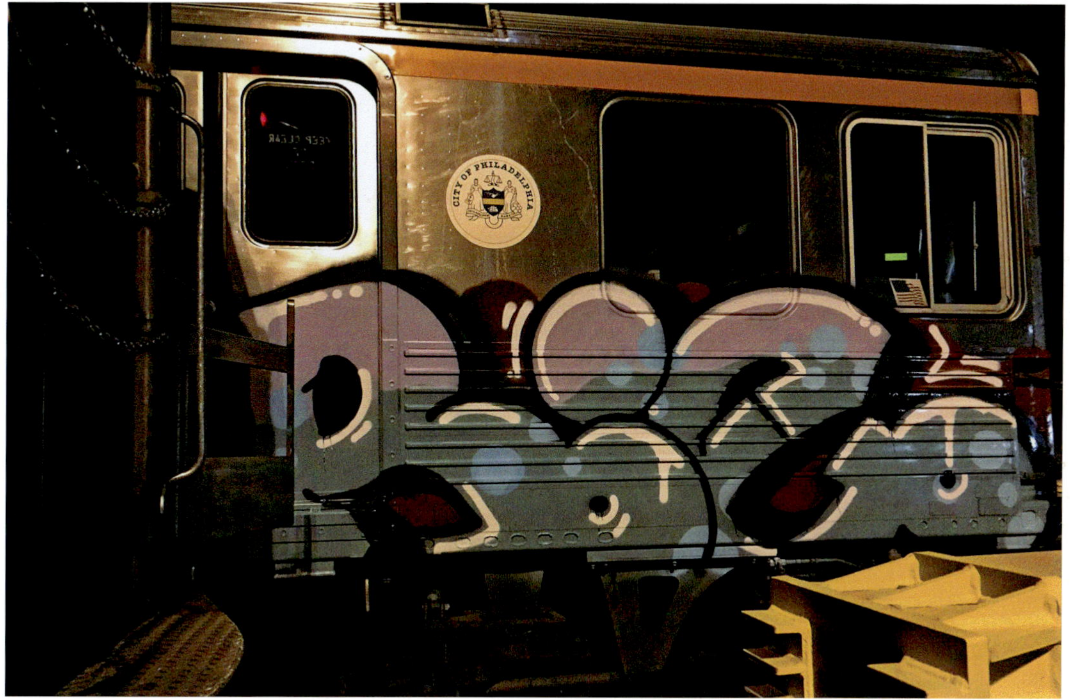

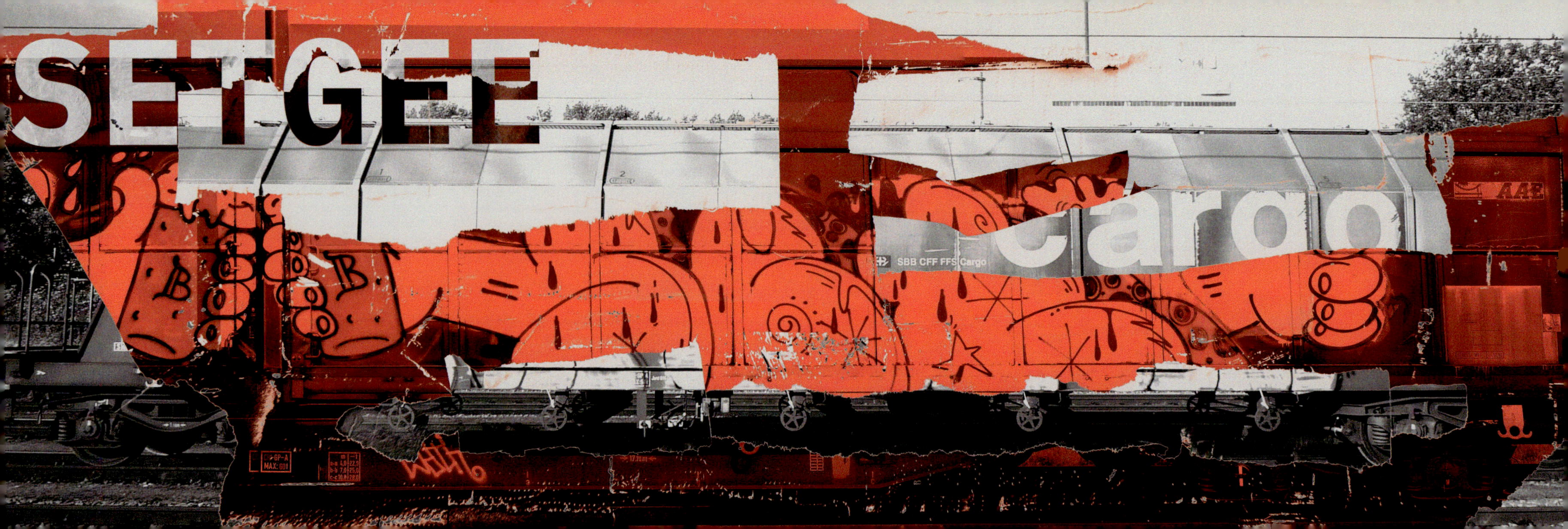

SETGEE
暴走破坏者

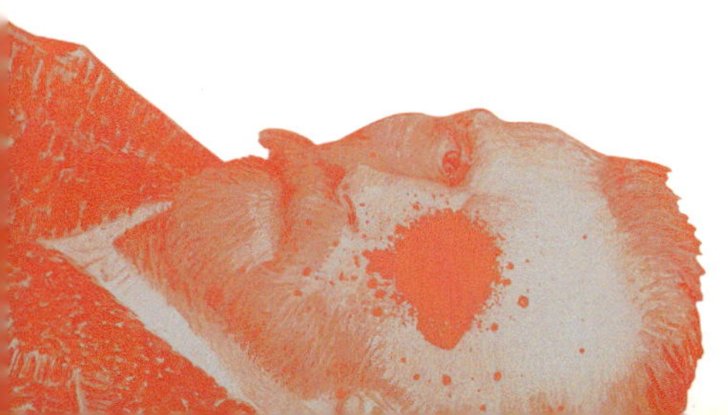

您好SETGEE，请自我介绍一下。你是个什么样的人？ :)

我是来自阿姆斯特丹的 SET，但由于涂鸦圈有太多人用相同的名字，所以我在后边加了 GEE。起初我以为这个名字会更特别，但是现在我真的不太喜欢它，因为填色的时候需要耗费更多的喷漆。

你是哪年加入涂鸦这个疯狂的游戏，如何开始的?

1983 年，我开始在自己的教学楼中写 BIG MAC 3（之前还有另外两位写手叫 Big Mac），但是第一次真正做 piece 是一年后，当我们班一起去梵高博物馆时。在建筑物的前面，有 LONE（DELTA），SHOE 和 ALOHA 所喷绘的涂鸦作品。我以前从来没见过这样的东西，并且随之产生敬畏。

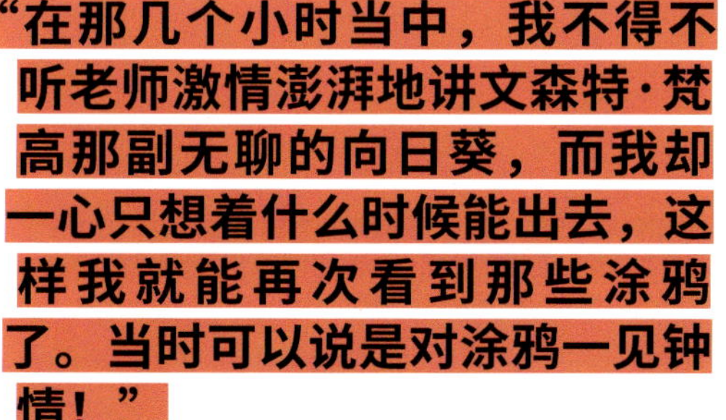

> **"在那几个小时当中，我不得不听老师激情澎湃地讲文森特·梵高那副无聊的向日葵，而我却一心只想着什么时候能出去，这样我就能再次看到那些涂鸦了。当时可以说是对涂鸦一见钟情！"**

您是 MSN 团队的成员，这个团队对于欧洲涂鸦历史有着非常重要的意义。你们的涂鸦奠定了非传统涂鸦风格的基础，不顾一切的态度，对喷火车的执着，以及在互联网出现之前就已经存在的世界影响力。您是如何加入到这个团队的?

我和其他团员最初的见面是在阿姆斯特尔车站踩点的时候。自从我会定期去隧道涂鸦之后，他们有一天晚上约着我带他们画一次。当时的计划是在皇后节（Queens Day）的前一天晚上去，这是荷兰著名的传统节日。很多人会来阿姆斯特丹玩，他们将会看到我们的作品。但不巧的是我的社会福利被驳回了。这意味着下个月我没有任何收入，生活也没有任何保障。如果我在隧道中摔断了腿那麻烦大了。于是我偷了一瓶伏特加酒，并改变了计划。我告诉他们，我会在早些时候从内侧打开紧急出口，指给他们进去的路，然后自己一个人去城里一醉方休。

这些家伙（REAZE，MELLIE，EROR 和 SEKS）起初对我不打算加入他们感到失望，但是当他们听到伏特加的时候，就露出了酒鬼本性，每个人都想分一口。作为一个贪婪的荷兰人，我开始比其他人喝得更猛，因为怕全都被他们喝了。很快我就彻底醉了，因为基本一整瓶酒都是我一个人喝掉的。我当时站在门口，当每个人都在下楼梯时，MELLIE 再次让我加入他们的行列。"我身上没带喷漆，下回吧。"我回答。然后 EROR 回到楼梯上说"没事儿，哥们，我带的漆足够我们俩人的了。"

> **"我倒在地上很多次，EROR 不得不把我拉起来，将我背在背上，因为我再也无法正常行走了。我做了一些特别荒谬奇丑无比的 throw-up，而 MSN 伙计们做了一些非常不错的 piece"**

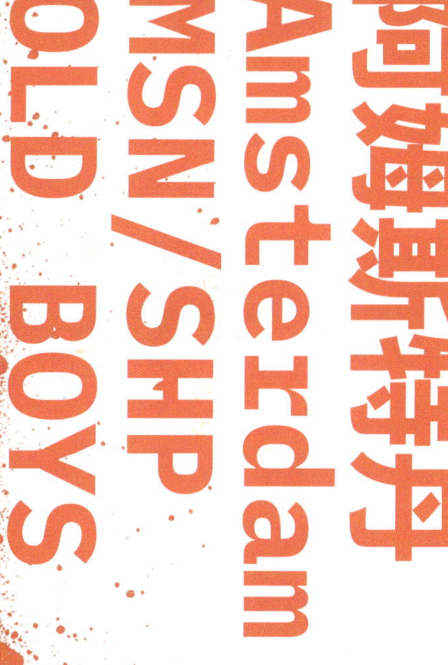

这个时候酒劲儿开始上来了，我还没有意识到就已经到楼梯下面了。从那开始一切都变得模模糊糊。我只记得我开始在隧道中四处写签名，而其他人都只想去 Waterlooplein 站画银色的涂鸦。我倒在地上很多次，EROR 不得不把我拉起来，将我背在背上，因为我再也无法正常行走了。我做了一些特别荒谬奇丑无比的 throw-up，而 MSN 伙计们做了一些非常不错的 piece。喷了两个车站后，他们所有的喷漆罐都空了，该是时候离开了。我们出去以后，这些家伙帮我找到了回家的夜班车。他们一直在笑，但我不知道为什么。即使在公交车上，人们也把我看作是个变态，不断地嘲笑我。直到第二天早上醒来时，我才彻底明白了为什么。因为我在隧道中摔倒了很多次，所以我完全被铁轨上的污垢所覆盖，衣服也毁了，全是铁轨上的棕色的焦油，脸完全是黑色的，就像是扫烟囱的人一样。他们下午给我打电话了解我的状况，并通知我通过了测试，已经成他们的一员了！

"除了整天偷喷漆和食物，晚上喝醉外，别的真的什么也没做"

之所以能够在城市里活跃地涂鸦是因为我是一个无业游民，每年都会在城市里搬来搬去。除了整天偷喷漆和食物，晚上喝醉外，别的真的什么也没做。我经常在回家时背着一个装满漆的背包用来涂鸦。那时，这座城市到处都是涂鸦。似乎没人在乎你在街上写名字。人们没有手机，警察也不得不处理城市里更大的问题，例如与毒品有关的犯罪。我也很荣幸认识像 PONE，SKEE 和 OASE 这样的人，他们总是在非常的积极。相较于他们我总是粗心大意，在没有工作的时候被抓。我周围的每个人都过着无忧无虑的生活方式，到处都有人在被废弃的地方歌舞升平。这个城市提供了许多可以做涂鸦的老房子。我觉得那些年真的很幸运。

"我蹲在第三条轨道上。而眼前的一切是那么美。在他喷涂鸦的过程中，火车上冒出的烟雾环绕着他，像是一只反射着光芒的巨兽"

1995 年左右我去了纽约，因为 YALT 在那生活了一年。他知道皇后区一个隧道中能够轻易涂鸦的地点。于是我们决定用银画满车厢，在那我们可以站在站台上，并轻易的画到顶部。当我们在隧道里时，我实在惹不住想去厕所，这让我想放弃任务然后回去。不幸的是，YALT 不同意，所以我不得不在隧道里找个地方拉屎。当他起稿的时候，我蹲在第三条轨道上。而眼前的一切是那么美。在他喷涂鸦的过程中，火车上冒出的烟雾环绕着他，像是一只反射着光芒的巨兽。

当我终于开始画的时候，我偏执地觉得车站上的乘客可以看到我们。而隧道里亮着灯，我总感到有一盏直射着我们。我毫不犹豫地从墙壁上取下了灯管，这让我在黑暗中更加自在。但随之我也碰到了麻烦，因为那截车厢太暗，几乎什么也看不见。我别无选择，只能把灯管放回去。但当我把它放回去时，它就像频闪仪一样闪烁。YALT 愤怒地说："你在做什么，你个傻瓜?!"于是我不得不在彻彻底底的黑暗里喷，那也是我有史以来做过最差的整车涂鸦。不过YALT的涂鸦再次成功的完美。当我们想通过紧急出口出去时，我们发现它被堵了。所以不得不走了一个不知道会通向何处的出口。当我们打开小门时，正对着一栋教学楼，前面有一辆保安的车。幸运的是，那家伙正在检查另外一侧，所以我们借机偷偷溜了出去。

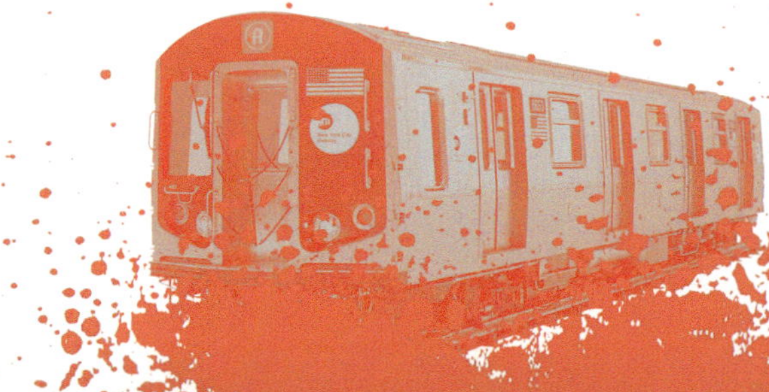

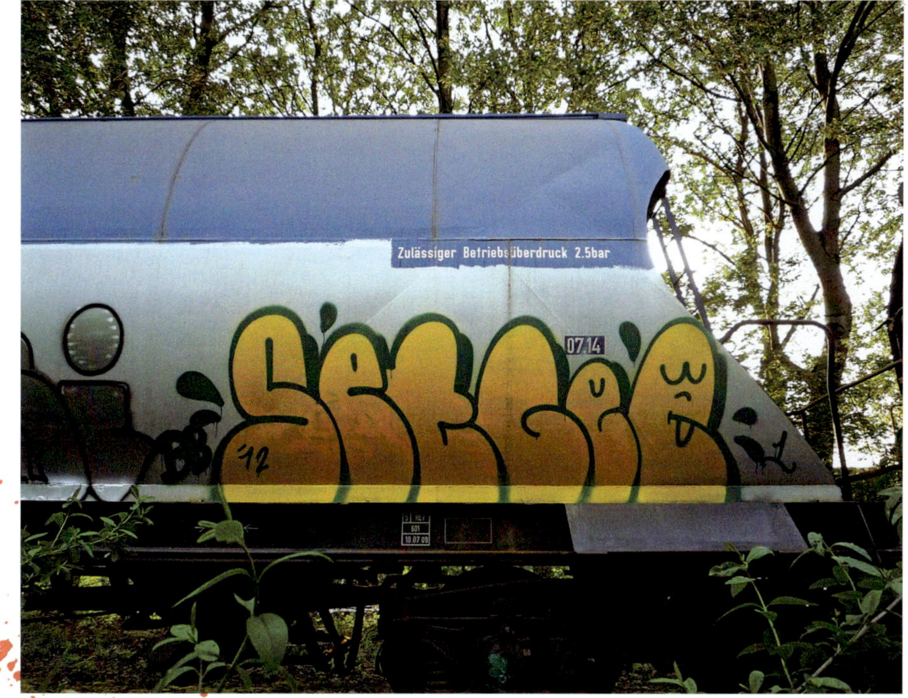

您与罗马的 TRV 团队是什么关系？

1995 年慕尼黑举办了一场大型的涂鸦聚会，其间有许多涂鸦大神，而 DELTA 也被应邀参加。于是我决定周末也去那放松一下。那次活动中我遇到了来自罗马的 PANE 和 JOE。他们的英语很差，但是我们一拍即合，他们邀请我一起回意大利。因为他们的朋友有一间大房子，我可以在那随意地待几天。SEL 听到了这件事，并告诉了 DELTA 和 SENTO，他们毫不犹豫地决定加入我的行列。谁不想去罗马玩还可以免费住一间新的房子呢？

随之我们偷走了用于做主题涂鸦的喷漆，并准备前往意大利首都。只不过当我们到达时，才发现他们口中的豪宅，只是工地里的一间房子。甚至没有自来水，没有厕所，也没有通电。

那时候刚好是年初，天气冷得要命，但是我们以某种苦中作乐的想法，从中获得最大的乐趣。我们甚至比原计划的停留时间待得更长，几乎习惯了睡在地面上。因为几乎每一天，TRV 团队的伙伴都会带我们去位置特别好的火车区间涂鸦，那种感觉就像到了天堂一样。

在一起的最后一个晚上是在 Nuovo Salario 火车区间。STAND 告诉我们在这里你只有 30 分钟的时间来完成一幅涂鸦，多一秒钟都不行。不幸的是他忘了 SENTO 也在我们的队伍里，他大概是地球上涂鸦速度最慢的人。在画他的放客风格涂鸦时他还停下来找我。当他看到我在另一辆车上画 throw-up 的时候，说："哟，看起来不错啊，让我在你旁边也喷几个吧。"我们最终在院子里呆了至少两到三个小时。当晚 STAND 没突发心脏病还真算是一个奇迹。

"我们甚至比原计划的停留时间待得更长，几乎习惯了睡在地面上。因为每一天，TRV 团队的伙伴都会带我们去位置特别好的火车区间涂鸦，那种感觉就像到了天堂一样"

您也属于 SHP 和 OLD BOYS 团队：对于这些团队你有什么特殊的情感吗？

对我来说，这些团队是关于友谊的。SHP 中的大多数人都不再涂鸦了，但出于情感原因我还是会喷这个名字。它使我想起曾经无忧无虑的生活。OLD BOYS 是我们（SKEE，JAKE 和我）的团队名字，因为那些一起涂鸦的的大多数人都比我们年轻得多。在雅典和我一起涂鸦的人都只年轻我一半的岁数。这瞬间让我觉得我好老！

目前您的涂鸦生活如何？ 会常去画货运火车吗？ 还是更倾向于街面涂鸦？ 您已经活跃了几十年，现在是什么状态？

我一直在尝试每周至少做一幅涂鸦。但是要让我在晚上11点以后离开家门却变得越来越难了。这也是为什么我会选择在货运火车上涂鸦的原因，因为他可以让你在白天喷，而且还可以在车身上保留很多年。

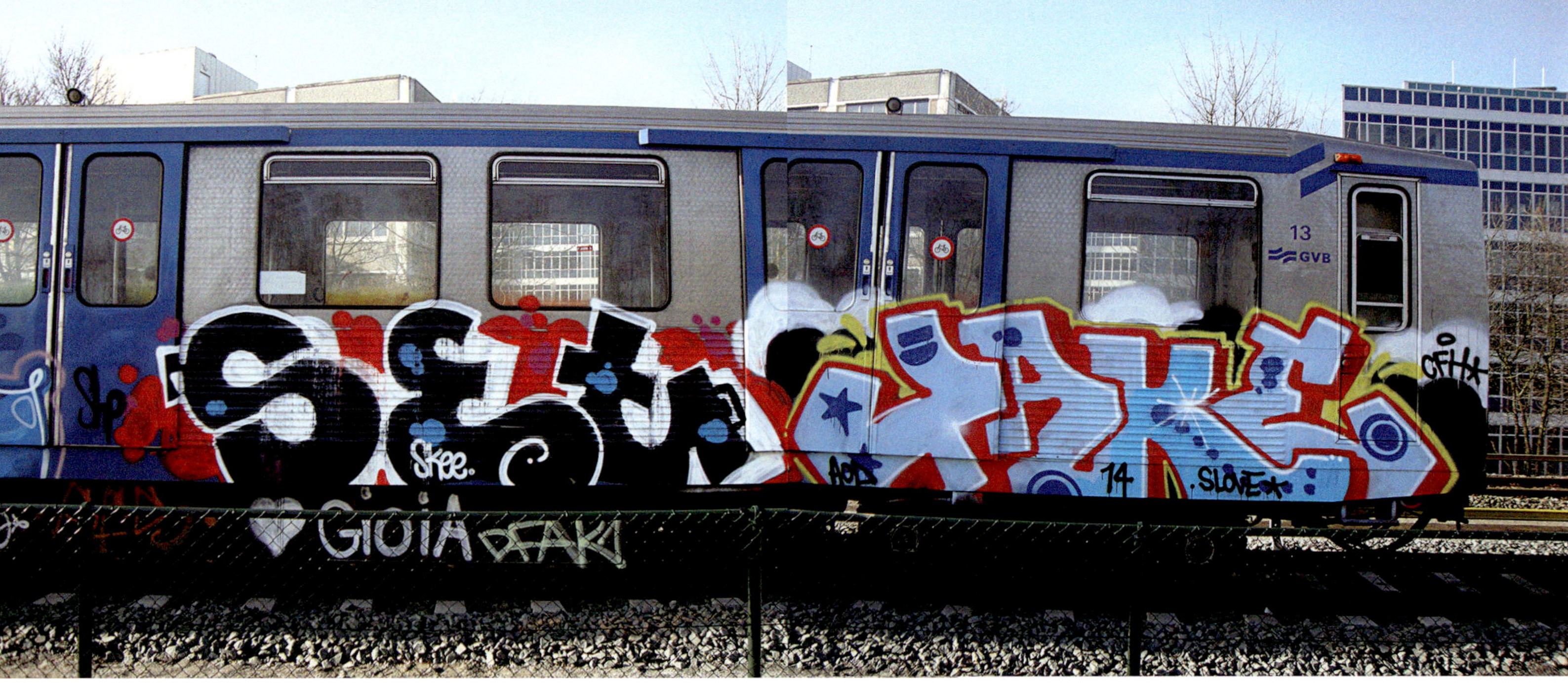

SETGEE
The footloose vandal

**Hello SETGEE, please introduce yourself.
What kind of guy are you? :)**

I'm SET from Amsterdam but since there are so many people writing that same name in the graff world I added the GEE to it. At first, I thought the name sticks out more, now I really dislike it because I need more cans for the fill-in.

Which year did you got involved in this graffiti madness? How did it happen?

I started to tag BIG MAC 3 (there were two other Big Mac before me..) in my school building in 1983 but my first real encounter with pieces was a year later when I went with my class to the Van Gogh museum. On the front of the building, there were these colorful pieces done by LONE (DELTA), SHOE, ALOHA. I had never seen anything like that before and was totally in awe of the pieces.

"For hours I had to listen to my teacher talking enthusiastically about the boring sunflowers of Vincent Van Gogh and all I could think was when we would go outside so I can see those pieces again. It was really love at first sight!"

You're part of the MSN crew, a group that is really important for the European graffiti history. Your crew paved the way regarding unorthodox styles, don't-give-a-fuck attitude, devotion to train-bombing, and international networking way before the internet. How did you got involved with the crew?

I think we started to see each other at the Amstel Station while we were benching for trains. Since I've been going to the tunnels regularly they asked me to take them with me one night. The idea was to go on the night before Queens Day, a famous holiday in the Netherlands. Lots of people would come to Amsterdam and would see our stuff. Then on that day I just heard my welfare check was revoked. So no money for the upcoming month and I wasn't insured. So if I would break my leg in the tunnels I was in big trouble. I stole a bottle of vodka and changed my plans; I would get them into the tunnel from an emergency exit I had opened from the inside earlier that day, show them in and then get shitfaced by myself in the city.

The guys (REAZE, MELLIE, ERROR, and SEKS) were disappointed at first that I didn't join them but when they heard about the vodka of course the guys were keen on having a sip too. Being the greedy Dutch guy I start to have bigger gulps than the rest, afraid they would drink it all by themself. Within no time I was completely drunk because I drank almost the whole bottle by myself. When I stood there at the hatch door, and everybody was going down on the stairs, MELLIE asked me again to join them. "I don't have any paint on me, so maybe next time." I replied. Now EROR came back on the stairs and said: "No worries man! I got enough for both of us."

"I felt so many times on the ground, EROR had to pick me up and carry me on his back because I could not walk normally anymore. I did some totally ridiculous, ugly throw-ups while the MSN boys did some really nice pieces."

The alcohol was doing his work because before I knew it I was already on the stairs going below. From there everything became a blur. I know I started to tag everywhere in the tunnel while the rest was going for the Waterlooplein station doing silver pieces. I felt so many times on the ground, EROR had to pick me up and carry me on his back because I could not walk normally anymore. I did some totally ridiculous ugly throw-ups while the MSN boys did some really nice pieces. After hitting two stations all their cans were emptied and it was time to leave. When we were outside the guys helped me find my night bus to go home. All the time they were laughing but I didn't know why. Even on the bus people looked like I was some kind of freak and laughed at me. When I woke up the next morning I understood why. Because I felt so many times in the tunnel I was completely covered in dirt from the tracks, my clothes ruined, brown from the tar on the tracks, face totally smeared black like I was a chimney sweeper. They called me in the afternoon to check up on me and told me I was in the crew, I passed their test so to speak!

The reason I was up in the city is that I was unemployed and lived every year in a new place in the city. I really didn't do anything except steal paint and food all day and get drunk in the evening. I would always have a backpack full of paint to finish when I walked home. Back then the city was filled with graffiti. Nobody seemed to care if you would put up a tag. There were no mobile phones and the cops had to deal with bigger problems in the city like drug-related crimes. I also was privileged to know guys like PONE, SKEE, and OASE, who were always up for some actions. I was more reckless than, there was no job on the line when I would get caught. Everyone around me lived this carefree lifestyle, there were tons of parties in abandoned places everywhere. The city was boarding up so many old buildings where you can do pieces on. I really feel lucky that was around in those years.

Around 1995 I went to NYC because YALT was living there for a year. He knew a spot in a tunnel in Queens that was supposedly very easy. We decided to do silver whole cars because you could stand on a platform. When we were in the tunnel I really had to go to the toilet and I wanted to go back and abort the mission. Unfortunately for me, YALT did not approve so I had to find a place to take a shit in the tunnel. While he was sketching up I was taking a shit while sitting over the third rail. It was such a beautiful sight to see; him painting and seeing the paint fumes coming from the train, the big metal beast with the lights shining on me.

When I finally started to paint I got all paranoid that they could see us from the station. There were lights in the tunnel and I had the feeling one was directly pointing at me. Without hesitation, I took the fluorescent tube from the wall so I would be more in the dark. I only then discovered that now my part of the train was too dark and I couldn't see anything. I had no choice but to get the tube back into the fitting. But when I was putting it back in it was now flickering like a stroboscope. YALT reacted furiously: "What the hell are you doing fool?!" Now I had to paint the car in complete darkness and did the worst whole car ever. YALT of course burned again. When we wanted to go out through the emergency exit we found out it was blocked. We had to take an exit we did not know where it would lead us to. When we opened the hatch we were right across a school building with a security car in front of it. Luckily the guy was checking the other side so we could sneak out.

What is your connection with the TRV crew from Roma?

In 1995 there was this big graffiti jam in Munich and DELTA was invited to paint there amongst many other big names. I decided to go there and just chill for the weekend. When I was there I met PANE and JOE from Rome. Their English was very bad but we bonded instantly and they invited me to travel back with them to Italy. One of their friends had a big house where I could easily chill for a few days. This came to the attention of SEL, who told DELTA and SENTO and without hesitation, they decided to join me. Who wouldn't want to go to Roma and stay in a brand new house for free?

"We [...] almost got used to sleeping on the ground. Every day the TRV boys took us to all these nice layups and yards and it felt like paradise."

After that, we stole the paint that was initially going to be used for a big mural at the jam and we were ready to visit the Italian capital. Only when we arrived we soon discovered that our luxury residence was nothing more than a house in the middle of a working site. No running water, no toilet, no electricity.

It was at the beginning of the year so it was cold as hell but somehow we had to laugh about it and made the best out of it. We even stayed longer than we planned and almost got used to sleeping on the ground. Every day the TRV boys took us to all these nice layups and yards and it felt like paradise.

The last night together was at the Nuovo Salario train yard. STAND told us we would have 30 minutes to do a piece and not a second longer. Unfortunately, he forgot he was dealing with SENTO. Man slowest painter on the planet. While painting his funky piece he stopped and came looking for me. He saw me doing throw-ups on another car: "Yo, those look nice, let me put a couple of them next to you." We ended up being there in the yard for at least two to three hours. It is a miracle that STAND didn't have a heart attack that night.

You're also into groups like SHP and OLD BOYS: any thoughts about these crews?

To me, these crews are about friendship. Most of the guys from the SHP don't write anymore but I like to put up the name for sentimental reasons. It reminds me of those years of carefree living. OLD BOYS is the name we (SKEE, JAKE, and me) just gave ourselves because most of the people we paint with are way younger than we are. In Athens, I've painted with guys that were half my age. I felt so old!

How is your graffiti life at the moment? Freights? Streets? You've been active for decades, how is it now?

I always try to do at least one thing a week. But it is getting harder to motivate me to get out of the house after 11 pm. That's why the freights are always nice. You can do them during the daytime and they will run for years.

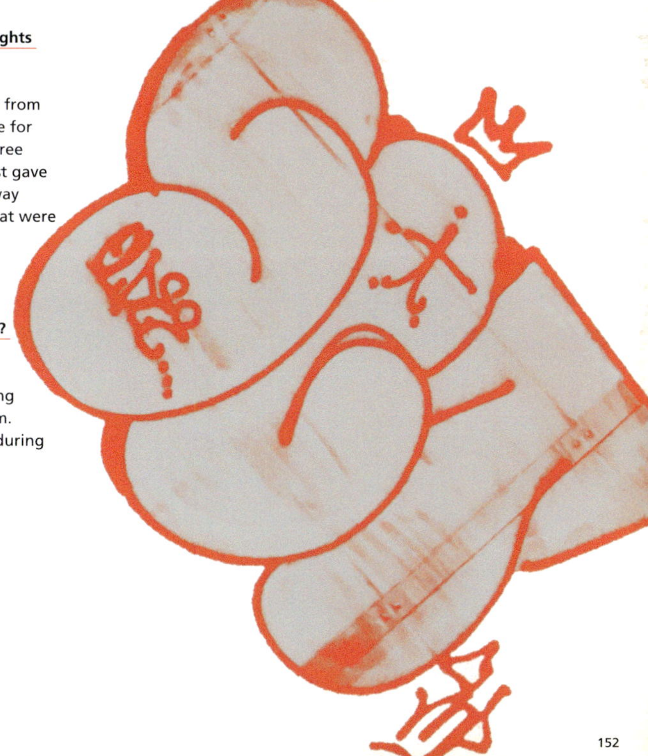

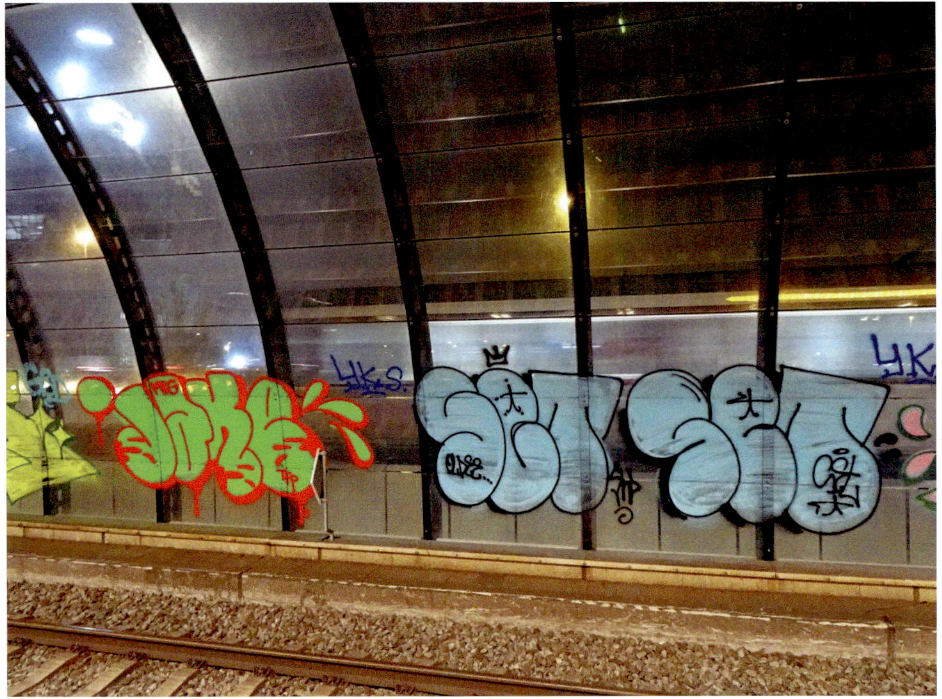

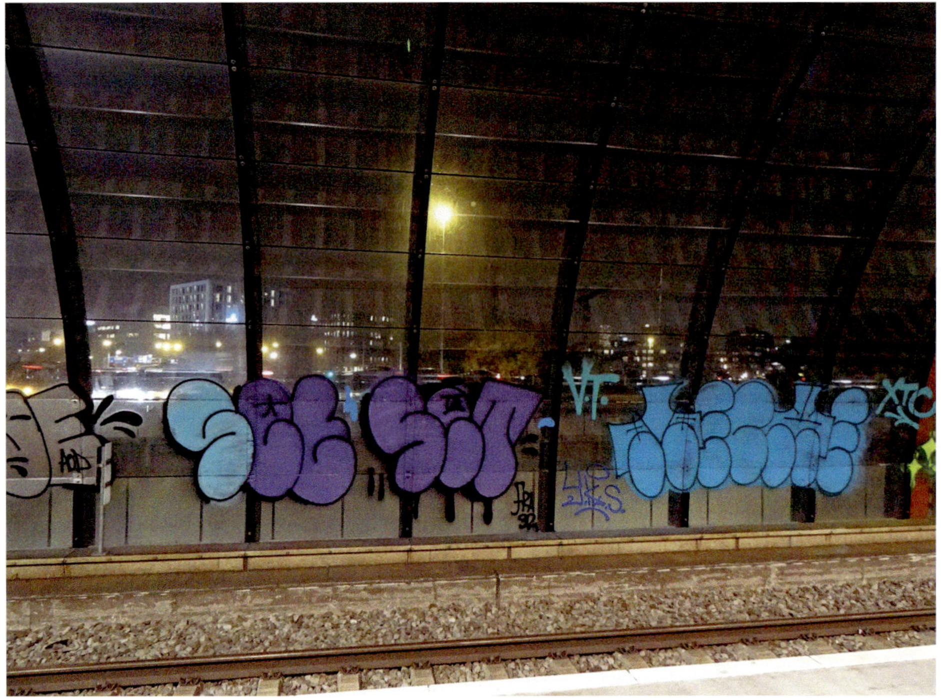

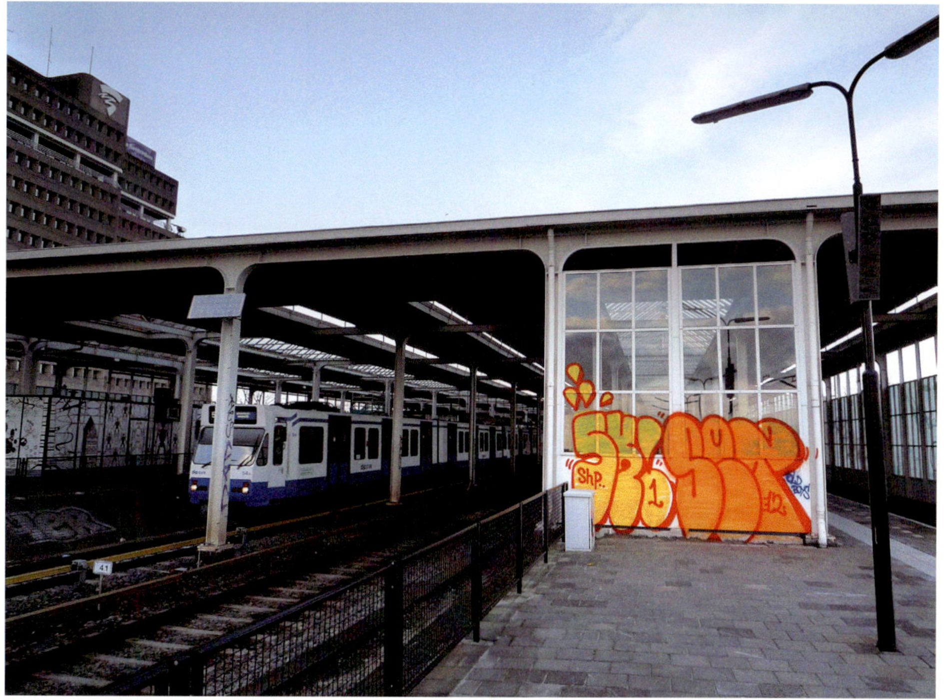

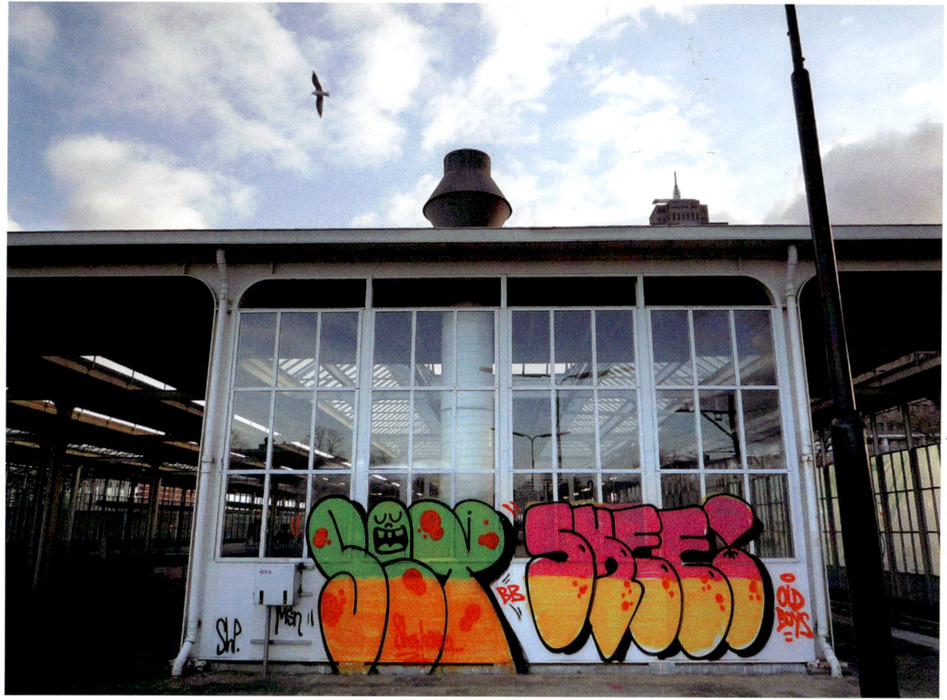

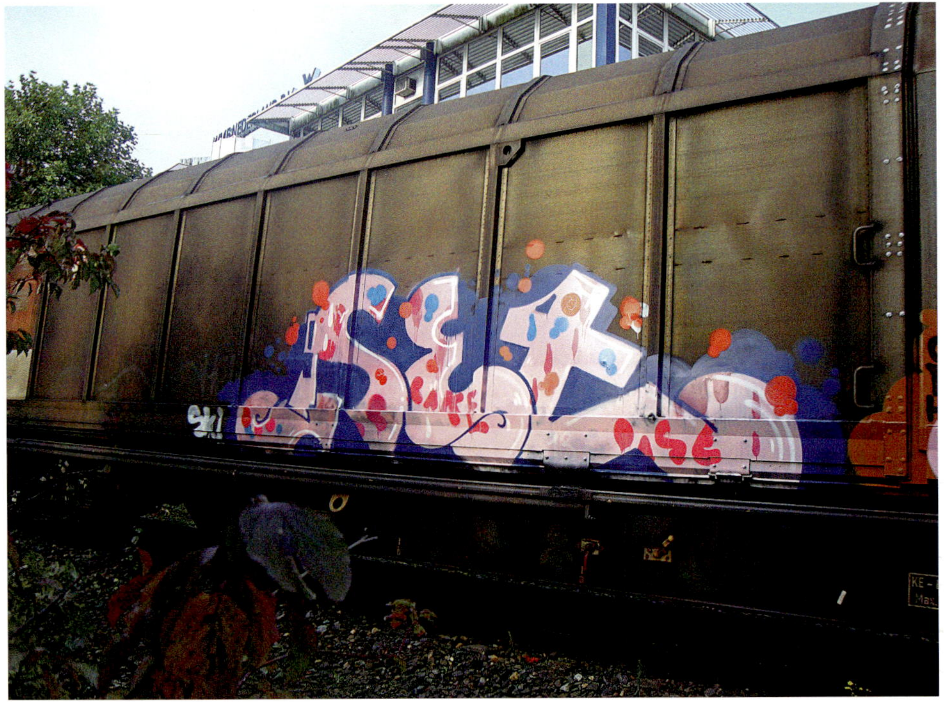

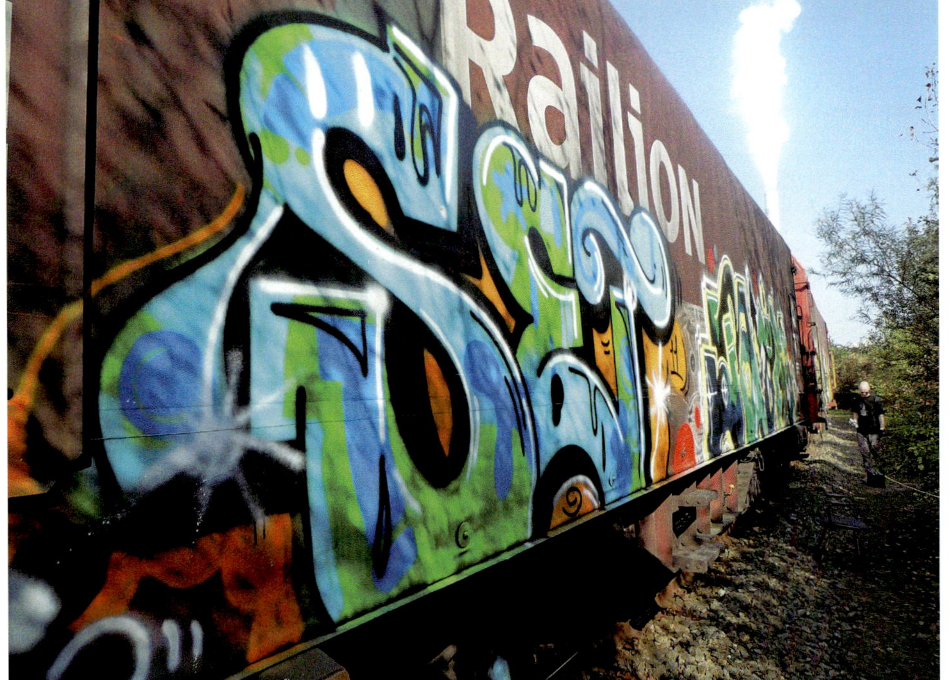

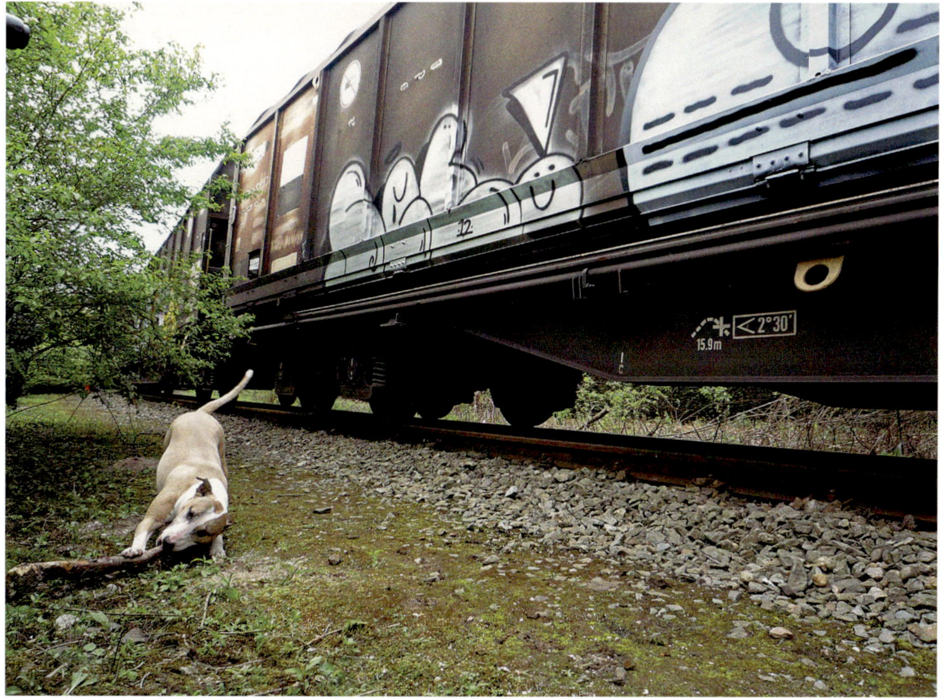

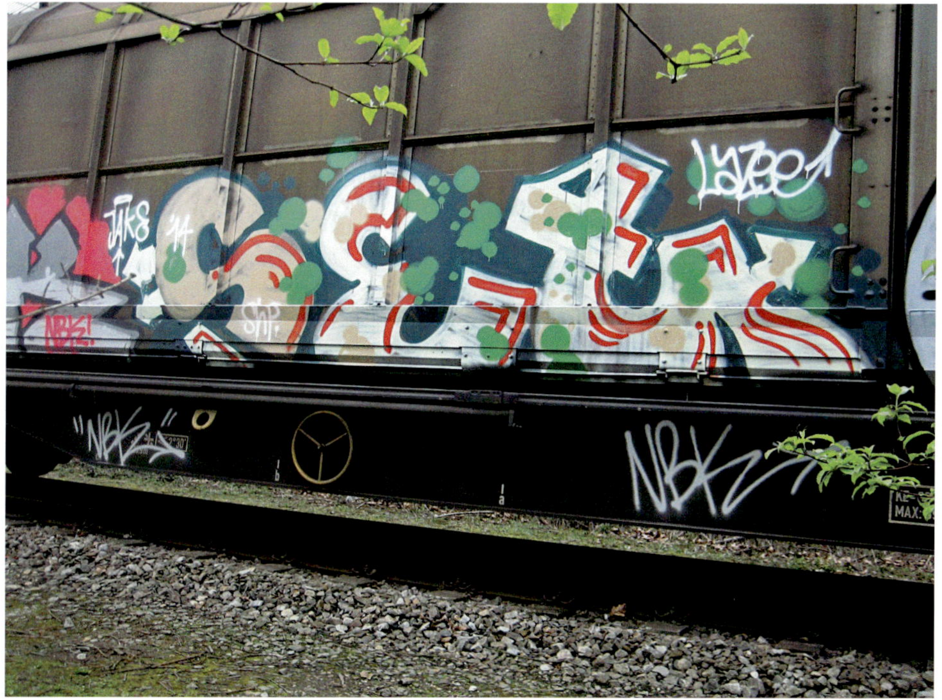

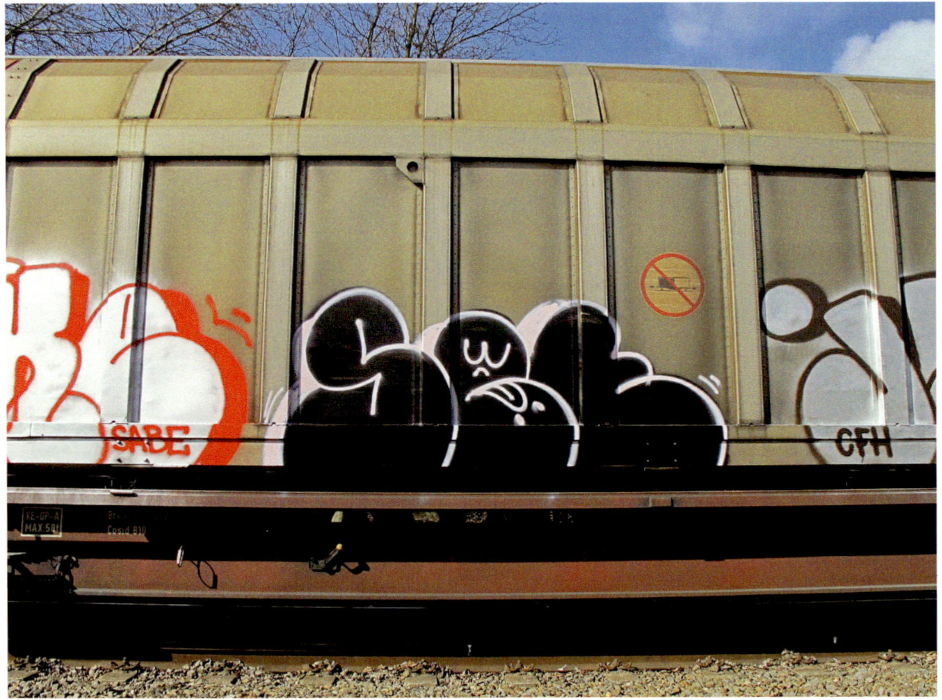

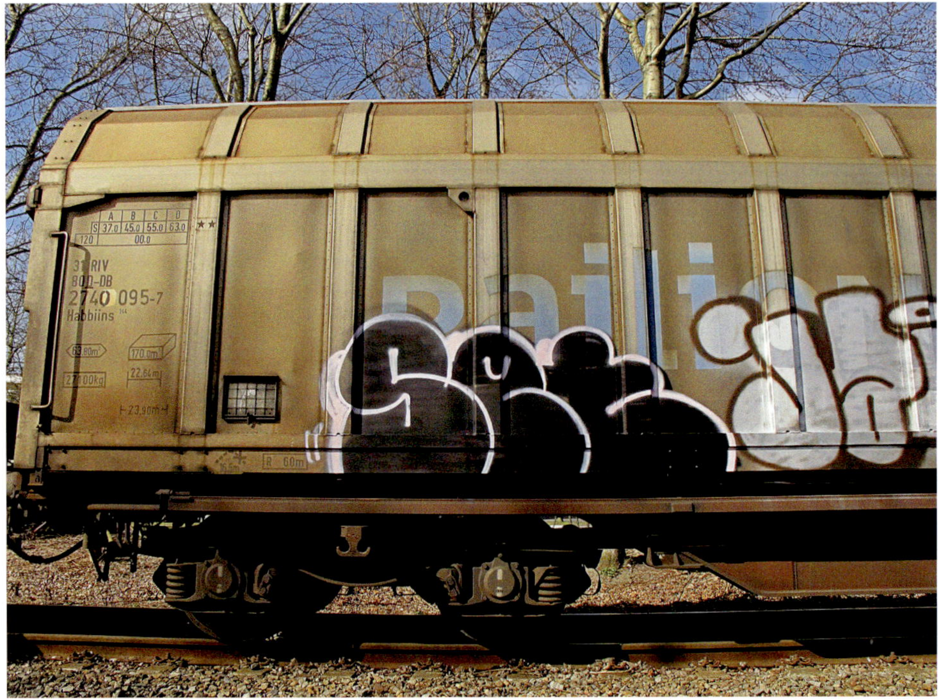

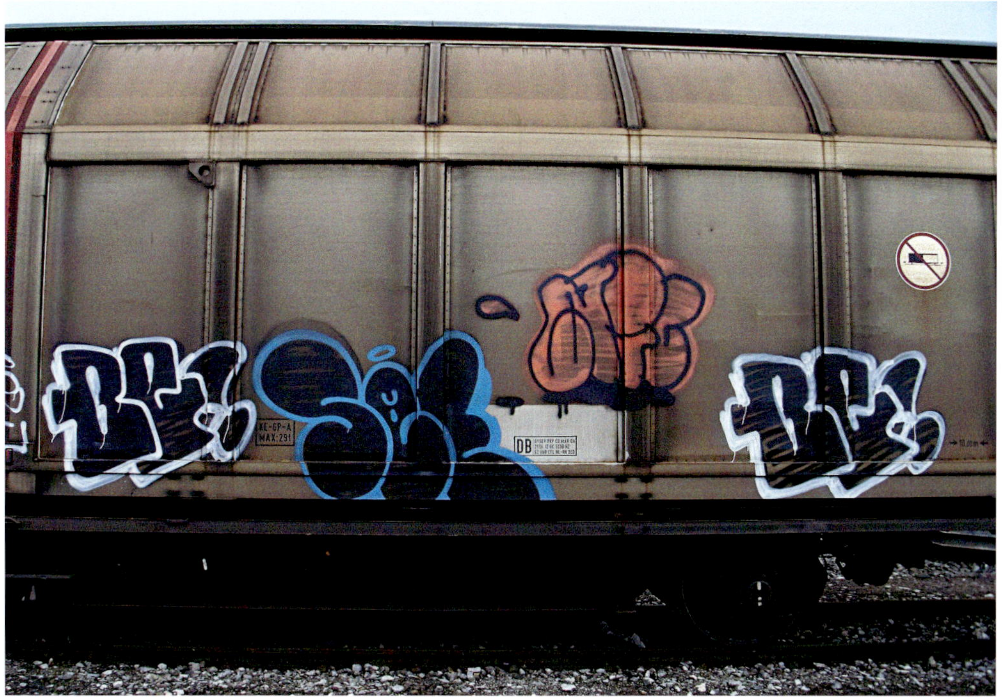

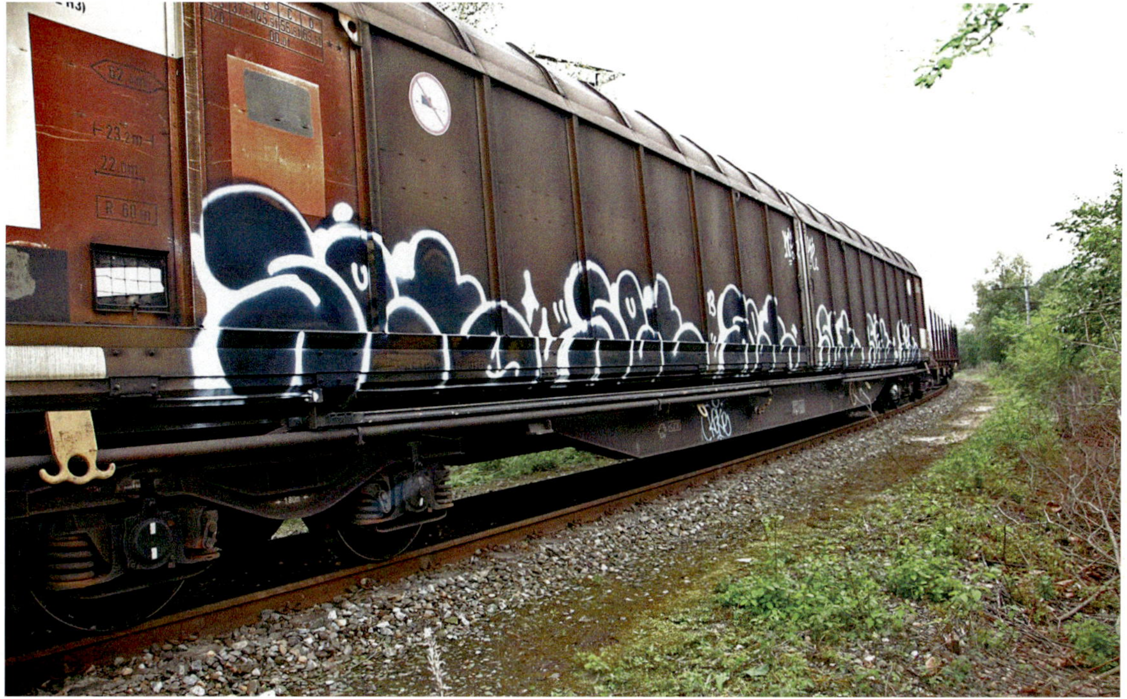

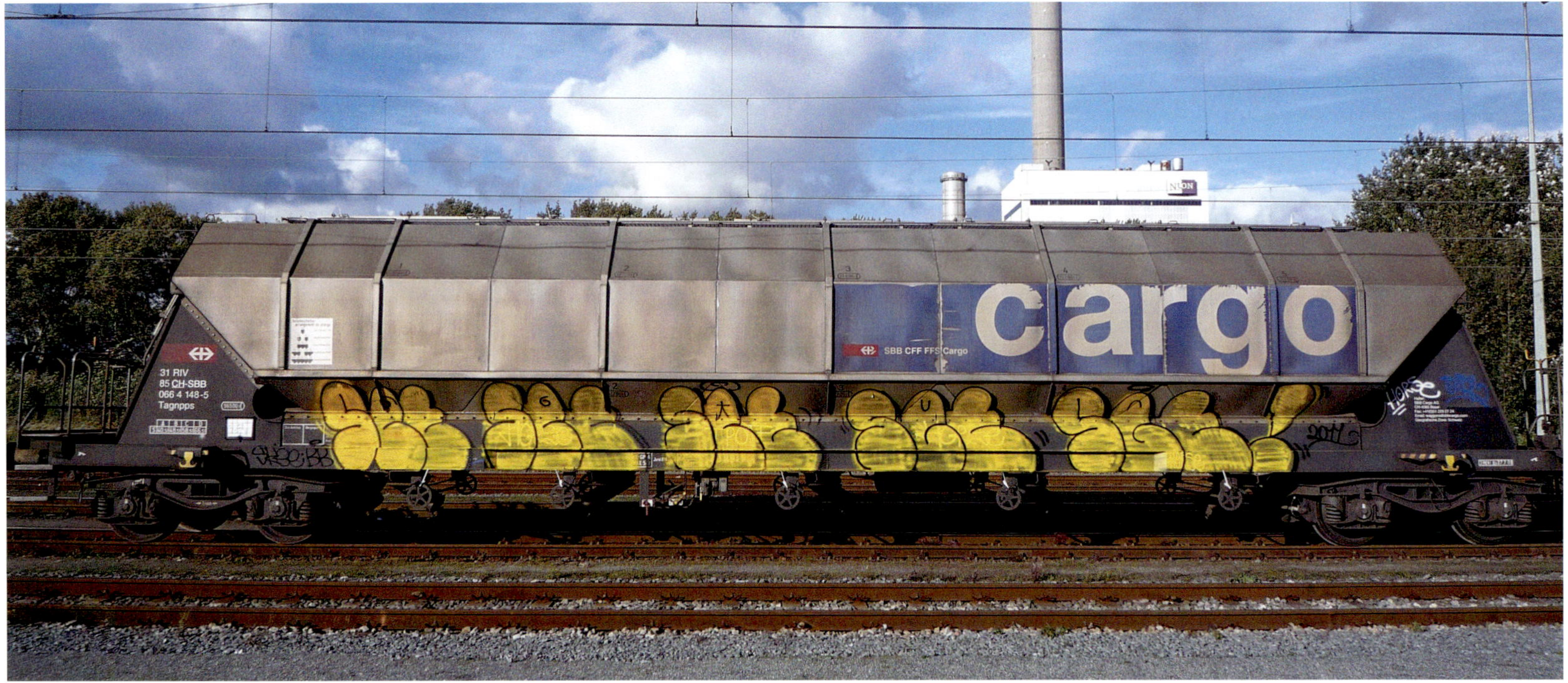

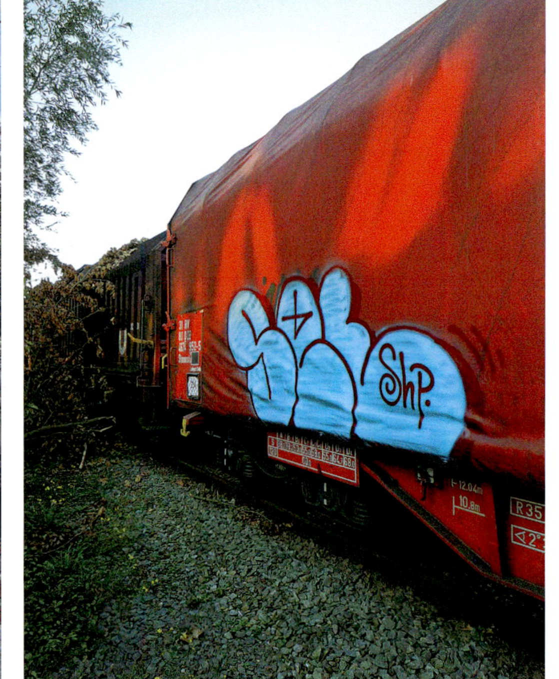

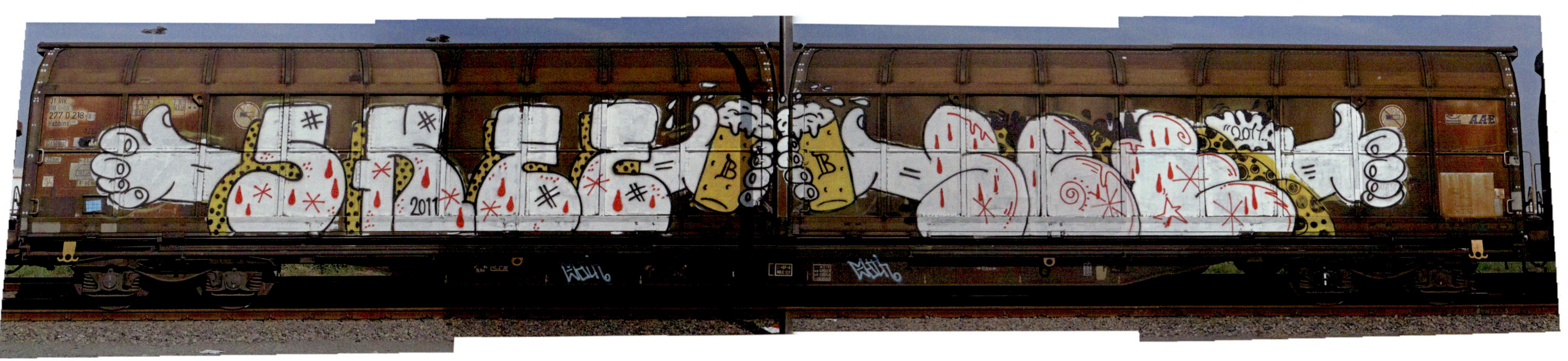

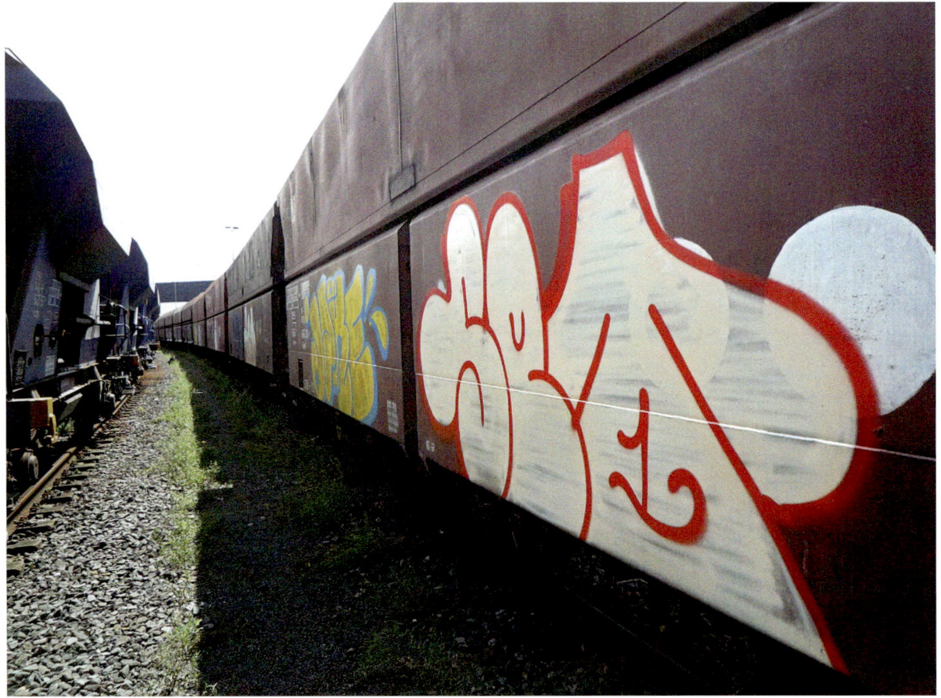

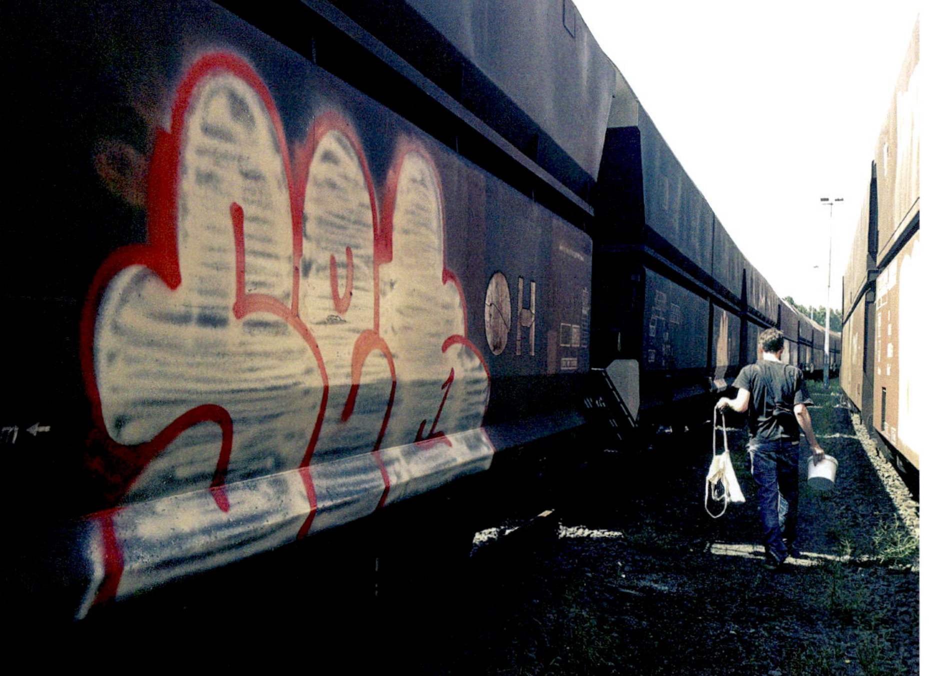

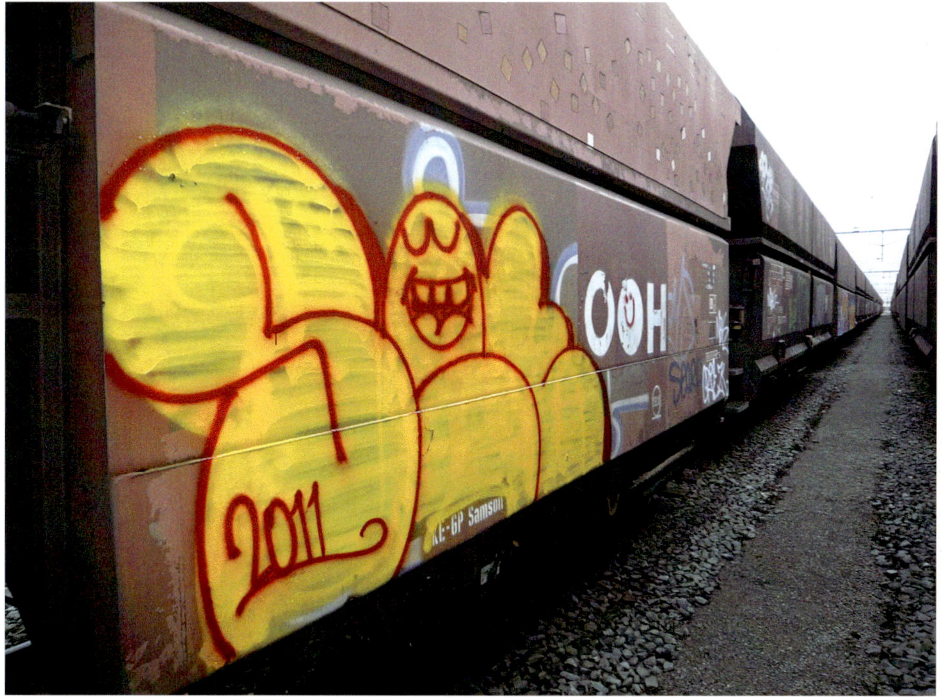

2011
COOH
Fysiobus

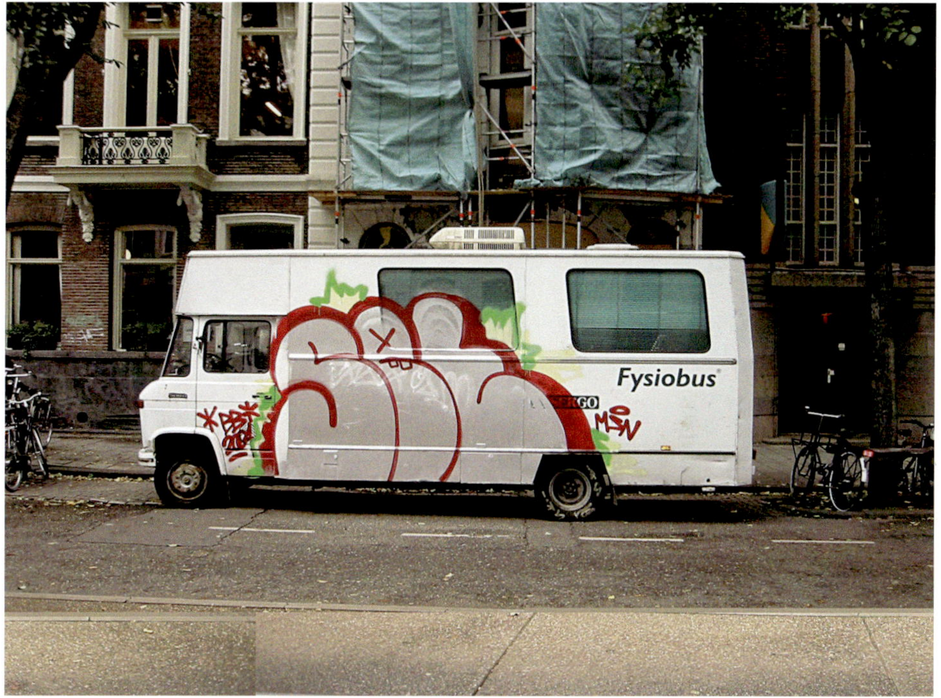

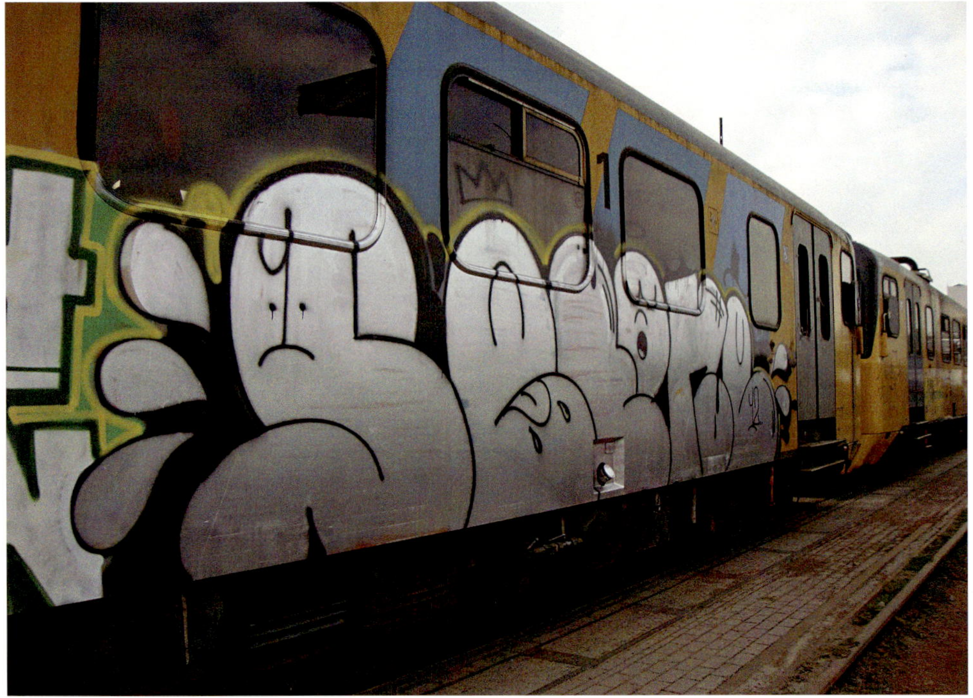

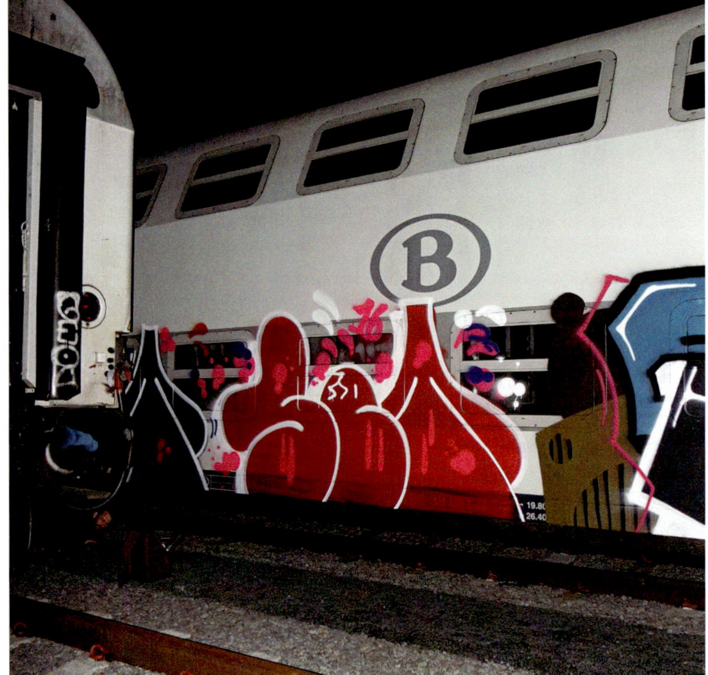

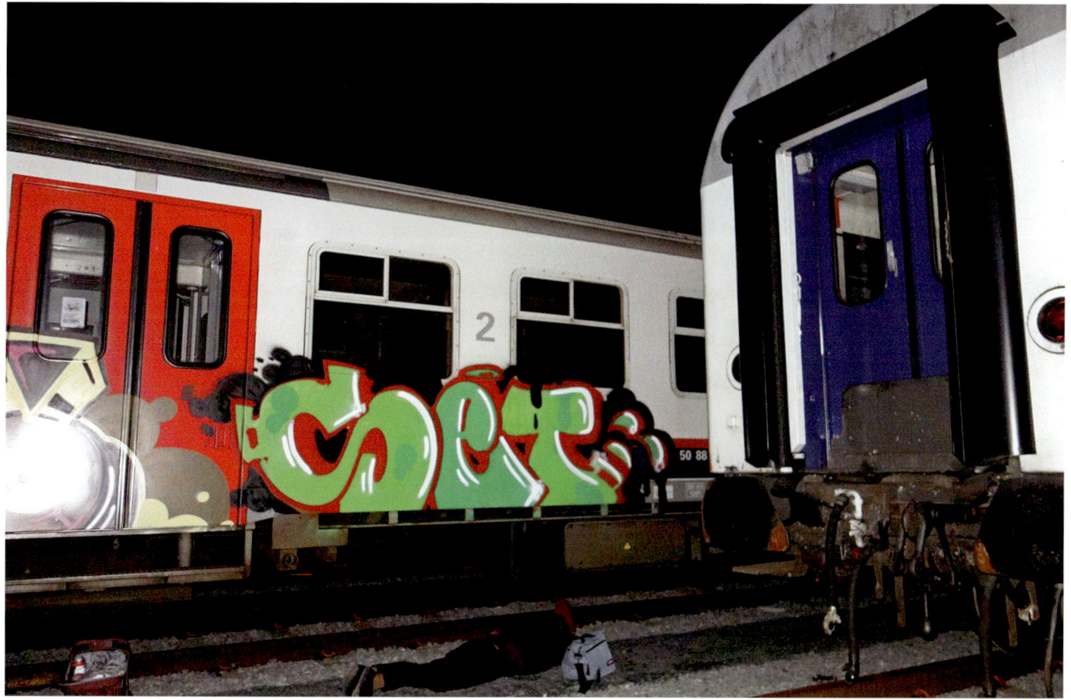

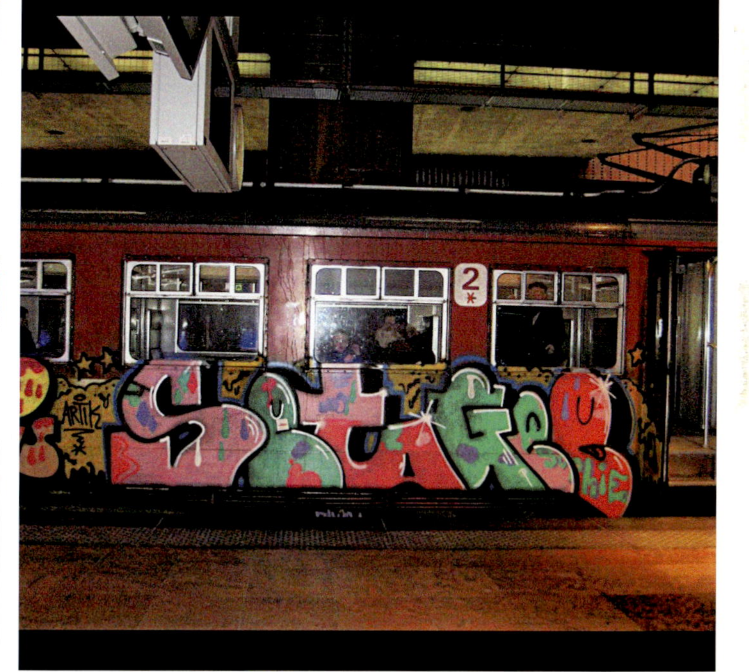

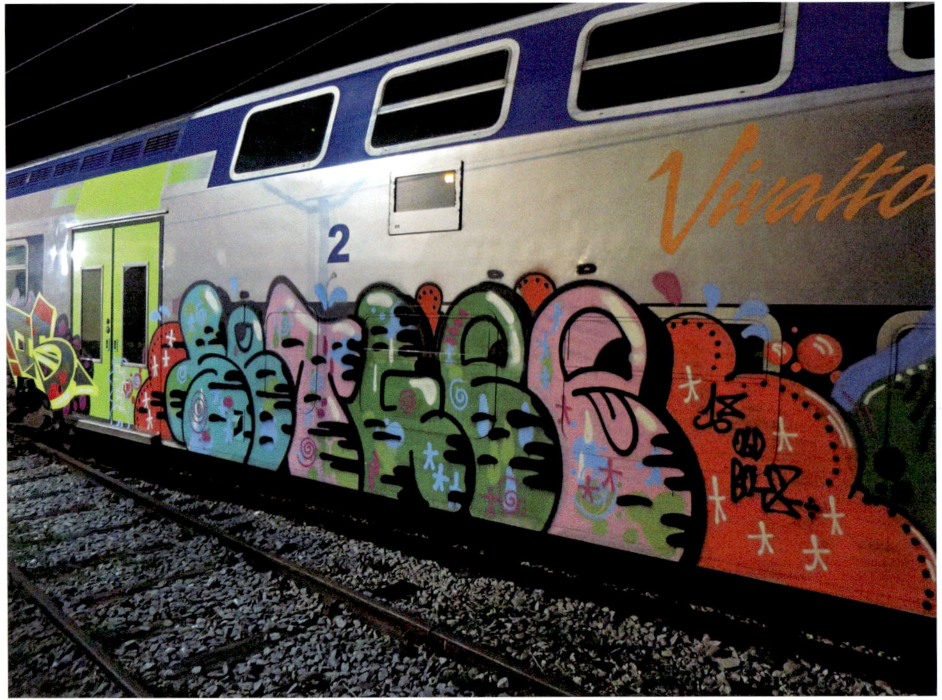

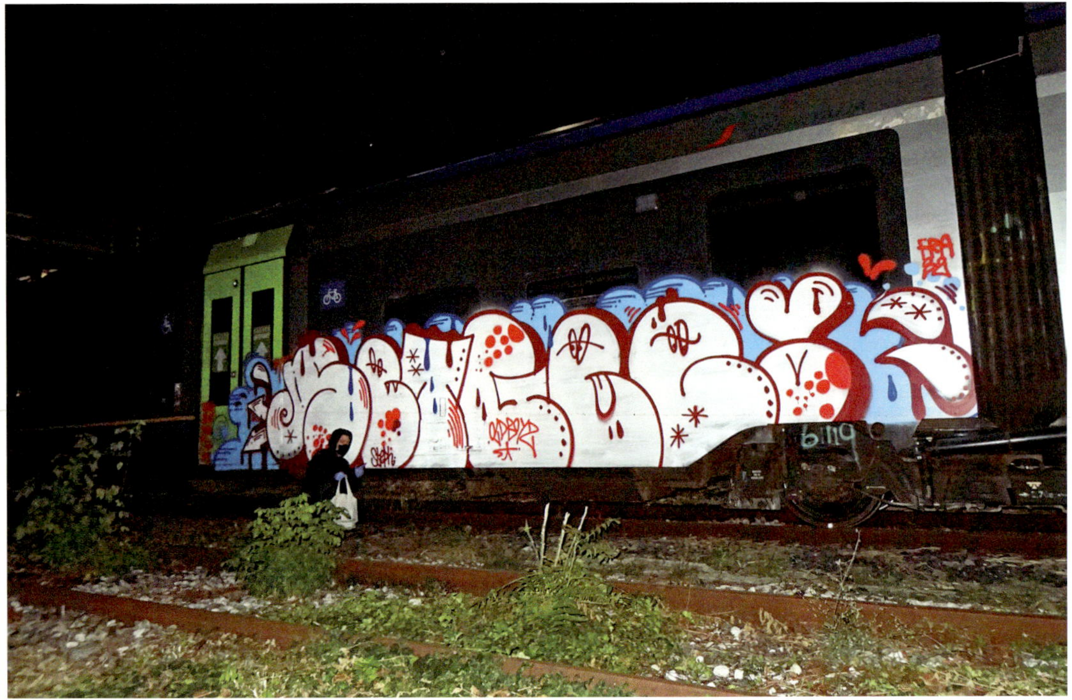

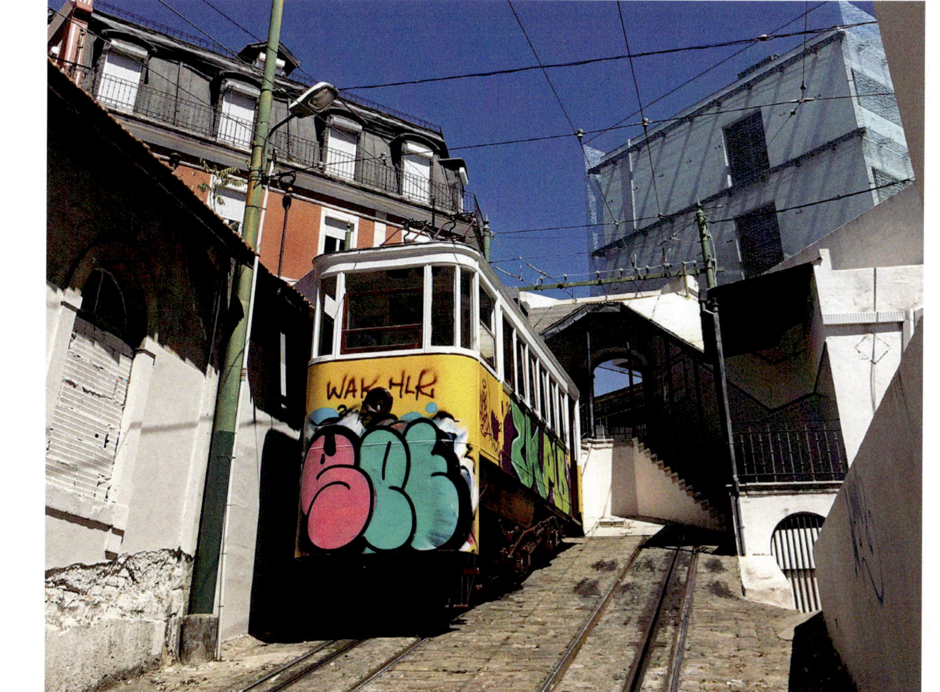

The Unsung Vandals of China

ASKO & ELVIS

被埋没的中国武达尔王

编辑部对涂鸦的热爱，在《无妥协方式》里已经不是秘密了。但我们不会把商业化的东西混在其中，也不会把任何时髦流行的趋势夹杂其中，这当然这也包括你所热爱的街头艺术家，纹身师，或者说唱歌手。但我们对这本杂志的厚重感到抱歉，编辑部只是在努力去涵盖更多的内容。这也是为什么这一辑我们选择了 ASKO 和 ELVIS 来代表中国的涂鸦氛围。他们的作品很疯狂，风格暴力却充满个人特色，但最重要的是他们完全不去做任何多余的修饰和包装。

"ASKO 的作品很癫狂，就像是一个来自平行维度的原始人空降在了中国的首都"

最初在北京的街头看到 ASKO 的作品时，我们花了好一段时间才认识到他。因为从他做涂鸦的第一天起就没按套路出过牌，ASKO 的作品很癫狂，就像是一个来自平行维度的原始人空降在了中国的首都。经过几年的历练，ASKO 的风格也进化了，他现在更着重于在一些疯狂的位置上喷涂鸦，并且生活也指引着他来到了涂鸦圣城——纽约，在那里他继续努力炸街。这是一个充满烂涂鸦的时代，但他已经能够自由自在的在这片创作的海洋里遨游，并且保持原生的风格和向往自由的精神。

"ELVIS 的作品就像是当"肯尼迪之死"乐队在演奏"我打败了法律"时，你正站在冲撞区的中央"

另一方面，ELVIS 则是数量和野蛮力的体现。他的涂鸦绝对是我们见过最朋克的作品之一。当我们漫步在一条高档的奢侈街道，周边都是琳琅满目的古着精品店时，却突然撞见 20 多个用马克笔写着"ELVIS"代号的涂鸦字在不同表面上，这不禁逗乐了编辑部的我们。显而易见，他到处留下自己的印迹，而他却并不在意写的是否漂亮。他做的都是最粗燥原始的涂鸦，并尽可能多的画满中国的每个角落。难道你不喜欢这种涂鸦吗？即使是，那也是你的问题，你是没有办法阻止他的脚步。而他就像射进黑洞的一颗子弹。在中国没有多少写手拥有这样的毅力，他的作品就像是当"肯尼迪之死"乐队在演奏"我打败了法律"时，你正站在冲撞区的中央。

这期无妥协杂志，我们有幸邀请到了 ASKO 和 ELVIS 和我们一起，我们也希望你能沉浸于被埋没的中国汪达尔武士的世界里。

It is no secret that at *No Apologies* we like graffiti. We do not mix it with commercial stuff, we do not mix it with the latest design trends, with your favorite street artist, contemporary artist, tattoo artist, or rapper. Sorry, we are a bit thick and we struggle to manage more than one thing at once. Said that is easy to understand why we selected ASKO and ELVIS to represent the Chinese scene. The guys are bold, their style is raw and fresh, and they don't know what sugar-coating is.

"ASKO's stuff is lysergic, like a savage from a parallel dimension that has landed in the capital of China"

The first time we saw ASKO's work around the streets of Beijing it took us a while to figure him out. Since day one he has been completely out of the box, his stuff is lysergic, like a savage from a parallel dimension that has landed in the capital of China. A few years have passed and ASKO's style has evolved. He is now focusing on faster productions over crazy spots and life has brought him to the mecca of graffiti, New York, where he kept bombing hard. He has been able to surf over the sea of bullshits of this graffiti era and he retained the raw power and free spirit of his early days.

"ELVIS' work is like being in a mosh-pit while the Dead Kennedys play *I Fought the Law*"

ELVIS on the other side is the embodiment of quantity and brutality. His graffiti is like one of the most punk stuff we have ever seen. You walk along this gentrified, lovely street full of boutiques that sells over-priced vintage clothes and suddenly you spot 20 fat tags of ELVIS over whatever and an amused sneer shows up on our faces. He is everywhere and he doesn't care about doing pretty stuff. What he does is crude graffiti, as many as he can and all around China. Do you not like it? It is your problem, you can't stop him, he is like a bullet shot into a black hole. Not so many writers in China have his stamina, his work is like being in a mosh-pit while the Dead Kennedys play *I Fought the Law*! Just what graffiti should be.

At *No Apologies,* we are honored of having ASKO and ELVIS down with us and we hope you'll enjoy this journey into the world of the unsung vandals of China.

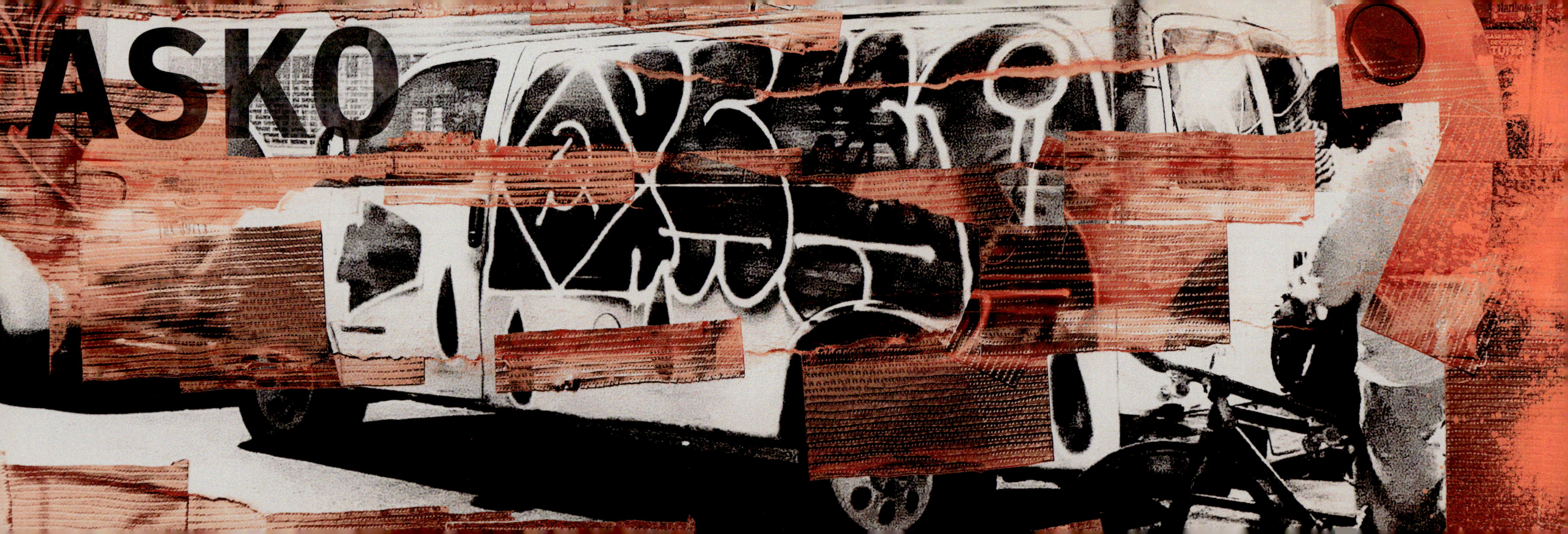

ASKO

ASKO
契丹孤狼

ASKO 是你一直以来的代号，最近你也开始尝试一些新的中文 tag，这些中文对于你来说有什么意义吗？

涂鸦是个辣妹子。一个写手对辣味的选择最能代表他的个性和品味，Tabasco 辣椒仔是我的选择，我是它爸 ASKO。我是一名来自东北的契丹林牙，身边的一位辽史学家与他的研究勾起了我对家乡和民族的一腔热血，这些中文的 tag 都是契丹的身份象征和耶律律辽国的盛世写照。

哪些写手对你的影响最大？

我喜欢和有趣并且谨慎的写手搭档，因为一起享受涂鸦很有乐趣，同时更需要彼此信任。我尤其享受和风格相似的朋友用同样的颜色搭配来分享同一个位置，这样的涂鸦创作在整个环境中看起来会更有故事性和角色感。

> **"因为除了涂鸦本身以外，许多心态和想法都更值得学习"**

谁会跟你一块画涂鸦？

我受到很多风格写手的影响，比如 TIE，STER，KLESK，ZOMBRA，OGER，AY Crew 等都曾给我过醍醐灌顶的感觉。但身边一起战斗过的同伴其实对我都有不同程度影响，因为除了涂鸦本身以外，许多心态和想法都更值得学习。身边的全能型写手一定是影响我最多的，比如纽约的 LOT29（EHC）和北京 WRECK（KTS）。

你在美国街头参与的创作与在中国境内的创作有什么不同呢？是否因为地域的变化而影响了你的涂鸦风格？

在美国，她被无数人捧上神坛，却也惨遭蹂躏。我必须要努力突破重围，重复创造偶遇机会，并站在显眼的位置，只为了让她多看我一眼，让自己能够有一瞬间脱颖而出。

在中国，她被排挤到消逝殆尽，却也无人问津。

> **"我必须要努力张开臂膀，不论风吹还是雨打，也要助她美丽绽放，只为了做她最后的稻草，让自己不会因为失去她而悔恨"**

在我们的第一辑中写手"灵丹"也曾在纽约生活与创作，并通过中文涂鸦来作为他的传播工具，在美国也由很多亚裔写手在街头创作，这种亚洲身份是否在你们创作中带给你任何特殊的灵感？

首先向我的哥哥灵丹表示赞许和支持，作为纽约华人涂鸦第一人，他对涂鸦很有一套，而且花样百出，我想涂鸦也一定很迷恋他吧。从纽约来看，我认为亚裔的写手们都挺有风格的，对于我来说，灵感不好说，但看到日本，韩国，台湾以及越南籍或裔的写手在美国对涂鸦上下其手，各显神通，着实使我有一种危机感，认为自己有必要在这个世界舞台上展示一下来自华夏契丹写手的技巧与魅力！

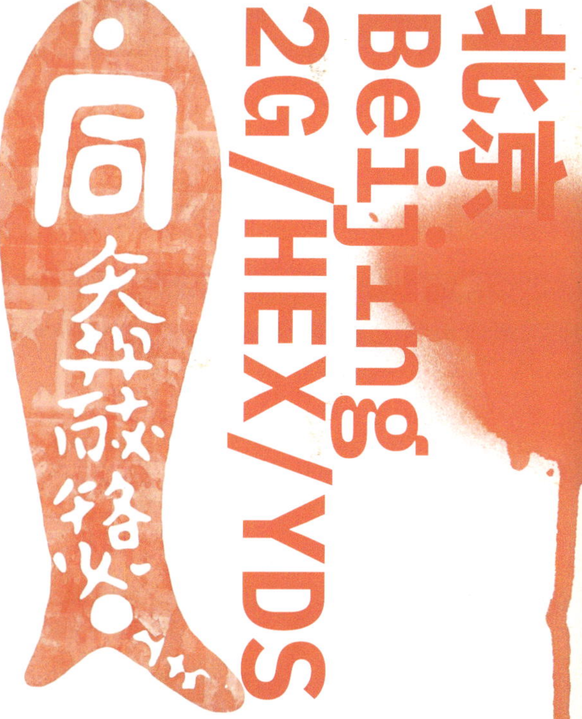

你在选择画涂鸦的地点也发生了很大改变，能不能聊一聊你最喜欢的一个位置？

我最喜欢的位置并不是那些暴力生猛的位置，而经常是最调皮捣蛋让我操心的那类。

"有一个房顶的位置我一直很想去刷大字，但不凑巧两次都还没完成就遇到了警察，倒也都侥幸逃脱了，但总共花了我三次才完成了这个位置，让我又爱又恨…"

在你看来涂鸦的存在是否是一种对社会的破坏还是一种对社会的检讨？

我个人感觉都不是，或者说都不重要。涂鸦是社会（城市）的孩子，也许受到社会的溺爱，也许受到社会的冷落，但不论如何她都以她自己的姿态存在在城市的角落，而且只要还有我们这些人懂得去欣赏和呵护她，就足够使她每一个短暂的绽放都富有意义了！而她对于社会的意义，就留给社会去体会吧。

面对当下美国居高不下的疫情，是否对你上街涂鸦造成影响？

最大的影响就是很多冠状写手（Corona Writers，在疫情期间更加活跃的写手）的出现让我感觉能写的地方少了很多……

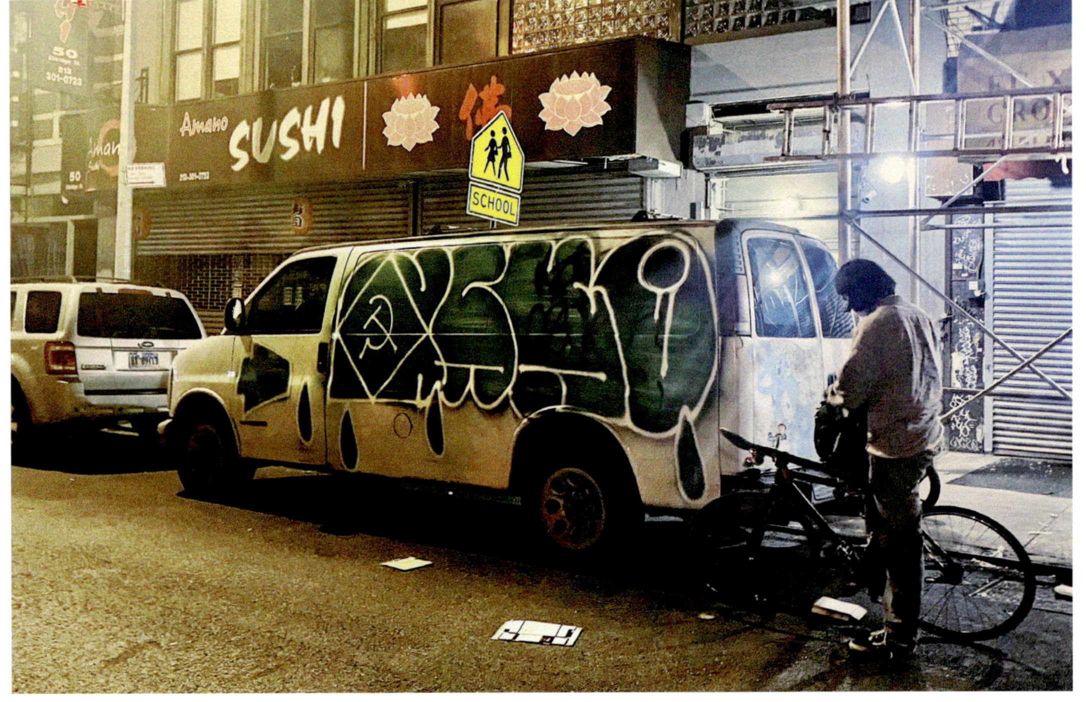

ASKO
The Khitan lone wolf

You have been tagging 'ASKO' for a while but recently, you have written some new Chinese tags. What do these new tags mean for you?

Graffiti is like a hot girl and I chose the name of a hot sauce because it represents well my idea of what a writer is 她爸 (ta bà) ASKO is my favorite tag. I'm 她爸 (literally 'her daddy')-ASKO (tabasco).

I'm a Khitan[1] writer from the north-east of China. I have a friend who is a historian who specialized in the Liao dynasty[2] and his studies have triggered my interest in my hometown's history and lineage. These Chinese tags are the status symbol of a Khitan and portrayal of the prosperity of the Liao Dynasty.

Who are your partners in crime?

I prefer partners that are funny and cautious in missions. It is fun to paint together but at the same time, it requires mutual trust. I especially like sharing the good spots with friends that have a similar style and coordinating the colors with them. In this way, the works tell a story and they reflect our personalities.

"Except for Graffiti itself, attitude and mentality are much more valuable to me"

Which are the writers that influenced you the most?

I was influenced by many writers with fresh styles, such as TIE, STER, KLESK, ZOMBRA, OGER, AY Crew, etc. They all amaze me. As a matter of fact, each one of the writers that I have gone on a mission with has, more or less, affected me as a writer, and as a human being. Except for Graffiti itself, attitude and mentality are much more valuable to me. The writers around me that have definitely influenced me the most are LOT29 (EHC) from NYC and Wreck (KTS) from Beijing.

What's the difference between your graffiti-life in the US and China? How your work has been influenced by these two different contexts?

In the United States, graffiti is held up to the altar by many but it has also been badly ravaged. I have to fight hard to stand out among many, keep creating opportunities for encounters, and get-up onto striking spots. Only in this way graffiti get to give me a glance and I could stand out for a moment.

In China, graffiti are excluded and almost vanished, and still, no one will care about it. I had to try my best to embrace it, no matter the wind or the rain blows, I helped graffiti here to bloom in its own way.

"Even if this is its last breath I would never accept that graffiti will die"

In our first issue, also 灵丹 (EXAS) often used his Chinese tag when bombing around New York and the US, and nowadays, on the streets of the United States, there are many other talented Asian writers. Did your Asian identity give you any special inspiration for your work?

First thing first, I want to give a big shot out to my man EXAS, as the first Chinese who bombed New York City. He really got skills and he is full of tricks. Graffiti and EXAS is a story of mutual love.

Talking about New York City, I feel like many Asian writers got fresh styles. I'm not sure about inspiration, but seeing that Japanese, Korean, Taiwanese, and Vietnamese writers were bombing hard with their own style on this world stage, really pushed me to embrace my personality and my style as a Khitan writer on this graffiti frontline.

During your career, you have dedicated yourself to many different surfaces. Can you tell us something about your favorite kind of actions?

My favorite spots are never the ones where you need to go hard and sick. I prefer the ones that require some smart tactics.

For a while, I wanted to hit this roof spot with a roller-brush piece.

"Unfortunately, I ran into cops twice and I wasn't even able to finish it. Luckily enough, I got away both times. I had to come back three times to close that piece"

I love and hate this kind of stuff..."

In your opinion, graffiti is simply a form of vandalism or it has also deeper implications?

I feel it's not so important to label graffiti. Graffiti is the child of the city and maybe the city loves it, or maybe it doesn't care about it. Either way, Graffiti lives in every corner of the streets, and —as long as there are people like us that appreciate and care for it— any manifestation of good graffiti, no matter how short it is, will be cherished as something gorgeous and meaningful. As for its significance to society, I leave to society their judgment.

How the epidemic in the United States has affected your work as a writer?

The biggest issue was the 'Corona Writers'[3] who started to bomb the streets even harder, and that left me with even less space to paint.

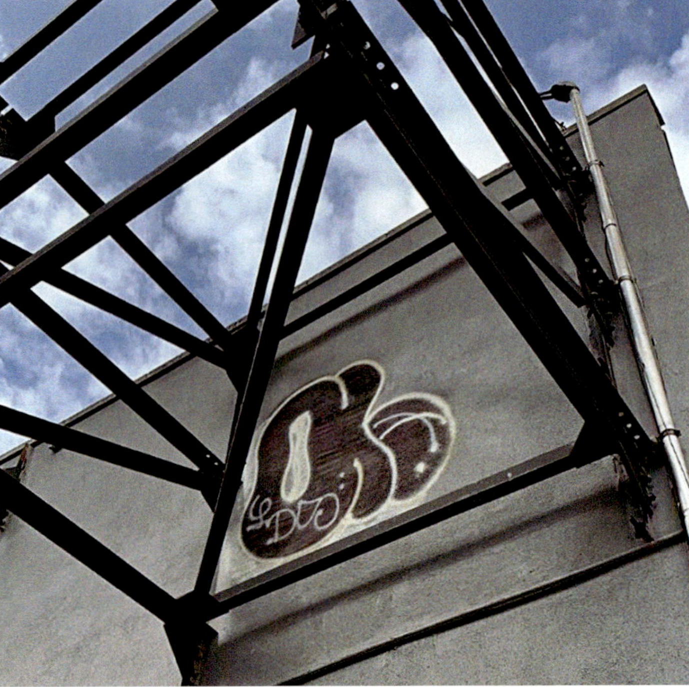

1. The Khitan people (契丹; *Qidan*) were a Para-Mongolic nomadic people from Northeast Asia who, from the 4th century, inhabited an area corresponding to parts of modern Mongolia, Northeast China, and the Russian Far East.

2. The Liao dynasty, also known as the Khitan (*Qidan*) State was an empire and imperial dynasty in East Asia that ruled from 916 to 1125 AD over present-day Northern and Northeast China, Mongolia, and portions of the Russian Far East and North Korea.

3. Graffiti writers who have been more active during the pandemic period.

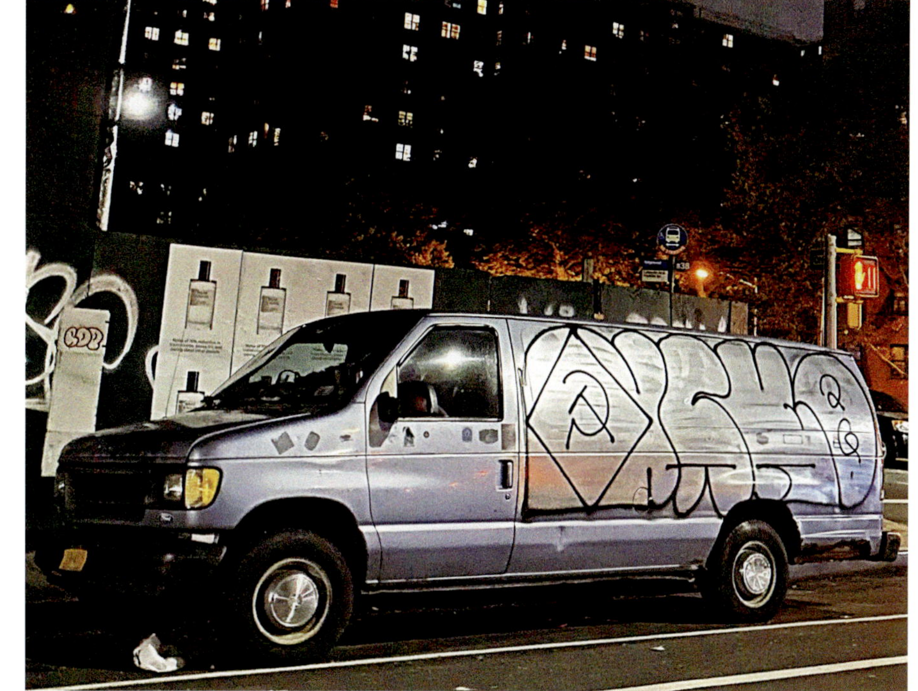
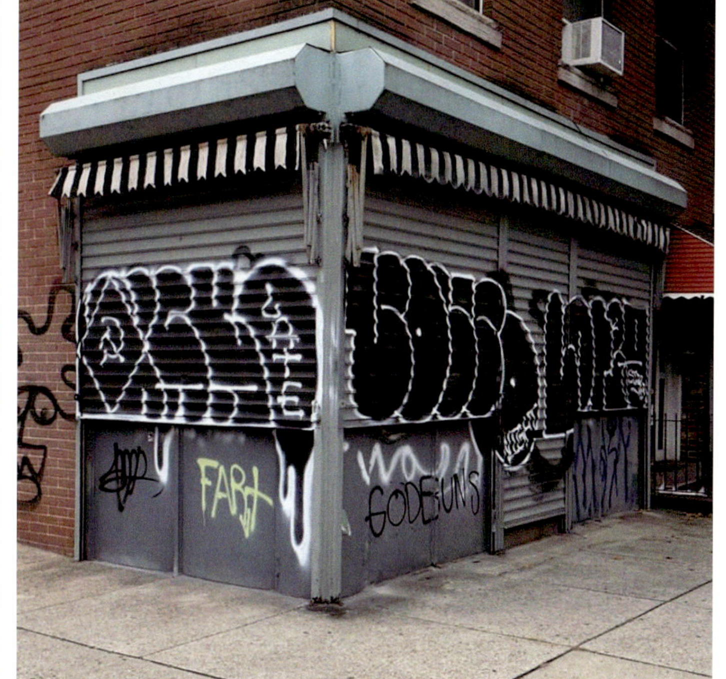
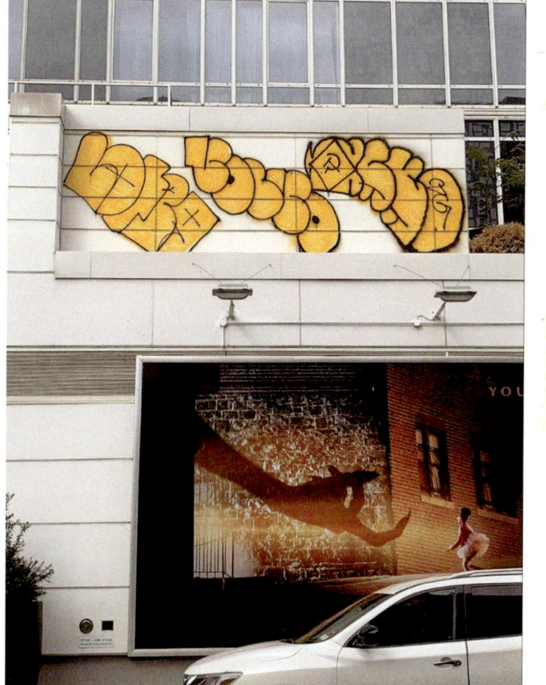

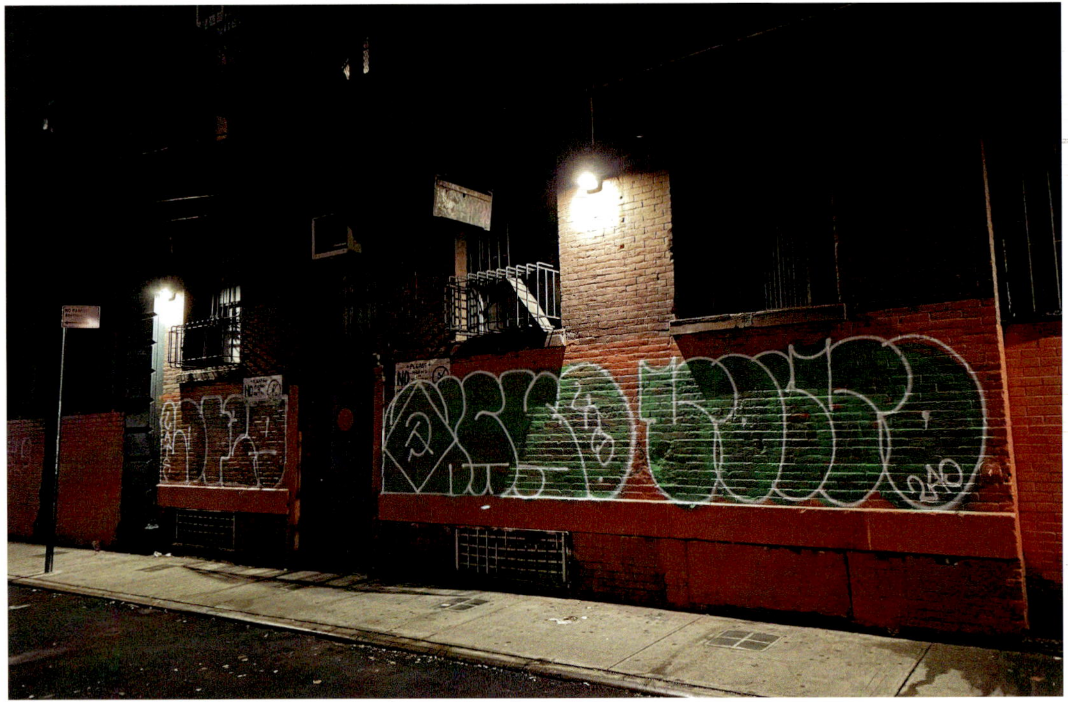
240

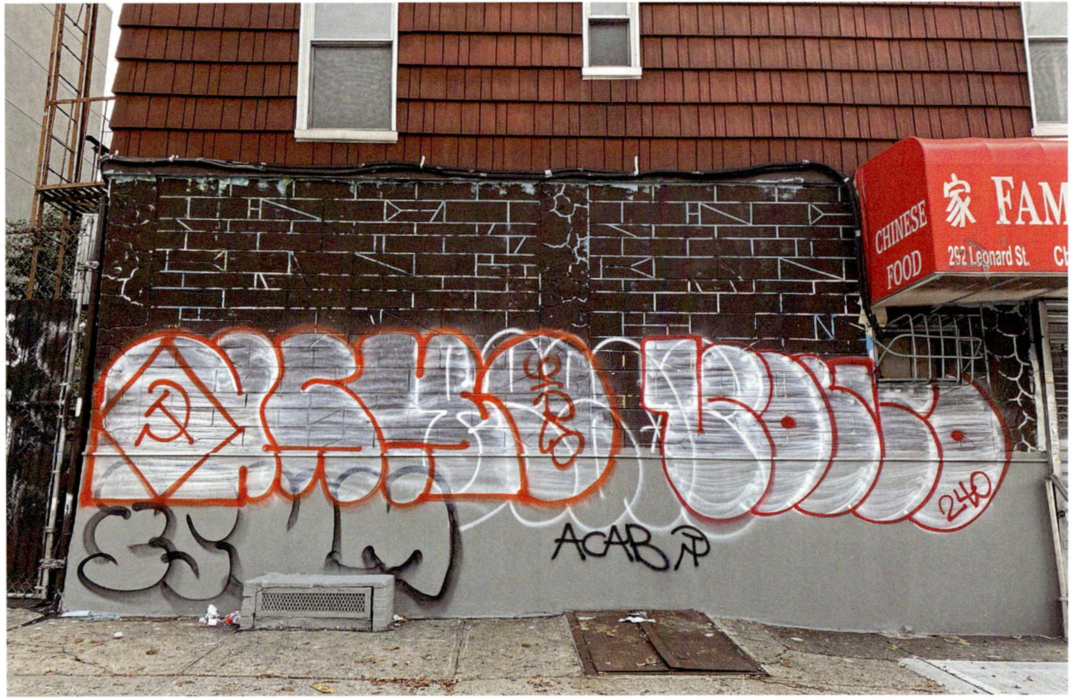
CHINESE FOOD
家 FAM
292 Leonard St.
ACAB
240

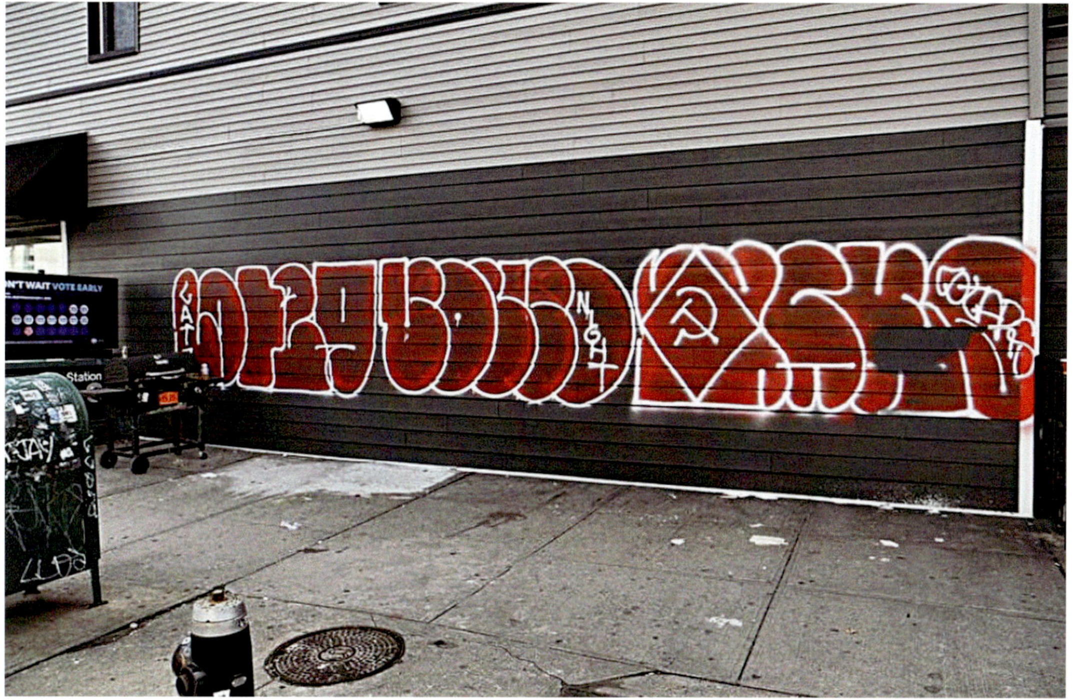
N'T WAIT VOTE EARLY
Station

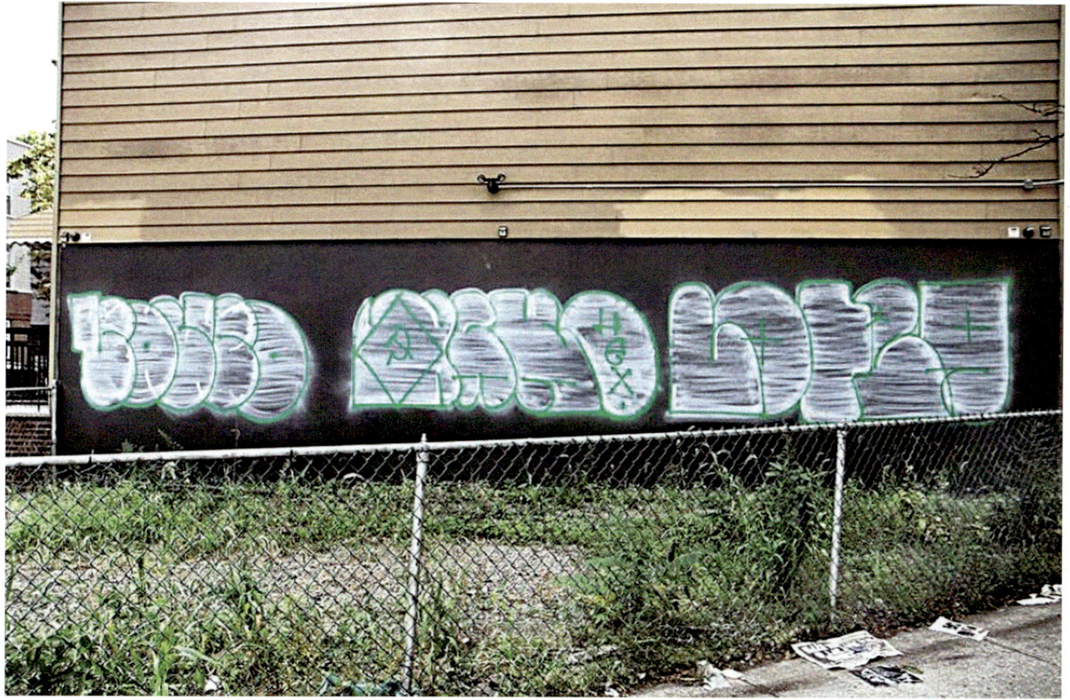

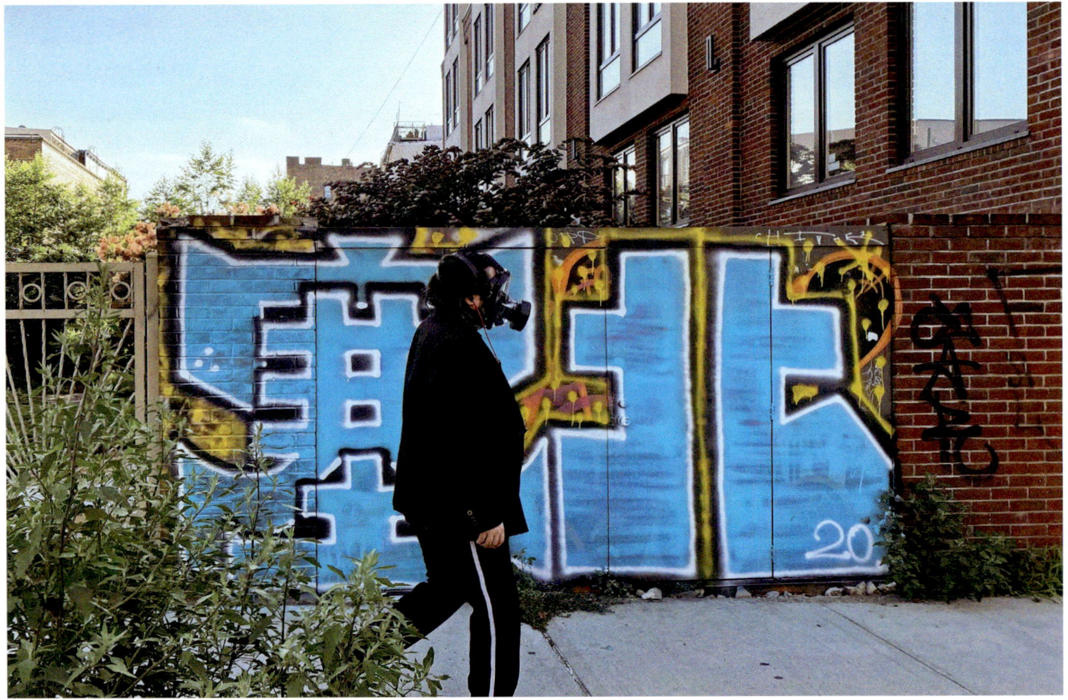

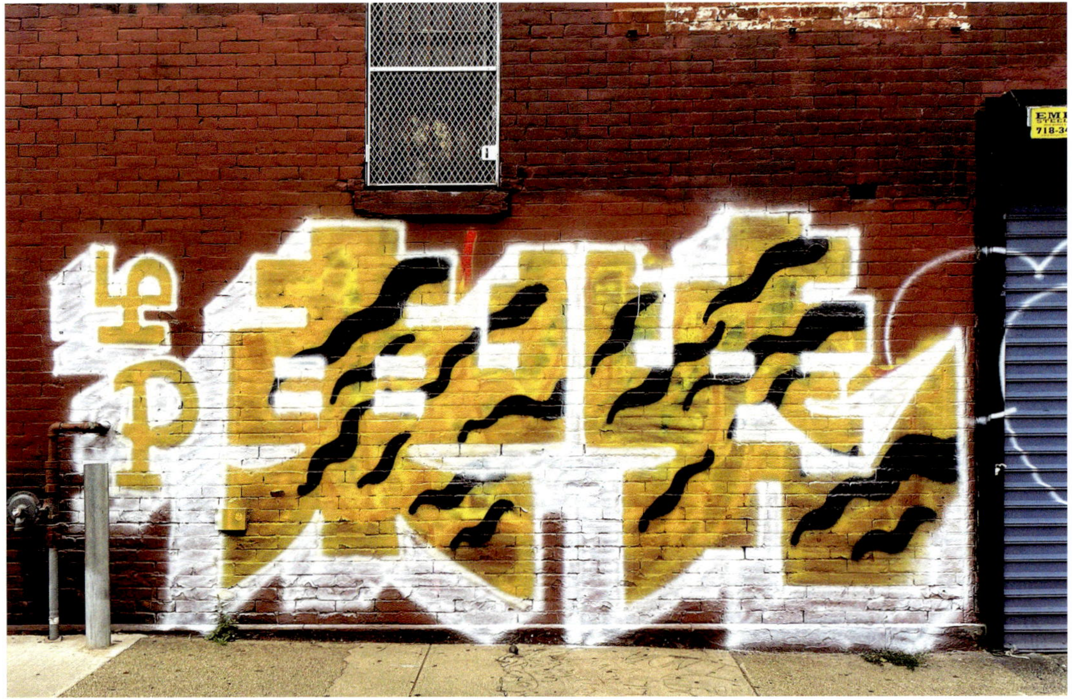

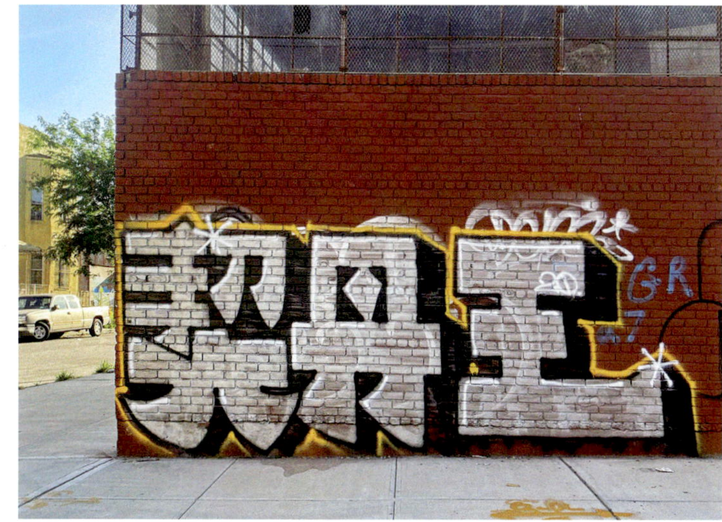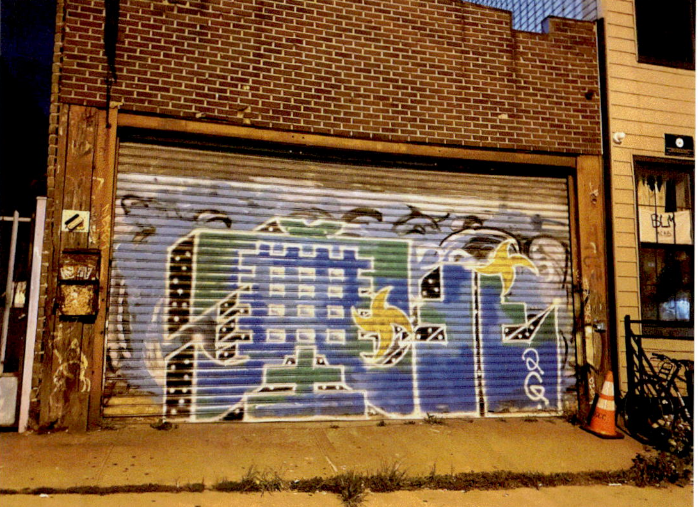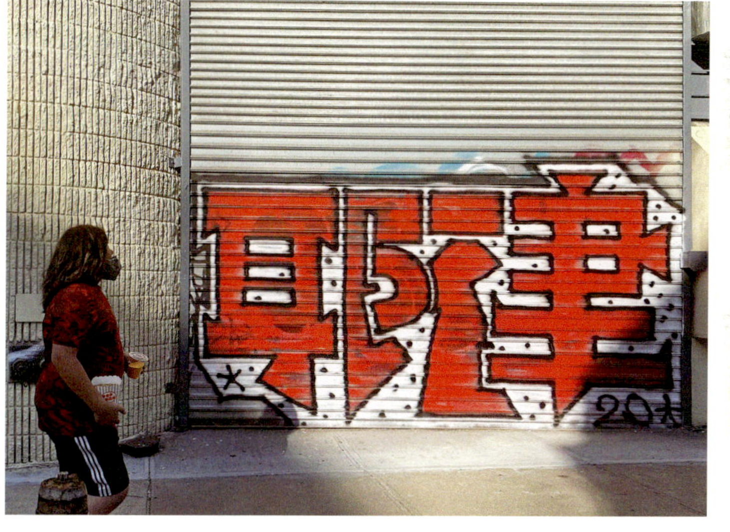

同样大小的中文涂鸦要比英文费时费力，很难像T-up一样迅速地复制，却更需要耐心和思考，而过程中与环境的羁绊也更难忘些。

Pieces in Chinese are more time-consuming and labor-intensive than their English counterpart. It is difficult to do a quick throw-up. It requires more patience and thinking, and the connection with the surroundings is deeper.

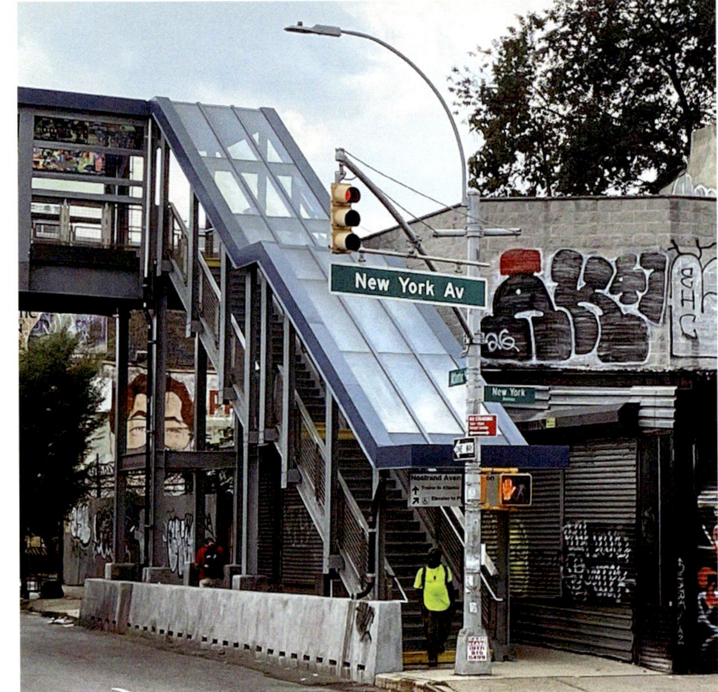
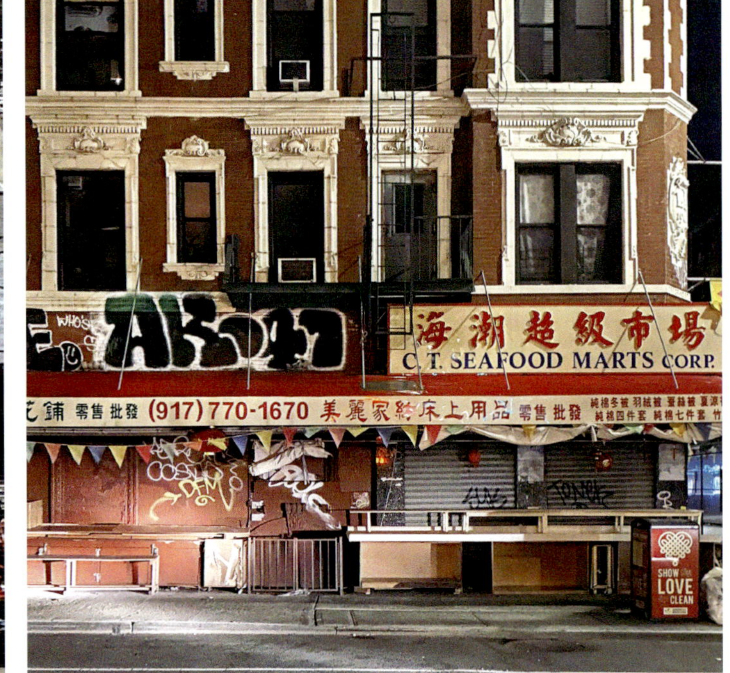
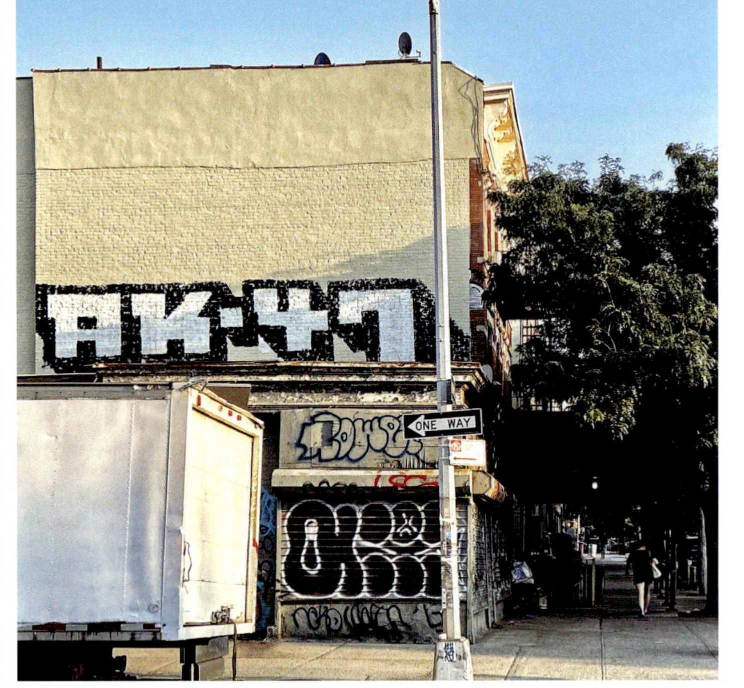

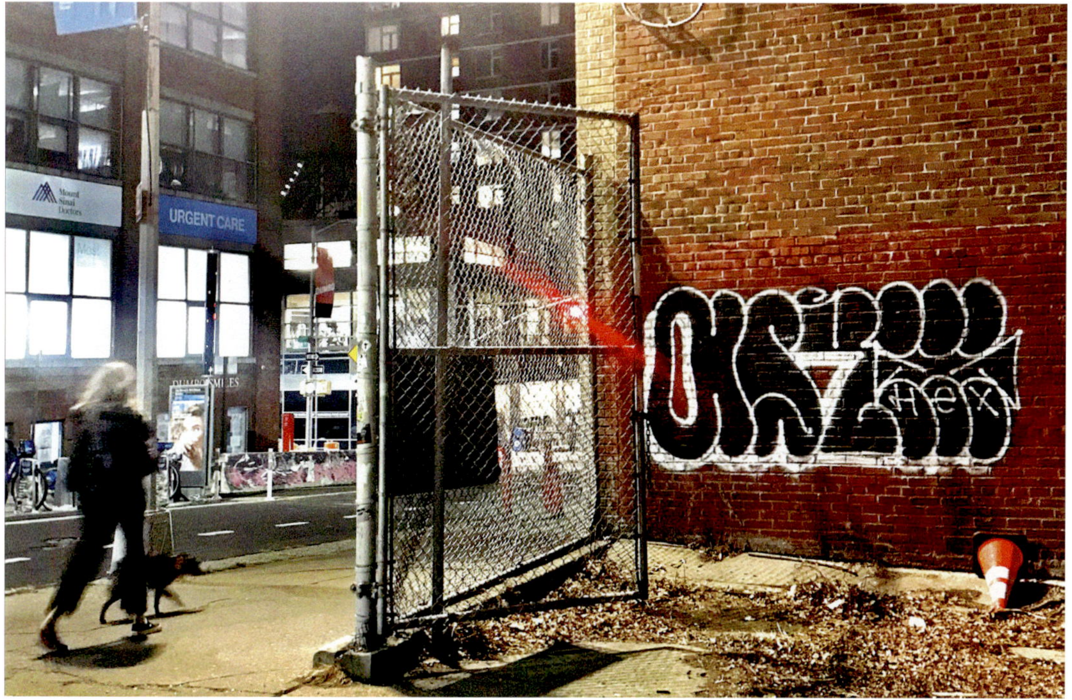

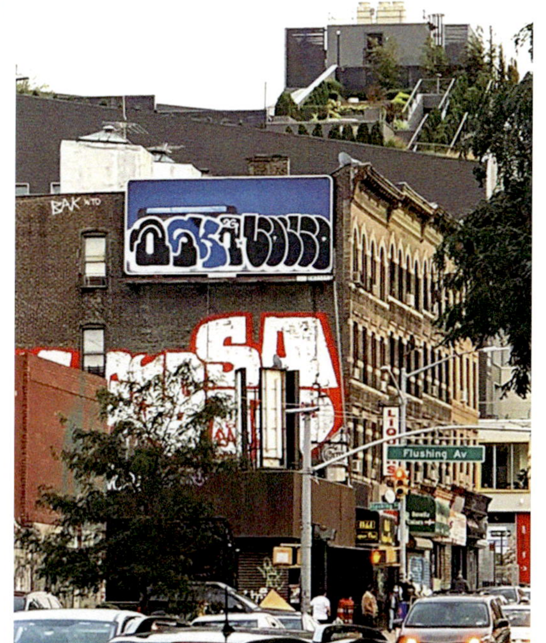
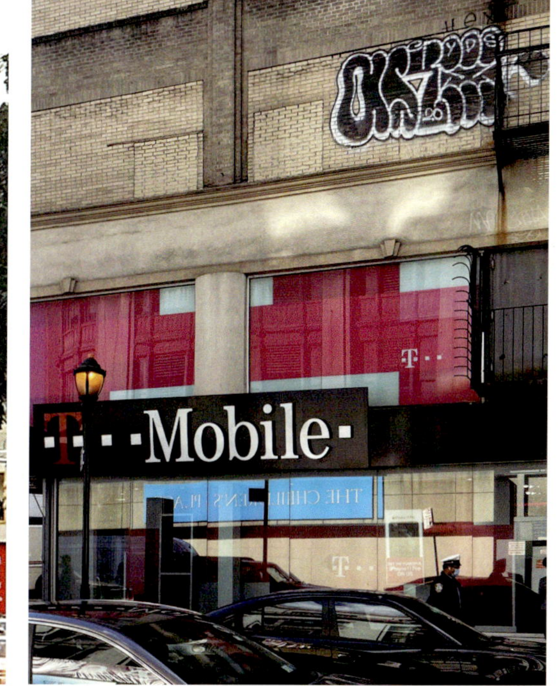

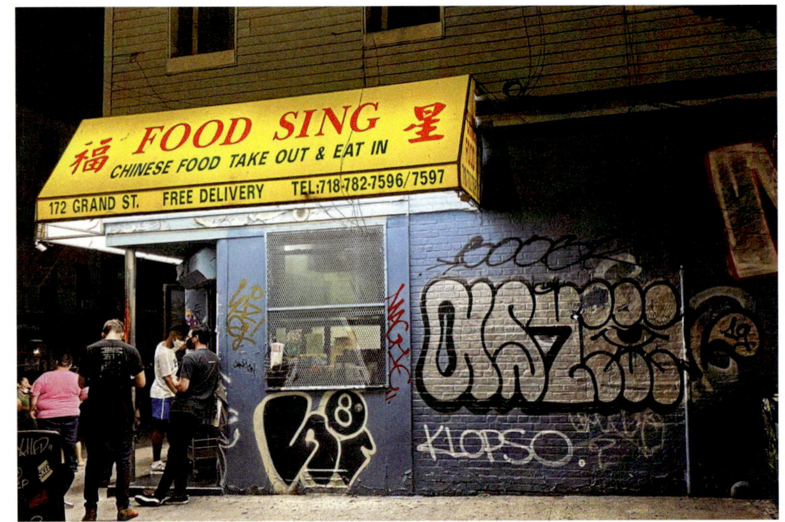
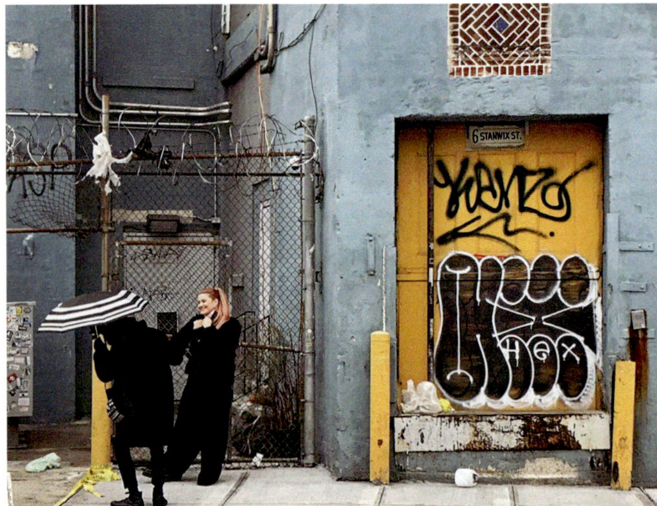
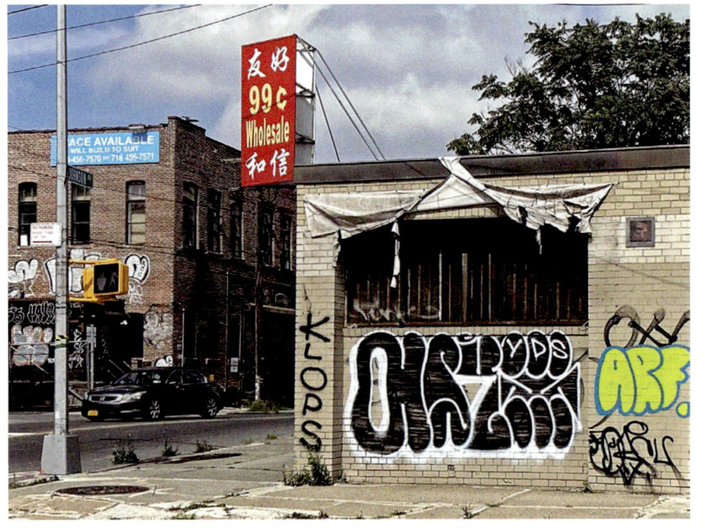

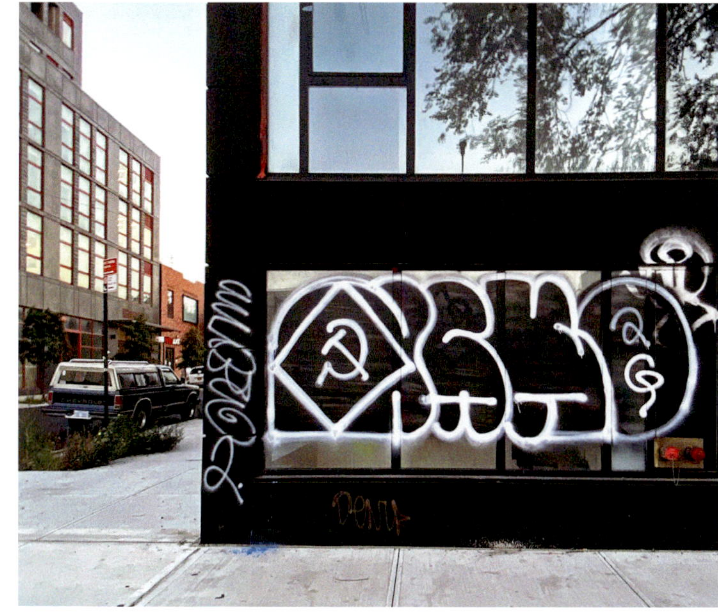
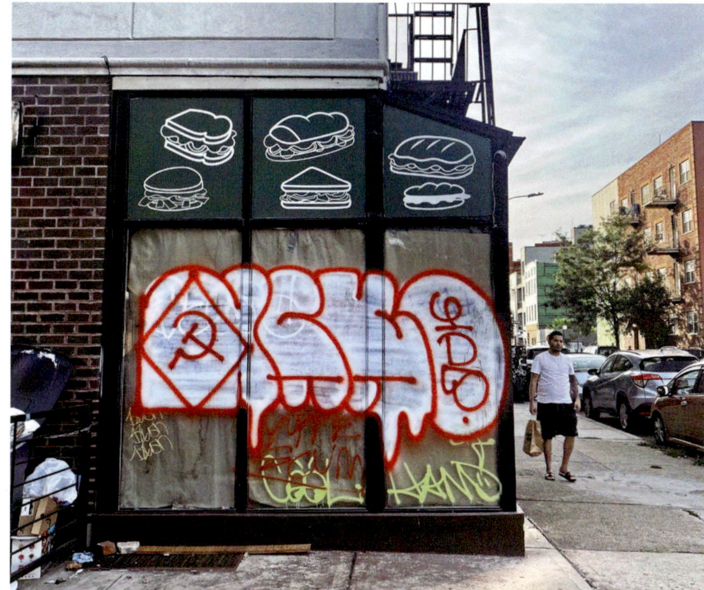
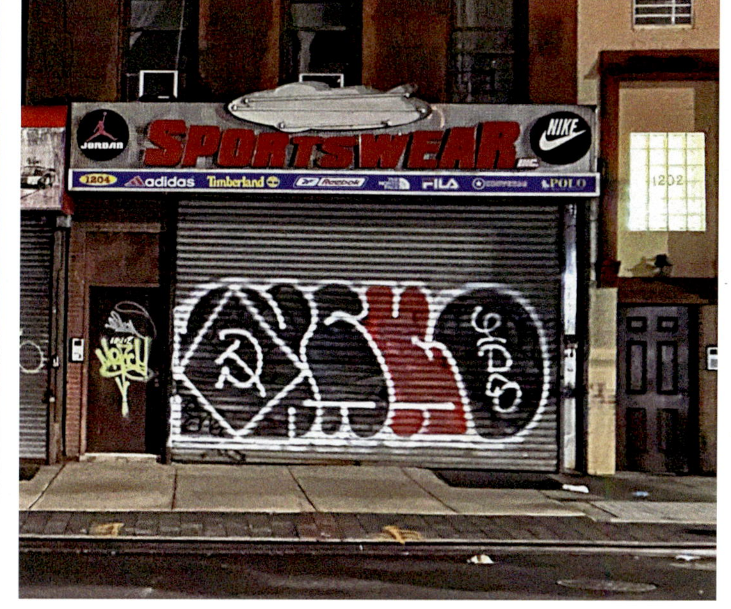
SPORTSWEAR
JORDAN
NIKE
1204
adidas
Timberland
Reebok
FILA
POLO
1202

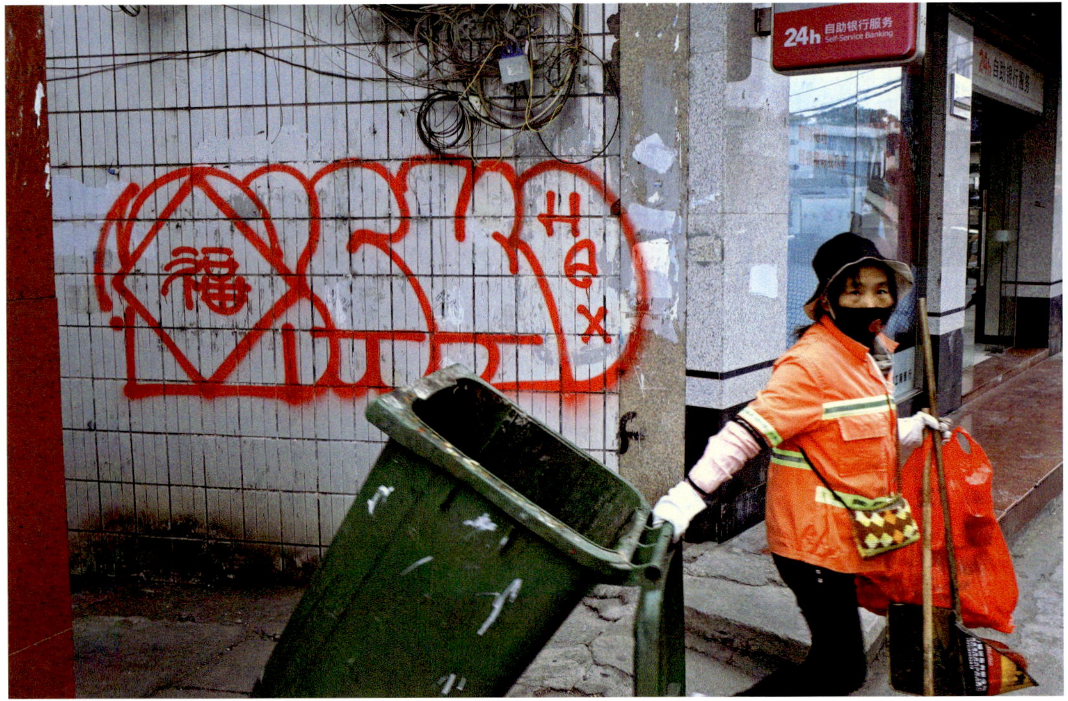
24h 自助银行服务
Self-Service Banking

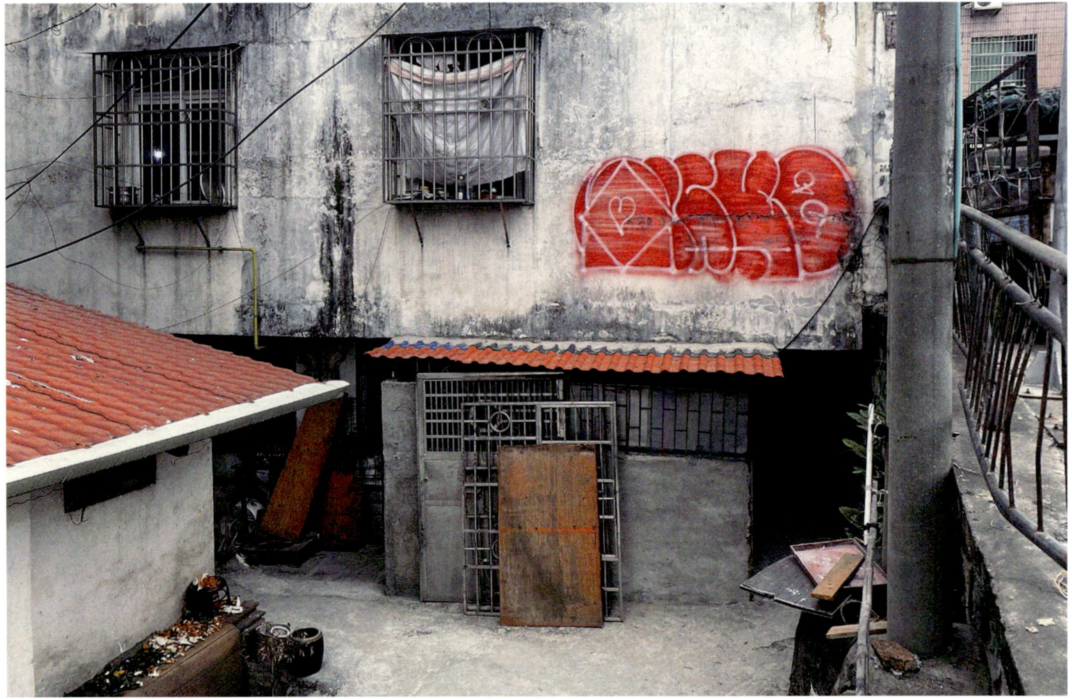

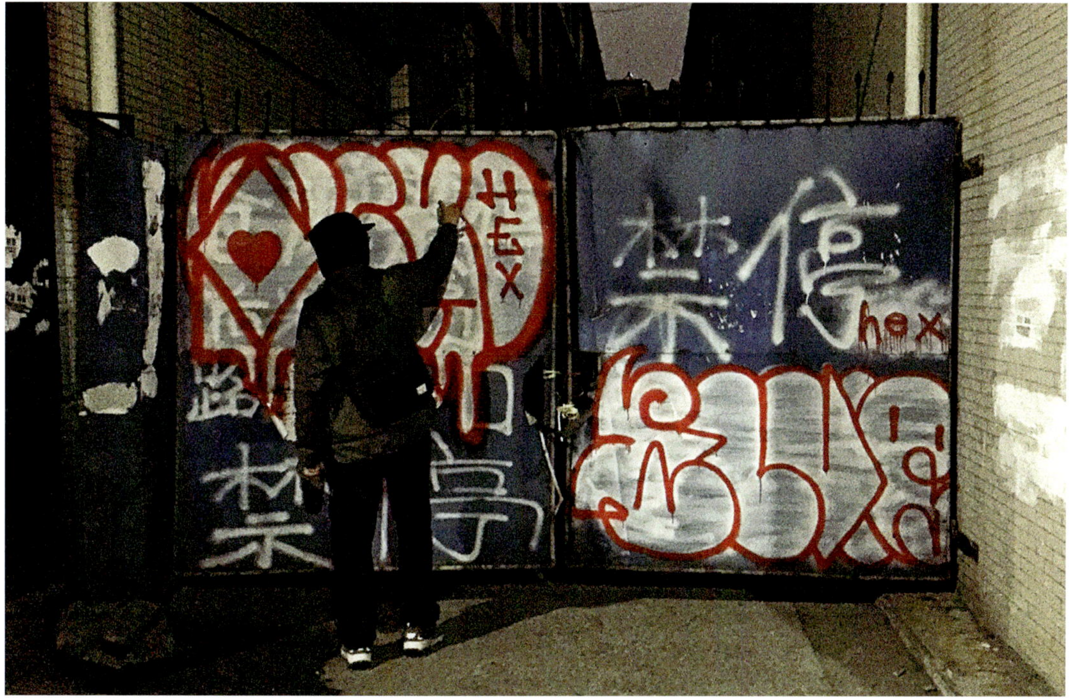
禁停
hex

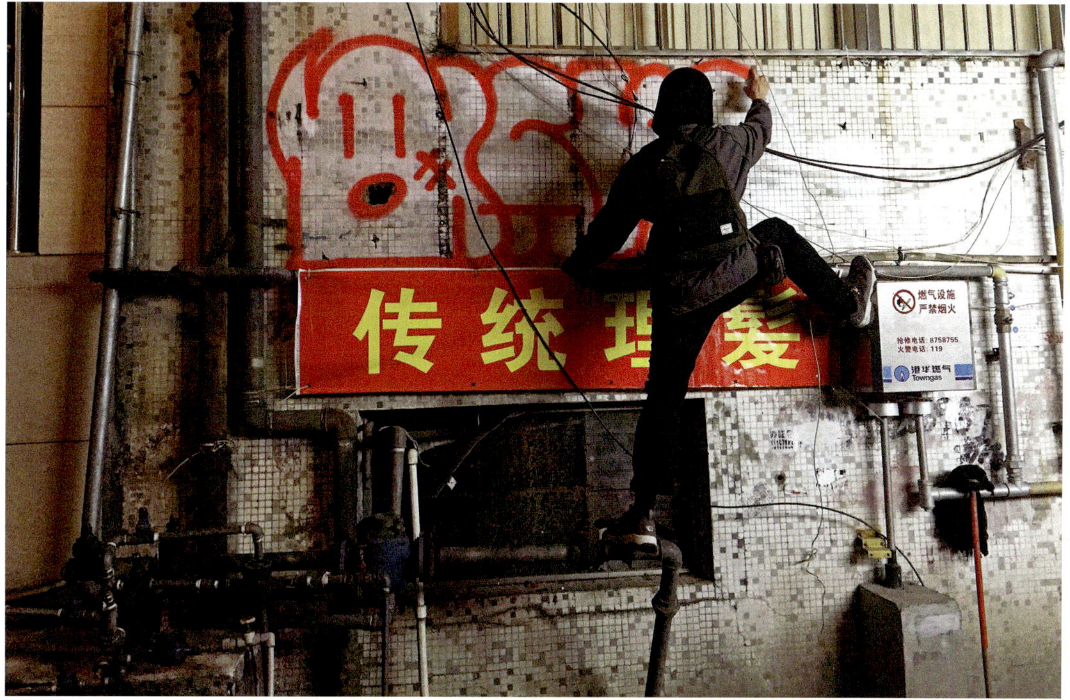
传统
燃气设施
严禁烟火
Towngas

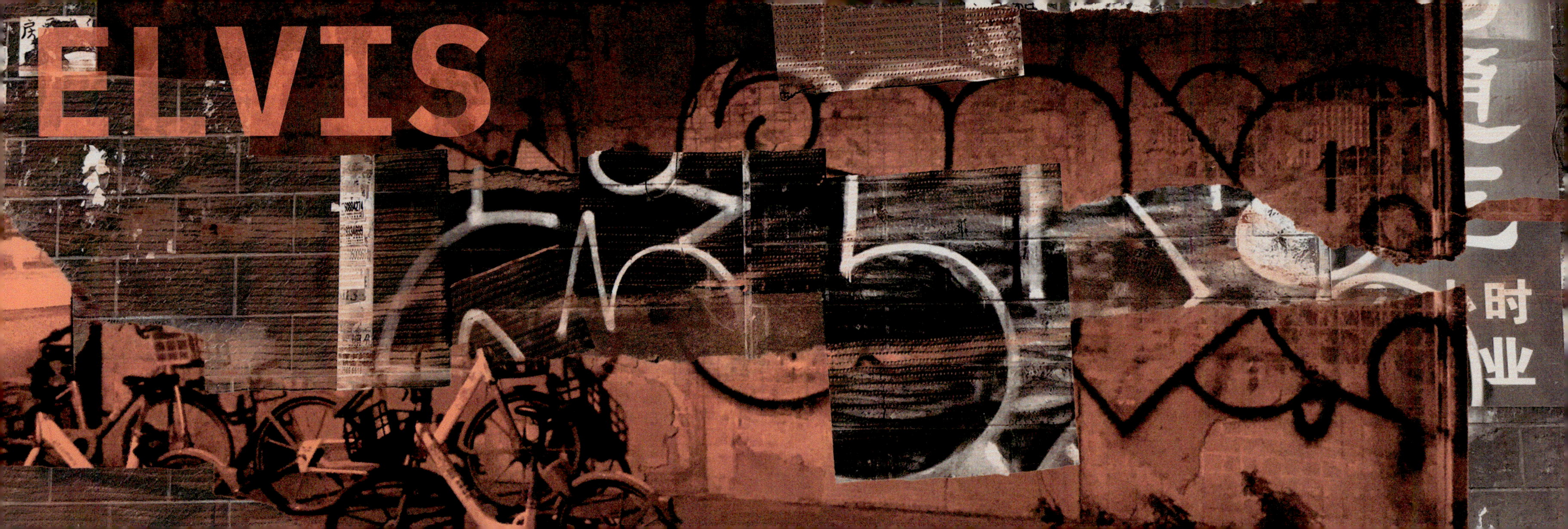
ELVIS

ELVIS
不退却的破坏

ELVIS 与"猫王"让我们直接联想到的是美国歌星，因为地理位置的关系，广州在中国的地图上也是最早接触流行文化的一座城市，在中西文化的碰撞下，是否对你的涂鸦生涯产生影响？

影响肯定有，但他是潜在的。

"怎么开始的也没关系了，重要的是我还没停止，也不会停止"

哪些写手对你的影响最大？

对我影响最大的写手无疑是旧金山的 TIE（RIP）；他的精神至今仍然指引着我。喜欢和志同道合的写手一块画涂鸦。涂鸦的氛围对我影响其实不大。除非有一条街道是充满了臭名昭著的写手的名字，那么我会更加的兴奋。

广州与香港的交流频繁吗？

我常去香港画涂鸦，当地有一些非常不错的写手，他们对待涂鸦非常认真谨慎。

中国南方不得不提的一只团队就是"GB"（鸽帮），你们专注在街头非法涂鸦的同时，也经常举办一些恶搞聚会，能不能聊一聊你们的团队趣事？

GB 集非法涂鸦和地下音乐于一身，当然还有恶趣味的娱乐节目。我们的成员有地下写手，纹身师、摄影师、滑手、音乐制作人、两爬饲育者、金融学教授等等各方面的人才。因此，一场属于多元文化的化学反应就此产生。最重要的是，成员们大多行踪诡秘，所以互相之间放鸽子的几率很大，当你看到 GB 的活动海报时，你就要小心了。

你现在也开始尝试很多与甲骨文有关的风格，这是否对你的涂鸦风格有所影响，是否有哪张字帖对你影响深刻？我们知道你同时也是一位纹身师，中国文化与纹身是如何在你身上发生质变的呢？

中国的书法对我的汉字涂鸦影响很大，法帖是唐朝才开始出现，但我着迷于商朝至晋朝的碑刻拓片，每一块碑，每一块摩崖石刻的风格都各不相同，千姿百态。其中对我影响最大的分别是《杨淮表记》《散氏盘》《广武将军碑》，那种歪扭错动的结字和艰涩的线性就是从这里面学习而来的。中华文化神秘而深远，其中很多天真稚拙的民间艺术作品正是纹身图案很好的采样来源，这两者的古拙味深深吸引着我，我也尽力地表现出他们这种共同的特性。

你的 tup 出现在中国很多城市，能不能说一说哪座城市是你最喜欢的？当你在旅行的时候是否有什么特殊的经历可以与我们分享？

哈哈，没有最喜欢，只有更喜欢，在路上的感觉永远是最好的。最近的一次特殊经历就是跟朋友在长沙晚上画完东西之后去和毛的巨型石雕一起 Chilllllll～

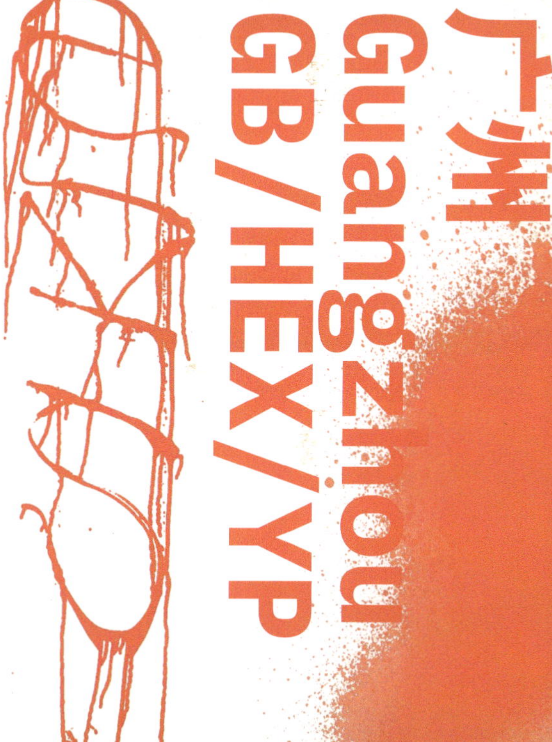

中国城市更新的速度一直很快，而从你的照片里我们也可以看到中国曾经有很多不同的城市肌理，关于重复被刷掉的墙面，涂鸦是否让你重塑这座城市，或者他是你很个人化的产物？

我对比起城市实在是太渺小，谈不上重塑，城市让涂鸦不断地消失，而我能做的只有让它不断地出现，应该说是城市在重塑我的涂鸦。

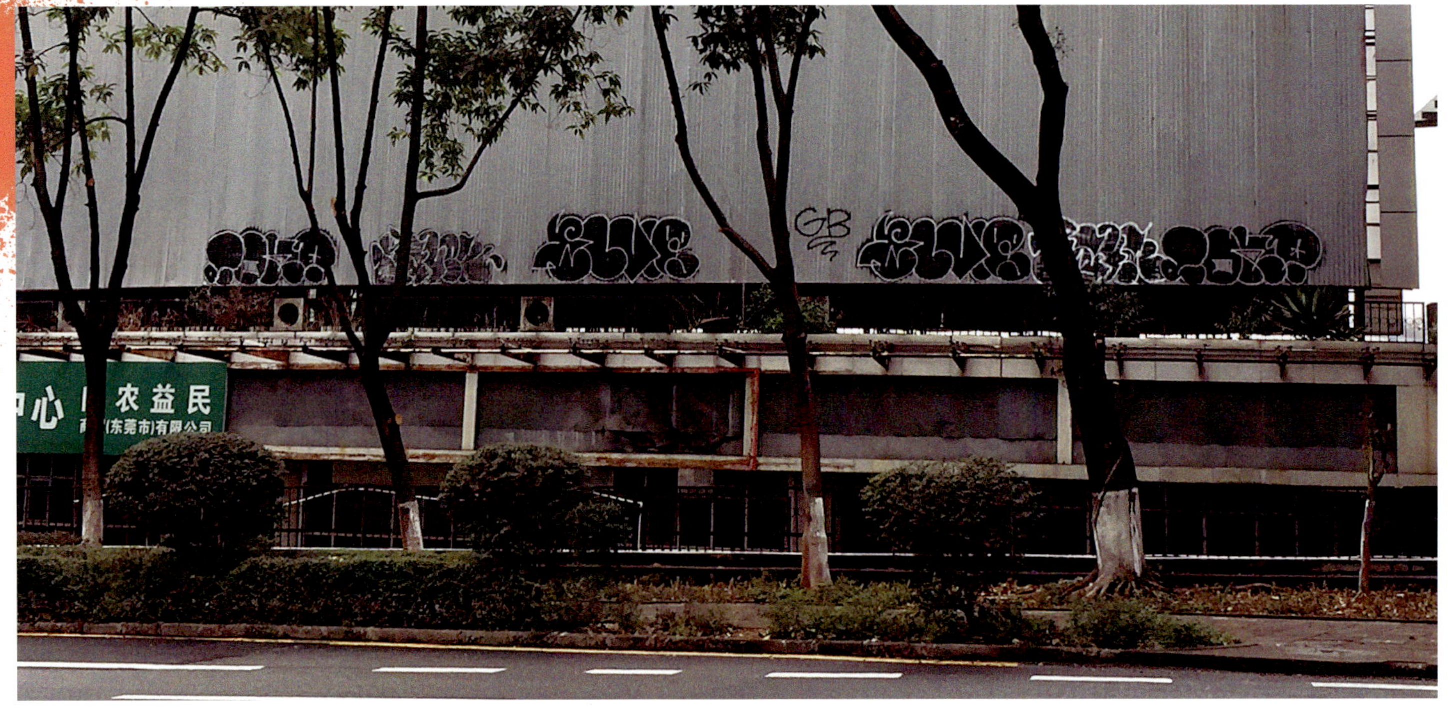

ELVIS
The unabated vandal

When you mention ELVIS a.k.a. 猫王 (mao wáng, The Hillbilly Cat), you also think about the American rockstar. Guangzhou (ELVIS' province) is also the first city that has been in contact with the American pop culture. Does the collision of Chinese and Western culture affected your work?

I have been influenced by western culture in some way, but it is quite subtle.

"For me, it doesn't matter where graffiti comes from, what matters is that I haven't stopped, and I never will"

Which are the writers that influenced you the most?

The writer that influenced me the most is definitely TIE (RIP) from San Francisco. His spirit still guides me all the time.

I also enjoy painting with writers that share a similar mindset but I don't really care about the graffiti scene. Unless I see a street that is covered with notorious tags, in that case, I get very excited.

Are the Guangzhou and Hong Kong scene connected in some way?

I paint a lot in Hong Kong. There are many amazing local writers there and they handle graffiti very seriously and with caution.

There is one crew that we have to mention when we talk about the South of China: GB (*Ge bang*, Pigeon Gang). GB focuses mainly on illegal graffiti, but you also organize parties pretty often. Can you tell us something more?

GB is a mixed crew about graffiti, underground music, as well as kuso[1] parties. Our members include writers, tattoo artists, photographers, skaters, music producers, breeders, finance professors, and so on. GB is also a multicultural chemical reaction. The most important thing is that our members are low profile and never act under the sun. There's a good possibility that they will never show up so be careful when you see a GB's poster.

You have been experimenting a lot with 甲骨文 (*Jiaguwén*, oracle bone scripts) related styles. How did this ancient script affect your graffiti? Which calligraphy books have influenced you the most? We know that you also a tattooer, how did Chinese culture and tattoos are connected in your work?

Traditional calligraphy has a deep influence on my Chinese-graffiti. 法帖 (*Fatiè*)[2] began to appear only during the Tang Dynasty but I'm more obsessed with the inscriptions from the Shang and Jin Dynasty[3]. Every inscription, every carved character has a different style. The books that influenced me the most are 杨淮表记 (*Yánghuáibiao jì*, The Record of Yang Huai), 散氏盘 (*sàn shì pán*, Sanshi Disk), and 广武将军碑 (*guang wu jiàng jun bei*, Guangwu General Monument). All my twisted knots and obscure lines come from this kind of stuff. Chinese culture is deep and mysterious.

Many of the naive folk-art works are also a good source of inspiration for tattoo design. The ancient allure of these two aspects of the Chinese culture really fascinates me, and I try my best to show this link through my works.

Your tag is up in many different places around China, which is your favorite city? Can you share with us some special experiences you had during your graffiti-trips?

Haha, I don't have a favorite city, I like a few but to be on-the-road gives you always good vibes. The best, recent experience I had has been chilling under a giant statue of Mao after a night painting with my homies in Changsha.

"In the city, graffiti vanishes constantly, and all I can do against it is to paint constantly"

Gentrification in China has been very fast and from your photos, we can see that China used to have many more different textures. Do you think that your work reshaped the city? Or your pieces are something rather personal?

I'm way too small to talk about 'reshaping' when compared to the city. In the city, graffiti vanishes constantly, and all I can do against it is to paint constantly. It's more like the city is shaping my graffiti.

1. *Kuso* is a term used in East Asia that emerged from the internet and describes all types of parody, usually of kitsch cultural products. In Japanese, *kuso* (糞, くそ) means "fuck", "shit" or "bullshit". It is also used to describe outrageous matters and objects of poor quality.

2. 甲骨文 (Jiaguwén, oracle bone scripts) was the form of Chinese characters used on oracle bones—animal bones or turtle plastrons used in pyromantic divination—in the late 2nd millennium BC and it is the earliest known form of Chinese writing.

3. 法帖 (*Fatiè*): book containing examples of calligraphic styles; It is usually meant to be used as a reference while practicing calligraphy.

4. A historical period that goes from the 2nd millenium BC to the 420 AD.

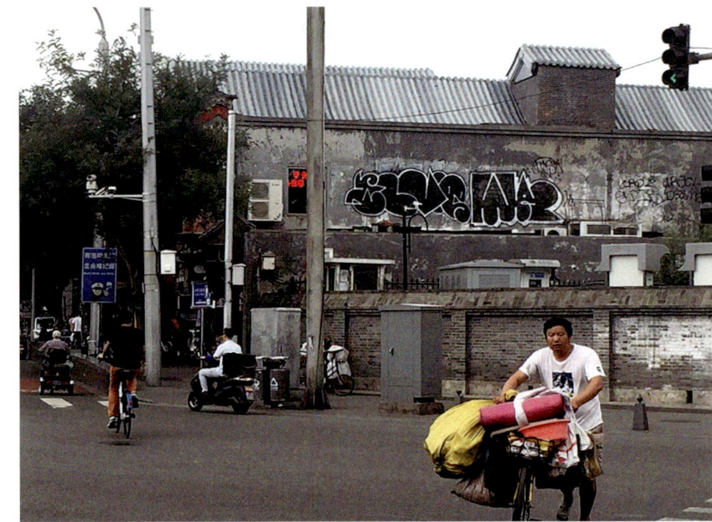

跟 WRECK 在一块的时候，总能遇到刺激惊险的位置，但他都游刃有余，他 hardcore 的精神能够占领街上每一个角落。

The spots that I painted with WRECK were cool and dangerous, but he knew how to handle them. WRECK's hardcore spirit can take over every corner of the street.

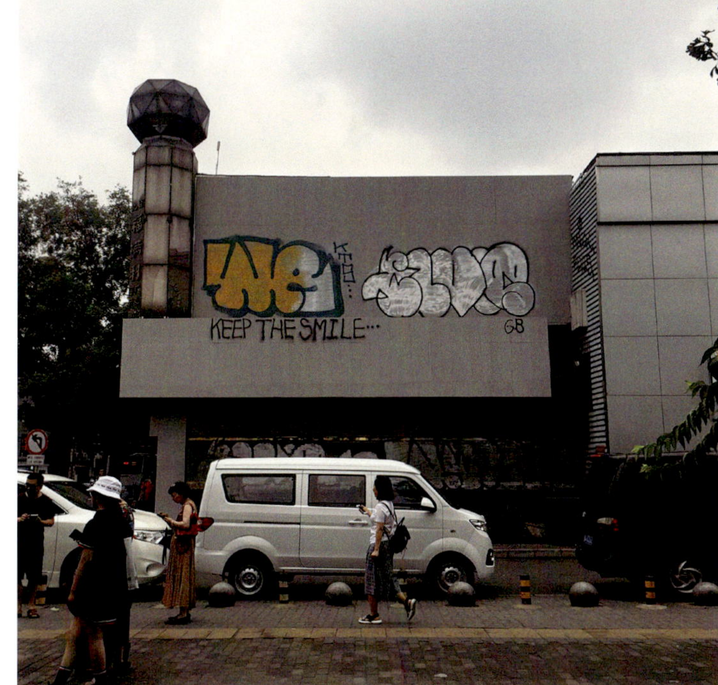

KEEP THE SMILE...
68

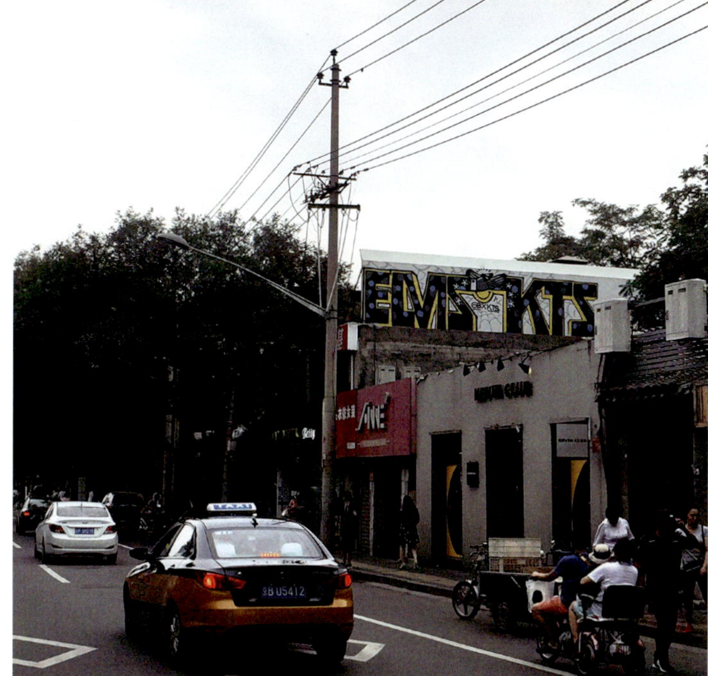

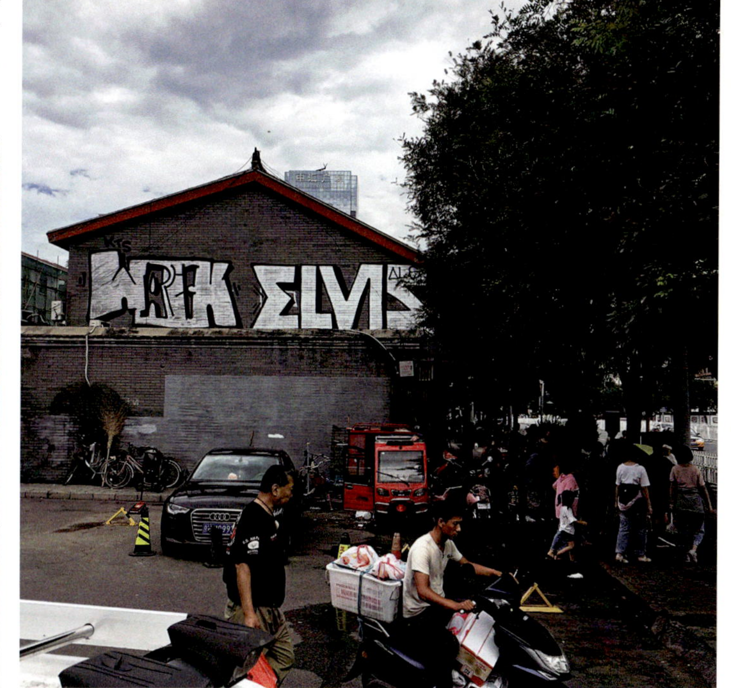

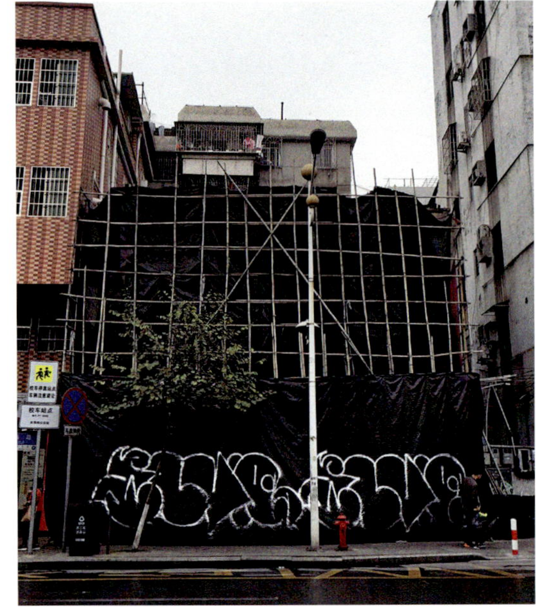
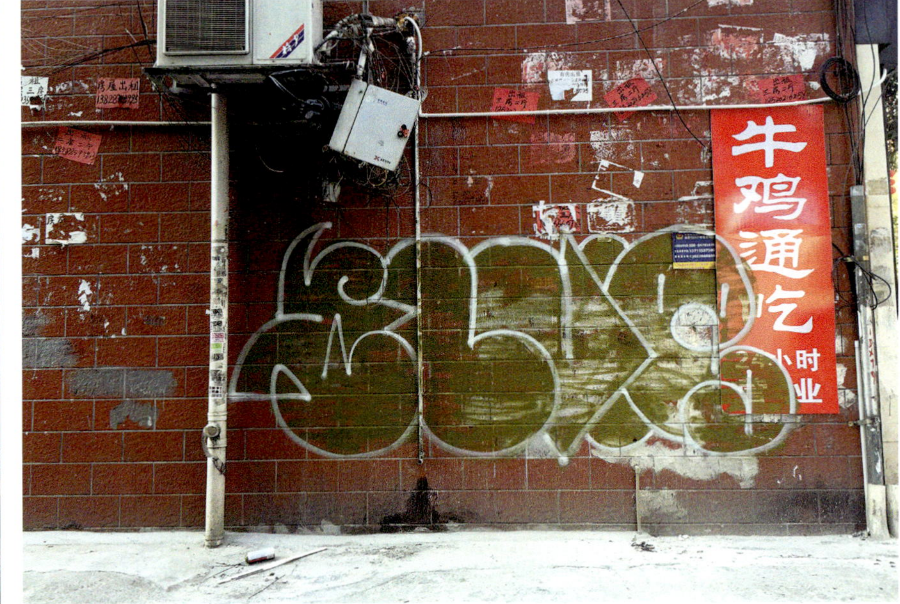
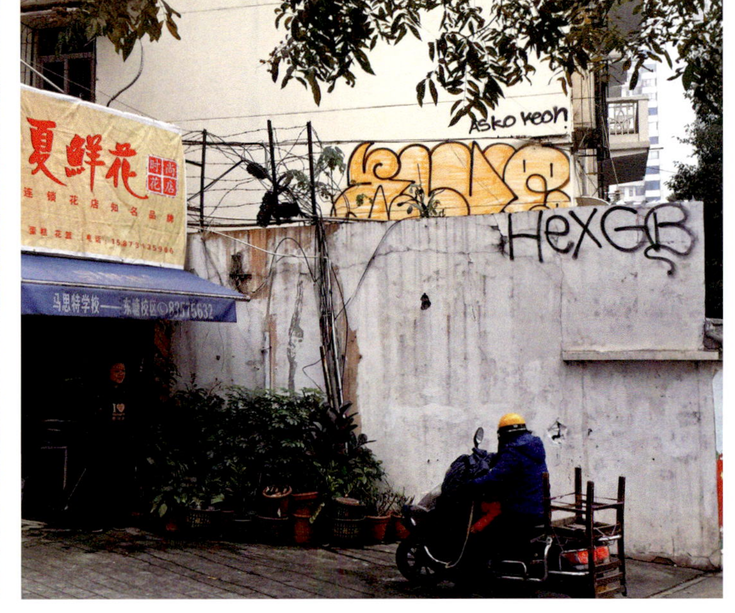

牛鸡通吃
小时营业
夏鲜花
ASKO keon
HeXGB

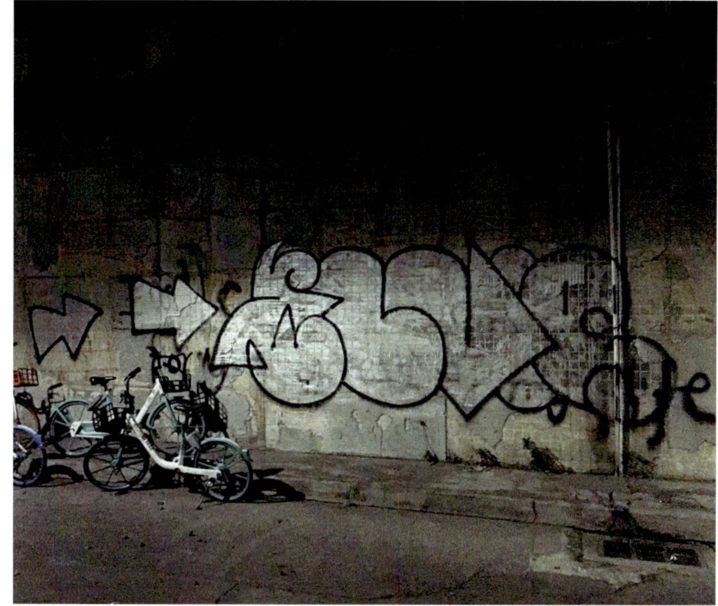
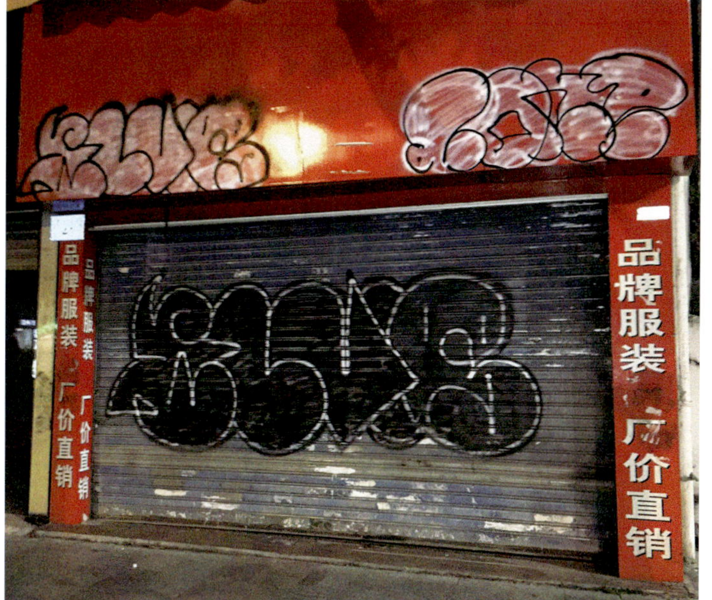

品牌
服装
厂价
直销
品牌服装 厂价直销

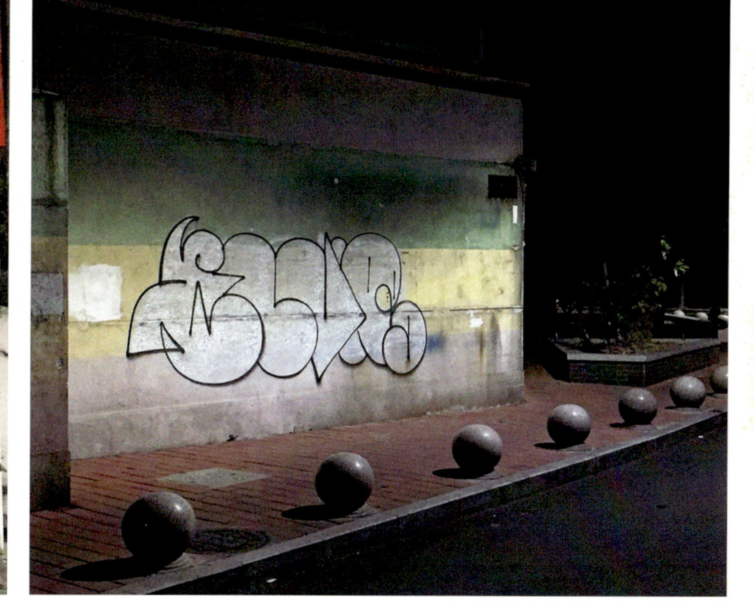

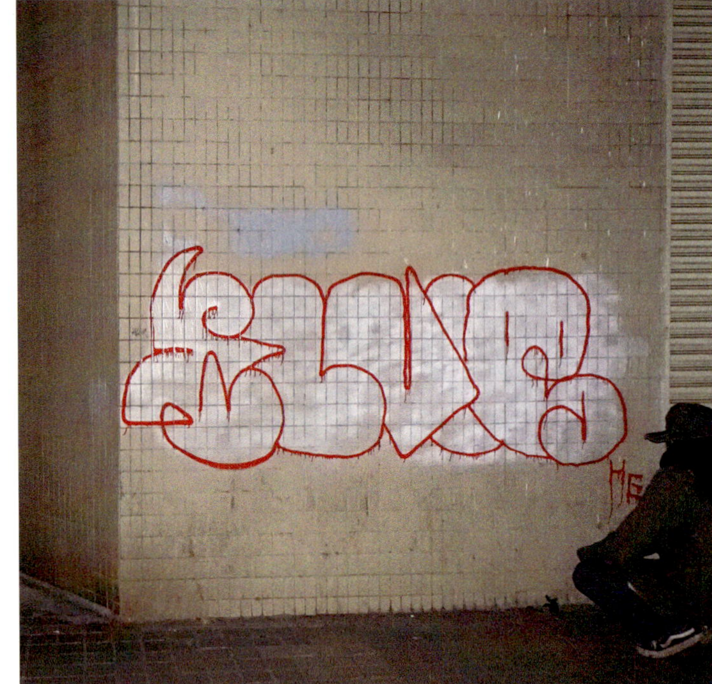
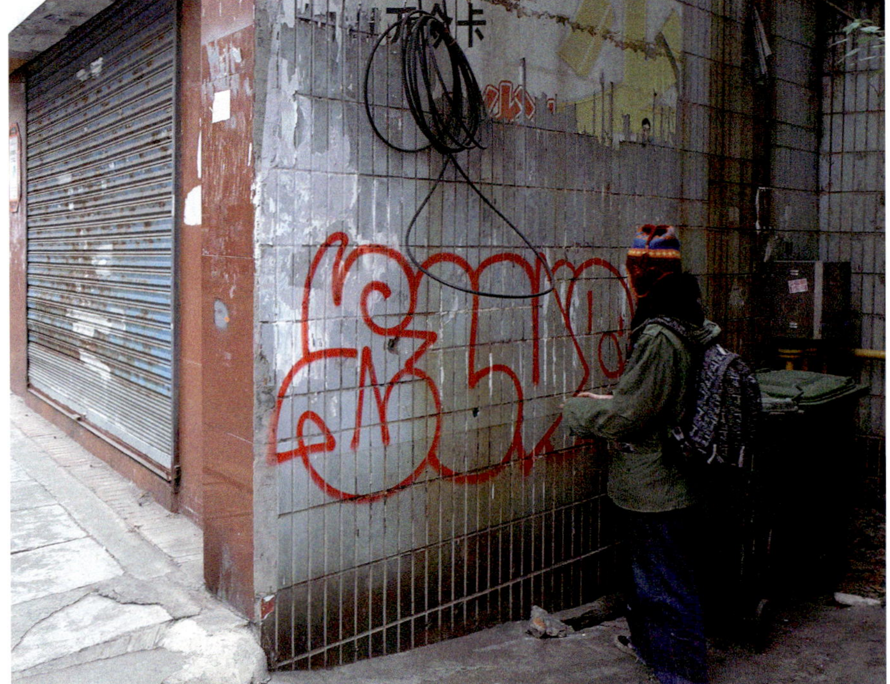
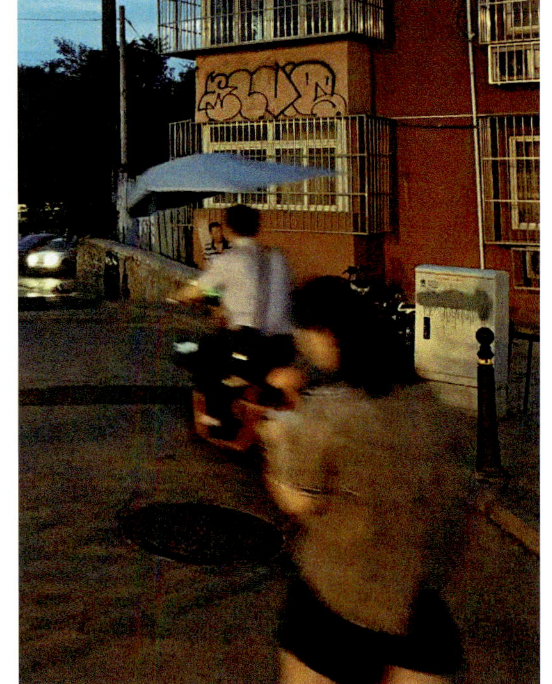

这种完美的大红砖墙总会令人产生强烈的破坏
欲，那天晚上我和 YETI 爬了上去，喝得烂醉的
CONE 则在下面把风。
—
When I see a big, red-brick I always feel a
strong desire of destroying it. That night
YETI and I climbed up to the wall while
CONE was very drunk on the lookout.

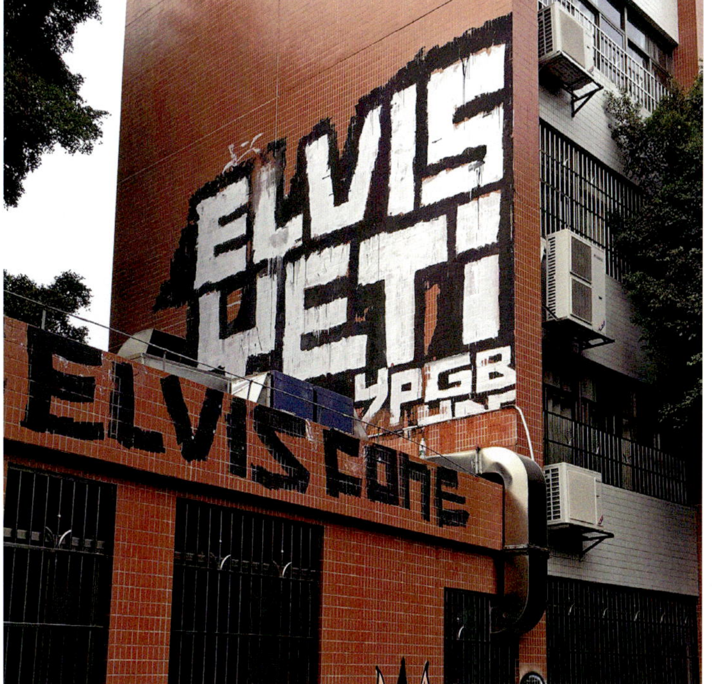

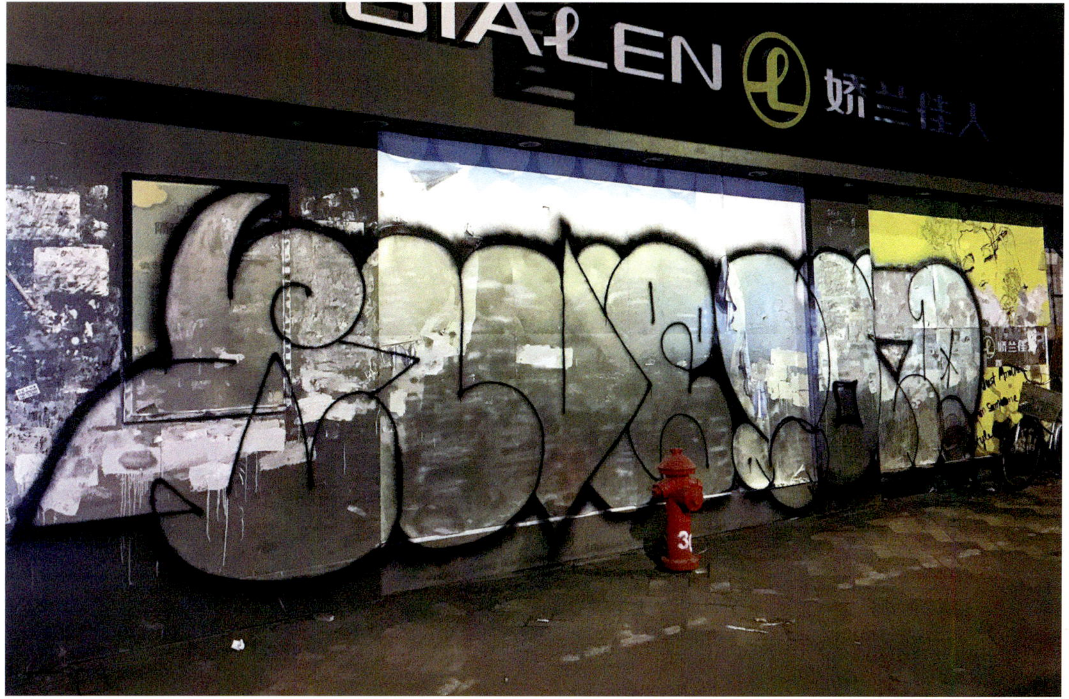

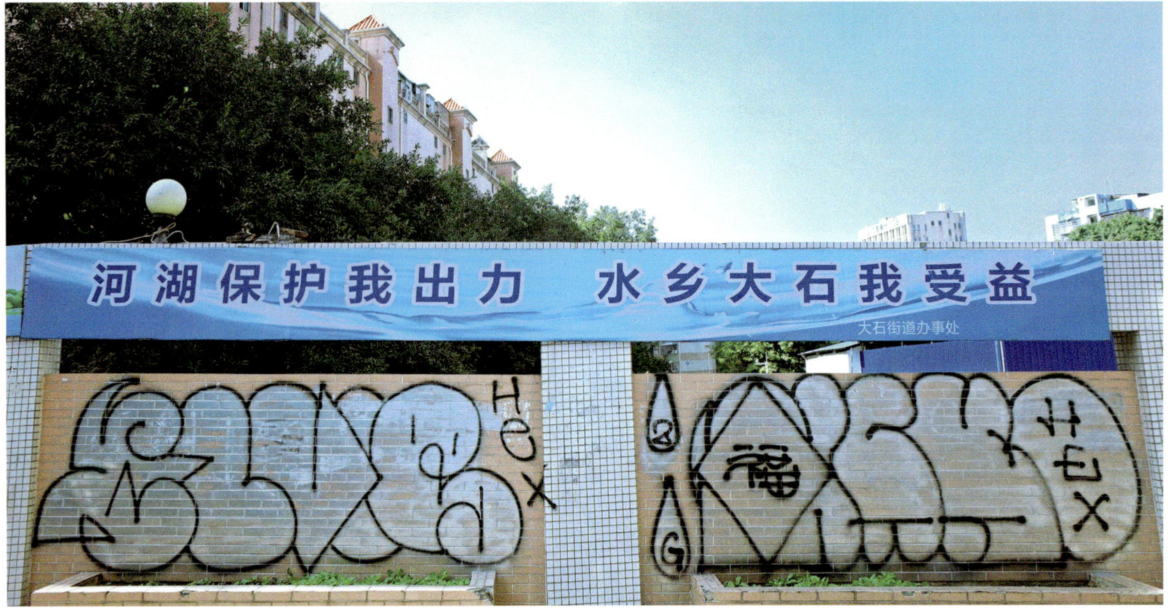

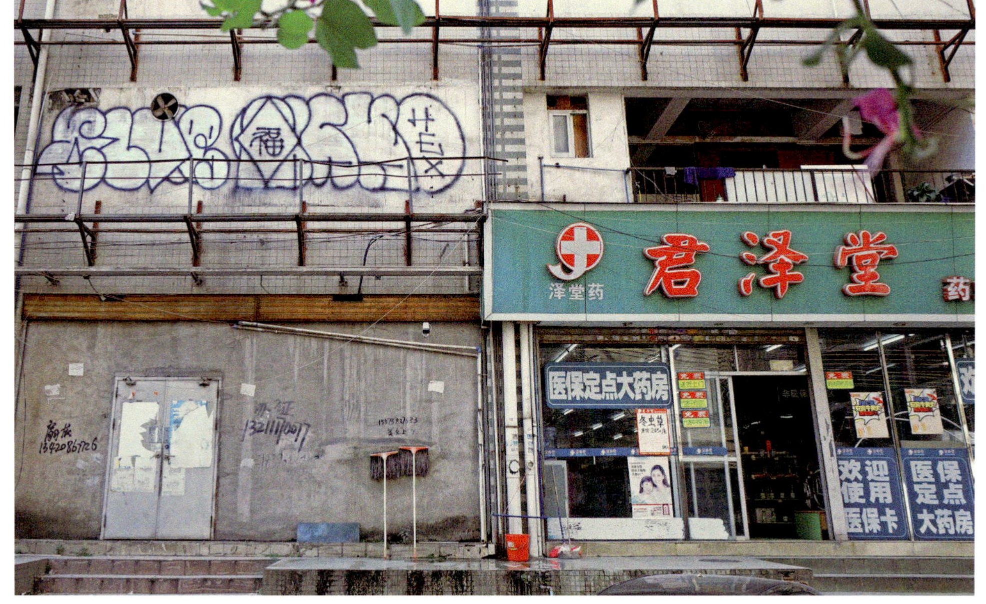
河湖保护我出力　水乡大石我受益
大石街道办事处
泽堂药
君泽堂
药
医保定点大药房
欢迎使用医保卡
医保定点大药房

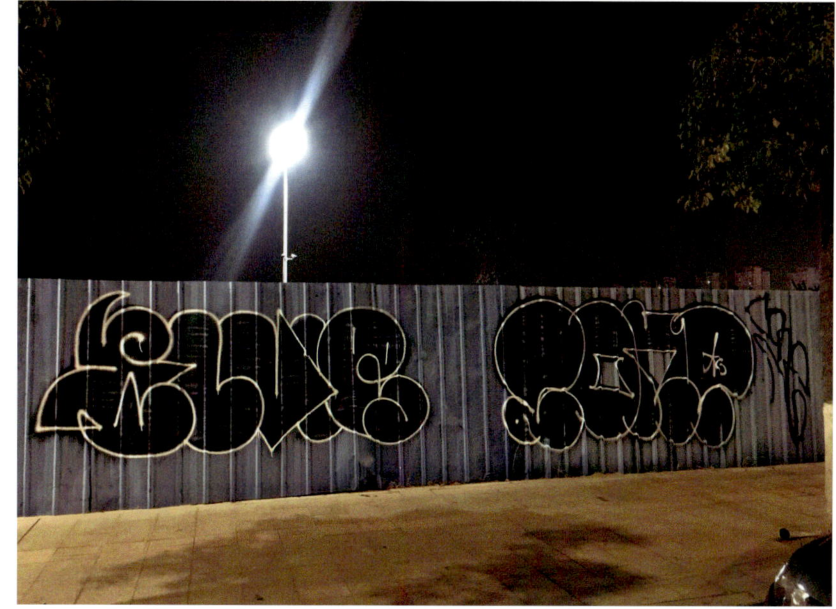
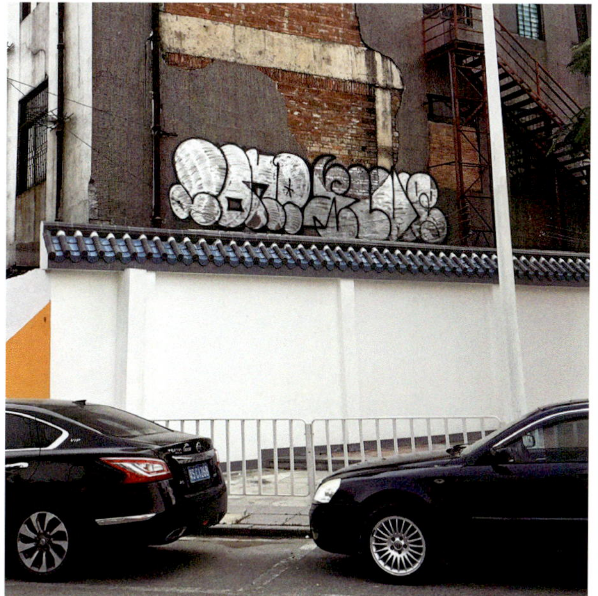
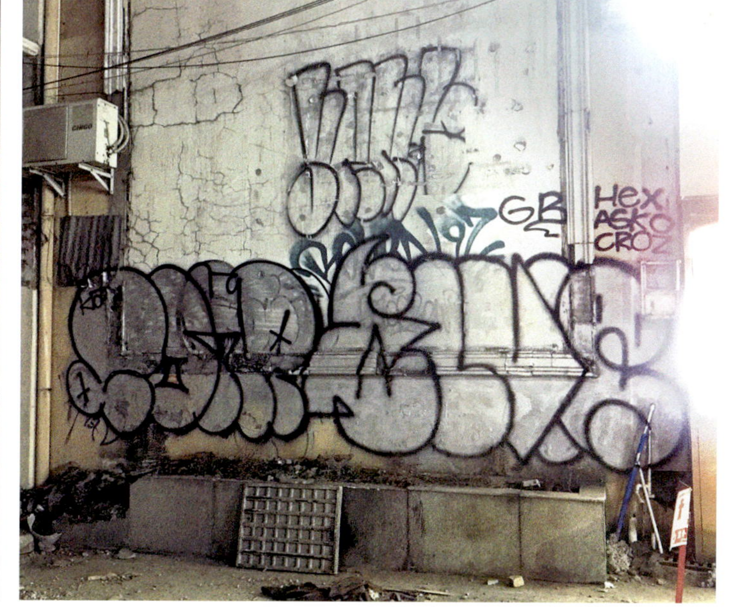

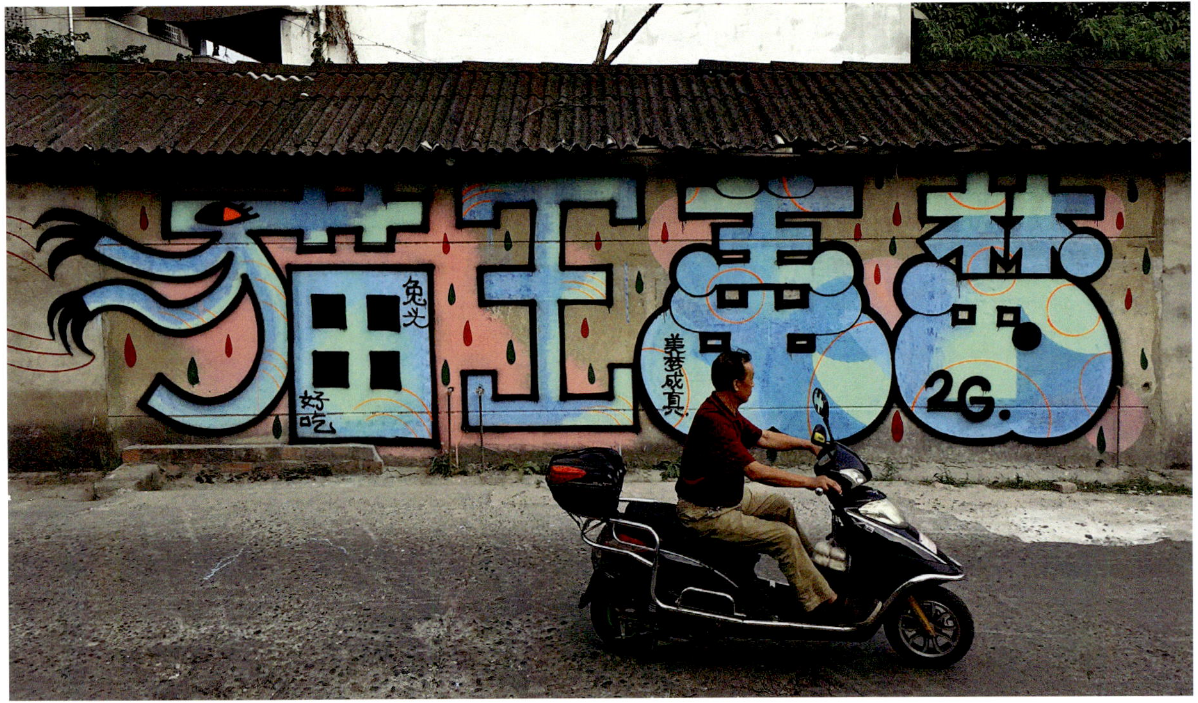

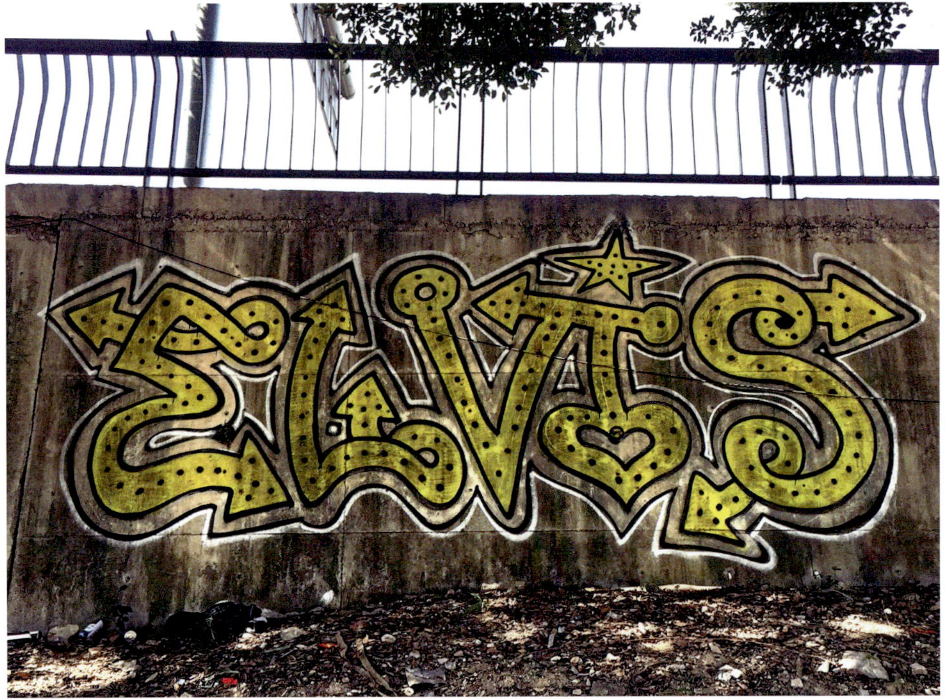

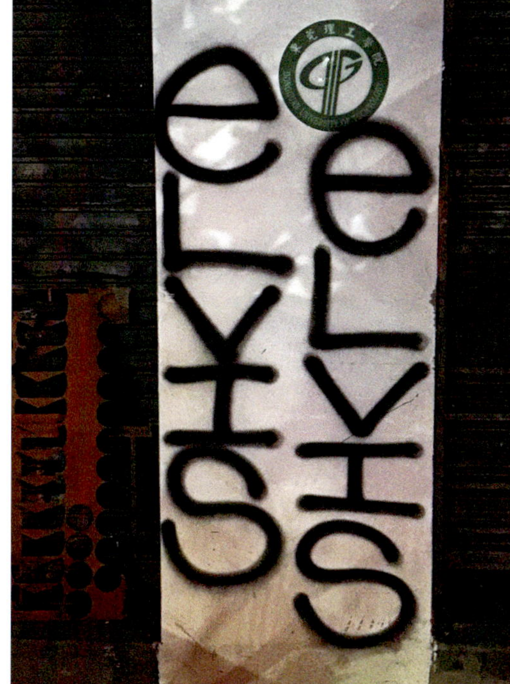
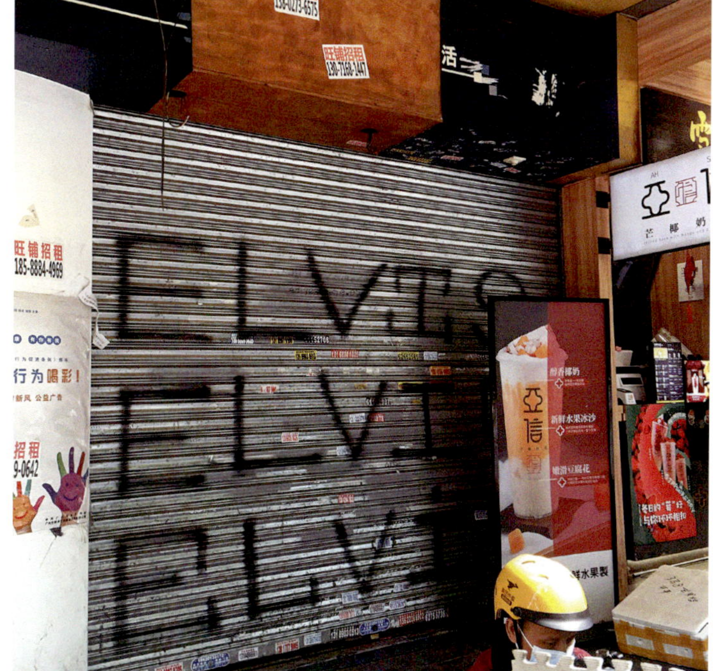
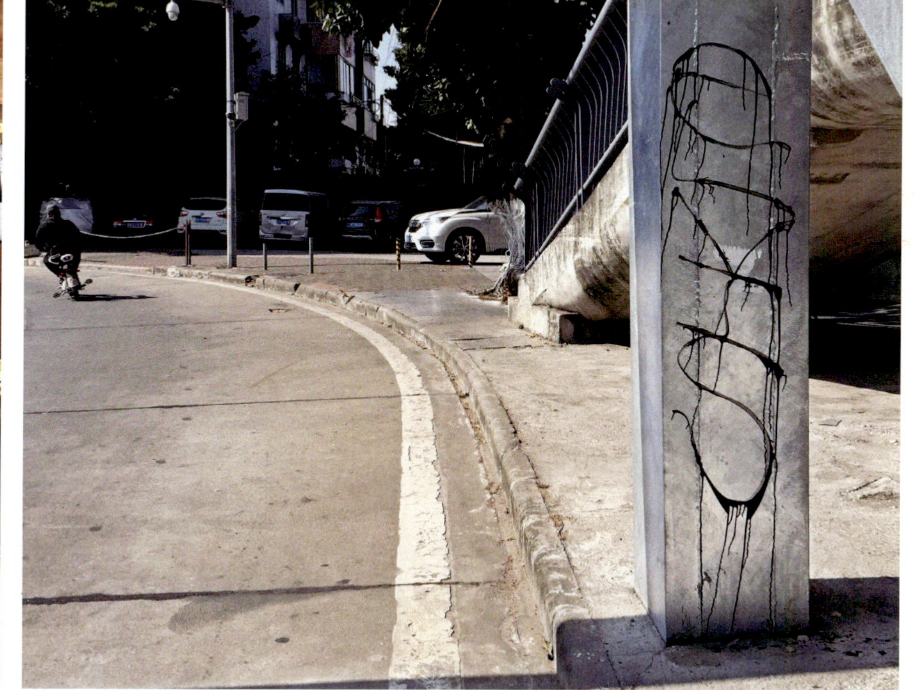

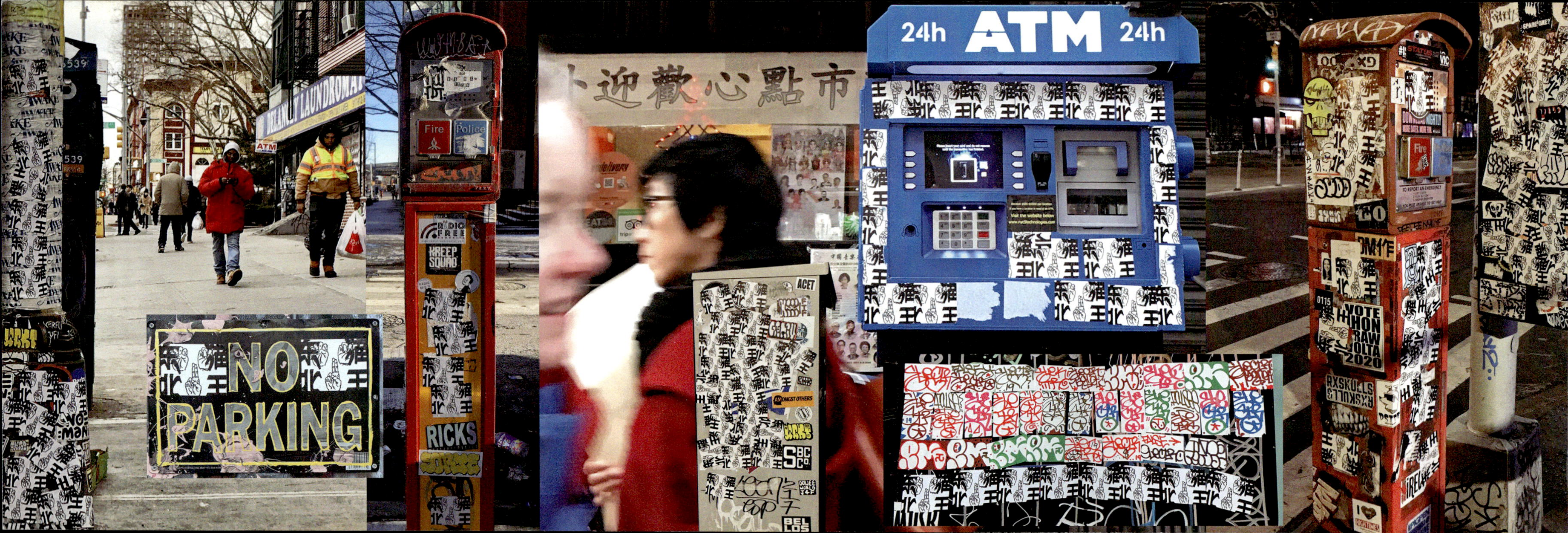

LAUNDROMAT
ATM
Fire
Police
RADIO FREE
KREEP SQUAD
RICKS
NO PARKING
ACET
AMONGST OTHERS
24h ATM 24h
VOTE HON RAW OLTA 2020
RXSKULLS

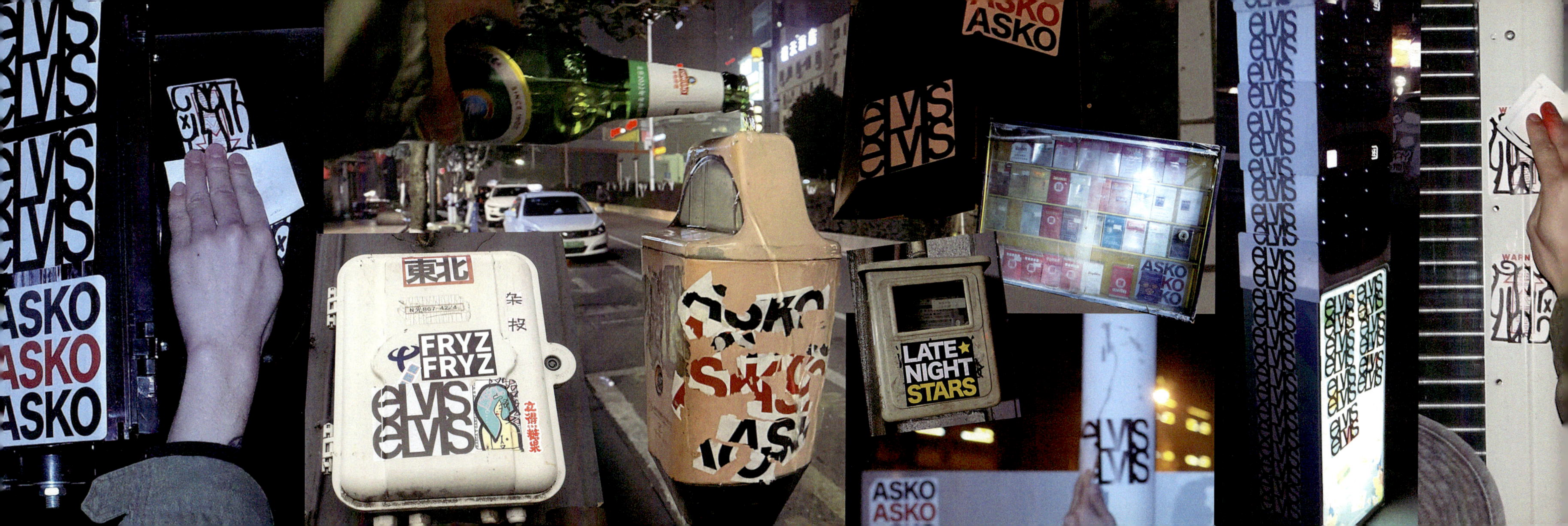

ELVIS
ELVIS
ELVIS
ASKO
ASKO
ASKO
ASKO
東北
FRYZ
FRYZ
ELVIS
ELVIS
ASKO
ASKO
ASKO
LATE NIGHT STARS
ASKO
ASKO
elvis
elvis
elvis
elvis
elvis
elvis

Domenico 'RYO' de Girolamo — 1981-2020

"WHEN YOU WALK THROUGH A STORM
HOLD YOUR HEAD UP HIGH
AND DON'T BE AFRAID OF THE DARK
AT THE END OF THE STORM
THERE'S A GOLDEN SKY
AND THE SWEET SILVER SONG OF THE LARK.
WALK ON, WALK ON,
WITH HOPE IN YOUR HEART,
AND YOU'LL NEVER WALK ALONE"

By REBUS

When I was asked to write a text to remember Domenico 'RYO' de Girolamo, I didn't hesitate for even a moment to accept but the first obstacle I encountered was to decide what kind of slant I should give to my writing. On which aspect of Domenico's character should I focus more? Better to talk about Domenico, the kind friend with whom in recent years, before and during his illness, I shared numerous dinners and endless chats, or will be better to describe Domenico, the writer and passionate promoter of graffiti culture?

Domenico was a big-hearted person and a trusted friend. It has happened to me very few times, if ever, to meet someone always so keen on helping others, such a generous person, in the literal sense of the word. Active since the end of the 90s, he was an important writer in his region, Puglia, but I think that the aspect of Domenico that may interest the most the readers of "No Apologies" is undoubtedly his love for graffiti. Anyone who met me knows how much into graffiti I am and in Domenico, I found someone clearly affected by the same virus and fueled by the same endless passion for this culture.

For more than a decade—through various publications with his publishing house, Wholetrain Press—he documented the international graffiti scene, analyzing it from every point of view. The research done by Wholetrain leaves to the public an incredible legacy; dozens of publications curated in every detail and physical products of great beauty and quality that are rarely seen in this sector of the publishing industry. Each book created by Domenico gives back dignity to a subject that unfortunately is often mistreated. Today, this kind of content is more and more often shared too frequently and in a superficial way.

I remember numerous and endless discussions about the spreading of the internet and social media and how it was important to continue the mission of research and storytelling. I fell in love with this world also thanks to books that miraculously passed through my hands when I was barely more than a child. It makes me happy to think that someone, one day, will experience my same epiphany thanks to the fantastic work of Domenico.

With his demise, an important pillar of this community left us but his work will always be available to anyone who wants to dive deep into, or simply get closer to, the graffiti culture. I like to think that a part of him is still here with me every time that I raise my eyes to my bookcase and I proudly glance through all the Wholetrain press titles in my collection.

By Rebus

当我被问及写一篇纪念 Domenico 'RYO' de Girolamo 的文章时，我毫不犹豫的接受了，但我遇到的第一个障碍，却是整片文章的切入点。是应该更多关注于 Domenico 的个性方面？还是说说这几年，在他生病之前和生病期间，我与这位狂热的文化推手在餐桌上聊了无数次的涂鸦话题？

Domenico 为人宽厚，也是一位值得信赖的朋友。我很少遇到一位从始至终都热衷于帮助他人并且慷慨的人。他从 90 年代末就开始活跃于普利亚区，在当地也是非常重要的一位写手。但我认为 Domenico 最让《无妥协方式》的读者感兴趣无疑是他对涂鸦的热爱。认识我的人都知道，我对涂鸦的热度，而反观 Domenico，他同样也受到了涂鸦这种病毒的影响，并时刻保持着对这种文化的同样激情。

数十年来，他通过 Wholetrain Press 出版了来自世界各地的涂鸦类型杂志，全方位的分析涂鸦所带来的的影响。Wholetrain Press 为大众创造出的了一份惊人的文化财富。数十个出版物不管在实体或细节上都经过精心的策划，而将最高的质量呈现给观者，这在出版行业也是少见的。而 Domenico 所经手的每一本杂志都给予了其最大的尊重。如今，涂鸦却越来越频繁地以肤浅的方式被分享。

我记得有关互联网和社交媒体的传播以及继续进行研究和讲故事的任务的重要性的无休止的无休止的讨论。我还爱上了这个世界，这也要归功于当我还只是个孩子的时候，书就奇迹般地通过了我的手。多梅尼科（Domenico）的出色工作使我很高兴地想到，某人某天会经历我同样的顿悟。

随着他的逝世，这个社区的重要支柱离开了我们，但他的作品将始终供那些想要深入了解涂鸦文化或只是更接近涂鸦文化的人使用。每当我抬起我的书架时，我都会以为他的一部分仍然在我身边，我很自豪地浏览了我收藏中的所有 Wholetrain 新闻标题。

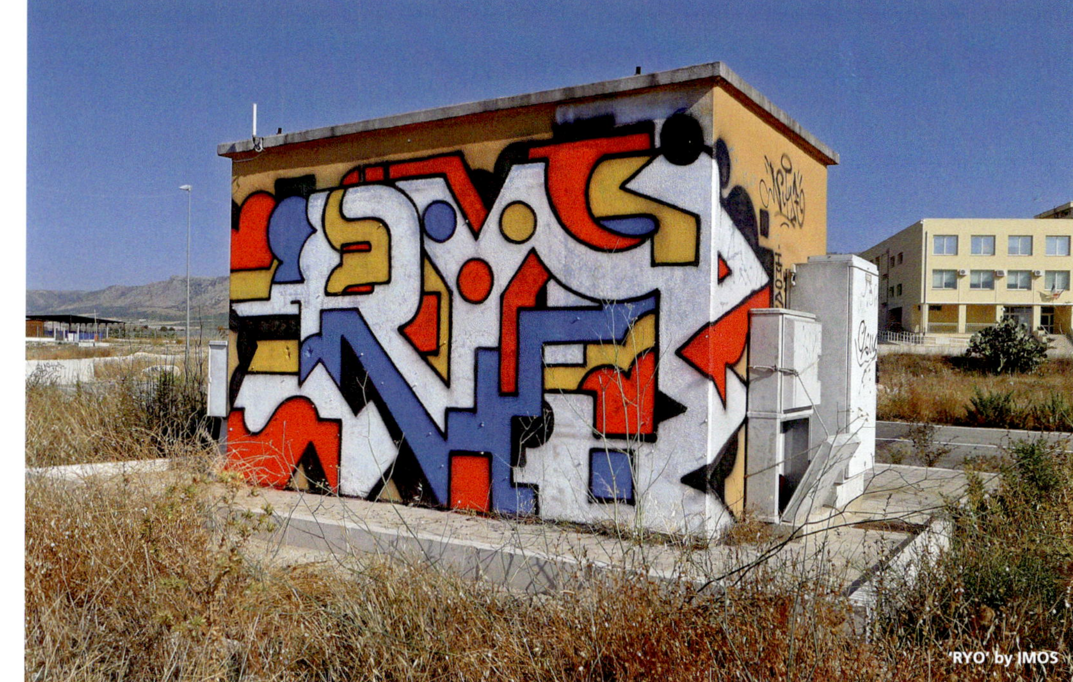

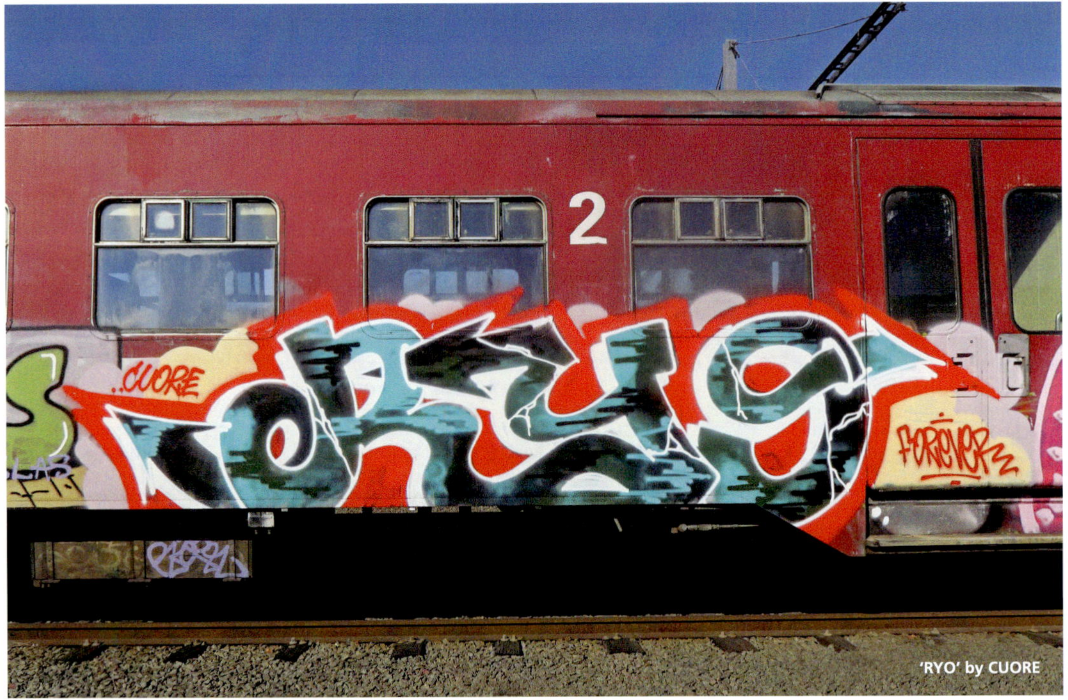

'RYO' by CUORE

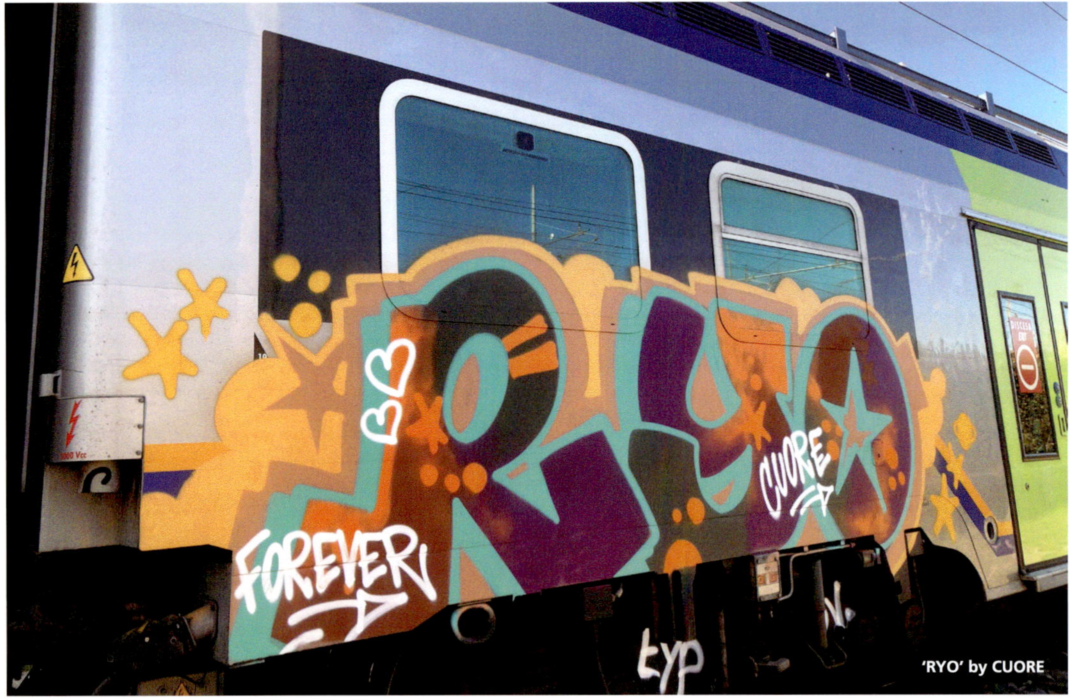

'RYO' by CUORE

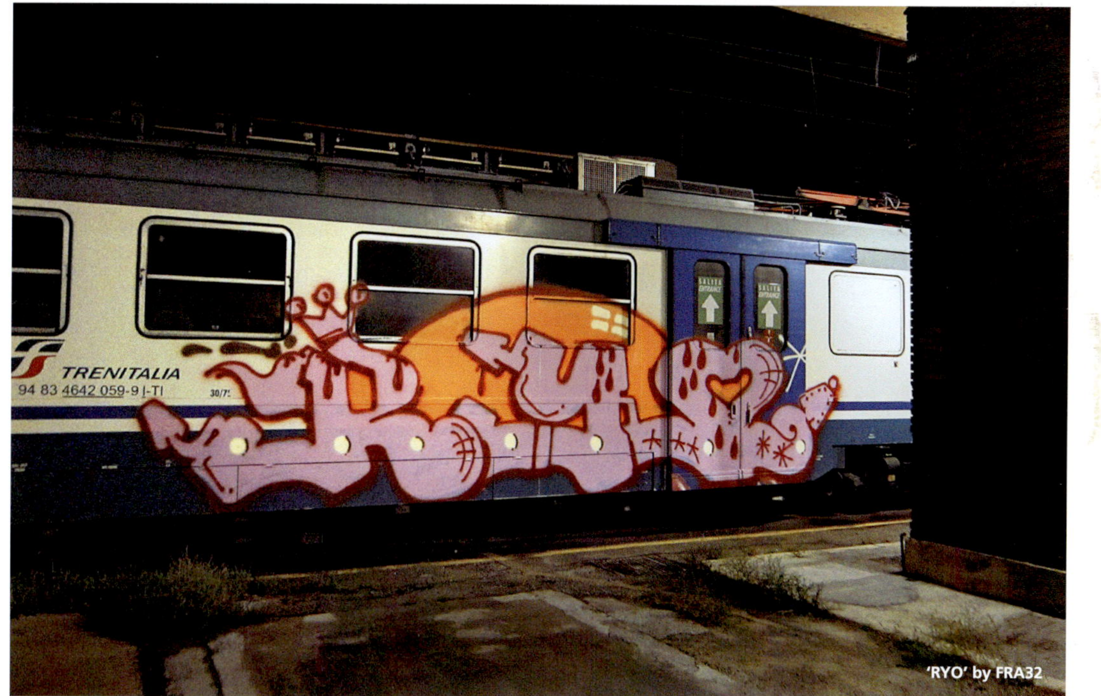

'RYO' by FRA32

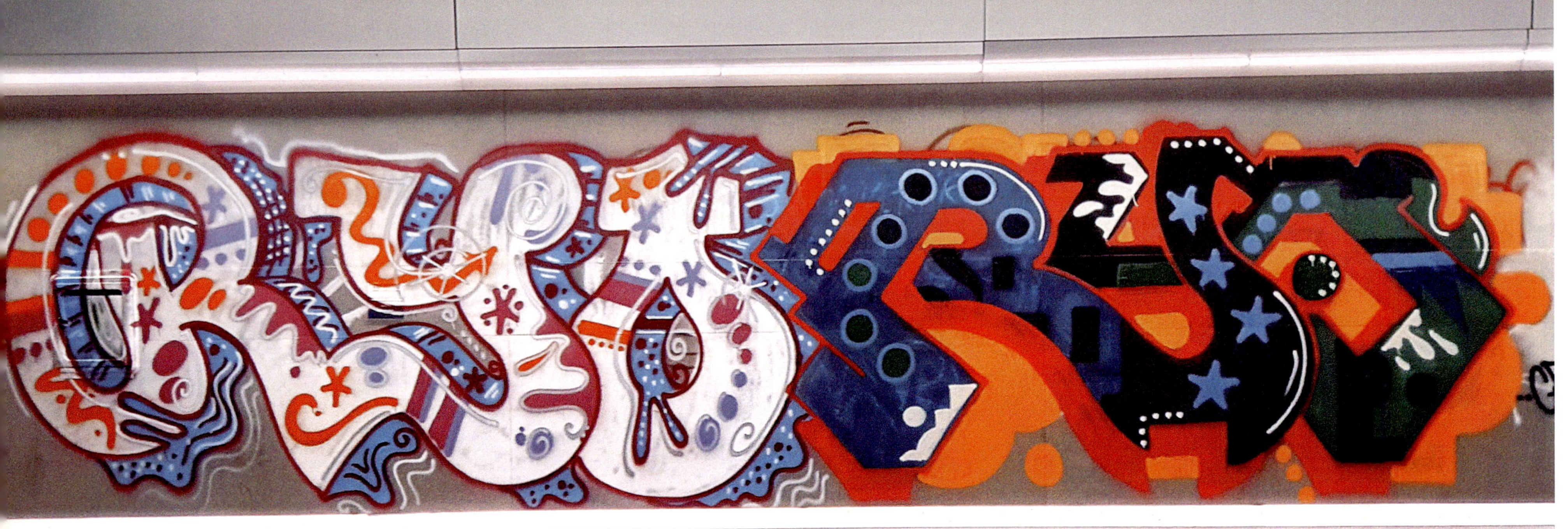

'RYO' by JON & IMOS

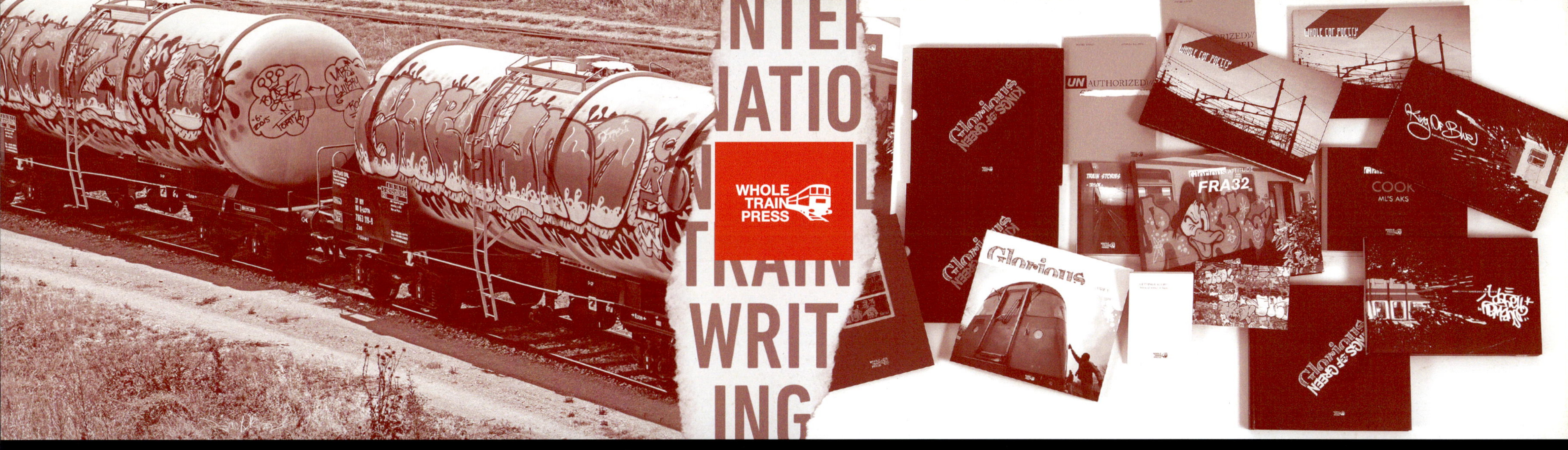
INTER
NATIO
TRAIN
WRITING
WHOLE
TRAIN
PRESS
www.wholetrain.eu
#wholetrainpress

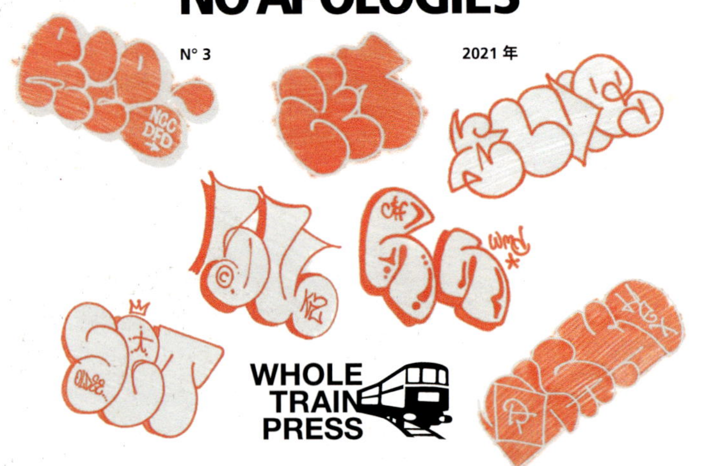

Editor:
Teresa Santoro

GLOBCOM
www.gcurbanworld.it

WHOLE TRAIN PRESS
www.wholetrain.eu

ISBN: 978-88-97640-23-3

印刷于 2021年 5月
Printed in May 2021

感谢 ZEIT（2G，FEK）， ASKO（2G，HEX，YDS）和 MASK（OFS，TDS）在这个杂志印刷品已经成为过去式的时代里，依旧孜孜不倦的为新一期杂志付诸努力。

感谢 FRA32（KNM，RSG，UG）和 BEAST（RSG，TDS，UG）对内容的支持和宝贵的建议。

感谢收录于本杂志的所有写手，为我们提供最硬的素材，将这些疯狂的内容拼凑在一起。

感谢我们的支持者：Still writing，Good Night Press，400 毫升，和天赋街头。没有你们，这本杂志就不可能呈现在读者面前。

最后，同样也是最重要的，感谢我们从始至终的合作伙伴: Tabula Rasa 画廊和 Whole Train Press。你们给了我们真正的支持和完全的信任，我们心存感激。

Thanks to ZEIT (FEK), ASKO (2G, HEX, YDS), and MASK (OFS, TDS) for working hard on a hopeless project like a printed zine in this era of likes and followers.

Thanks to FRA32 (KNM, RSG, UG) and BEAST (RSG, TDS, UG) for the support and priceless pieces of advice.

Thanks to all the writers in this zine to agree on being part of this madness and to provide us the finest material to work with.

Thanks to our supporters: Still Writin, Good Night Press, 400 ml, and The Gift. Without you, this magazine wouldn't have been possible.

Last but not least our partners from day one: Tabula Rasa Gallery and Whole Train Press. You gave us real support and complete trust, we don't take it for granted.

TABULA RASA Zines

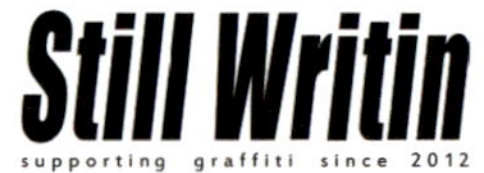
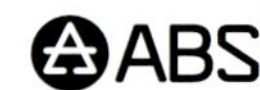
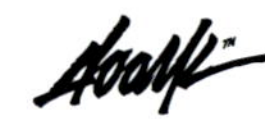
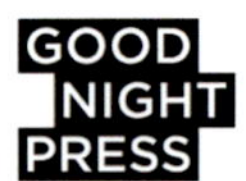